AF479141

This book was published on the occasion of the exhibition *How Many Billboards? Art In Stead*, organized by the MAK Center for Art and Architecture, Los Angeles, at the Schindler House, February—June 2010

Curator: Kimberli Meyer, Director MAK Center Los Angeles
Co-Curators: Lisa Henry, Nizan Shaked, Gloria Sutton
Public Art Consultant: Sara Daleiden

Editors: Peter Noever / Kimberli Meyer
Publication Coordinator/Editorial Advisor: Sara Daleiden
Editorial Assistance: Anthony Carfello, Philipp Levar, Marlies Wirth
Copy Editing: Elizabeth Pulsinelli
Graphic Design: Shannon Shelly, PS Los Angeles

Published by Verlag für moderne Kunst Nürnberg
Luitpoldstraße 5
90402 Nürnberg
Germany

Phone: + 49 911 - 240 21 14, Fax: + 49 911 - 240 21 19
Email: verlag@moderne-kunst.org
www.vfmk.de

Program website: www.howmanybillboards.org
ISBN: 978-3-86984-039-0

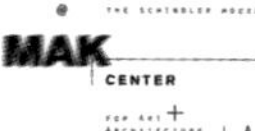

MAK Center for Art and Architecture, Los Angeles at the Schindler House
835 North Kings Road
West Hollywood, CA 90069
USA

Phone (323) 651-1510, Fax (323) 651-2340
Email: office@MAKcenter.org
www.MAKcenter.org, www.MAKcenterUFI.org

This publication is made possible in part by the Federal Ministry of Education, the Arts and Culture of the Republic of Austria.

Typeface: Helvetica Neue and Gotham
Paper: Gold East
Reprographics: Overseas Printing
Print: Four color
Binding: Case bound
Printed in China
First edition: 1,500 copies

Distribution: D.A.P. Distributed Art Publishers, Inc.
155 Sixth Avenue, 2nd Floor
New York, NY 10013
USA

Phone (212) 627-1999, Fax (212) 627-9484
www.artbook.com

How Many Billboards? Art In Stead

EDITED BY PETER NOEVER / KIMBERLI MEYER

CONTENTS

ART AND THE CITY

BY PETER NOEVER

With the conquest of art over billboards, a medium that is otherwise the exclusive reserve of commerce becomes, for a brief moment, non-commercial. Putting art on billboards also disrupts the routines of art viewing to which we have become accustomed. Art, for the most part, is kept behind the walls of institutions. When placed on billboards, art is released into the wild, into precisely that place where modern urban nomads spend time en masse.

As a targeted intervention in urban structures, *How Many Billboards? Art In Stead* represents the opposite of a conventional museum exhibition. It does so in accordance with the idea that an art institution can only truly realize itself by first abolishing itself. It is precisely because it avoids the exiled status of the museum that this project has achieved resonance among artists and viewers. For a period of time, art is no longer locked up in solitary confinement (in the museum), but rather is allowed to permeate real life, "out there." "An estimated 735,000 people will view the...exhibition every day."[1] The statistics make the battle of museums over market share seem ridiculous.

"I CAN'T HEAR, I CAN'T SEE"[2]: With the occupation of mass media (of which, in Los Angeles, billboards are a prominent part),[3] art reclaims some of its status in visual culture and gathers the attention of the widest possible audience. In this, art adheres to its mission of making the invisible visible and the mute voice of the Other audible.

By misappropriating its medium, *How Many Billboards?* writes artistic narratives into the hegemonic order of commercial discourse. In so doing, art re-conquers urban spaces that have been colonized by the economic realm, and renders the urban ecology more fit for humans.[4] The artists make public art out of that which is otherwise privatized, and rob commercialism of its very stage—that most commercial medium of the billboard.[5] Here, an artistic "urban guerrilla" flaunts the logic of corporate logos, and carries out "public attacks" on the dictate of consumption. In a reversal of the usual flow, a crash of established ways of experiencing things takes place. Kenneth Anger's billboard text—"ASTONISH"—proclaims the concept, and lauren woods is among those who proceeds to destabilize the conventional logic of signifiers. She does so with lines from a love poem written in Urdu, the language of Pakistan. Instant comprehensibility—a fundamental principle of advertising—is turned on its head, with the head then being placed on its own two feet.

When 21 critically involved, contemporary artists intervene via billboards in the visual, urban landscape on strategically distributed sites, multiple re-readings of the city result. The artists' billboards foster an awareness of the metropolis and the everyday environment of its inhabitants (mobility, work, leisure time, and consumption). At first glance, passers-by must surely muse as to whether the MAK billboards are art or commerce. Does it occur to them, as they pass, that in our world things could be vastly different? Providing art with space avows openness, stimulates one's sense of the possible, and creates an image of the city that is not organized exclusively according to functional and commercial criteria. In fleeting, sidelong glances, time-particles open up potentially free spaces, freeways out of the realm of commerce and utilitarianism.

1. Erica Zora Wrightson, "The Big Canvas," *LA Weekly*, March 18, 2010.

2. Excerpt of text on Yvonne Rainer's billboard.

3. Other cities have their specific media that characterizes the public space. In Budapest, for example, it is currently glowing neon signs; Vienna's mass public medium is the poster. Posters, however, were not always dominated by commerce—they were once a way through which every citizen could express him - or herself.

4. The exhibition also includes ecological themes, such as in the works by Allan Sekula (*Los ricos destruyen el planeta*) and Daniel Joseph Martinez.

5. After all, large-scale outdoor advertising exerts a force that blocks or shifts the gaze and can hardly be avoided. For this reason, some cities have banned billboards altogether.

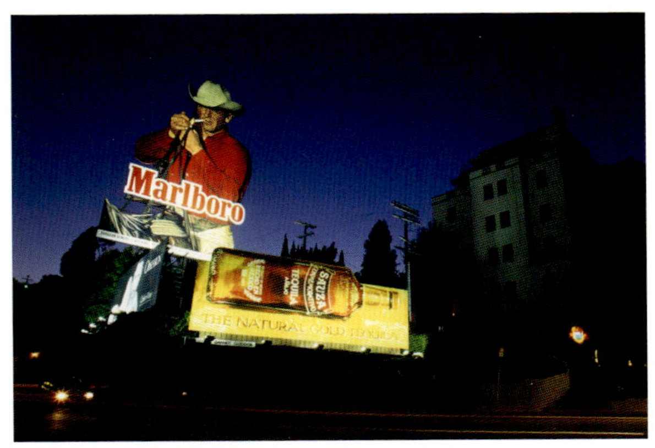

This infamous billboard was the exclusive territory of the Marlboro Man for decades, first with a cigarette, and later without. Today, an Apple billboard occupies the site. Times change, and with them their addictive substances.

Top: Marlboro cowboy billboard on Sunset Boulevard, 1990s
© Evan Hurd/Sygma/Corbis

Middle: Andrea Lenardin Madden
Former Site of Iconic Marlboro Billboard, Sunset Boulevard near the Chateau Marmont, 2008

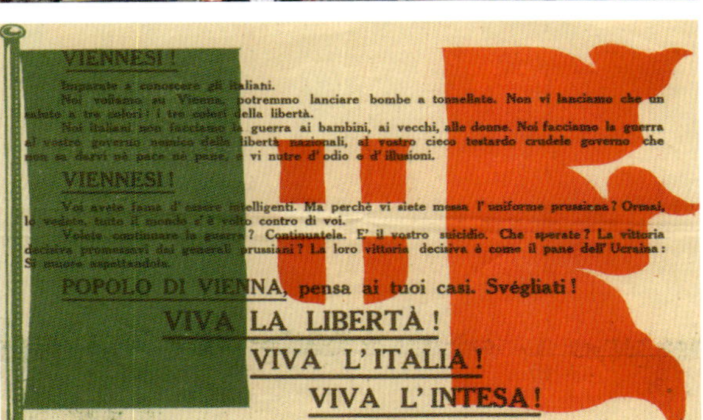

VIENNESI!

Imparate a conoscere gli italiani.

Noi voliamo su Vienna, potremmo lanciare bombe a tonnellate. Non vi lanciamo che un saluto a tre colori: i tre colori della libertà.

Noi italiani non facciamo la guerra ai bambini, ai vecchi, alle donne. Noi facciamo la guerra al vostro governo nemico delle libertà nazionali, al vostro cieco testardo crudele governo che non sa darvi nè pace nè pane, e vi nutre d'odio e d'illusioni.

VIENNESI!

Voi avete fama d'essere intelligenti. Ma perchè vi siete messa l'uniforme prussiana? Ormai, lo vedete, tutto il mondo s'è volto contro di voi.

Volete continuare la guerra? Continuatela. E' il vostro suicidio. Che sperate? La vittoria decisiva promessavi dai generali prussiani? La loro vittoria decisiva è come il pane dell'Ucraina: Si muore aspettandola.

POPOLO DI VIENNA, pensa ai tuoi casi. Svégliati!

VIVA LA LIBERTÀ!

VIVA L'ITALIA!

VIVA L'INTESA!

128

On August 9, 1918, the Italian poet Gabriele D'Annunzio flew over Vienna and bombarded the city with thousands of leaflets, drawing large crowds. This action, "The Flight Over Vienna," was a misappropriation of a medium, part artistic action and part propaganda mission.

Gabriele D'Annunzio
Volo su Vienna
© Archive Burzagli Family

OVERVIEW AND ACKNOWLEDGMENTS

BY KIMBERLI MEYER

In February 2010, the MAK Center for Art and Architecture at the Schindler House launched *How Many Billboards? Art In Stead.* This large-scale, urban exhibition debuted 21 new works by leading contemporary artists, presented simultaneously on billboards throughout Los Angeles. The billboard projects were accompanied by an overview exhibition at the Schindler House from February 27 through June 30, 2010; a series of public programs and bus tours; a promotional campaign on bus shelters; 10,000 brochure/maps distributed across the city; and a dedicated website providing up-to-date exhibition information and online navigational tools for handheld, electronic devices.

The proposition of the exhibition was that art should occupy a visible position in the cacophony of mediated images in the city. Scale matters in a big city; in order to make a discernable visual impact in the vast sea of signs, we determined that it was important that a large group of works be produced and that they all be on view at the same time. Our selection of 21 billboards was the largest group ever exhibited simultaneously in the history of Los Angeles.

Each artist was commissioned to create a new work that critically responded to the medium of the billboard and interpreted its role in the urban landscape. The exhibition followed decades of discussion amongst Los Angeles residents and officials about billboards and their impact on the city. *How Many Billboards?* investigated the political and artistic implications of these media surfaces that saturate the city's landscape, while also offering an alternative vision for displaying art in Los Angeles. Investigating art as an idea, as well as art as a medium for critical intervention, the exhibition also highlighted the interaction of Pop, Conceptualism, and Identity Politics in Los Angeles since the 1960s.

Participating artists were Kenneth Anger, Michael Asher, Jennifer Bornstein, Eileen Cowin, Christina Fernandez, Ken Gonzales-Day, Renée Green, Kira Lynn Harris, John Knight, David Lamelas, Brandon Lattu, Daniel Joseph Martinez, Kori Newkirk, Yvonne Rainer, Martha Rosler with Josh Neufeld, Allen Ruppersberg, Allan Sekula, Susan Silton, Kerry Tribe, James Welling, and lauren woods.

So that the exhibition could be seen via public transit, the billboard projects were sited on major boulevards with bus lines. The locations were constrained to central Los Angeles, which allowed the MAK Center to organize tours starting from the Schindler House. Since the billboard space was donated, we had no way of knowing where the artworks would be placed until a few days before installation. Thus the artists were told at the beginning of the process that they would not be able to choose a specific location for their billboard and respond to that particular site. Once the locations were identified, I did have some discretion in placing the works, although not all of them wound up where requested. Our agreements with the outdoor media companies stipulated that if the signs were rented while the art was still up, they could be taken down and re-installed in another location. This happened with the commissions by Michael Asher and Allan Sekula. Both locations of each project have been noted and photographed in "The Exhibition" section of this publication.

How Many Billboards? exemplifies the MAK Center's mission to explore the intersections and boundaries of art and architecture, to work with artists on specially commissioned projects, and to examine urban questions. However, it is the first major exhibition project the MAK Center has undertaken in public space. Mounting an exhibition of commissioned billboards in Los Angeles utilized the MAK Center's areas of expertise, and proved to be an art-centric, tangible way to contribute to thinking about urban space today.

With a full-time staff of four, the MAK Center could only realize an exhibition of this scale and ambition with the aid of its valued consultants and partners. Many played key roles in the development and execution of the project. Sara Daleiden, a long-time consultant for the MAK Center with a particular interest in art in public space, has been strategizing with me for five years on how to make the project happen, including what sorts of partnerships should be formed, and what the show could mean in relation to discourses around art in the public sphere. Nizan Shaked, curator, scholar, and professor of art history and museum studies, has been discussing the concept of the show with me for over a decade and was instrumental in helping articulate the curatorial premise that led to major grant funding for the project. Curators Gloria Sutton and Lisa Henry brought vital knowledge, ideas, and constructive criticism to the curatorial process.

The Emily Hall Tremaine Foundation Exhibition Award provided major production funding and opened the door for work to begin in earnest. I am grateful to the staff, Nicole E. Chevalier and Ashley Sklar, and the foundation's board for their faith in the potential of the project and their ongoing professionalism and attentiveness to the execution of the exhibition. Additional funding from the National Endowment for the Arts, the City of Los Angeles Department of Cultural Affairs, the City of West Hollywood Arts and Cultural Affairs Commission, the Los Angeles County Arts Commission, and the Audrey and Sydney Irmas Charitable Foundation allowed us to complete the exhibition and related components.

Critical to the realization of the project was the support of Rick Robinson of MacDonald Media. Rick's passion for art, combined with his decades of professional work in the outdoor advertising industry, made him a crucial interlocutor between the MAK Center and media companies. A media buyer and an artist in his own right, Robinson leveraged his charisma and good faith within the outdoor advertising industry to secure enough donated billboards to realize the show. His associate Kristy Nichols worked efficiently and with great charm to ensure proper coordination between the printer, the MAK Center, and the outdoor companies. I am grateful to Clear Channel Outdoor, CBS Decaux, CBS Outdoor, Fuel Outdoor, General Outdoor Advertising, Regency Outdoor Advertising, and Van Wagner Communications for donating space.

Communication is a crucial element of an outdoor exhibition. The stellar team of Bettina Korek, Melissa Goldberg, Sarah Williams, and Karen Constine of ForYourArt worked with the MAK Center on publicity, contributed many creative ideas, and introduced the MAK Center to a host of new technological tools. The enthusiastic and endlessly patient Shannon Shelly of PS Los Angeles designed the graphics for the project, including its logo, brochure, map, website, outdoor campaign, and this exhibition catalogue. Michael Hanrahan built the highly functional website. Roman Jaster provided valuable services on the blog and book design. Sarah Lehrer-Graiwer authored astute observations on the artworks as the project's blogger in residence. Considerable energy was devoted to photographing the works in situ, and these images serve as a major tool for communicating the project. Architect Gerard Smulevich's carefully constructed photographs were displayed in the Schindler House exhibition and appear in this publication. Architectural photographer patricia parinejad's spontaneous, city-climbing photographs of the exhibition are featured in this catalogue as well. Artist Ann Trondson and director Mark Escribano produced the video interviews with artists shown online and at the Schindler House. Trondson's substantial research guided her questions, which evoked thoughtful answers and provided apt editorial direction for the videos. Escribano's professional directing, shooting, and editing produced a high-quality set of published videos. Thanks also to Jena Lee, Cat Lee, Mimi Teller, Vivian Babuts, and Ido Sasson for their help with programming, and to Mark Daybell, Allan Finamore, Valerie Green, and Roddey Reid for their assistance with the artists' submissions.

Auxiliary programming was an important part of contextualizing the exhibition for a broader public. It was a pleasure to partner with The Museum of Contemporary Art (MOCA), ALOUD at the Central Library, Southern California Institute of Architecture (SCI-Arc), the Goethe-Institut, and the Master of Public Art Studies Program: Art/Curatorial Practices in the Public Sphere at the University of Southern California's Roski School of Fine Arts. Thanks go to Aandrea Stang in the education department of MOCA for coordinating the screenings of film and video by some of the participating artists, Louise Steinman and Justin Veach of ALOUD for hosting the first public issues panel, Wendy Heldmann for coordinating the panel at SCI-Arc, Annette Rupp of the Goethe-Institut for helping to host panelist Mirjam Struppek, and Joshua Decter at USC for collaborating on artist Renée Green's talk at the Schindler House. The politics of billboard space in Los Angeles is a rich topic, and we wanted to address it with those who have been considering it for a long while. Anne Bray, director of Freewaves, curated two panel discussions exploring the social, political, and economic aspects of outdoor advertising. Conversations between panelists Toby Miller, Rick Robinson, Christine Pelisek, John Tehranian, Bill Roschen, Mirjam Struppek, Alan Bell, and Dennis Hathaway were lively and thought-provoking. Touring on bicycles was a great way to see the show; we thank Amanda Smith and Sean Deyoe for organizing a wonderful Sunday morning bike tour.

Since the MAK Center was new to producing a large exhibition in public space, the project advisory board and partners assisted in trouble-shooting potential problems and acting as advocates and spokespersons for the project. Thanks go to board members Anne Bray, Freewaves; Karen Constine, ForYourArt; Susan Gray,

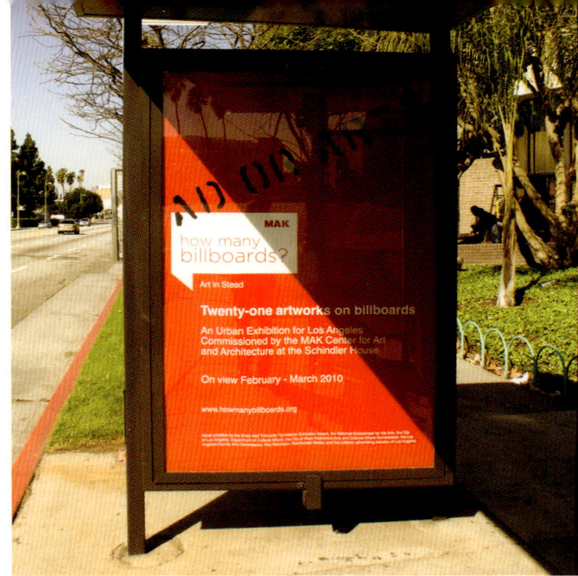

Bus shelter as part of *How Many Billboards?* ad campaign.

Community Redevelopment Agency of Los Angeles; Pat Gomez, City of Los Angeles, Department of Cultural Affairs; Letitia Fernandez Ivins, Los Angeles County Arts Commission Civic Art Program; Brigid Labonge, graphic artist; Emi Fontana, West of Rome; Michael McDowell, LA INC; Sarah MacPherson, Hollywood Property Owners Alliance; Shannon Shelly, PS Los Angeles; Zipporah Lax Yamamoto, Metro (Los Angeles County Metropolitan Transportation Authority); Rick Robinson and Kristy Nichols, MacDonald Media. As a partner, Metro promoted the exhibition through its transit brochures and website, and LA INC featured the project in its promotion of Los Angeles arts in 2010.

The exhibition catalogue benefited from the superlative editing skills of Elizabeth Pulsinelli. Esmail Najmi provided insightful commentary on a number of the essays. Thanks go to Janet Owen Driggs, Christine Steiner, Joshua Decter, and Anne Bray for adding entries to the publication that helped round out the discussion of art in public space.

Special thanks go to MAK director Peter Noever for his ongoing support of the idea, and MAK Center program coordinator Anthony Carfello for managing the details of the project with acumen, panache, and deep commitment to the project goals. Finally, I am grateful to all the participating artists for their generosity of spirit and for taking the challenge seriously.

SPEECH IN THE CITY

BY KIMBERLI MEYER

How Many Billboards? Art In Stead simultaneously presents 21 newly commissioned works by contemporary artists on billboards across the city of Los Angeles. This urban exhibition is designed for the characteristic sprawl, culture, and communication mode of Los Angeles. Conceived while sitting in traffic, the exhibition responds to the mandatory nature of the public viewing of corporate messaging. It views signage in the city as speech in the city. Images and language installed as outdoor advertising comprise one of the most visible forms of communication in urban space. The artworks in *How Many Billboards* operate as artistic speech in a corporate speech environment. In considering the works in this essay, I will explore several questions: As messages, how do the billboards operate? What gives them their authority? How may their meanings be refracted and absorbed by their localities and viewing publics?

A strong public outreach effort—including bus and bike tours, a related exhibition at the Schindler House, various public programs around the city, viral media updates, and a devoted website that includes a user-friendly map and videotaped interviews with the artists—aids the exhibition's visibility and impact. All of the artists' billboards are located on major boulevards so that the show can be seen via public bus routes. During its run in February, March, and April, the exhibition generated 735,000 "impressions" a day, totaling at least 22,050,000 default viewers.[1] (As points of comparison, the J. Paul Getty Museum receives an average of 4200 visitors a day, and the MAK Center at the Schindler House averages 32).[2] By all measures, the project delivers a noticeable interruption to the monolith of outdoor advertising in Los Angeles, and gives contemporary art a high profile, if short-term, platform.

Los Angeles is a sprawling, arid, freeway-dominated, palm-tree-ornamented, low-rise city. Its public spaces are diffuse and difficult to identify, and are most commonly felt not as spaces at all, but rather as corridors of transit. More than public space, Los Angeles has public right-of-ways. The communal zone of vision includes private property along public right-of-ways. Outdoor advertising dominates this zone with thousands of billboards and a growing number of building-sized supergraphics. The fact that urban-scaled advertising can impose itself so deeply into daily life means that the individual is in some ways enclosed by the commercial. The conventional divisions between public and private space in the city, commonly defined by roads, buildings, and property lines, break down in urban media space.

The ubiquity of advertising media in urban space today puts it in a special category of messaging. Since it is all around us, we should think of outdoor advertising as closer to broadcast media than print media. In radio and TV, much of the spectrum has been licensed for commercial purposes, yet a part has also been designated for the benefit of the public. Thus we have public and listener-supported radio, public television, and cable access. That public concerns warrant a voice alongside private ones in media programming has been well established. Such a model could be applied easily to outdoor media to diversify urban messaging.

Let's consider urban speech in grammatical terms. Speech in English travels mainly in two moods: the indicative and the imperative. In the indicative mood, facts are delivered. In the imperative mood, commands are issued. If we consider the syntax of city signage in these terms, the indicative mood would be found in administrative communications about geography, traffic rules, names, and locations ("Here is the freeway"), and the imperative mood would be found in commercial advertising ("Buy this"). *How Many Billboards?* presents art in the imperative mood, giving it a commanding stance that signals action.

The billboard by lauren woods offers a vibrant example of art in the imperative mood. It presents two lines of white, Arabic script on a black background. The phrase translates as:

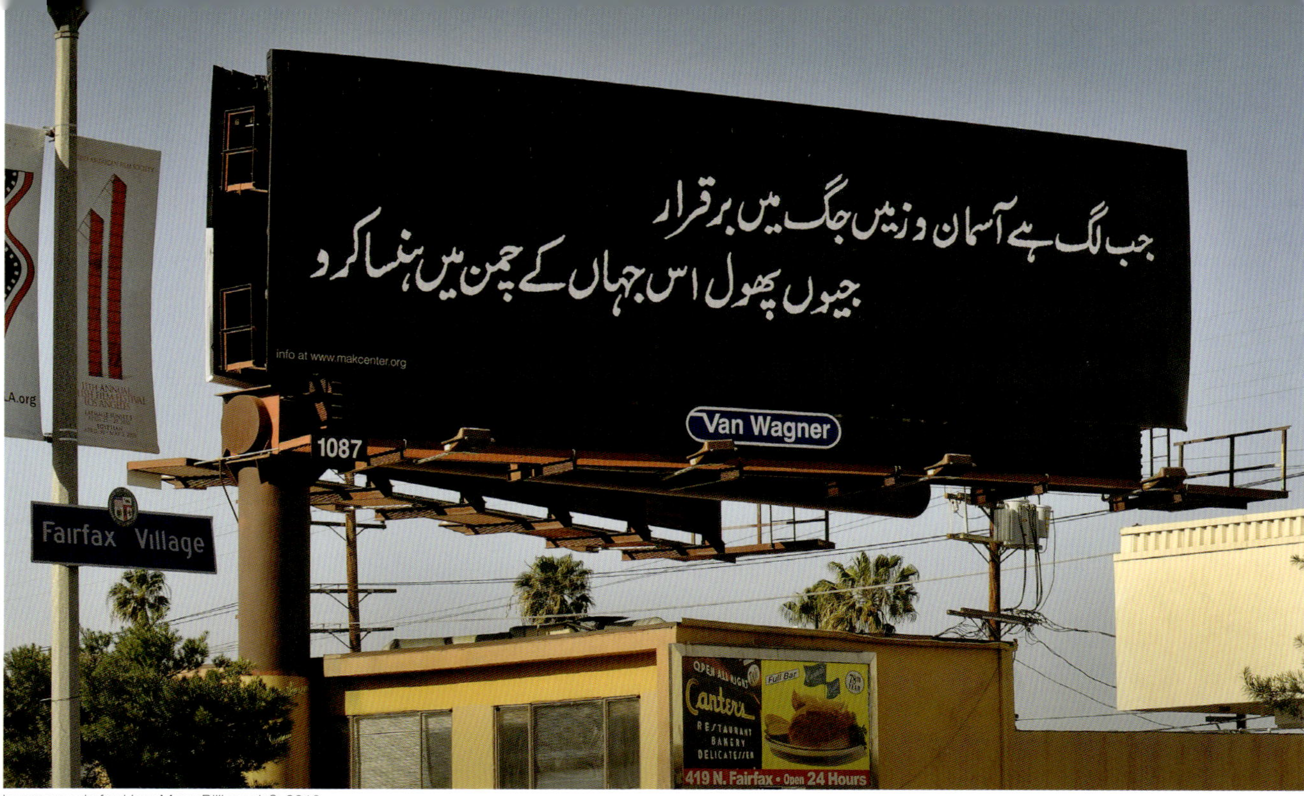

lauren woods for *How Many Billboards?*, 2010.

As long as the earth and the sky last,
Smile like a flower in the garden of the world.

These lines are from a love poem by Vali Dakhni, an Urdu poet of the medieval period. Woods became interested in Urdu poetry when she heard an interview with President Barack Obama. When questioned about Pakistan, Obama professed a love for Pakistani food and Urdu poetry. Woods began looking into the poetry and developed an appreciation for the form. Her commission for *How Many Billboards?* marks the first time she has incorporated this interest into her artistic practice.

The Arabic words are shown without English translation. Presented on a billboard, the undecipherable words cause us to realize that we don't understand everything going on around us. Most who see it cannot read the verse, and so are left with their own associations and musings as to what it might mean. The message might therefore seem ominous to some. The imperative mode of the billboard magnifies its power. We wonder what it is telling us, and what we should do if we don't know. Not knowing opens up a wide arena for speculation. Indeed, the billboard has sent a strong message to some, generating the largest share of calls to the MAK Center of any of the artworks. We have heard from viewers who feared it, and were angry to have seen it at all. Refrains included: "Why isn't it in English?" "This is America!" "I'm a New Yorker; I survived 9/11 and that billboard makes me angry." In a way, the work is equally accessible, because it is equally unintelligible to the majority of viewers. At the same time, it is not an easy artwork to deal with, in that it forces the viewer to interrogate her own preconceptions about the Other, specifically an Islamic Other. The work is designed to evoke feelings of xenophobia and encourage processing that fear through examining its roots and conditions. If the viewer fails to self-reflect, she may become righteous and angry. As such, the mode

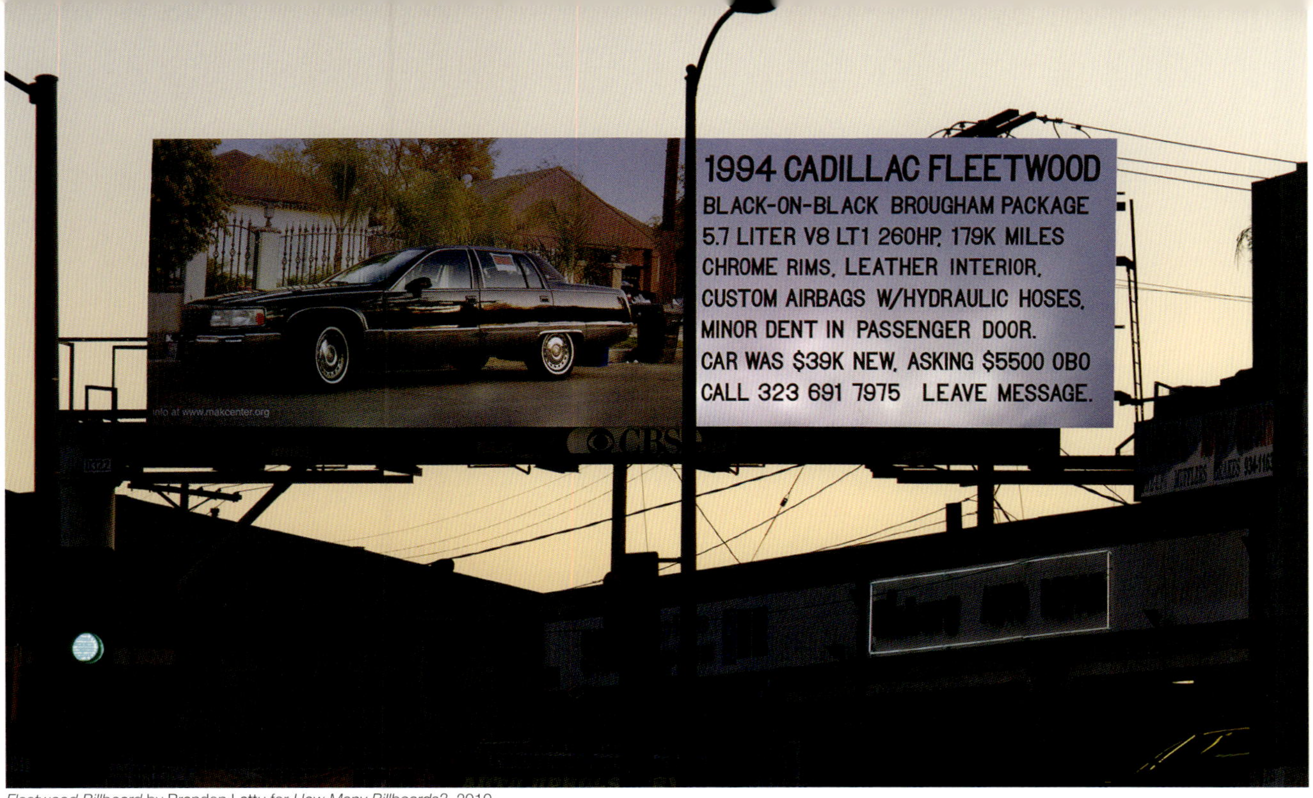

Fleetwood Billboard by Brandon Lattu for *How Many Billboards?*, 2010.

of messaging that woods employs walks a fine line between appealing to both the best and worst instincts and passions of the viewing public.

If outdoor advertising is the site, messaging is the medium (to play on Marshall McLuhan's famously prophetic declaration "The medium is the massage"). Typically, artists don't seek to convey a direct message, yet in the context of a billboard show, their works are set up to perform in that way. Site supersedes content and intent, in the sense that whatever appears on the billboard is read according to the conventions of the billboard as site.

Brandon Lattu's *Fleetwood Billboard* takes a site normally reserved for corporate speech and gives it over to individual, commercial messaging. Adopting the style and format of a classified ad, the artwork is an advertisement for a 1994 Cadillac Fleetwood. The car pictured is actually for sale; the text accurately describes the vehicle; the number listed is for a cell phone Lattu designated for the purpose of receiving messages about the ad; and inquiries related to purchasing the car are relayed to its owner by the artist. The artwork facilitates a sales transaction; as such it operates in the imperative mood with a message of "Buy this." Lattu maintains the marketing function of the billboard, but downshifts the product line from new to used, and from mass-produced to customized.

Cadillac Fleetwoods went out of production in 1996, but during their heyday they served as presidential transport, hearses, and ultimate luxury mobiles. Today, this classic car is no longer a symbol of wealth and power in the mainstream. However, it is popular with lowriders, a subcategory of California custom car culture. Lowriders come out of East Los Angeles, and their customized cars are considered a form of creative expression reflecting Mexican-American cultural pride. Lattu's interest in the Cadillac Fleetwood stems from its role as an indicator of how popular icons shift in meaning over time.

Unlike most corporate advertising billboards, the work provides the viewer with an opportunity to reply. In fact, the board has generated many calls, and the messages left offer insights into how it is being interpreted. People are used to seeing teasers—ads in which the subject of a promotion is unclear until it is unveiled in a subsequent ad—and many wondered if this board fell into that category:

It's really just a Caddy? It's not for something else, really? Wow!

The absurdity of using ad space worth well over the amount of the item for sale was commented upon in messages such as this one:

Just gotta know. Craigslist, Ebay, Cartrader, you just

had to go with a billboard. Um, look, there's a lotta of intelligent ways to go about things in life but spending money on a billboard and putting it on the middle of the street to sell a, whatever, Fleetwood for 5500 dollars seems a tad irrational and perhaps stupid. Um, I wish the best for you in life and I hope your retardation is fixed over time.

Many callers accepted both the message and its mode, while acknowledging the unconventional use of the ad space:

Ahh Ahh. #### Dang it. Pretty uh, hey what's up. Sorry, just spilled some water on my pants here, but just calling to see what inspired you to advertise in that manner. Because I am all about the Cadillac, but uh, yeh, just wondered about your approach there. So let me know if the car is sold, uh, condition of it, uh, what's going on, you know, etc. So give me a call back if you get this message. Phone number is — ——. You know, just history of stuff. Maybe Carfax, uh, acquisition date, trip, mileage, etc. and, uh, why you advertise it like that, but hey! to each his own, alright.

In notable distinction to a promotional campaign seeking many customers for many products, Lattu's ad functions as a direct means for commerce between one individual and another. The conventions of advertising have been disrupted, and the callers know it. The public response to both the woods and the Lattu commissions begs another question. Like the proverbial tree falling in the forest, is art still art if you don't know that it is? Does it matter whether people know that these billboards belong to a contemporary art exhibition? My

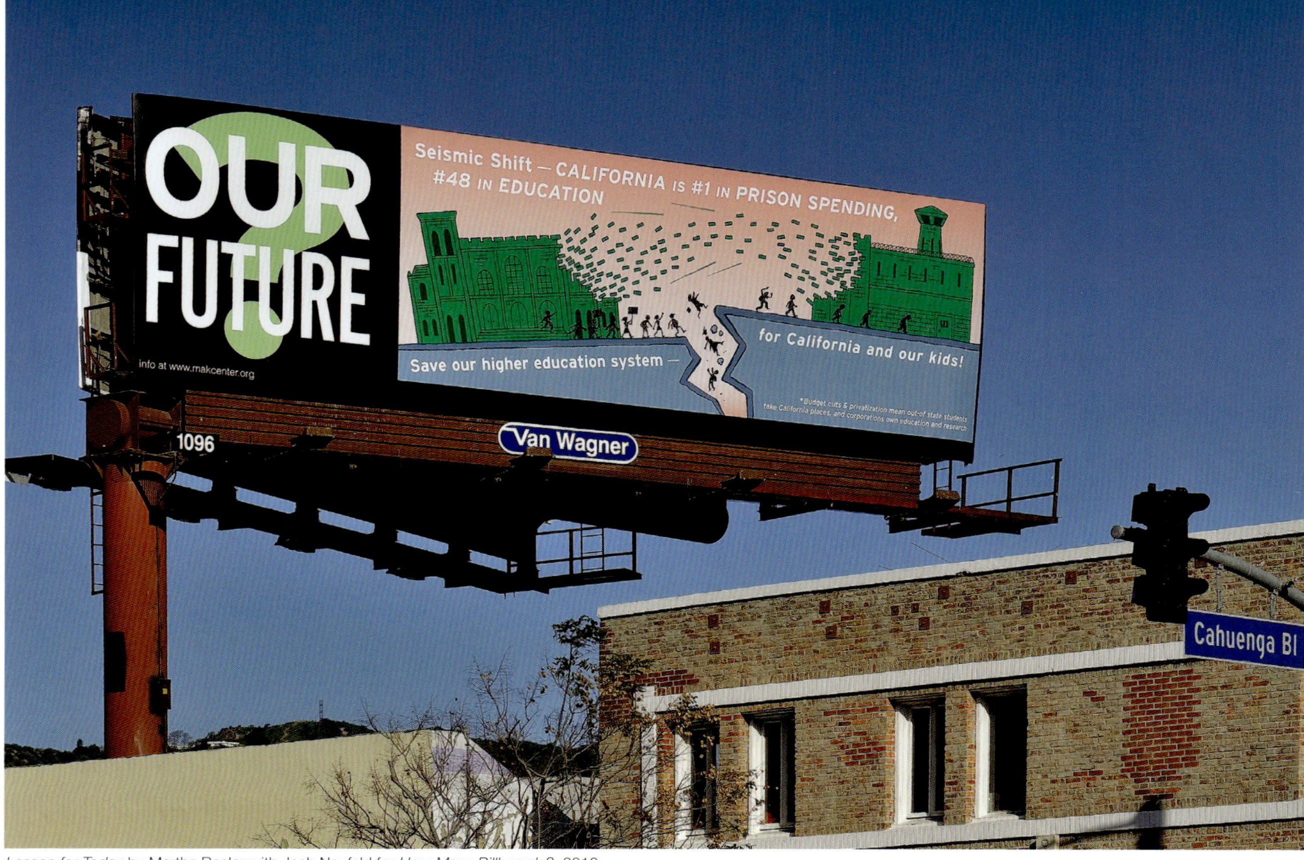

Lesson for Today by Martha Rosler with Josh Neufeld for *How Many Billboards?*, 2010.

answer is that what is most important is that viewers perceive a disruption, and are prompted to think more about their environment than they normally would by looking at a conventional ad. If they are turned on to art in the process, wonderful. The small, printed line "info at www.makcenter.org" that appears on all of the billboards offers a clue for those who seek it out.

Viewers could conceivably identify Martha Rosler and Josh Neufeld's *Lesson for Today* as non-art. The artists speak directly with their bold words: "Seismic Shift—CALIFORNIA is #1 in PRISON SPENDING, #48 in EDUCATION" and "Save our higher education system—for California and our kids!" In smaller type it reads: "Budget cuts & privatization mean out-of-state students take California places, and corporations own education and research." The graphic drawing shows bricks flying off of a school and onto a prison, and children literally falling through a big crack in the ground.

The imperative mood is adopted both linguistically ("Save our higher education system") and structurally (it assumes the authoritative voice of a public service announcement). It backs up its directive with key facts and posts an image illustrating the problem. In an interview with the MAK Center, Rosler makes clear that she wants to communicate with a broad public. Her stated intent is to make people think about the state of public education in California and how it will affect them. "The system will be sold, in effect, to people who can pay from other states, and your kids won't have access," she says in the interview.[3] However, the piece doesn't operate like a typical issue advocacy ad or public service announcement—there is no ballot initiative to vote for or against, no toll-free number to call, no organization to join. The viewer is called upon

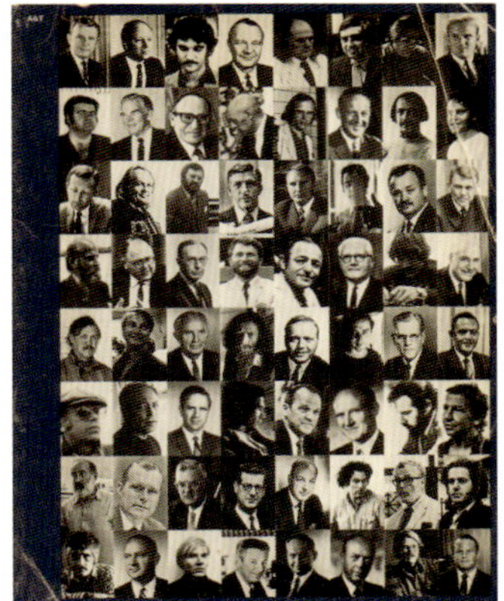

Cover of LACMA's *Art and Technology* exhibition catalog, 1971
Los Angeles County Museum of Art,
Los Angeles California, U.S.A.
Digital Image © 2009 Museum Associates/LACMA/Art Resource, NY

to reflect on the facts posed, and figure out how to act accordingly.

Rosler and Neufeld first conceived of this work in 1999 for *Projections: Intermission Images II.* Organized by Karen Atkinson with Side Street Projects, the exhibition featured slide shows that were projected during intermissions at movie theaters in Los Angeles. At the time, state budgets indicated that cuts and hard times were looming for education, while the prison system continued to be well funded. The topic was controversial; the artwork was censored. Fourteen years later, the crises with the education and prison budgets have become urgent, as global financial woes wreak havoc on state coffers and the number of incarcerated continues to grow rapidly. Recent news stories have highlighted the fact that, since high school dropout rates in Los Angeles have been high for decades and are statistically related to rates of incarceration, dropout rates factor in to the business plans of private prison-building corporations. Clearly, Rosler and Neufeld's message is as relevant now as it was in 1999. On exhibit for the first time more than ten years later,

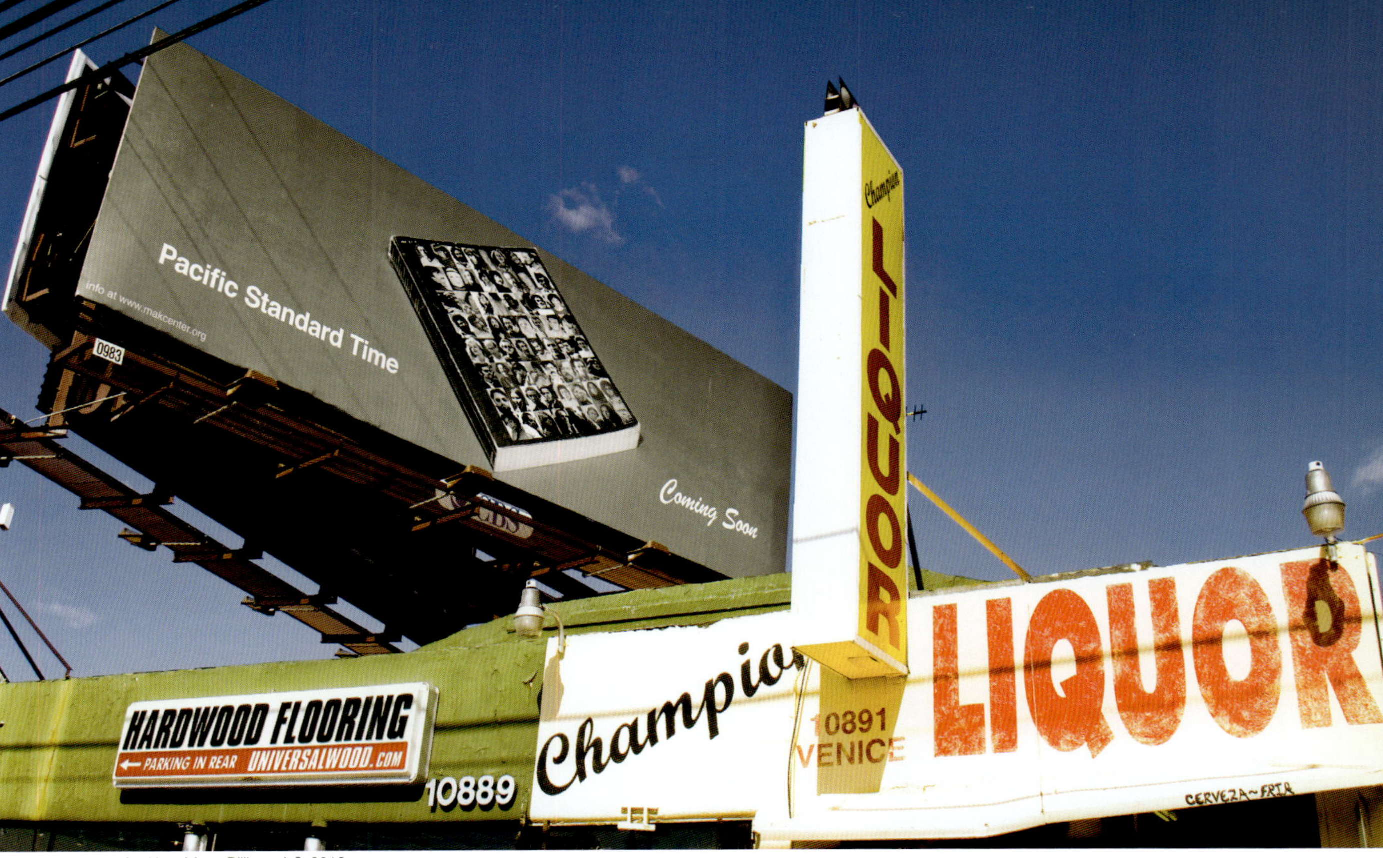

Allen Ruppersberg for *How Many Billboards?*, 2010.

the work has not, to our knowledge, received any negative attention.

Allen Ruppersberg's billboard addresses a more specific group of viewers by delivering an unsolicited advertisement for an upcoming cultural event. On the billboard, the phrases "Pacific Standard Time" and "Coming Soon" flank an image of a worn book with a grid of faces on its cover. The image is an alteration of the catalog *A Report on the Art and Technology Program of the Los Angeles County Museum of Art, 1967–71*, which documents a project at LACMA that paired artists with high technology corporations. Ruppersberg's text refers to the massive exhibition project *Pacific Standard Time: Art in L.A., 1945–80,* organized by the Getty Foundation and the Getty Research Initiative and set to open in 2011. The multi-venue project will focus on the history of post-WWII art in the region. Whereas the cover of the original *Report on the Art and Technology Program* features a grid of portraits of some of the artists, scientists, and corporate officials who participated in the program, Ruppersberg's alteration includes faces of artists who are in the demographic of the *Pacific Standard Time* exhibition. (*How Many Billboards?* participants Michael Asher and Martha Rosler appear in the grid.) The image of the book on the billboard is strikingly large and detailed; the cracked and frayed edges of the volume are visible, as are the faces. In this work, Ruppersberg ties together two large-scale cultural projects by major Los Angeles museums that are 40 years apart. As a message within *How Many Billboards?*, the work brings three exhibitions in concert. It also points to the fact that Ruppersberg, who has now been an influential figure in Los Angeles art since the 1960s, is being historicized along with his milieu.

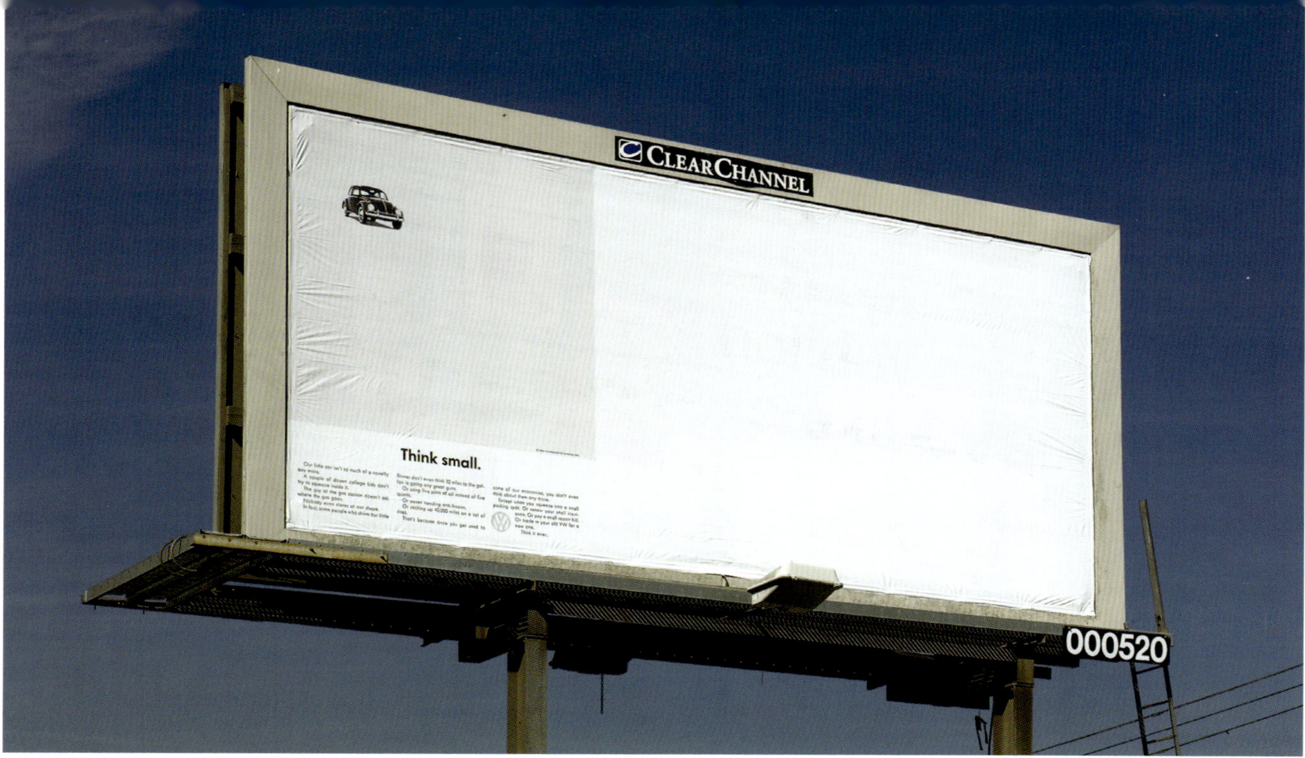

Michael Asher for *How Many Billboards?*, 2010.

Here, institutional speech is overtaken by artistic speech in several ways. As a participant in the MAK Center's *How Many Billboards?*, Ruppersberg uses the artist's platform and related funding to promote another institution's upcoming exhibition project. As a participant in *Pacific Standard Time*, he is promoting the Getty's activities without their knowledge or expressed permission. In an era in which branding and graphic identity are paramount, such unauthorized messaging—even when positive—seems mildly subversive.

In the case of Michael Asher's commission, artistic speech presents a historical image of corporate speech. The work displays a 1962 magazine advertisement from the "Think Small" campaign designed by Doyle, Dane, and Bernbach (DDB) for promoting the Volkswagen Beetle in the United States. Asher presents an image of the ad on the left side of a billboard. The ad includes a photograph with a small VW Beetle in the upper left corner, and text at the bottom of the page with the headline "Think small." The ad, like the billboard, is mostly white space. The tag line is strident, the imagery minimal, and the tone humorous and self-effacing. The body of the text reads:

Our car isn't so much of a novelty anymore. A couple of dozen college kids don't try to squeeze inside it. The guy at the gas station doesn't ask where the gas goes. Nobody even stares at our shape. In fact, some people who drive our little flivver don't even think 32 miles to the gallon is going any great guns. Or using five pints of oil instead of five quarts. Or never needing anti-freeze. Or racking up 40,000 miles on a set of tires. That's because once you get used to some of our economies, you don't even think about them anymore. Except when you squeeze into a small parking spot. Or renew your small insurance. Or pay a small repair bill. Or trade in your old VW for a new one. Think it over.

When the campaign was launched in 1959, it ran counter to the ballooning, post-war, consumer-driven economy. Its dual message was not only "Buy this," but also "You don't need as much as you think." That message took hold in the counterculture of the 1960s and '70s, as it provided a way to resist the ideals of consumer capitalism, as well as to address growing concerns about the industrialized world's impact on the environment. The tone of the campaign was considered counterintuitive at a time when marketing strategies either delivered information in a straightforward way, or attempted to create consumer desire through product aggrandizement. The ad campaign is considered one of the most influential of the twentieth century, and is credited with starting a creative revolution in advertising in which copywriters and art directors work closely together. The ad still has popular currency, appearing in the cable television series *Mad Men* (AMC) as the competition for the ad men protagonists, and in an episode of *This American Life* (produced by Chicago Public Radio) in a story about the true authorship of the ad's concept.

Asher's piece brings several ideas to our attention. First, by re-presenting this 50-year-old ad campaign, it points out that conspicuous consumption thrives and still merits critique. Asher's re-presentation comes at a time when the 40:1 leveraging of the financial sector, combined with widespread, unmanageable personal debt, nearly sank the U.S. and global economies. The piece asks: What have we learned, or failed to learn, since 1960? With unemployment high and financial futures uncertain, it seems to advocate the notion of living on limited means without sacrificing good design and simple pleasures. As concerns about environmental problems, including climate change, become increasingly urgent, it speaks to a growing need to bring ecologically sustainable practices into daily life, including conserving resources and scaling down. Secondly, the presence of an ad inside of an artwork draws a comparison between advertising and art. Voices in contemporary art have claimed that sophisticated advertising borrows heavily from the leading edges of art (and in several cases it has been demonstrated in court). Asher's piece suggests that the exchange is mutual, positing that the ad's use of white space, its minimalist composition, and the text's ironic tone in the positioning of its product, all foreshadow developments in art that were still on the horizon in the early 1960s.

Thirdly, Asher's artwork points to ideology and the transformation of a consumer item. Volkswagen translates from the German as "people's car," and it was first conceived and commissioned by Adolf Hitler in 1933 as an affordable car for an average Aryan family. The Beetle model went into production in 1938, however its production was quickly interrupted by the start of World War II. During the war, the base of the car was used for military vehicles, while a small number of Beetles were produced for the Nazi elite. The genocidal aggression of Hitler is in sharp dissonance with the ideals of the progressives, hippies, and environmentalists who later gravitated toward the Beetle in the 1960s and '70s. The "Think Small" campaign may well be responsible for helping the VW Beetle to shed its sinister associations. Communication in the imperative mood produced a phenomenon; Asher's use of that directive prompts a reflection on the power of the message.

In the midst of the vast banality of repetitious commercial speech, the singular artworks in *How Many Billboards?* shatter the inevitable numbness that occurs with media overload. Though essentially two-dimensional works, the scale, visibility and context of their installation on billboards bring the works into a vividly three-dimensional realm. Often, their immediate environments affect their meaning and reception. Although I had the opportunity to make some suggestions about which works went in which of the slots made available by the billboard companies, ultimately their locations were determined by a combination of factors, most of which were out of our control. As a result, chance was a factor in their installation. For example, woods's Arabic script assumes greater force based on its proximity to Israeli-owned shops and restaurants. The serendipitous placement of Lattu's Fleetwood ad over a smog-check auto mechanic shop has the effect of reinforcing its advertising message and giving the sense that the message belongs to the shop. In many of the works, nearby signage seems to be in dialogue with the artworks; the randomness of the conversation lends a Dada-like quality to the situation. In all cases, the presence of the artworks has the effect of highlighting the city around them.

In spite of a long history of community mural-making, and beyond uninspiring programs that requires that 1% of construction budgets go for public art, Los Angeles has not sustained a dedicated infrastructure for presenting art in public space. In contrast to cities such as New York, which hosts a number of organizations that commission and show art in public, and Muenster, Germany, which has committed itself to the Muenster Skulptur Project, Los Angeles has not yet developed this resource. In Los Angeles, billboards provide a consistent, recognizable standard to view commissioned art. Their regularity and industrial standardization, combined with their spectacular ability to get people's attention, make them an ideal place to site an exhibition and introduce contemporary art to a local public.

In their book *Learning from Las Vegas* (1972), Robert Venturi and Denise Scott Brown ponder if signs are replacing architecture as public symbols. A look around the cityscape of Los Angeles provides a convincing answer. *How Many Billboards?* proposes a reconsideration of today's urban media space by interrupting it with critical, contemporary art. It emphasizes a subtractive approach of inserting art into public space by choosing to displace advertising rather than add more visual noise to the already cluttered environment. Ultimately, *How Many Billboards?* issues a call for a more active engagement between art and urban media space.

[1] Based on industry calculations provided by Rick Robinson, West Coast General Manager / National Creative Director, MacDonald Media, in an email on March 8, 2010.

[2] Mike Boehm, "MOCA Exhibit Drew World-Class Numbers—But Not in L.A." *Los Angeles Times*, April 1, 2010.

[3] Videotaped interview with Martha Rosler, February 26, 2010 http://www.howmanybillboards.org/rosler-neufeld.html.

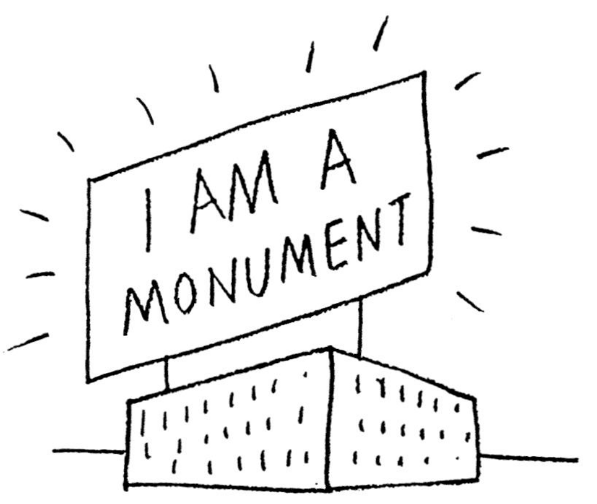

Image from *Learning from Las Vegas* by Robert Venturi and Denise Scott Brown
Published by the MIT Press, 1977
Courtesy of Venturi, Scott Brown and Associates, Inc.

THE EXHIBITION

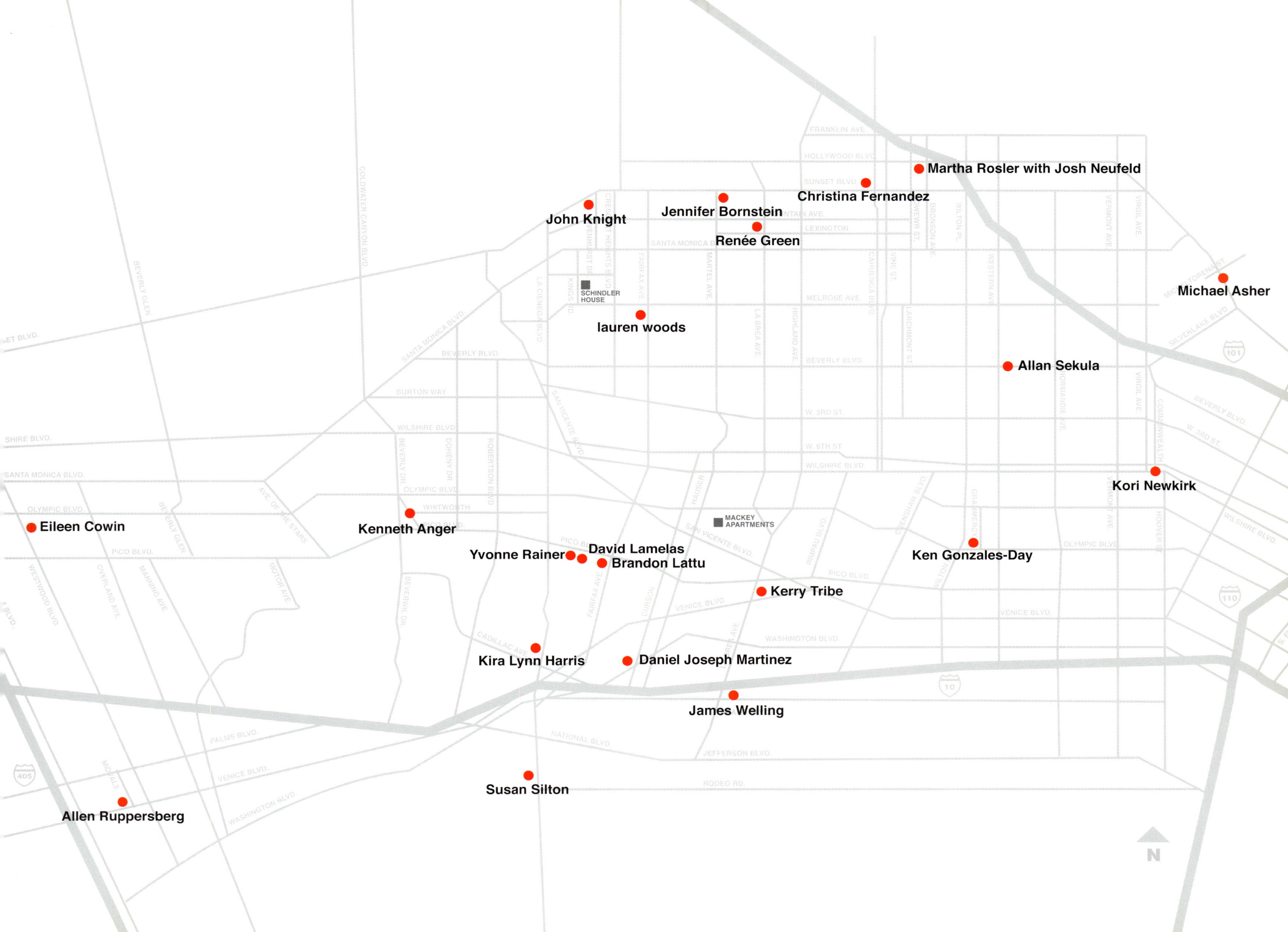
Martha Rosler with Josh Neufeld
Christina Fernandez
Jennifer Bornstein
John Knight
Renée Green
SCHINDLER HOUSE
Michael Asher
lauren woods
Allan Sekula
Kori Newkirk
Eileen Cowin
Kenneth Anger
MACKEY APARTMENTS
David Lamelas
Yvonne Rainer
Brandon Lattu
Ken Gonzales-Day
Kerry Tribe
Kira Lynn Harris
Daniel Joseph Martinez
James Welling
Susan Silton
Allen Ruppersberg
N

KENNETH ANGER

Kenneth Anger is a trailblazer of queer avant-garde film; he debuted his film *Fireworks* (1947) more than two decades before the landmark events of Stonewall in 1969. Numerous films that he has written and directed over the years have risen from underground to cult status. In Anger's rich oeuvre, images function not only as symbols, visual icons, or indices, but also as affective strobes meant to amaze and hypnotize the viewer.

In his billboard project, the word "ASTONISH" is spelled in all caps in bold, neon orange, sans serif font. The word fills most of the frame; the artist's scripted signature in lilac hovers diagonally across the bottom corner. The design enhances the impact of the word "astonish" beyond its denotation, and its meaning is activated here in several different ways. It echoes Anger's filmic strategy of montage as magic, where he employs consecutive or flashing images to enchant the audience. Here, a single word serves to bewitch. Yet, at the same time, the word informs the viewer about the action that is taking place, collapsing conventional art historical distinctions between affect and critical distance. Anger's ambivalent relationship to the spectacle of Hollywood, visible in his films as well as in his famous book *Hollywood Babylon* (Paris, 1959), is here directed towards the media. "ASTONISH" can function as recognition of the media's ability to astonish, as a critique of its power over the public, or perhaps, as a call for the media to step up its game and create something that can truly astonish. Multiple potential referents for the bold neon statement are raised to the power of two when cross-referenced with Anger's signature. Commonly standing for presence, it plays at once on the outmoded, Modernist gesture of signing an artwork—evidence that "the artist has been here" and proof of the artwork's originality—and on the notion of the autograph, which is alive and well in celebrity culture. Detached from the artist's hand, processed, enlarged, and reproduced, here, the commoditization of the autograph is amplified, reflecting the Postmodern emphasis on the multiple, the reproducible, and the conceptual as modes of art-making, and the ways in which those practices have come to be bought and sold.

BY NIZAN SHAKED

LOCATION: Beverly Drive, north of Pico Boulevard, on the west side of the street, facing southeast.

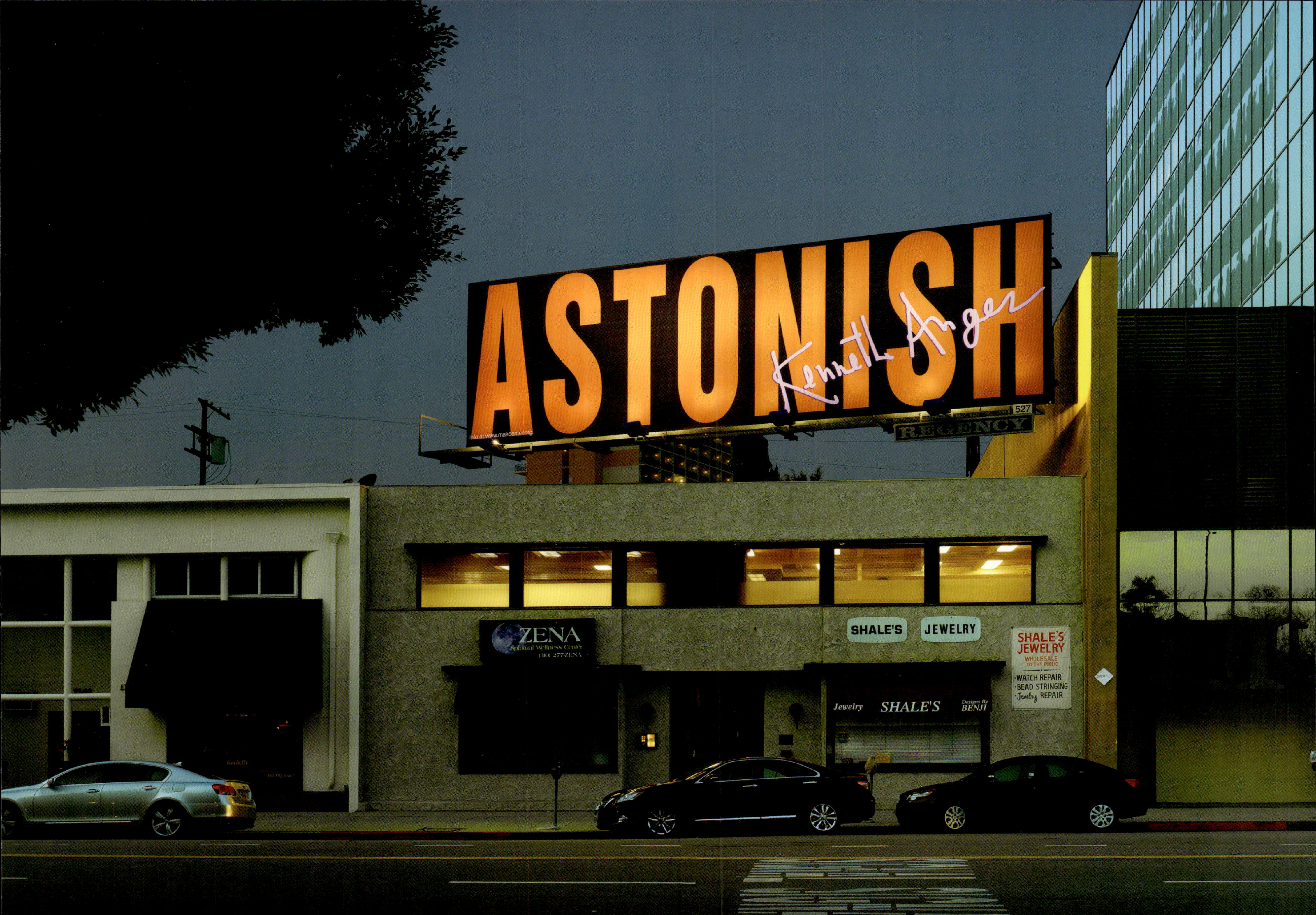
ASTONISH
Kenneth Anger
527
REGENCY
ZENA
SHALE'S
JEWELRY
SHALE'S JEWELRY
WATCH REPAIR
BEAD STRINGING
Jewelry REPAIR
Jewelry
SHALE'S
Designs By BENJI

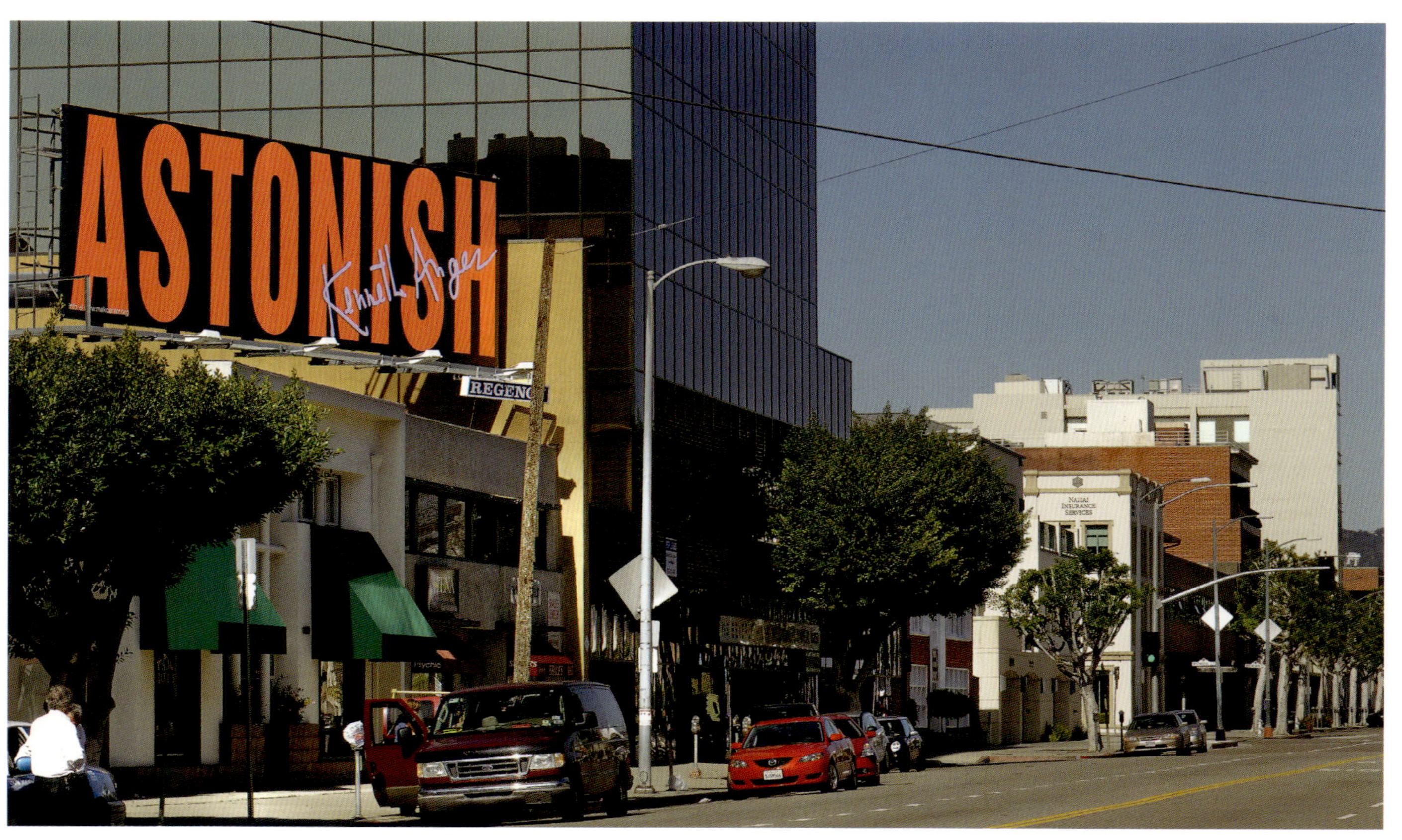
ASTONISH
Kenneth Anger
REGENC

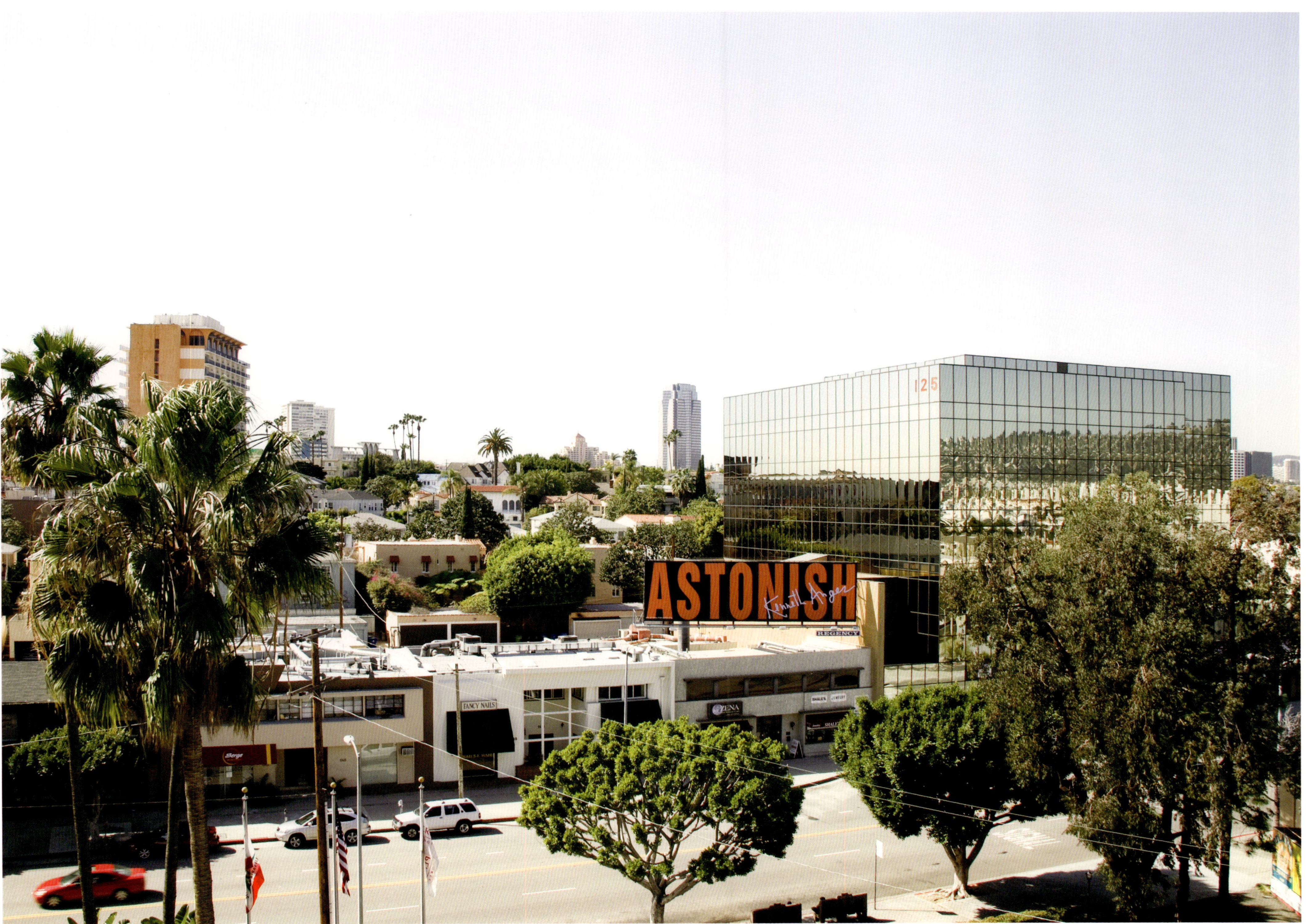
125
ASTONISH
Kenneth Anger
REGENCY
FANCY NAILS

MICHAEL ASHER

Michael Asher works site-specifically: he answers an invitation to exhibit by analyzing the host venue, identifying key areas of interest, and instigating a proposition that responds to the exhibition site. Most of his works are singular exhibitions in museums; in the case of *How Many Billboards?,* the site of exhibition is advertising space. Asher's piece is a reproduction of a 1962 print advertisement by Doyle, Dane, and Bernbach for the marketing of Volkswagens in the United States. "Think small" was the tagline in the ad and it became the concept of the campaign. Asher's piece performs a kind of time travel, stretching back a half a century and replaying a historical campaign for our present consideration. When the "Think small" ads came out, America was firmly committed to a post-war economy perpetuated by the rapid growth of consumerism. Going against that grain, the "Think small" message encouraged investment in a reliable, affordable car rather than an oversized, flashy one. Visually and linguistically, the message of the campaign was to consume less, not more. Yet the ad's critique of big consumerism performed well for corporate capitalism: many cars were sold, and the ad itself is credited with creating a sea change in the way advertising is created.

Asher's choice of ads reflects several ideas. Firstly, the revisited ad can be read as a challenge to the excesses of consumer capitalism. The VW bug became the iconographic vehicle for a 1960s counter-culture, as its efficient approach to economy rang true with subcultures that were becoming aware of humanity's impact on the planet. Today the "Think small" message resonates, as concerns with global sustainability are heightened, the United States grapples with a major economic crisis, and the model of unfettered growth, massive consumerism, and the debt that fuels such an economy are questioned. Secondly, its reinstallation prompts a comparison of art and advertisement, and suggests the influence of one upon the other. The use of white space, the composition of the picture plane, and the ironic tone, foreshadow developments to occur in contemporary art in the 1960s and after. Thirdly, the subject of the ad is a Volkswagen, which originated from Nazi Germany as a "people's car" serving the dark ambitions of Adolf Hitler. Asher interrogates the transformation of VW from Nazi ideal to hippie mobile, reflecting, as he notes in an unpublished artist statement, on the "iconic and discursive status that constitutes its contemporary reception."

BY KIMBERLI MEYER

LOCATIONS: Glendale Boulevard, north of Silverlake Boulevard, on the west side of the street, facing south. Originally located on Sunset Boulevard, east of Micheltorena Street, on the north side of the street, facing east.

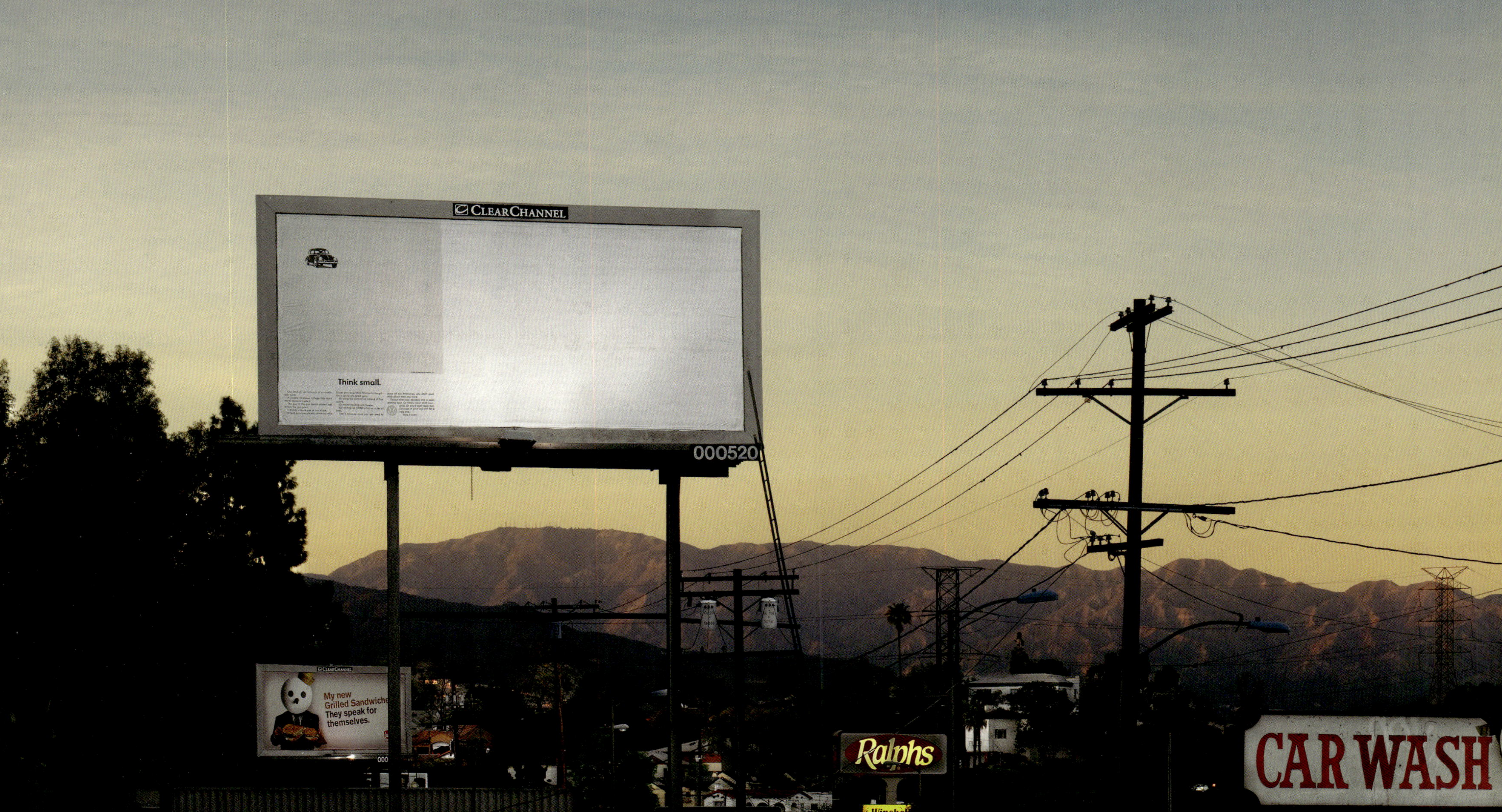
CLEARCHANNEL
Think small.
000520
My new
Grilled Sandwiche
They speak for
themselves.
Ralphs
CAR WASH

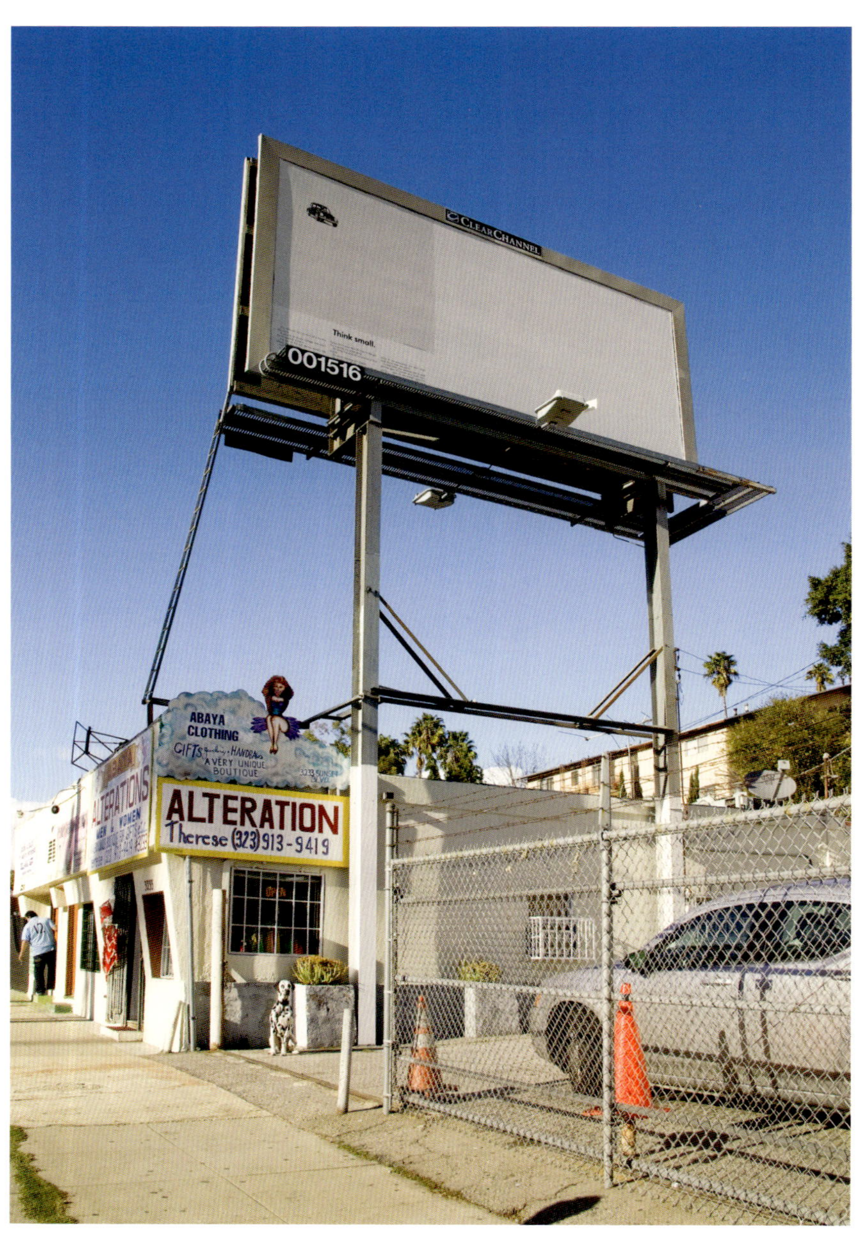
CLEAR CHANNEL
Think small.
001516
ABAYA
CLOTHING
GIFTS
A VERY UNIQUE
BOUTIQUE
ALTERATIONS
MEN & WOMEN
ALTERATION
Therese (323) 913-9419

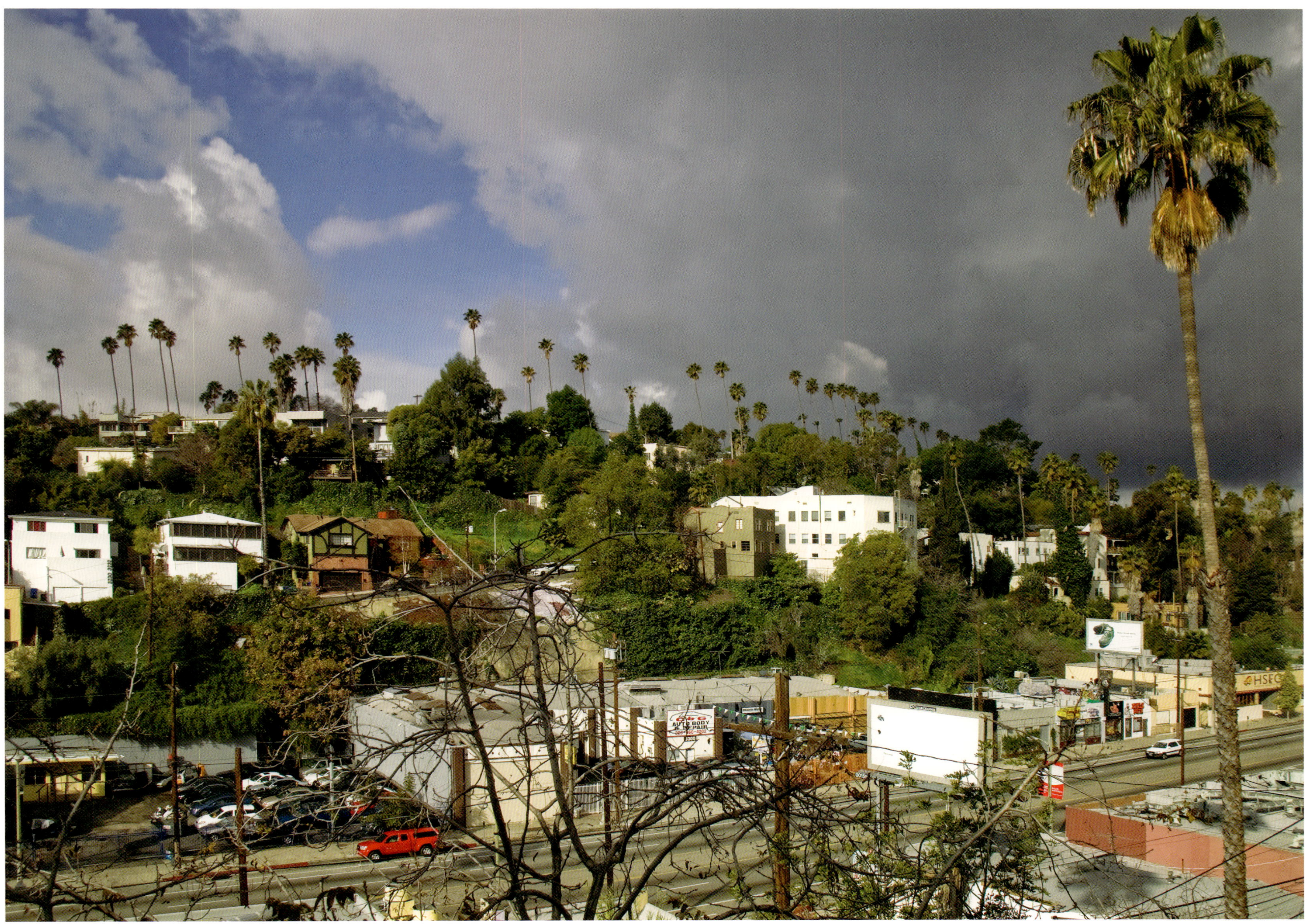
C&G
AUTO BODY
& REPAIR
3300
HSFC

JENNIFER BORNSTEIN

Since the late 1990s, Jennifer Bornstein has been engaged in producing serialized images in a variety of media, including sculpture, photography, 16 mm film, and most recently, intaglio printing. While doing research for a film project in 2003, Bornstein studied various 19th-century periodicals, in particular the engravings that illustrated these publications. That year she began the arduous task of learning the techniques of incising and copperplate printing in order to generate intaglio prints that she often uses as studies for her films.

Counterbalancing the "slow art" of the etching with the vehicular pace of billboard viewing is an example of how Bornstein's conceptual rigor is infused with a sly sense of humor. For *How Many Billboards?* Bornstein produced an etching that was then copied and enlarged. A precious medium intended for close study at intimate range is now stretched incongruously across several yards and exposed to the elements. Its subject is an Eiki 16 mm film projector atop a simple wood crate (an utilitarian material that often appears in Bornstein's sculptures). The fragmentary words "The End" are projected solemnly across the muted darkness rendered by Bornstein's meshwork of crosshatches, signaling celluloid's imminent demise in today's digital environment. The words and gothic type reverse engineer the technological progression of the history of media. Film's death knell is delivered in the even more antiquated process of copperplate etching. Bornstein's font choice also underscores typography's signficance within the history of Conceptual Art. Ed Ruscha's *The End* (1991) shows the same phrase and font; the bottom register is cut off and repeated at the top, mimicking film's movement in frames. Ruscha's painting is emblematic of Conceptual Art's ability to generate metaphorical meaning from words and type. Bornstein's expertise in copperplate etching offers a significant counterpoint to the narrative of de-skilling often identified with Ruscha and West Coast Conceptualism.

BY GLORIA SUTTON

LOCATION: Sunset Boulevard, west of Martel Avenue, on the south side of the street, facing east.

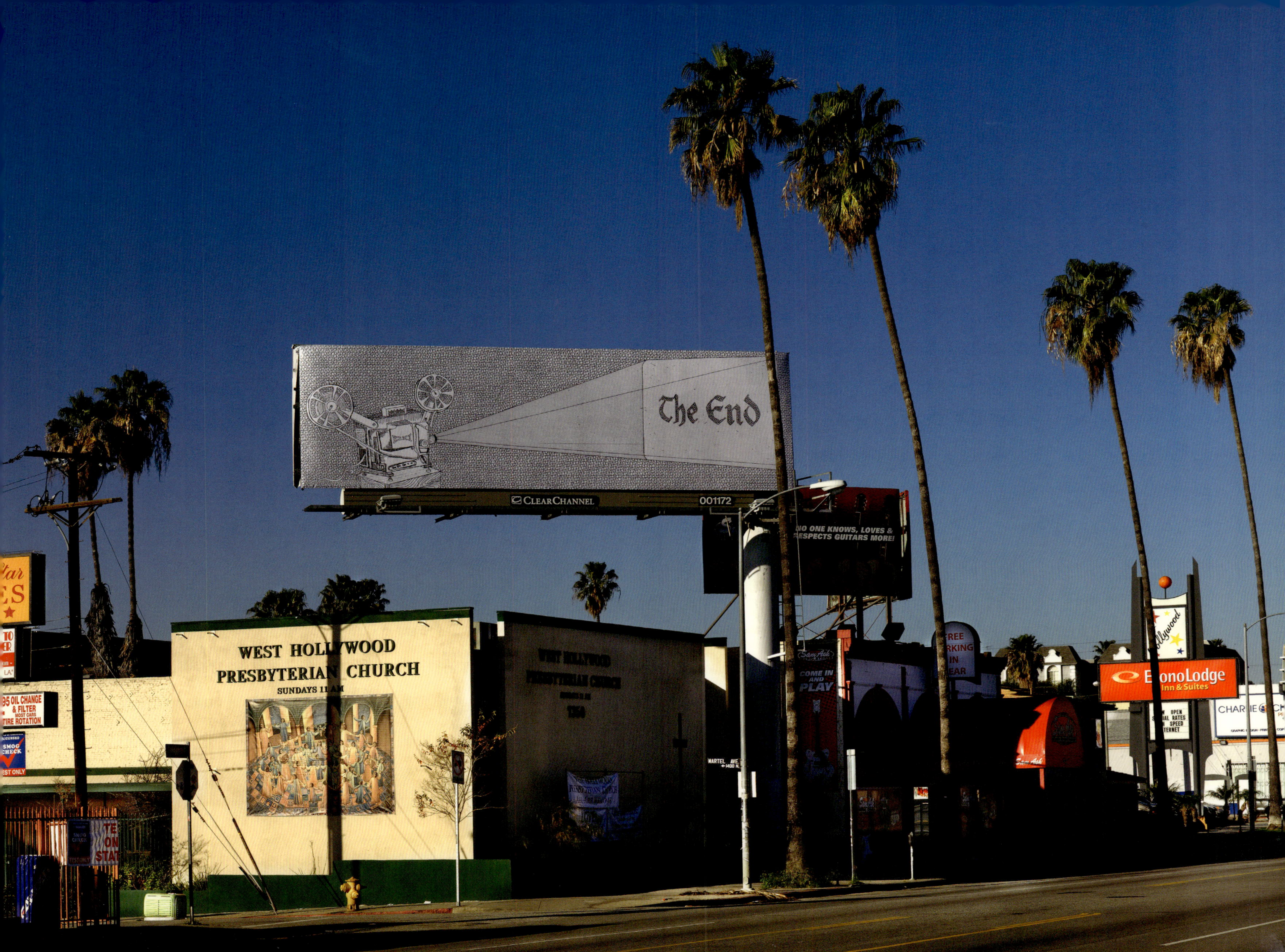
The End
CLEARCHANNEL
001172
NO ONE KNOWS, LOVES &
RESPECTS GUITARS MORE!
WEST HOLLYWOOD
PRESBYTERIAN CHURCH
SUNDAYS 11 AM
COME IN
AND
PLAY
EconoLodge
Inn & Suites
SMOG
CHECK

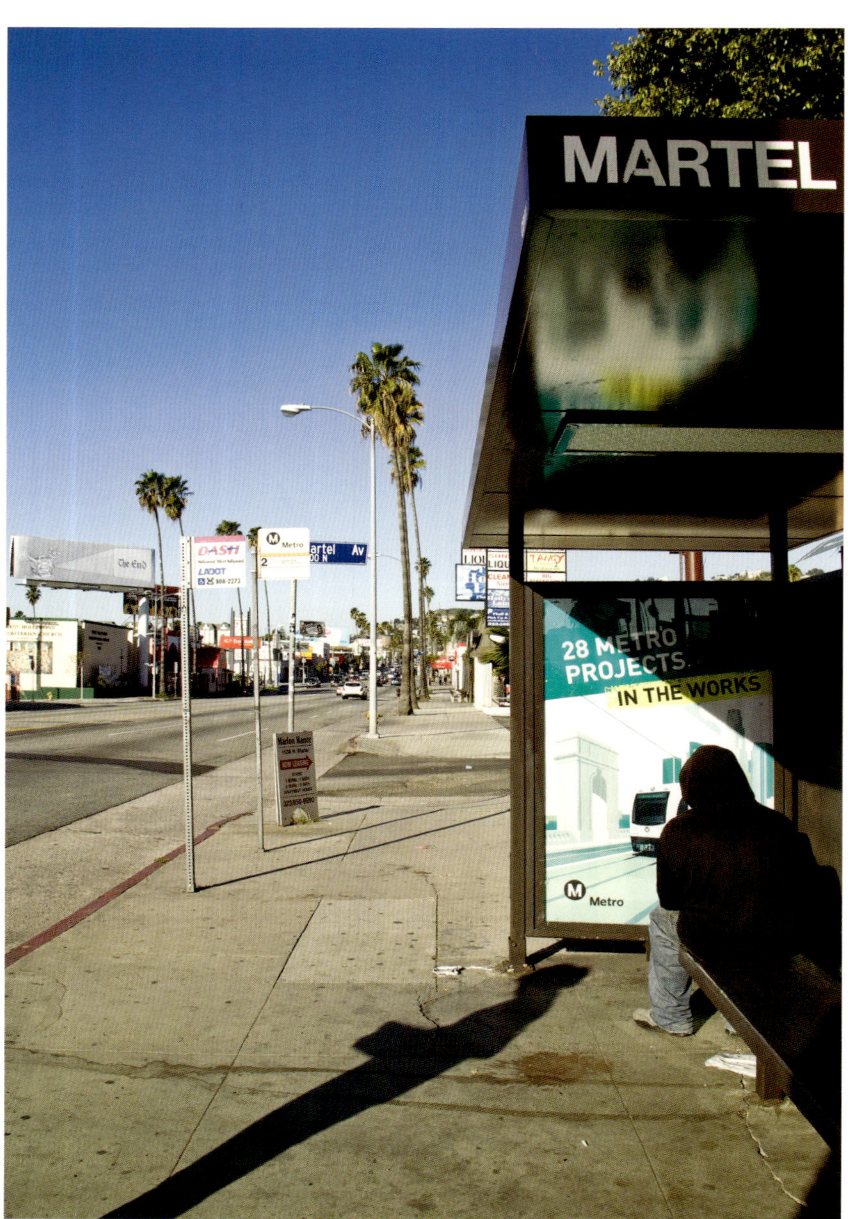
MARTEL
28 METRO
PROJECTS.
IN THE WORKS
Metro

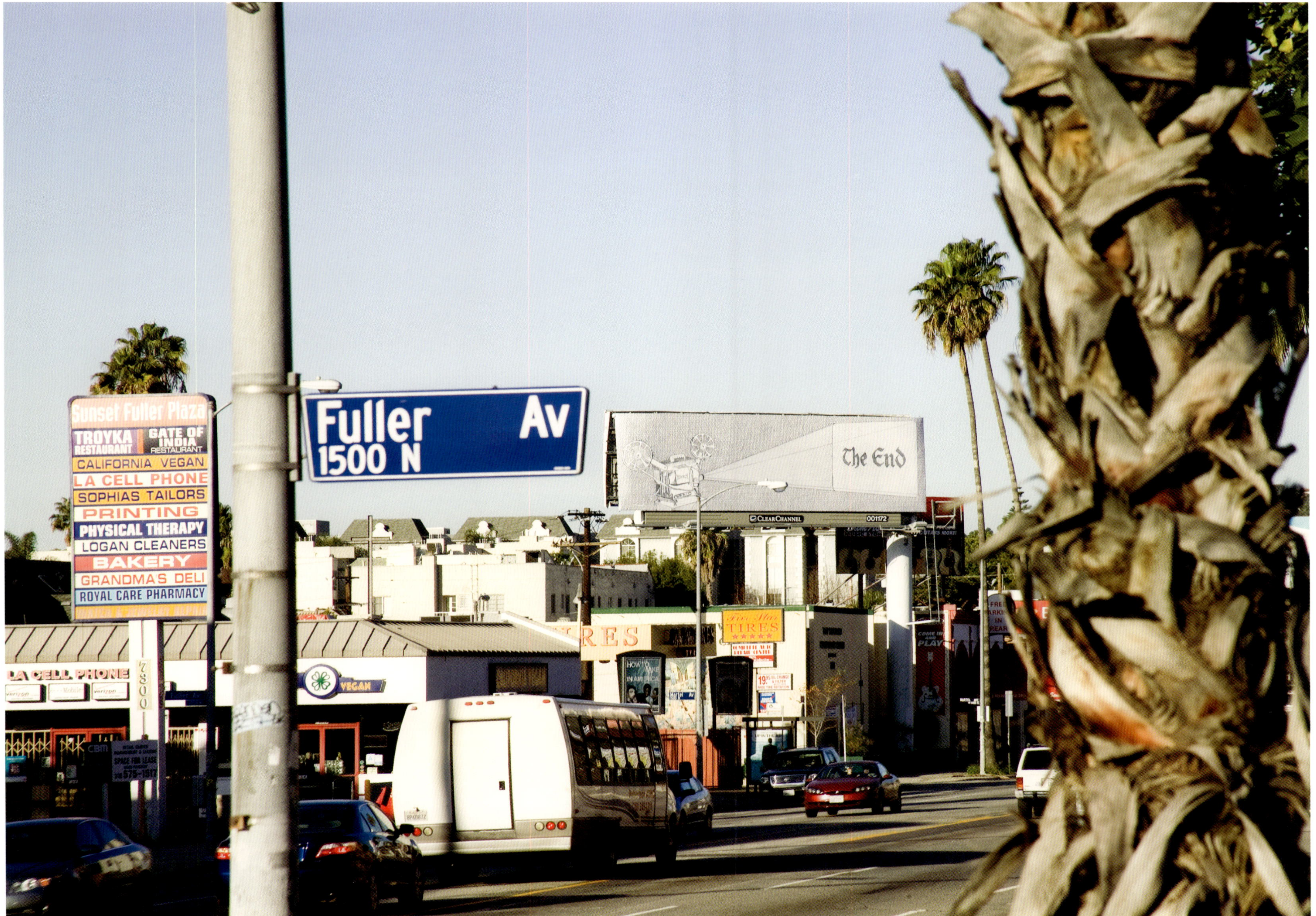

Sunset Fuller Plaza
TROYKA RESTAURANT
GATE OF INDIA RESTAURANT
CALIFORNIA VEGAN
LA CELL PHONE
SOPHIAS TAILORS
PRINTING
PHYSICAL THERAPY
LOGAN CLEANERS
BAKERY
GRANDMA'S DELI
ROYAL CARE PHARMACY
Fuller Av
1500 N
The End
CLEARCHANNEL
001172
TIRES
LA CELL PHONE
VEGAN

EILEEN COWIN

The works of photographer and video artist Eileen Cowin range from dramatic photo tableaux to installations and multi-channel videos. Cowin's conceptual approach to photography and video has not diminished her interest in human emotion. Her diverse body of work includes a commissioned billboard for the Los Angeles County Museum of Art's expansive exhibition *Made in California* (2000). That billboard featured a poignant diptych called *Yearning for Perfection II.* In the first image two hands hold a photograph of a seascape; in the second a woman, her back to the camera, stands facing the sea.

That image is a stark contrast to her contribution to *How Many Billboards?*. For the current exhibition, Cowin combines a cropped face with a single line of text. From the extreme right we see the partial profile of a white man with his mouth open. The words "I love you too," printed in pink, float in the black expanse of the background. At billboard scale, the image is commanding yet ambiguous. Cowin elevates a familiar phrase to the point where we become aware of how subtle variations in tone and facial expression can dramatically affect a sentiment that seems universal. The piece reveals Cowin's interest in both intimacy and the disintegrating boundaries between public and private space.

BY LISA HENRY

LOCATION: Westwood Boulevard, south of Olympic Boulevard, on the east side of the street, facing north.

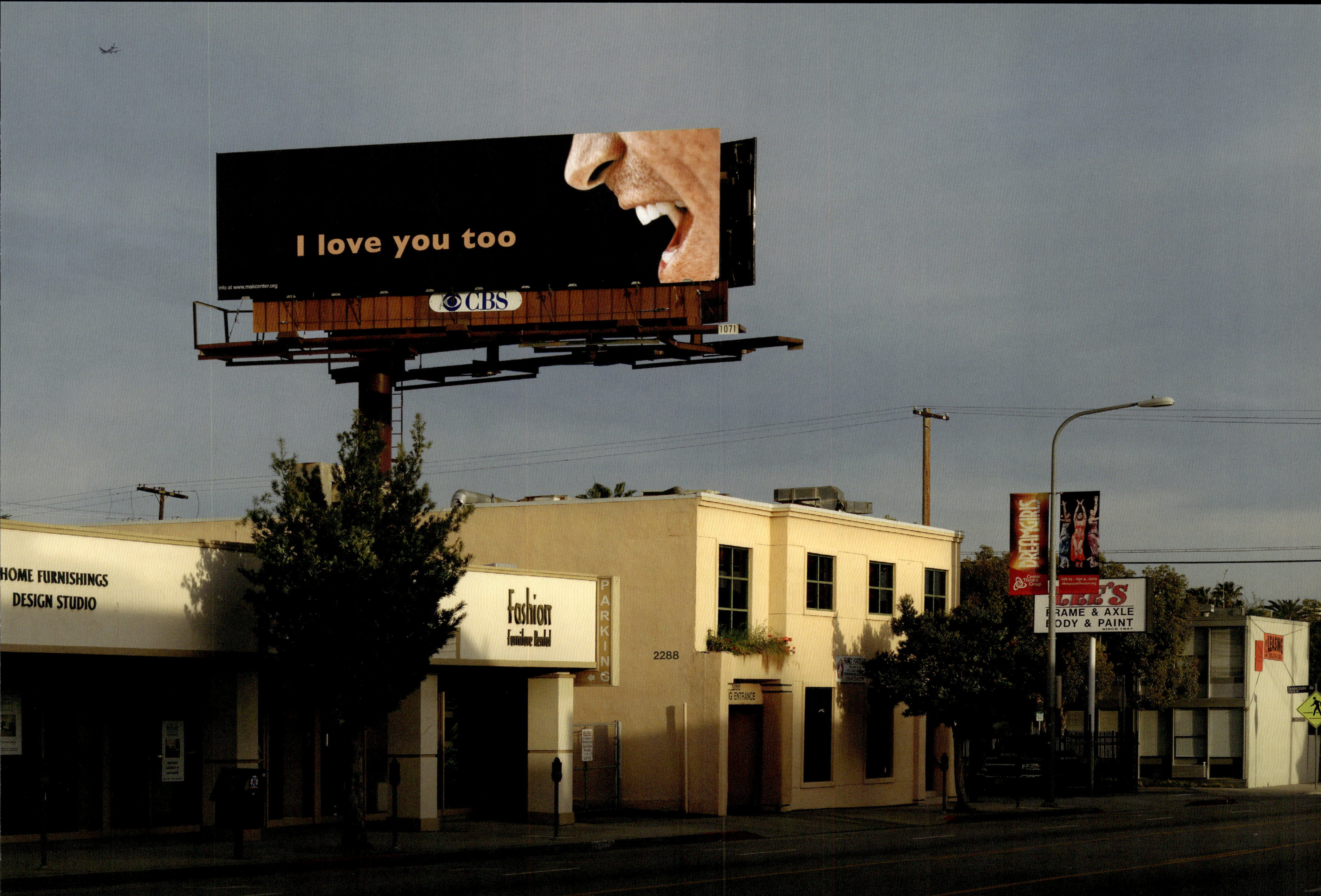
I love you too
CBS
1071
HOME FURNISHINGS
DESIGN STUDIO
Fashion
Furniture Rental
PARKING
2288
DREAMGIRLS

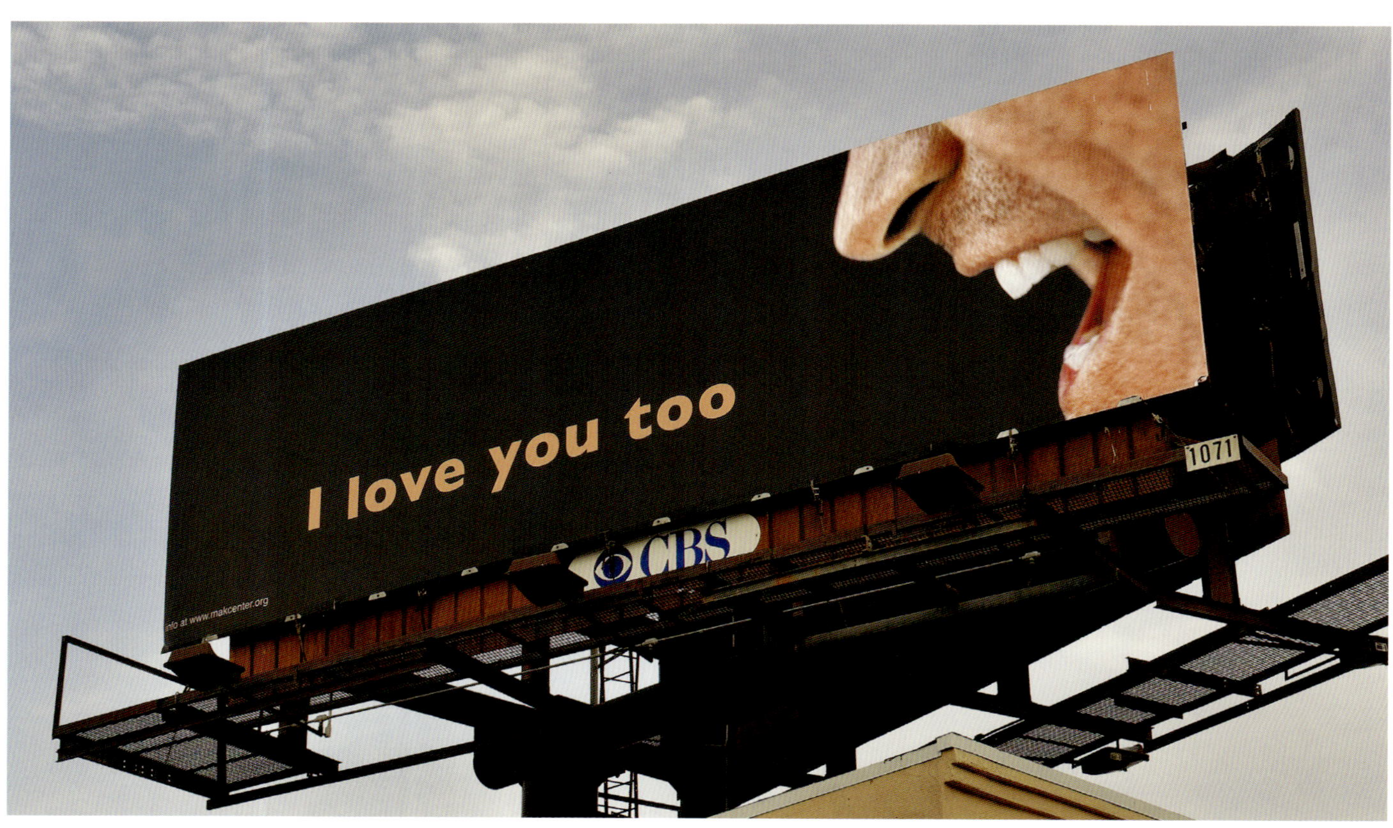
I love you too
CBS
1071
info at www.makcenter.org

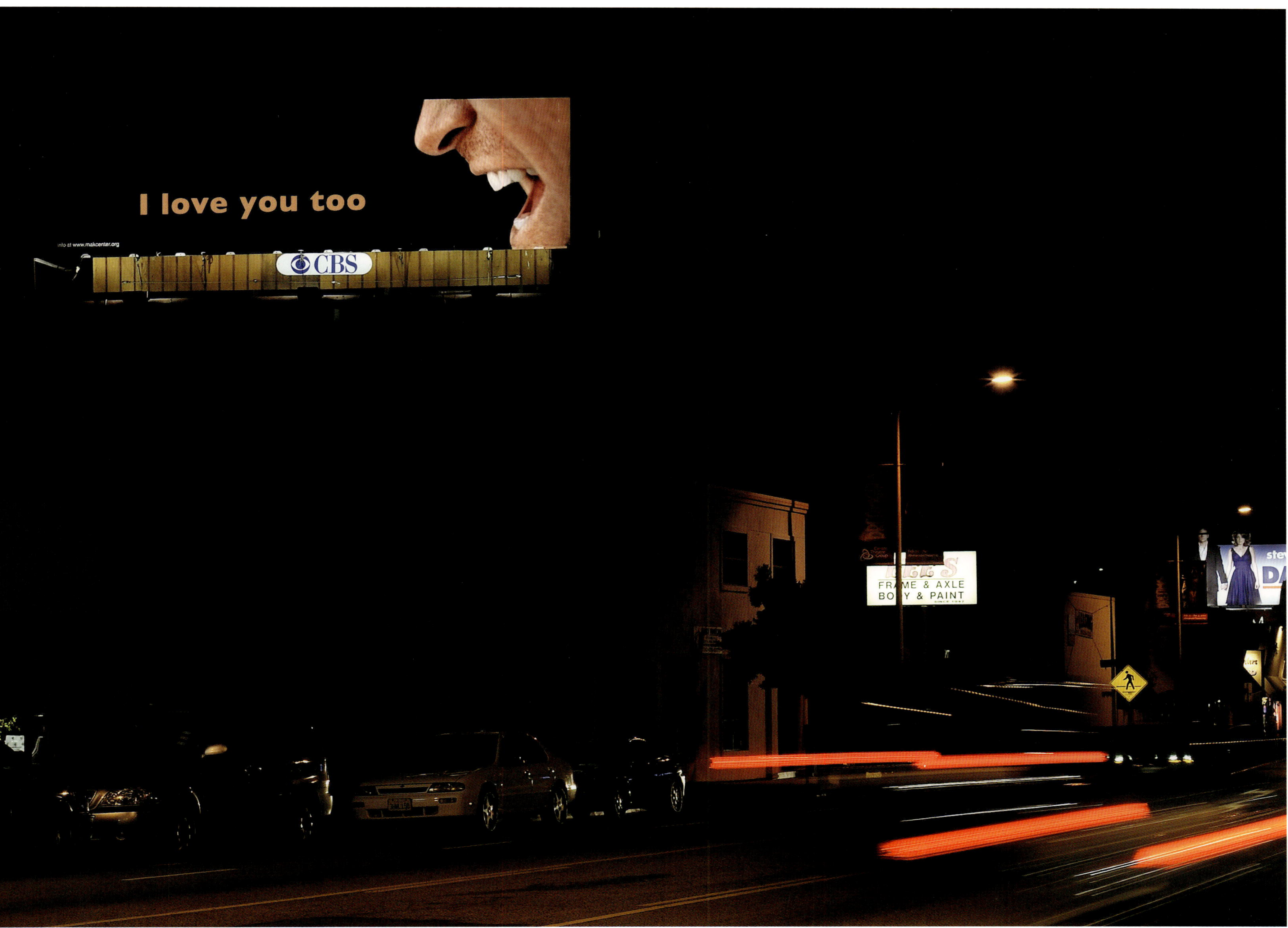
I love you too
info at www.makcenter.org
CBS
FRAME & AXLE

CHRISTINA FERNANDEZ

The practice of Christina Fernandez combines genre photography with formats such as the photo-roman to tell histories and stories of migration and immigration. Working in documentary and formal modes, her urban and landscape photography carries subtle social and political commentary through choice of subject matter, light, framing, and focus on detail. Her billboard, *Coldwell Couch,* fuses two square-format photographs from her recent series *Serano*, capturing two distinct vantage points onto the characteristically Los Angeleno geography of an El Sereno neighborhood.

Taken at the same site ten months apart, the two sides of the diptych are a complex meditation on our present socio-economic condition. In the left-hand photograph, a post displaying a Coldwell Banker Brokerage sign cuts across the foreground of the frame; from a distance, an overturned loveseat echoes the shapes of houses sunk into a lush ravine of natural and cultivated vegetation. The warm tones of dry summer weed in the right-hand image indicate the passage of a significant amount of time, yet the couch is still there. Framed close up, the couch's bleached out pattern uncannily echoes the foliage of the castor bean plant behind it. The push-pull between the natural and the man-made is everywhere in this piece, reflecting the structure of its context. Los Angeles was the first American city built not on the European model, as were Chicago and New York, but on the Jeffersonian model of a center-less city in the midst of vast countryside. Refusing to "return to nature"—to either collapse or decompose—the couch turns into a ruin, a monument to the failure of the Homestead American Dream. At this moment in history, the Coldwell sign unavoidably evokes the collapse of the housing market and its far-reaching aftermath.

BY NIZAN SHAKED

LOCATION: Hollywood Boulevard, west of Bronson Avenue, on the south side of the street, facing west.

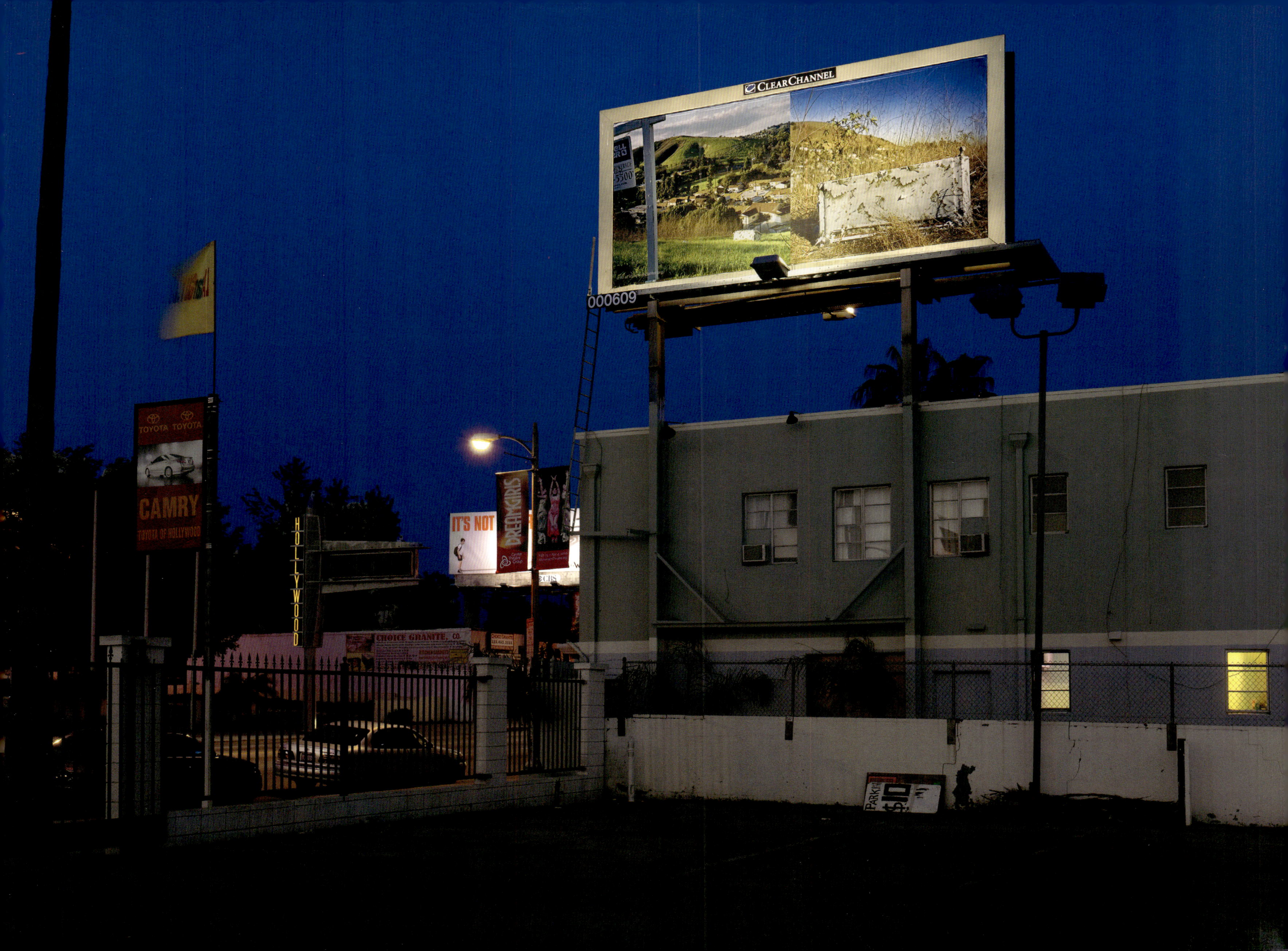
CLEARCHANNEL
000609
TOYOTA TOYOTA
CAMRY
TOYOTA OF HOLLYWOOD
HOLLYWOOD
IT'S NOT
DREAMGIRLS
CHOICE GRANITE, CO.
$10

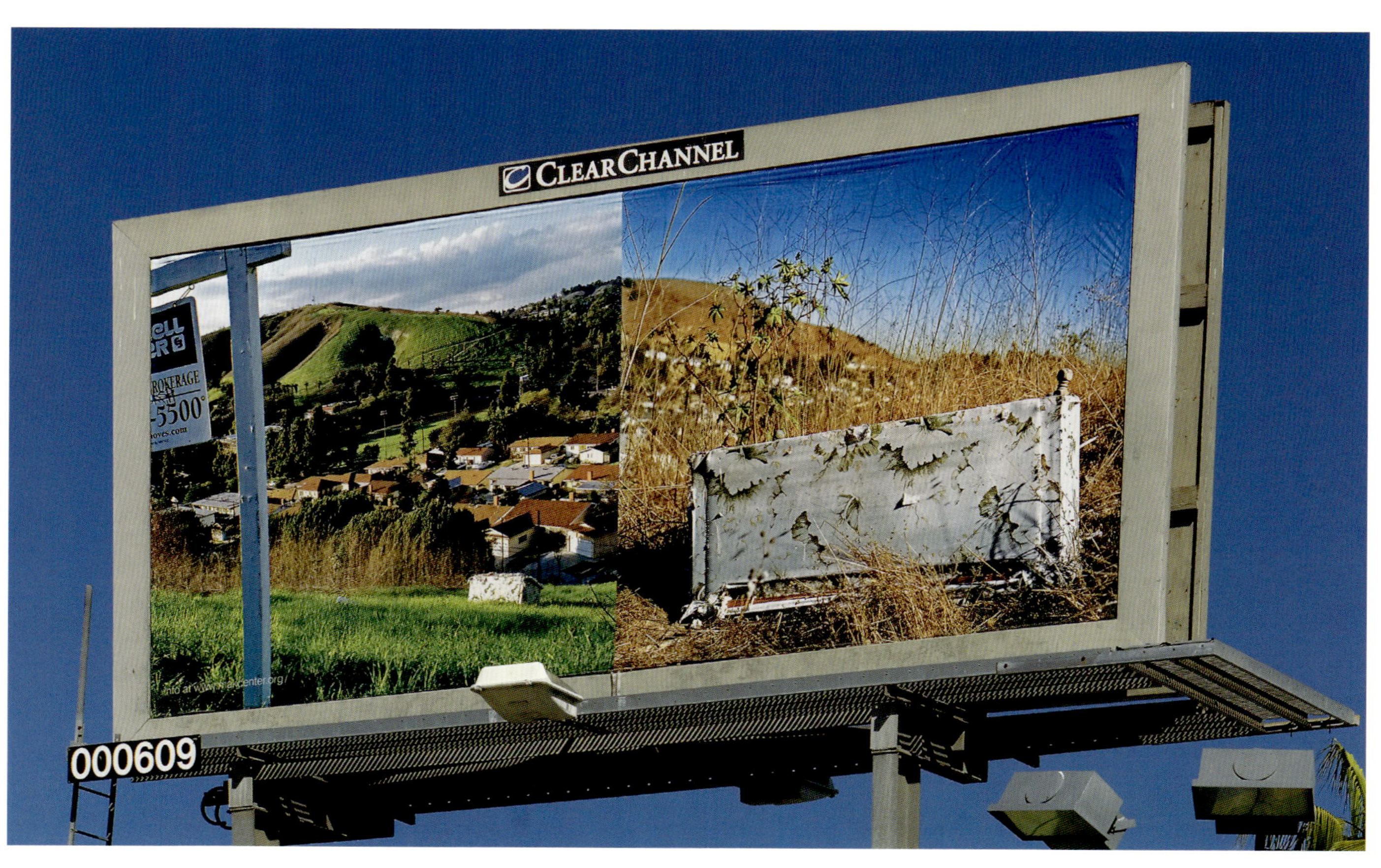
CLEARCHANNEL
000609

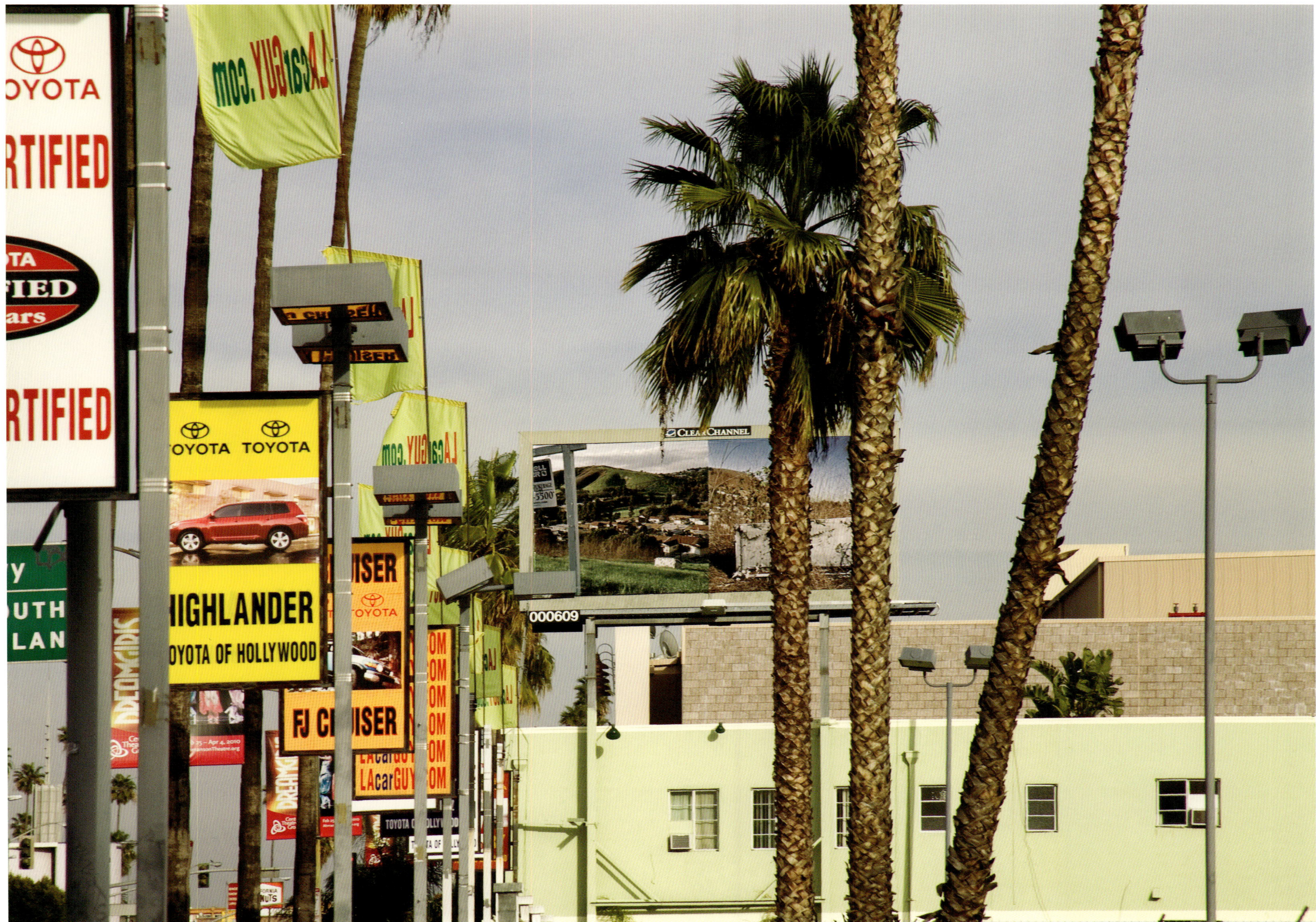

TOYOTA TOYOTA
IGHLANDER
OYOTA OF HOLLYWOOD
TOYOTA
FJ C ISER
LAcarGUY
CLEAR CHANNEL
000609

KEN GONZALES-DAY

The rigorous, inter-disciplinary practice of artist and scholar Ken Gonzales-Day brings historical research and theoretical analysis of representation to bear on his photographs. At the same time his knowledge as a practitioner provides the visual insight required by his scholarly projects. His book *Lynching in the West: 1850–1935* (Duke University Press, 2006) was nominated for a Pulitzer Prize. It investigates, among other things, the role of photography in its relationship to the discourse of race and the dire consequences of racism.

Gonzales-Day's billboard project brings these histories into the present, reflecting upon how residues of oppression linger in varying forms, despite the many changes that society continues to undergo. His subjects, *Bust of a Young Man* (bronze with silver inlay eyes, by the Italian artist Antico) and *Bust of a Man* (black stone-pietra da paragone, Florence 1758, by the Englishman Francis Harwood), are owned by the J. Paul Getty Museum. Gonzales-Day photographed them as part of his *Profile Series* during a residency as a Getty Research Institute Scholar. The historical sculptures refer to the artistic styles and philosophies of the Renaissance and the Neoclassical period, both of which in their turn revived the achievements of Greek and Roman culture. The imaged sculptures serve as a reminder that despite the manifold social advancements we have witnessed, it is still with the vocabulary of the past that we speak today. The figures in profile also allude to the dawn of photography and the earliest technologies used to mechanically reproduce human likeness. In the billboard, a Photoshop composite of the figures facing each other ignites an erotic charge as they stare into one another's eyes. As photographs of sculptures engaged in a virtual dynamic, these profiles are thrice removed from their human referents, a fact which is emphasized by the brilliant highlights that bounce off the material-objects' surfaces.

BY NIZAN SHAKED

LOCATION: Olympic Boulevard, west of Gramercy Place, on the north side of the street, facing east.

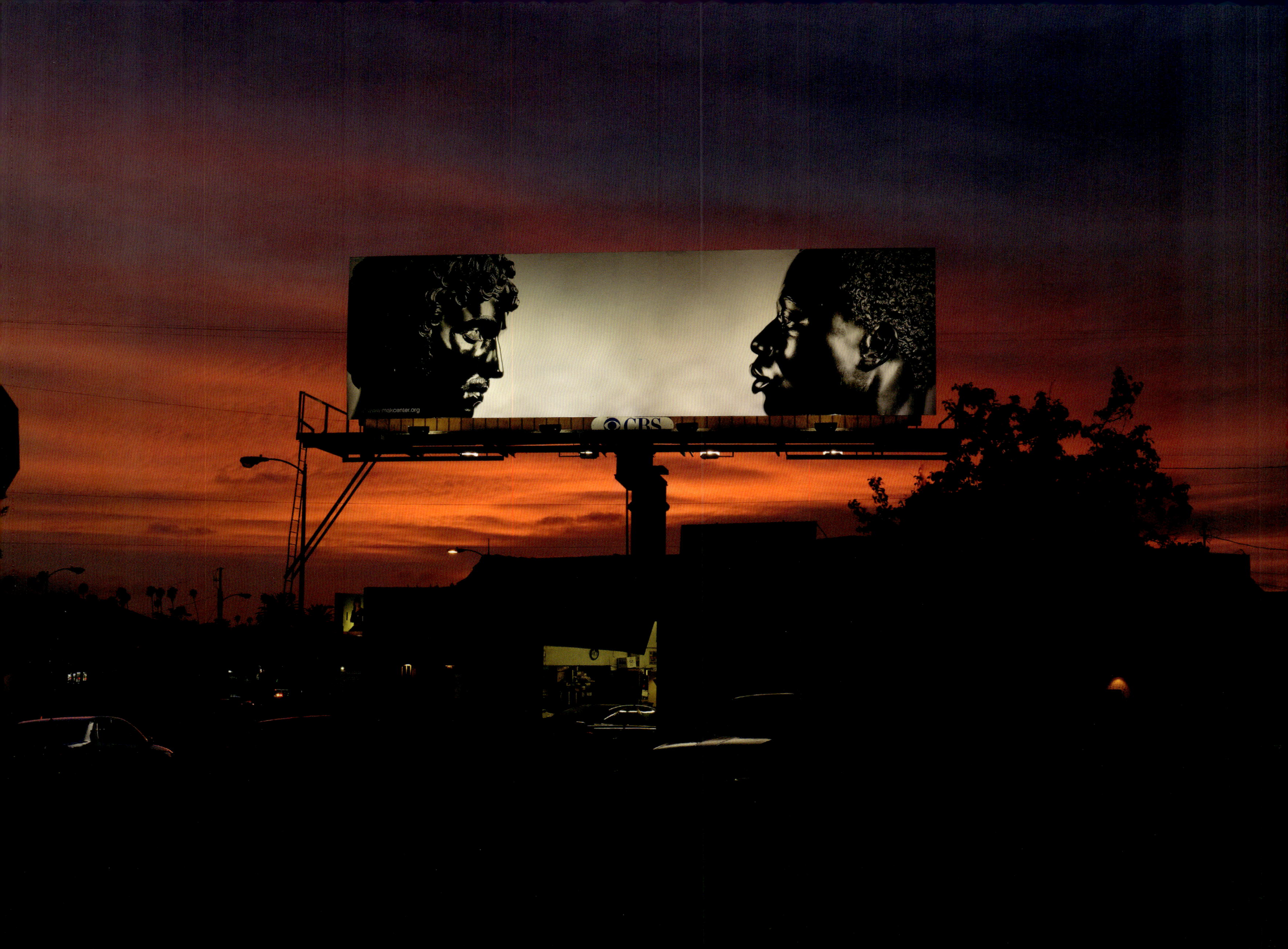
www.makcenter.org
CBS

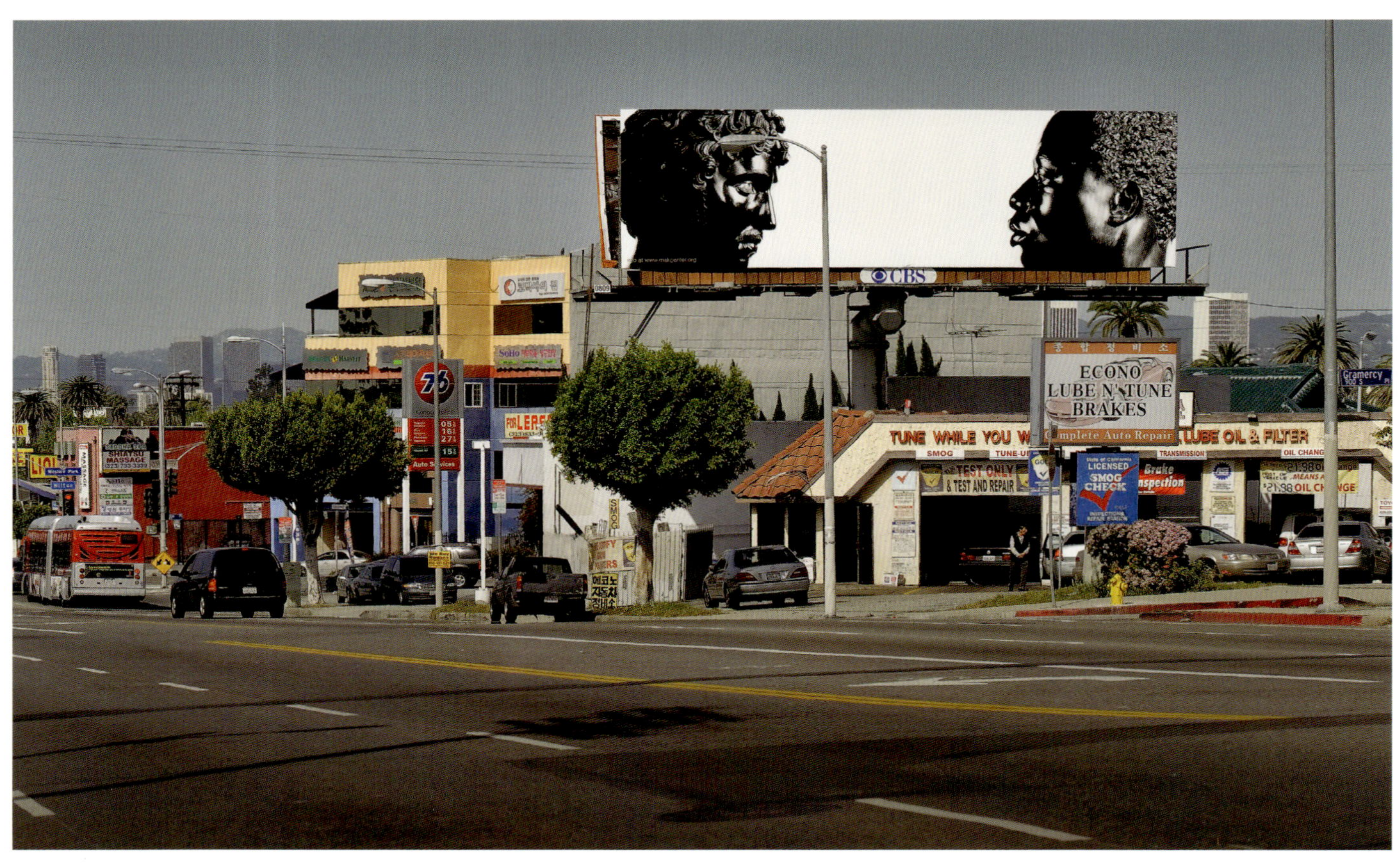
CBS
76
ECONO
LUBE N' TUNE
BRAKES
Complete Auto Repair
LUBE OIL & FILTER
TEST ONLY
& TEST AND REPAIR
LICENSED
SMOG CHECK
Gramercy

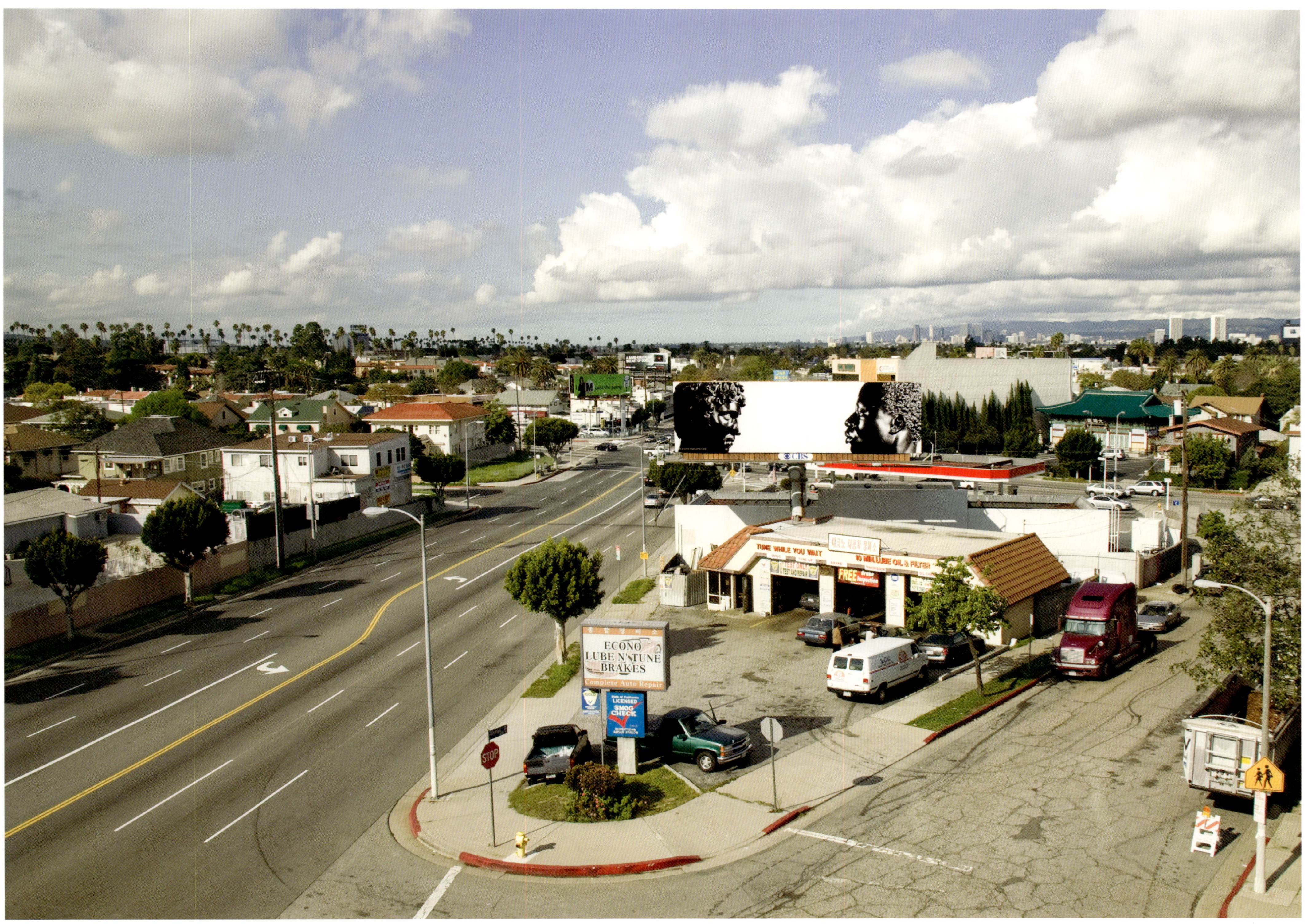
ECONO
LUBE N'TUNE
BRAKES
Complete Auto Repair
TUNE WHILE YOU WAIT
FREE
LICENSED
SMOG CHECK
STOP
CBS

RENÉE GREEN

Renée Green's billboard features a grey seascape with outcroppings of land visible in the near distance. Dark water conforms to tracks made by the kind of ferry that shuttles tourists and commuters. The foreground is occupied by the outlines of several figures standing at the rear of the vessel. The image centers on a muted sun trying to break through dense cloud cover. This brooding, timeless scene is evocative of nineteenth century Romantic literature and painting, which developed in the wake of Western European industrialization and urban sprawl. However, two bands of text framing the image—"Strangers Begin Again" in yellow and "Native Strangers Hosting" in red—interrupt any sense of reverie. Like many of the banner pieces that Green has consistently produced since the early 1990s, the phrasing is purposely ambiguous, yet pointed. "Strangers" and "natives" are loaded terms. The status of each is never fixed but changes almost cyclically, especially when considered in terms of geological time rather than the recent histories of nations or states. The word "hosting" also carries multiple meanings. It demarcates the roles of visitor and guest, but also refers to a biological relationship in which a parasitic organism drains its host for its own survival.

The image is a still from a film that is part of a recent project by Green called *Endless Dreams and Water Between* (2009), which includes four film projections, sound works, banners, and drawings. Together these works trace several fictional characters' engagements with the islands of Manhattan; Majorca, Spain; the various isles dispersed around the San Francisco Bay and the California Pacific Rim; and the San Francisco peninsula, where Green currently lives and works. Green calls our attention to these landmasses precisely because they do not fulfill the fantasy of tropical exoticism. Each is insular and paradoxically cosmopolitan. Most importantly for Green, they are situated within bodies of water that connect human bodies, giving rise to themes of travel and migration. Green's ongoing interest in cultural flows and personal histories links this maritime project to her other important discursive works that use personal memories and narrative to pry open monolithic histories. For example, the archive-like installation and CD-ROM project *Import/Export Funk Office* (1992) traces the international dispersion of hip hop and its cultural and political significance through the presentation of books, magazines, photographs and videos.

BY GLORIA SUTTON

LOCATION: La Brea Avenue, north of Lexington, on the west side of the street, facing south.

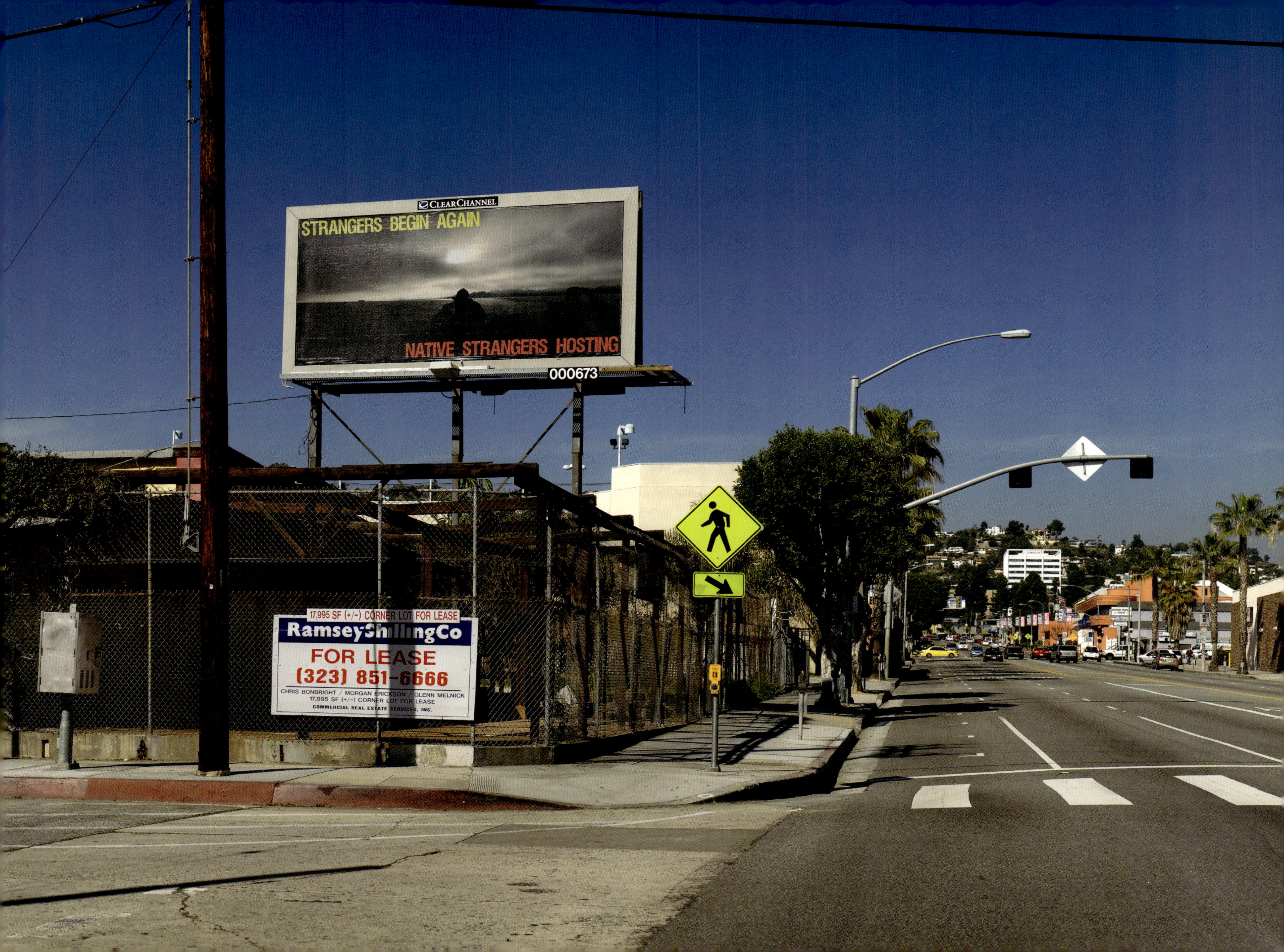
ClearChannel
STRANGERS BEGIN AGAIN
NATIVE STRANGERS HOSTING
000673
17,995 SF (+/-) CORNER LOT FOR LEASE
RamseyShillingCo
FOR LEASE
(323) 851-6666
CHRIS BONBRIGHT / MORGAN ERICKSON / GLENN MELNICK
17,995 SF (+/-) CORNER LOT FOR LEASE
COMMERCIAL REAL ESTATE SERVICES, INC.

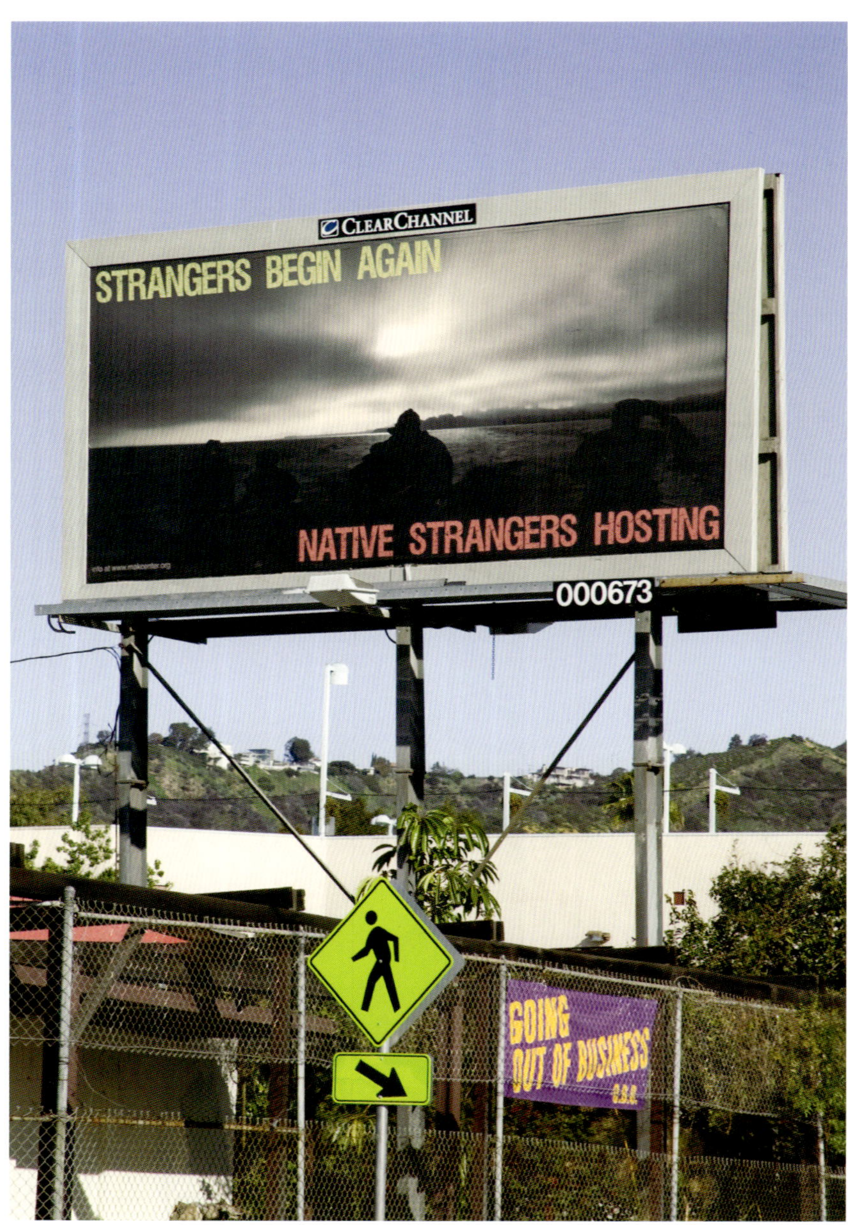

CLEARCHANNEL
STRANGERS BEGIN AGAIN
NATIVE STRANGERS HOSTING
000673
GOING
OUT OF BUSINESS

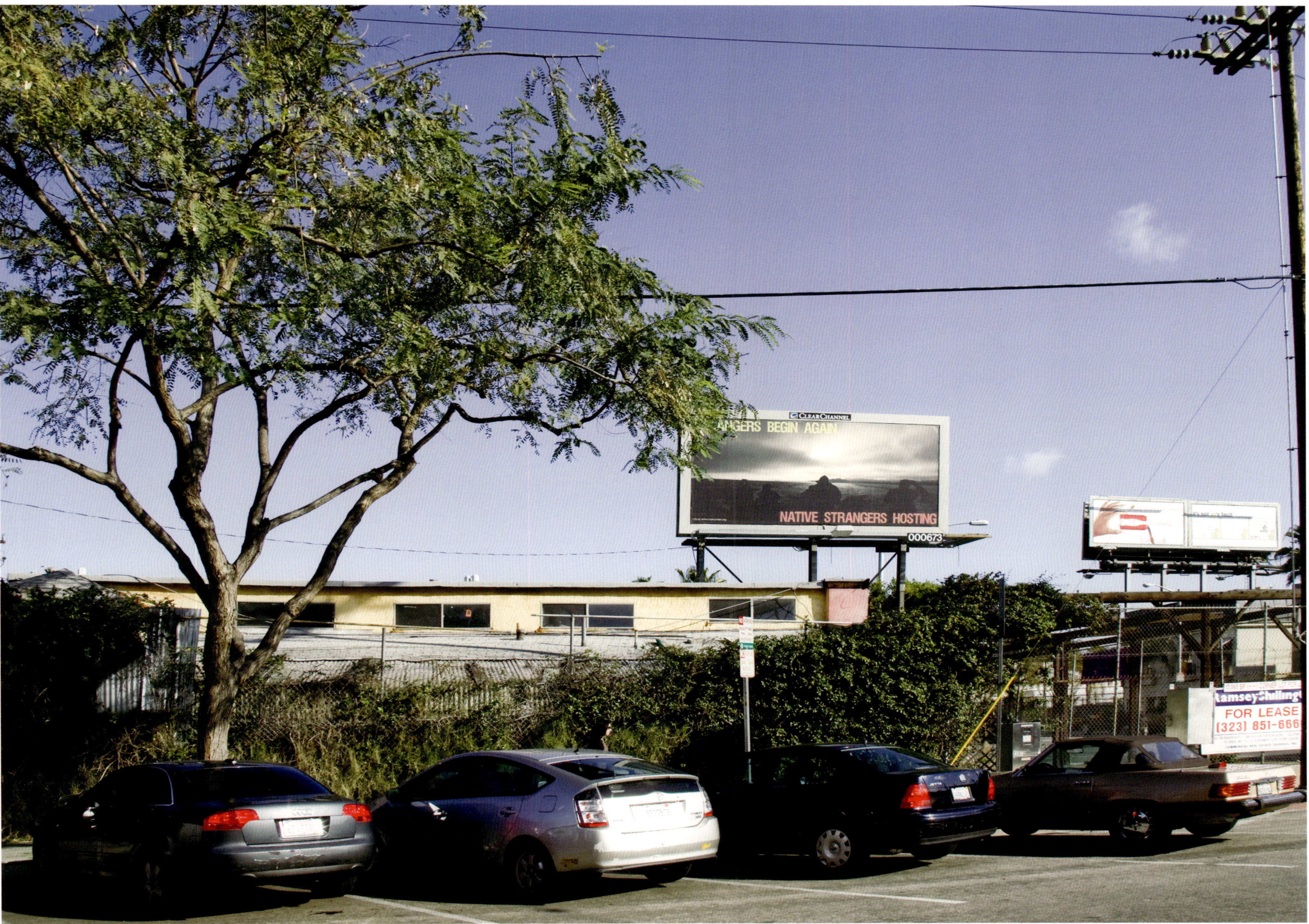
CLEARCHANNEL
ANGERS BEGIN AGAIN
NATIVE STRANGERS HOSTING
000673
FOR LEASE

KIRA LYNN HARRIS

Kira Lynn Harris's work centers on architecture, space, light, and perception, often resulting in installations and large-scale drawings. For her billboard piece, Harris highlights an icon of Los Angeles, the Watts Towers, built by Simon Rodia between approximately 1921 and 1954. The work is internationally known and loved as a prime work of "outsider art." A citizen's committee saved it from the wrecking ball in the late 1950s, and today it is owned by the State of California and administered by the Los Angeles Department of Cultural Affairs. The Watts Towers Arts Center, also overseen by the city of Los Angeles, was founded in the aftermath of the Watts Riots of 1965 in an attempt to use art to heal a battered community. More recently, the Watts House Project, initiated by artist Edgar Arceneaux and defined on the project website as a "collaborative artwork in the shape of a neighborhood redevelopment," has added new art activities to the neighborhood. Harris's billboard points to this aggregation of art-centered structures.

Her choice of subject reflects Harris's love of the towers, her interest in artworks that do not easily reside in one discipline or another, and her concern with the marginalization of community-based art projects from the mainstream art world. By placing the image of the towers on a billboard, she is pointing to a landmark that is both iconic yet possibly underappreciated in Los Angeles, and certainly in great need of financial support. The words "Community as Art" in boldface suggest that community building and placemaking can be viable art-making practices. The third element, ghostly variations of phrases that contain the words "community" and "art," give the sense that there are many possibilities for these ideas to come together.

BY KIMBERLI MEYER

LOCATION: La Cienega Boulevard, north of the 10 Freeway (Cadillac Avenue), on the west side of the street, facing south.

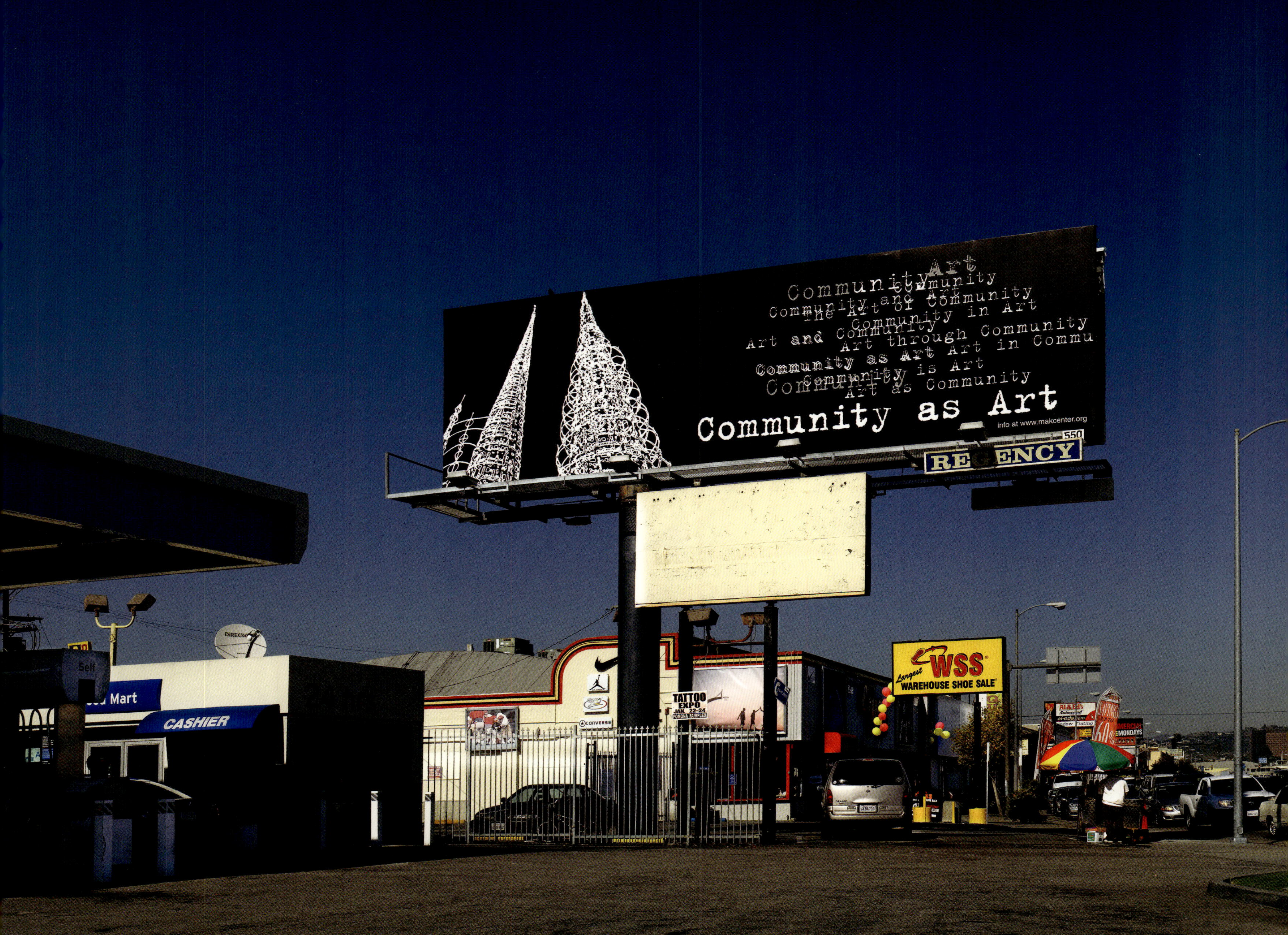

The Art of Community
Community in Art
Art and Community
Art through Community
Community as Art
Community is Art
Art as Community
Community as Art
info at www.makcenter.org
550
REGENCY
WSS
Largest
WAREHOUSE SHOE SALE
Mart
CASHIER
TATTOO
EXPO
CONVERSE

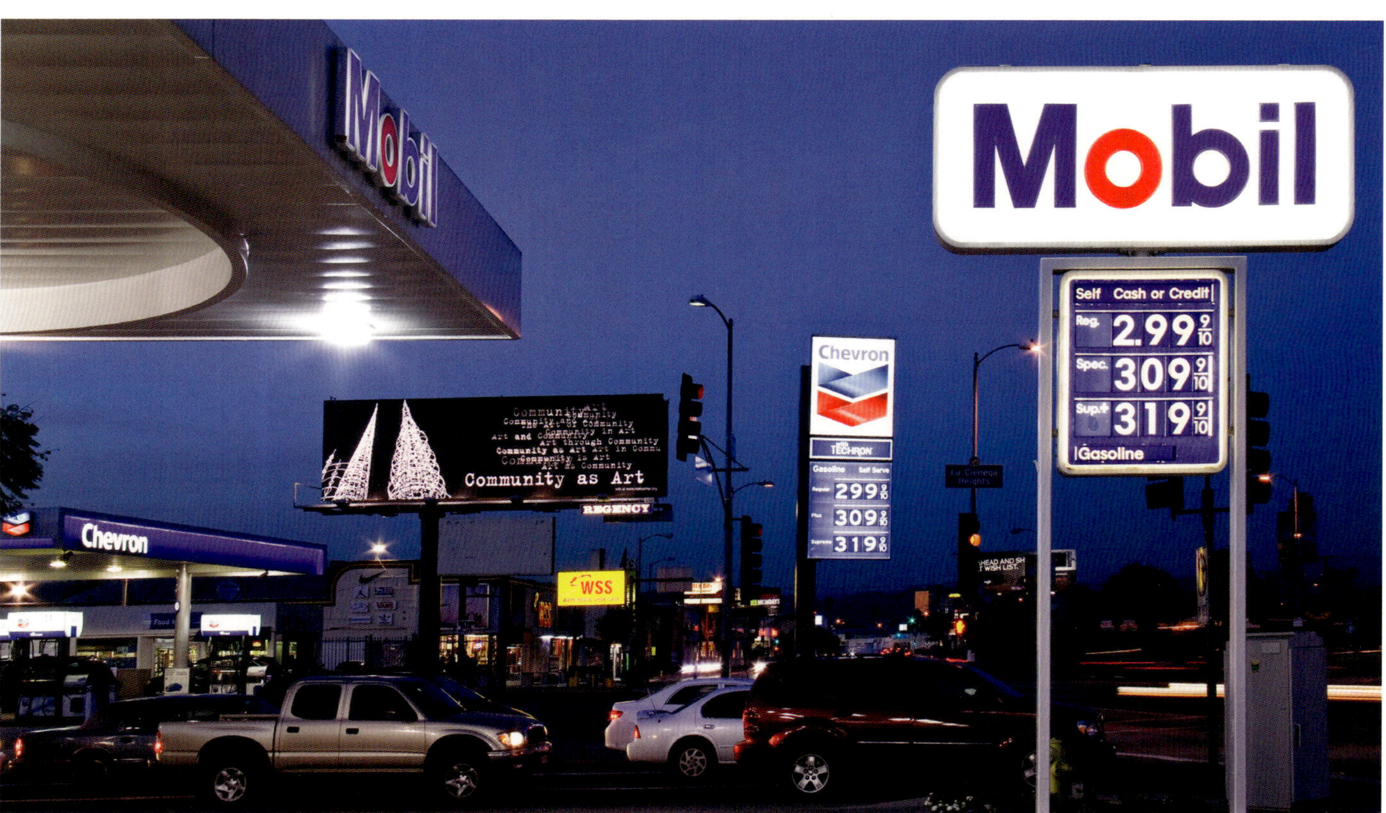
Mobil
Mobil
Self Cash or Credit
Reg. 2.99 9/10
Spec. 309 9/10
Sup.+ 319 9/10
Gasoline
Chevron
TECHRON
299
309
319
Chevron
Community as Art
REGENCY
WSS

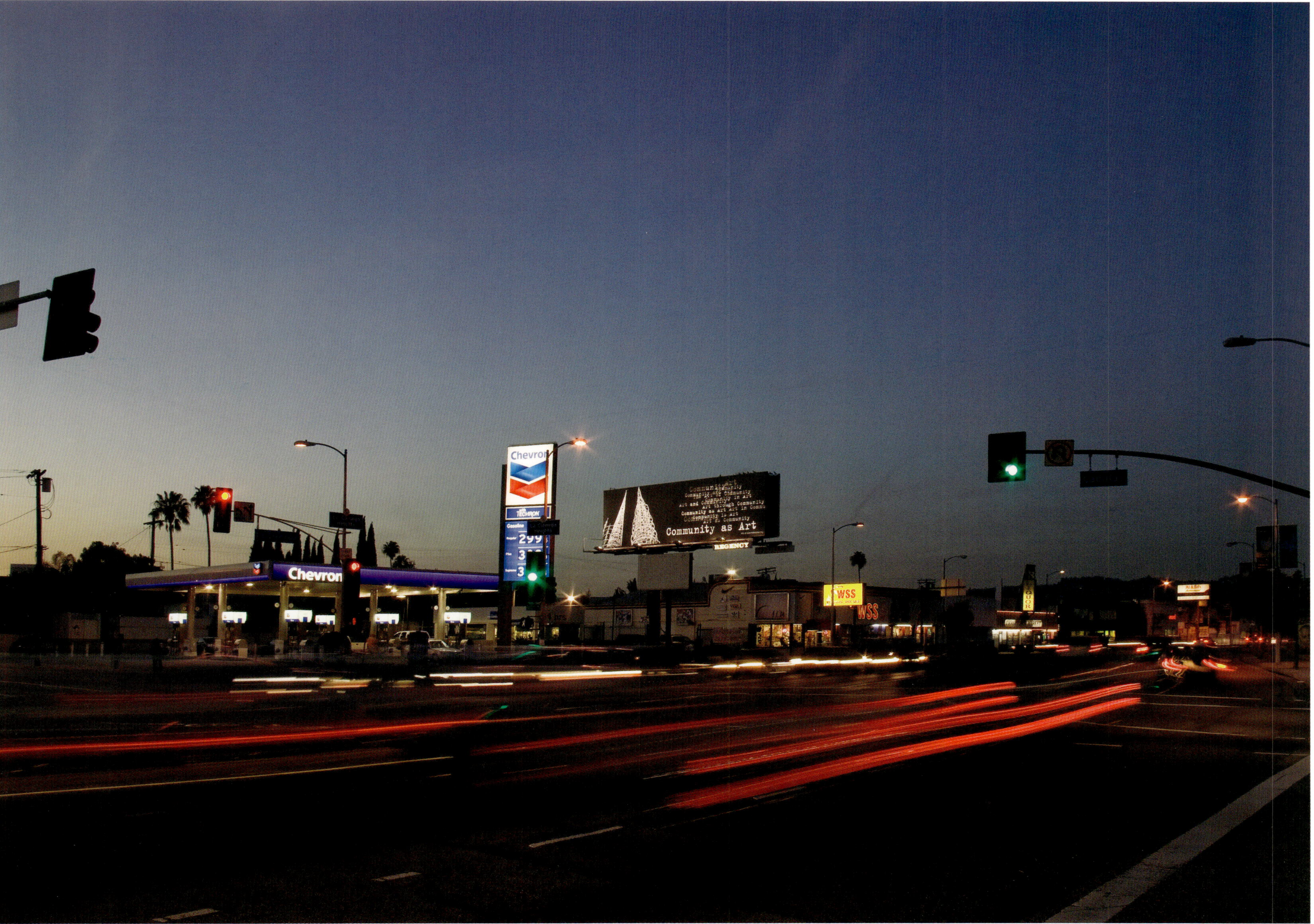
Chevron
TECHRON
Chevron
Community as Art
REGENCY
WSS

JOHN KNIGHT

Since the late 1960s, John Knight has engaged institutional critique—a strand of Conceptual Art that takes the art establishment as its subject of investigation. Through nuanced intercessions into the mechanisms of display and visual communication, his practice unpacks conventions and codes that give art its value, using art as a platform to reflect upon larger political and economic systems. Working "in situ," each project is based on analysis and intervention specific to the venue at hand; its aesthetic logic takes its cues from the structure of that of the gallery, museum, or other exhibition venue.

For the duration of *How Many Billboards?*, Knight has donated his billboard to the Middle East Children's Alliance (MECA), a nonprofit organization founded in 1988 to benefit children of the Middle East. In return, MECA chose to display a public relations ad to bring awareness to their MAIA project, which works to install water desalinization and purification systems in Gaza schools, kindergartens, and nurseries. Knight's gesture creates a paradoxical condition where the billboard is both the thing itself—an ad for a humanitarian organization—yet at the same time it is still a work of art. As an ad that points to the very real crisis of global water shortages, it serves to critique the exhibition itself, suggesting that the strategy employed by *How Many Billboards?,* which aims to reclaim media space for art, ultimately serves the same economy of meaning that leaves art aloof from politics and without any real ability to affect change on a structural level. As work of art and a public relations ad, the gesture isolates the function of the billboard itself as a means of communication, and points to the ways in which its existence has become naturalized and its domination of public space unquestioned.

BY NIZAN SHAKED

LOCATION: Sunset Boulevard, west of Havenhurst Drive, on the south side of the street, facing west.

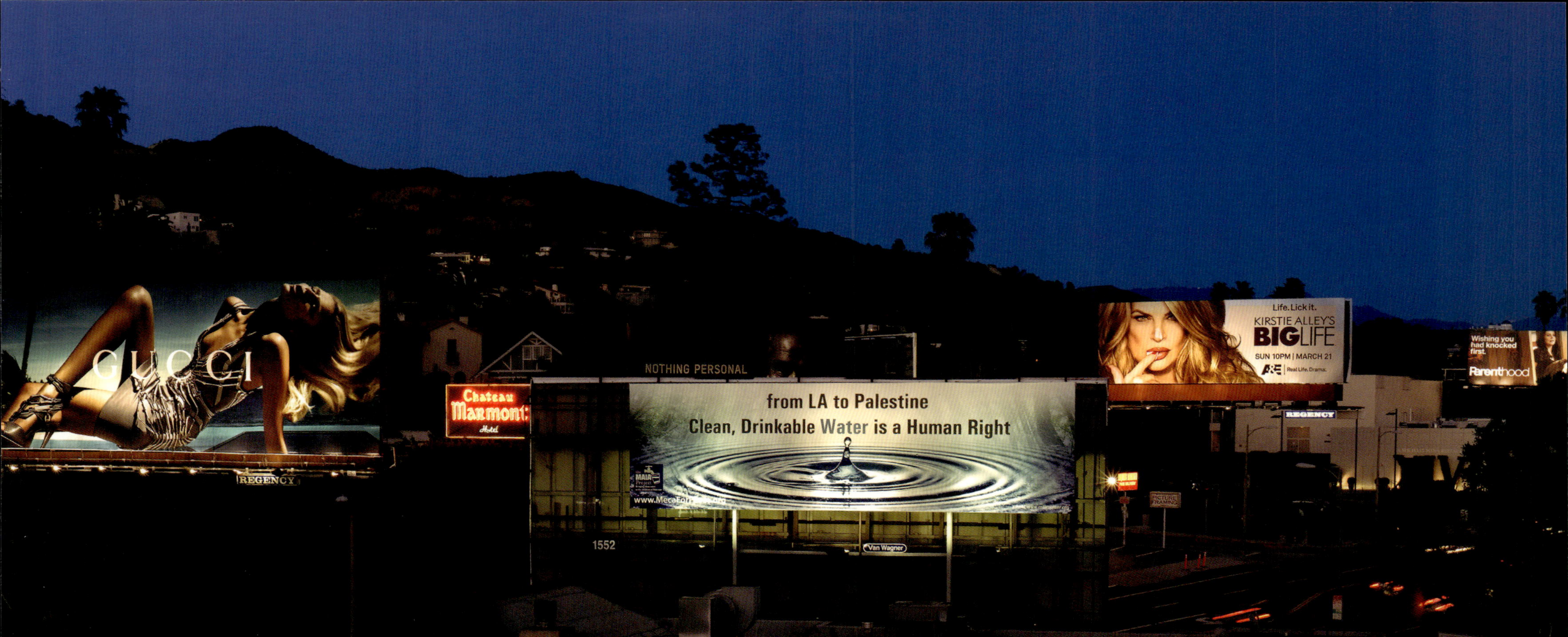
GUCCI
REGENCY
Chateau
Marmont
Hotel
NOTHING PERSONAL
from LA to Palestine
Clean, Drinkable Water is a Human Right
MAIA
Project
1552
Van Wagner
Life. Lick it.
KIRSTIE ALLEY'S
BIG LIFE
SUN 10PM | MARCH 21
A&E | Real Life. Drama.
REGENCY
PICTURE
FRAMING
Wishing you
had knocked
first.
Parenthood

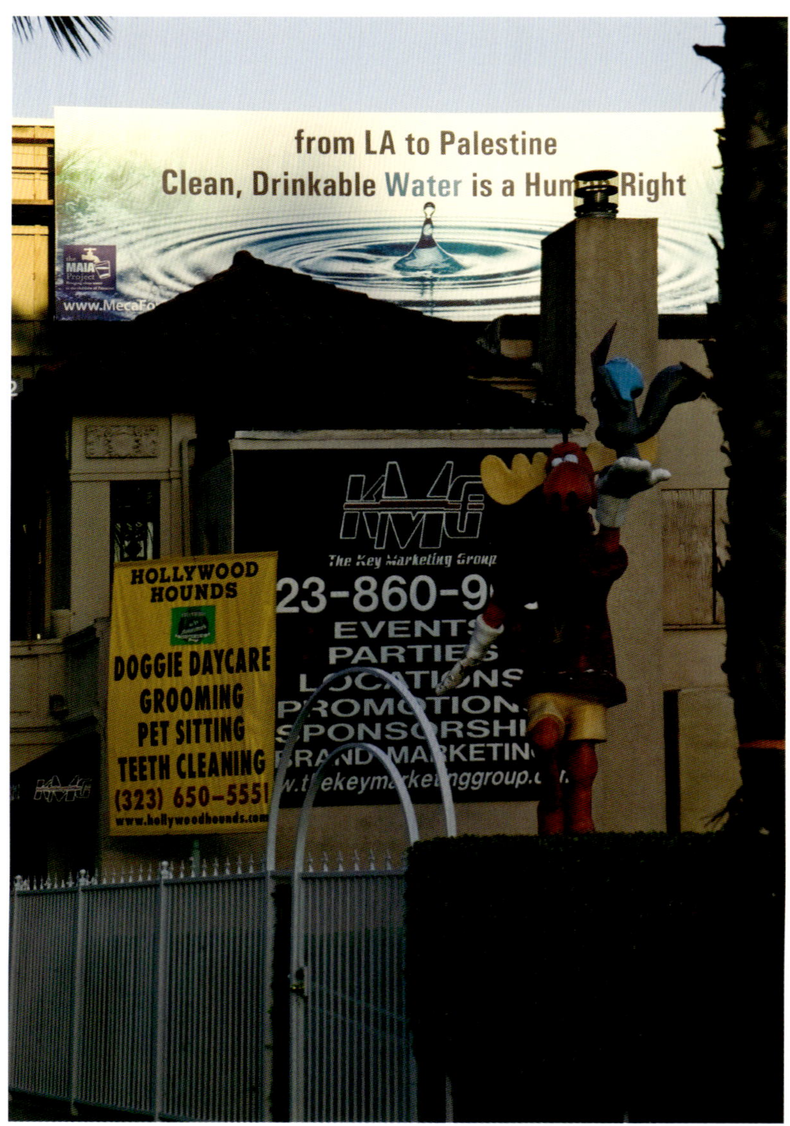
from LA to Palestine
Clean, Drinkable Water is a
HOLLYWOOD HOUNDS
DOGGIE DAYCARE
GROOMING
PET SITTING
TEETH CLEANING
(323) 650-5551
www.hollywoodhounds.com
The Key Marketing Group

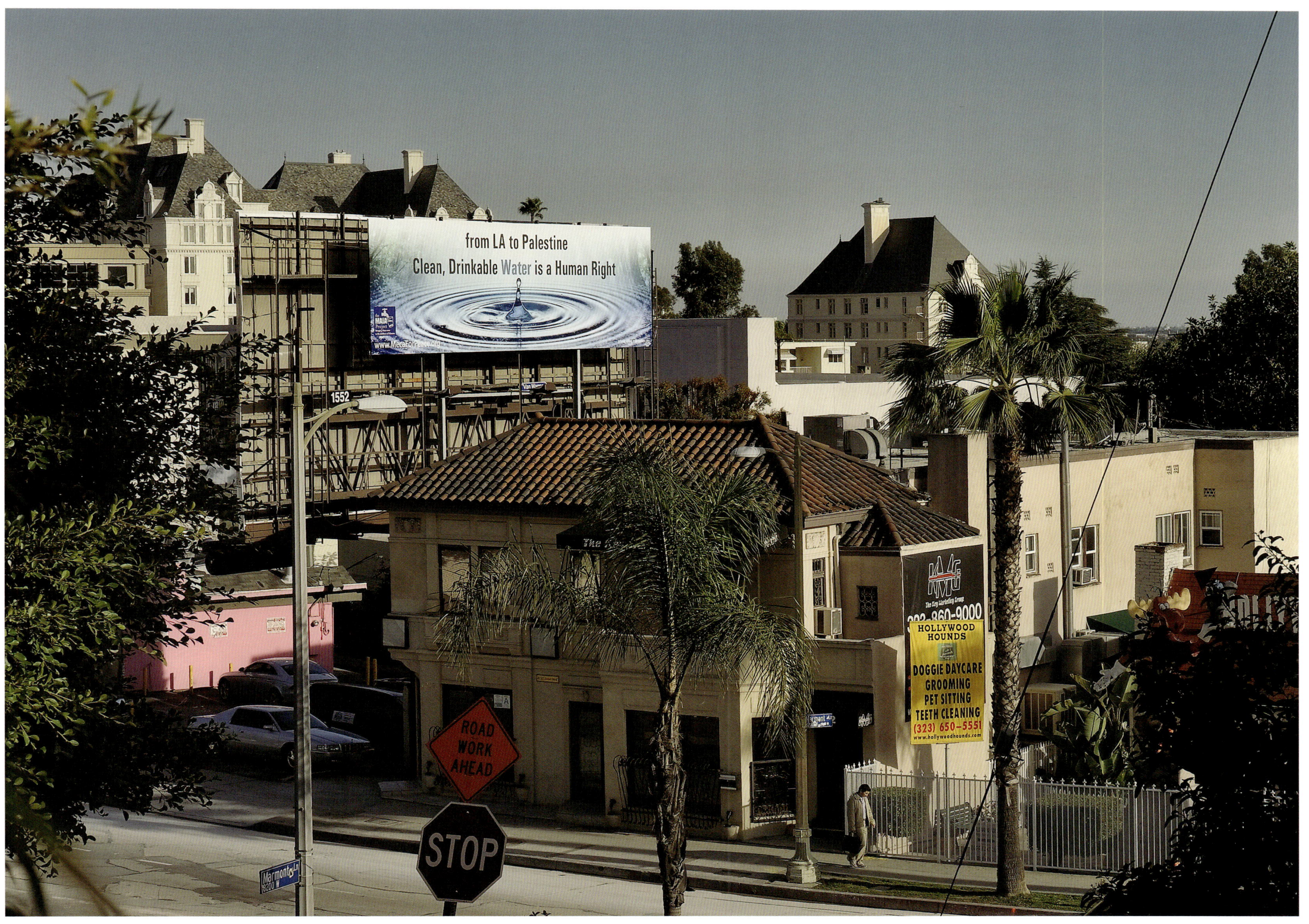

from LA to Palestine
Clean, Drinkable Water is a Human Right
1552
ROAD WORK AHEAD
STOP
HOLLYWOOD HOUNDS
DOGGIE DAYCARE
GROOMING
PET SITTING
TEETH CLEANING
(323) 650-5551

DAVID LAMELAS

David Lamelas has a restless and peregrinating artistic practice that addresses the parameters of time and space. He has investigated these topics in a range of post-minimalist installations, performances, photos, and films since his participation in Argentina's nascent avant-garde during the early 1960s. Lamelas is best known for the structuralist films and media installations he produced in London and Los Angeles during the late 1960s and early 1970s, which questioned art's capacity as both a means of communication and a medium for creating self-awareness. Key to these projects was Lamelas's interest in relating techniques and systems used by the film and television industry to the burgeoning discourse on public space and media technology. His installation *Office of Information about the Vietnam War at Three Levels: The Visual Image, Text, and Audio* (1968), for example, helped establish the practice of bringing real-time information (news reports and television footage) into the space of the gallery.

Lamelas has continued to critique conventions of representation in his more recent projects, which foreground demonstrations of stardom and celebrity. For *How Many Billboards?*, he takes aim at the archetypal rock star. Lamelas documents himself in the lead with hair slicked back and wearing a rolled-up, black t-shirt revealing generic tribal tattoos. The electric pink hue of his face and exaggerated pose of his body leaning into the microphone add to the overall distortion of the image of an aging rock god. The phrase "Think of Good" hangs in the atmosphere like a mantra or refrain from a clichéd song. Lamelas's insertion of himself into this particular role refers back to *Rock Star (Character Appropriation)* (1974), a suite of seven black-and-white self-portraits that depict Lamelas in the rock aesthetic of the mid 1970s—loose, long hair and skintight jeans. The terms Lamelas uses to describe both projects have little to do with acting or role-play, but rather with what he labels "character appropriation." In this manner, Lamelas points to two seemingly contradictory tendencies within Conceptual Art's critique of representation: the aspiration for self-criticality and emancipation from the art world's dependency on cult or star status, and a full-scale assimilation of the technologies of both media and spectacle culture.

BY GLORIA SUTTON

LOCATION: Pico Boulevard, west of Fairfax Avenue, on the south side of the street, facing east.

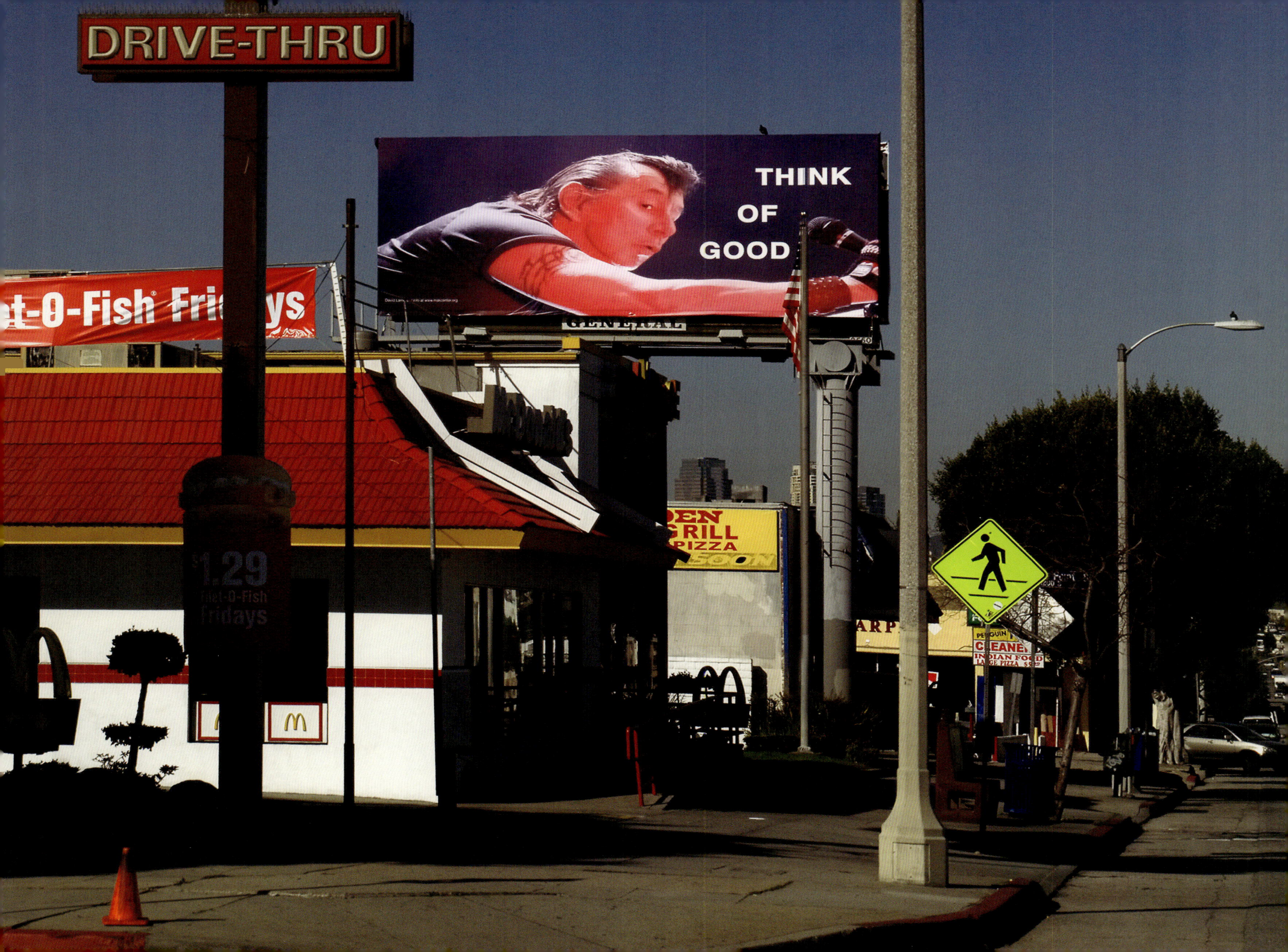
DRIVE-THRU
THINK
OF
GOOD
-O-Fish Fri ys
$1.29
Filet-O-Fish
Fridays
GRILL
PIZZA
CLEANE
INDIAN FOOD

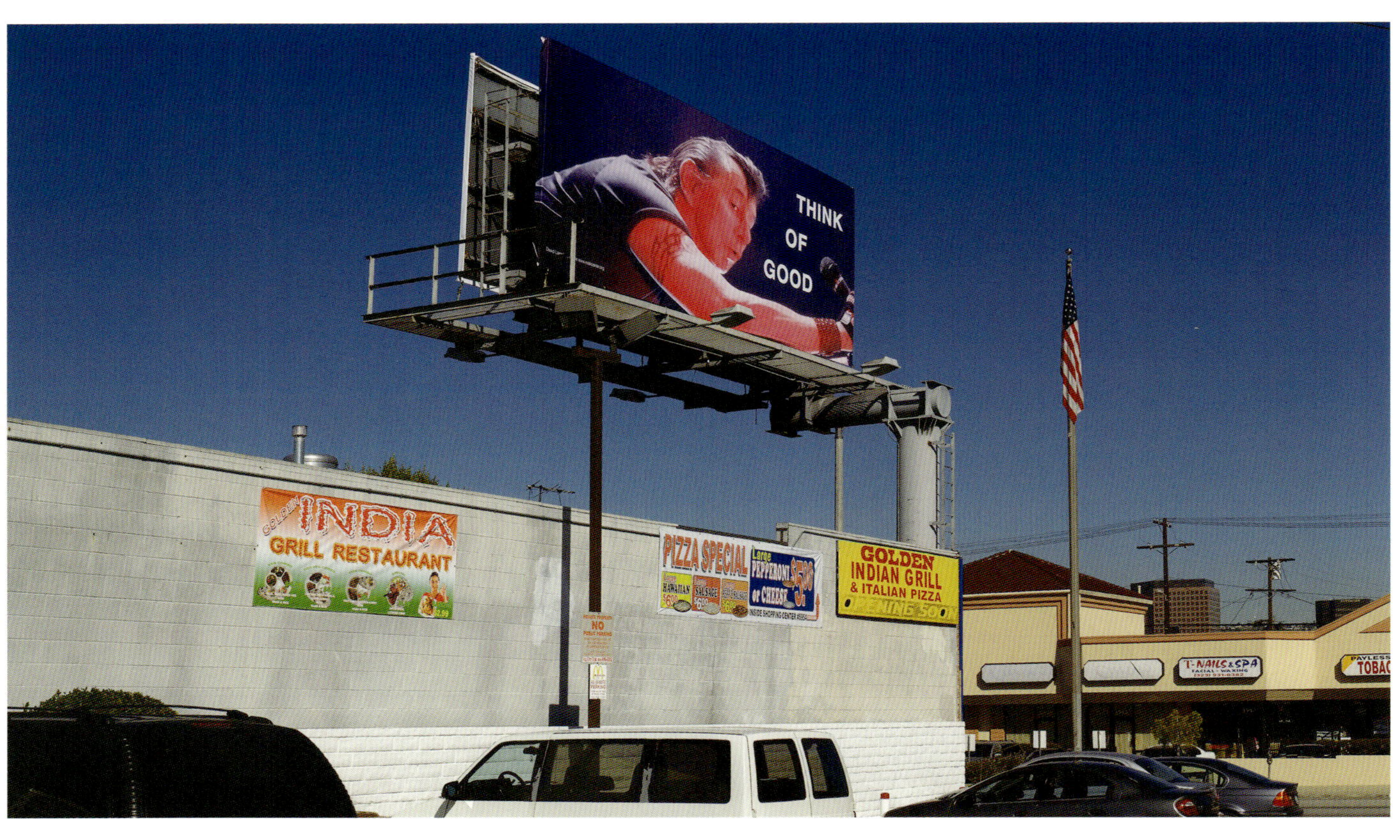
THINK
OF
GOOD
INDIA
GRILL RESTAURANT
PIZZA SPECIAL
GOLDEN
INDIAN GRILL
& ITALIAN PIZZA

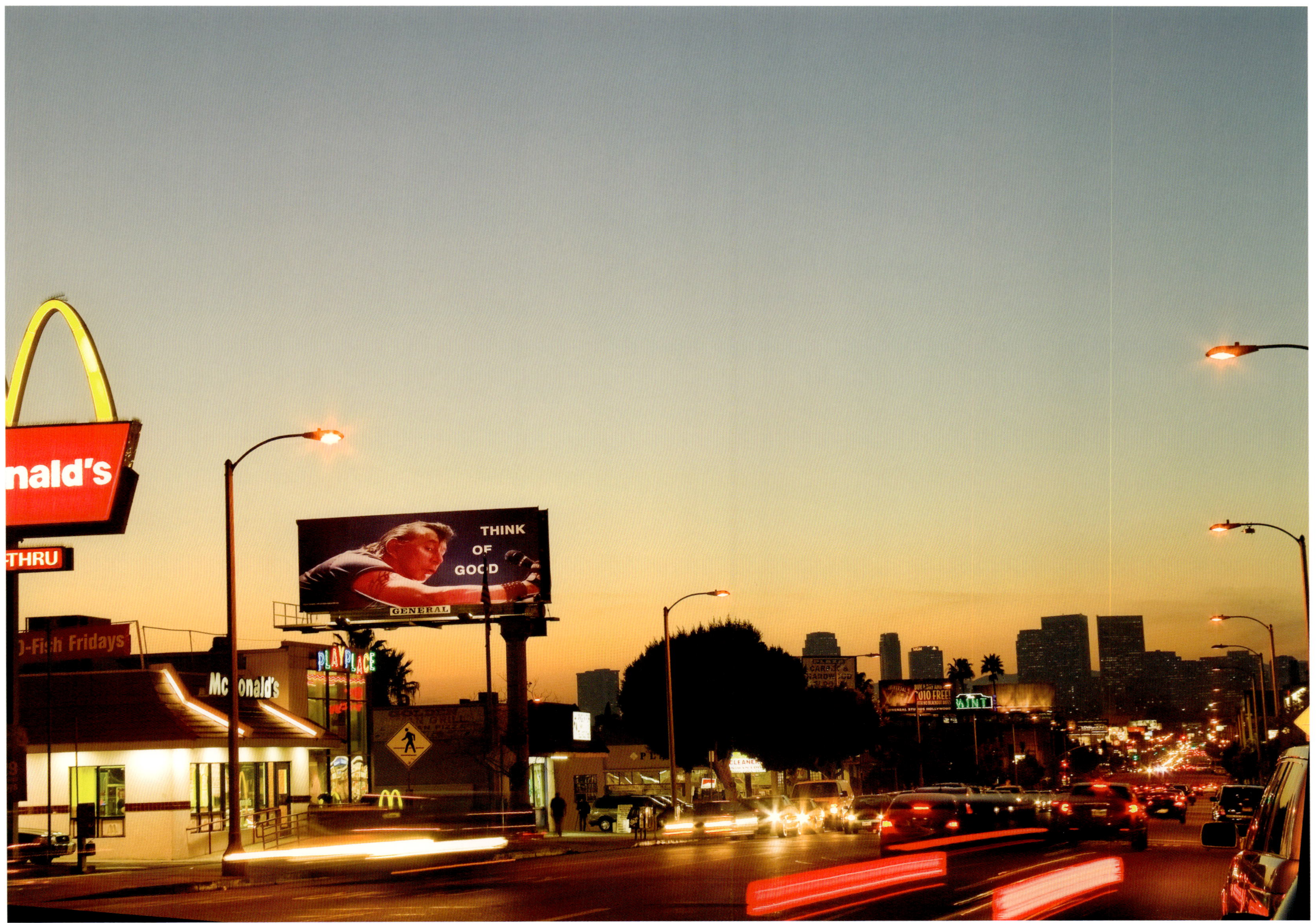

nald's
-THRU
THINK
OF
GOOD
GENERAL
-Fish Fridays
PLAYPLACE
McDonald's

BRANDON LATTU

Brandon Lattu uses both photography and the idea of photography to explore relationships between meaning and representation. His practice consists of disassembling and reassembling information from the visual, consumer, architectural, and urban realms. For *How Many Billboards?*, Lattu has chosen the automobile for his subject, both as a nod to the viewer who is quite likely navigating traffic while pondering the piece, and to allude to the corporate products that dominate billboards, whetting and capitalizing on human desire. The Cadillac Fleetwood shown in Lattu's piece, in production from 1927 to 1996, came to be associated with the pinnacle of luxury, repeatedly served as the U. S. President's transport, and was the most common base model for both the limousine and the hearse.The visual presence of a former icon of affluence on a present day billboard highlights the passing of time, and positions current objects of advertising as transient and soon to be relegated to history.

Today, the 1994 Cadillac Fleetwood is a classic car coveted by lowriders, a subset of California's car culture with roots in Mexican-American East Los Angeles. The lowrider is a symbol of creative expression and pride of cultural identity and community, especially for Chicanos. In Lattu's piece, this reference can be seen in the list of attributes that includes hydraulic hoses. Lattu's piece is an active advertisement; this Fleetwood is actually for sale and the owner can be contacted through the phone number given on the billboard. By using the conventions of a free classified ad for a billboard ad—itself the luxury model of printed advertising—Lattu underscores the shifting value of objects of consumer desire and the transformation of the meaning of such objects.
BY KIMBERLI MEYER

LOCATION: Fairfax Avenue, south of Pico Boulevard, on the west side of the street, facing northeast.

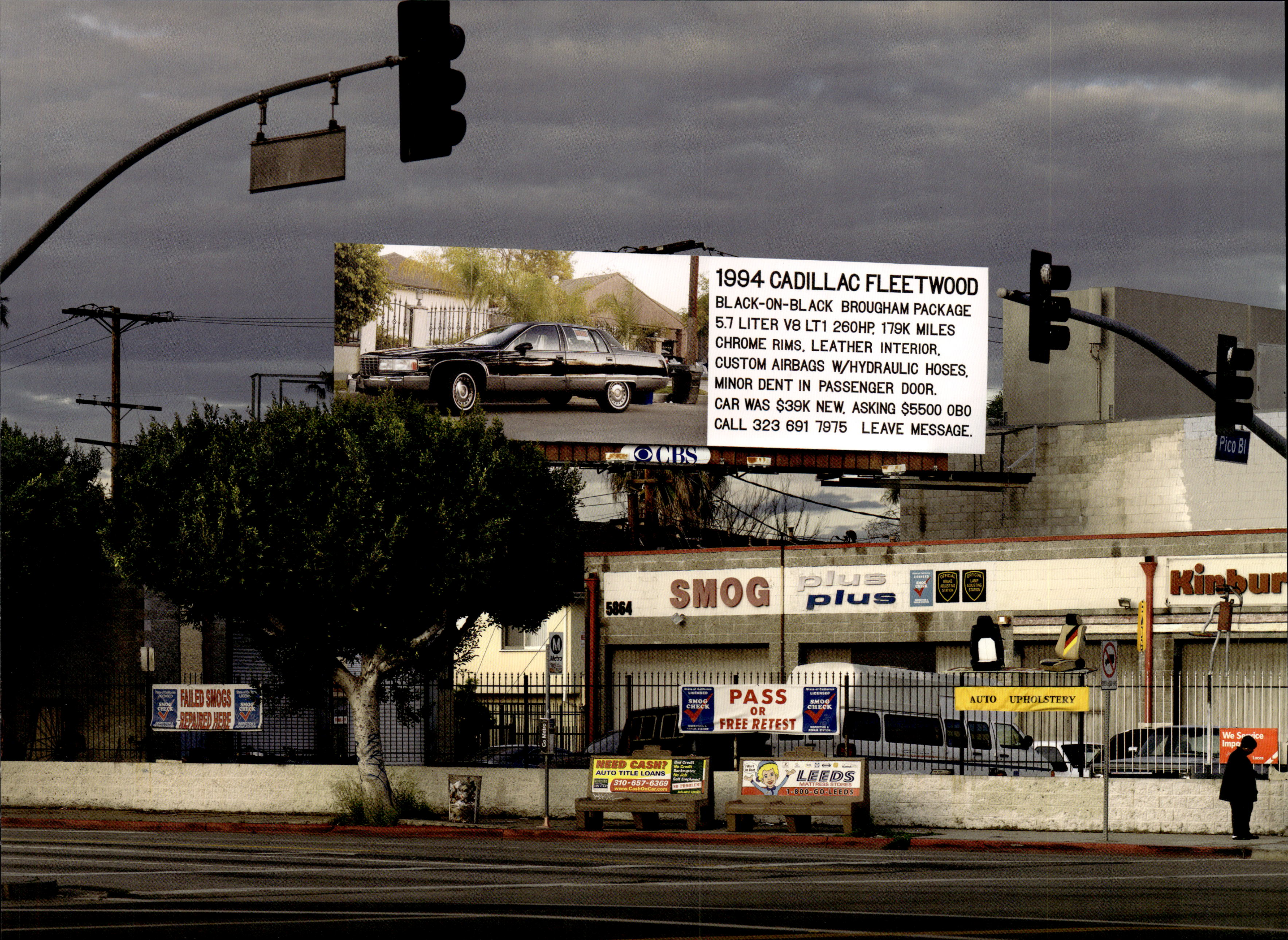
1994 CADILLAC FLEETWOOD
BLACK-ON-BLACK BROUGHAM PACKAGE
5.7 LITER V8 LT1 260HP, 179K MILES
CHROME RIMS, LEATHER INTERIOR,
CUSTOM AIRBAGS W/HYDRAULIC HOSES,
MINOR DENT IN PASSENGER DOOR,
CAR WAS $39K NEW, ASKING $5500 OBO
CALL 323 691 7975 LEAVE MESSAGE.
CBS
Pico Bl
5864
SMOG
plus plus
FAILED SMOGS REPAIRED HERE
SMOG CHECK
PASS OR FREE RETEST
AUTO UPHOLSTERY
NEED CASH?
AUTO TITLE LOANS
310-657-6369
www.CashOnCar.com
LEEDS
MATTRESS STORES
1-800-GO-LEEDS

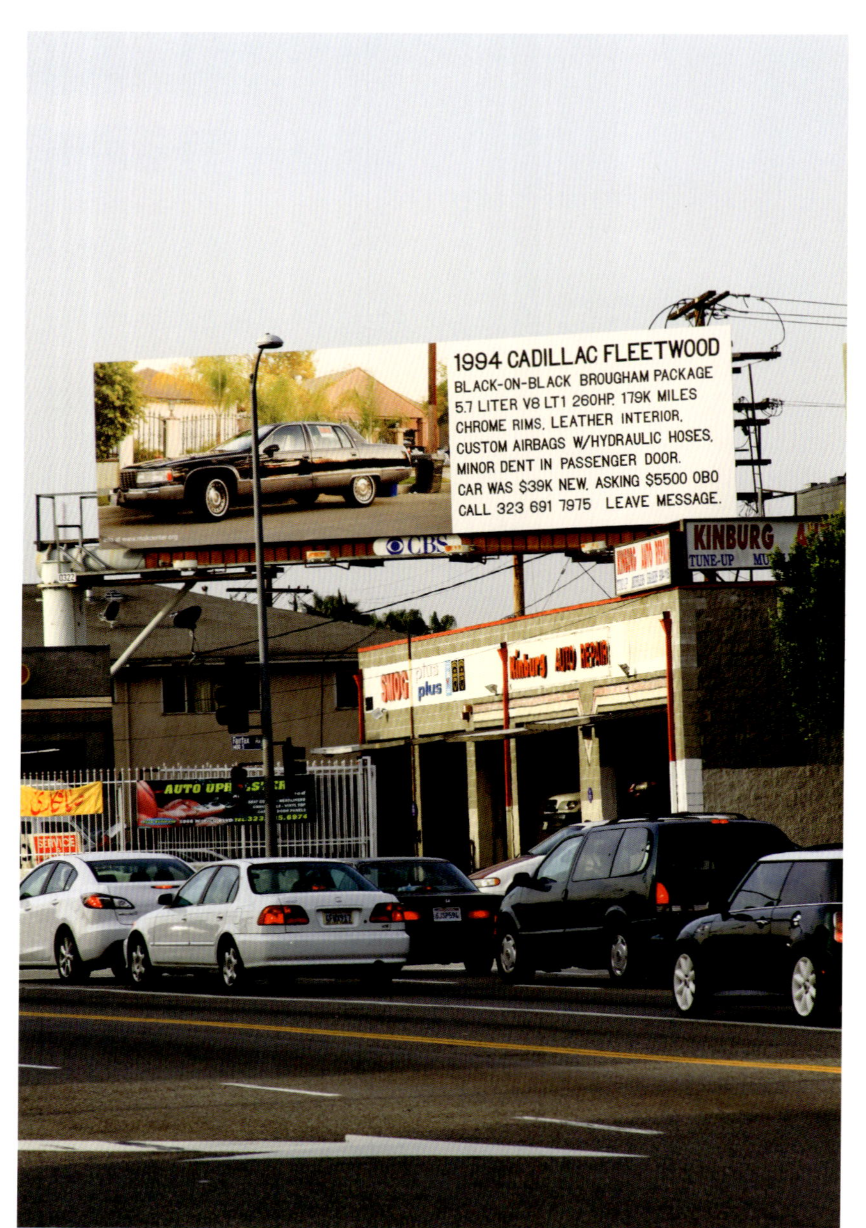
1994 CADILLAC FLEETWOOD
BLACK-ON-BLACK BROUGHAM PACKAGE
5.7 LITER V8 LT1 260HP. 179K MILES
CHROME RIMS, LEATHER INTERIOR,
CUSTOM AIRBAGS W/HYDRAULIC HOSES,
MINOR DENT IN PASSENGER DOOR.
CAR WAS $39K NEW, ASKING $5500 OBO
CALL 323 691 7975 LEAVE MESSAGE.
CBS
KINBURG
TUNE-UP
SMOG
plus
Kinburg AUTO REPAIR
AUTO UPHOLSTERY

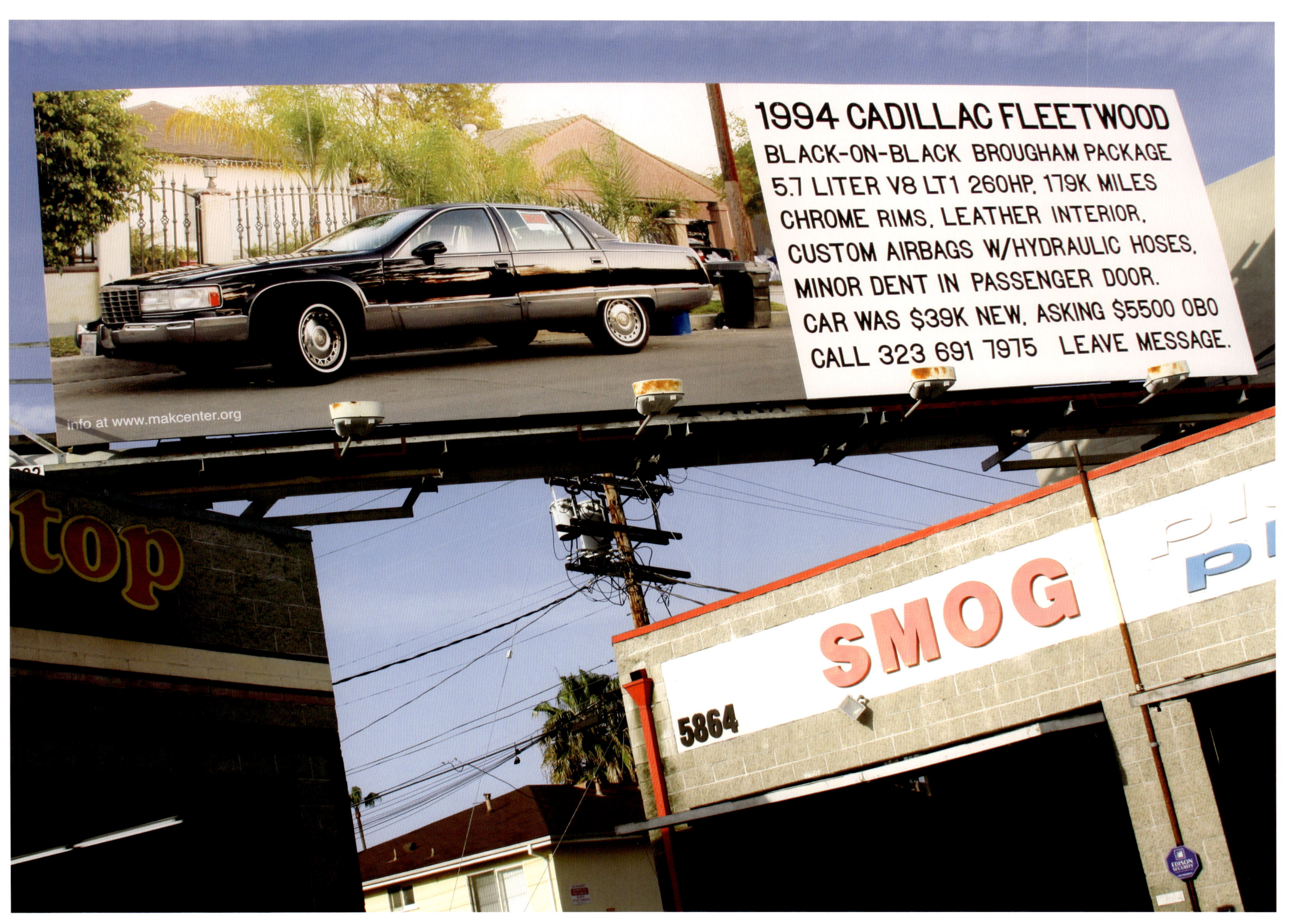
1994 CADILLAC FLEETWOOD
BLACK-ON-BLACK BROUGHAM PACKAGE
5.7 LITER V8 LT1 260HP, 179K MILES
CHROME RIMS, LEATHER INTERIOR,
CUSTOM AIRBAGS W/HYDRAULIC HOSES,
MINOR DENT IN PASSENGER DOOR.
CAR WAS $39K NEW, ASKING $5500 OBO
CALL 323 691 7975 LEAVE MESSAGE.
info at www.makcenter.org
top
SMOG
5864

DANIEL JOSEPH MARTINEZ

Traversing media and disciplinary boundaries for over 30 years, the artwork of Daniel Joseph Martinez has relentlessly insisted on the potential of art to agitate for political consciousness and action. Revisiting and remixing methodological conventions, his work proposes self-contradictory intellectual hybrids, resulting in the counter-dogmatic attitude characteristic of his diverse aesthetic oeuvre.

In Martinez's billboard collage, a military aircraft carrier turned sideways is in danger of pouring the fleet of Chinook helicopters on its bow into the ocean. Considered the workhorses of the U.S. Army, here the aircrafts are painted red, symbolizing that they have been repurposed for environmentalist activities. This military/environmentalist amalgam is corroborated by the rainbow design painted on the ship's side, which recalls Greenpeace's schooner the Rainbow Warrior. Fernando Pereira, the ship's photographer, tragically died when Greenpeace's original Rainbow Warrior was bombed and sunk at Auckland's Marsden Wharf in 1985 by agents of the French government. Despite the fact that the agents pleaded guilty to charges of manslaughter and willful damage, they were released in less than two years. With this referent in mind, the collage is inconclusive. Conflating the military with militant, it debates morality, authority, and justice. The image is offset by a text that reads: "The disappointment of a fanatical searcher of the truth, who saw through trickery of an authoritarian world filled with illusions." The various images, in their relation to the words, provoke a matrix of possible meanings. "Truth," this work demonstrates, may mean a different thing for Greenpeace, the French government, or for New Zealand justice, where the French agents were tried. With "disappointment" signaling that justice is nothing if not blind, it also brings to mind the recent arrests and criminalization of peaceful protestors in Copenhagen during the 2009 United Nations Climate Change Conference.

BY NIZAN SHAKED

LOCATION: Washington Boulevard, west of Curson Avenue, on the north side of the street, facing east.

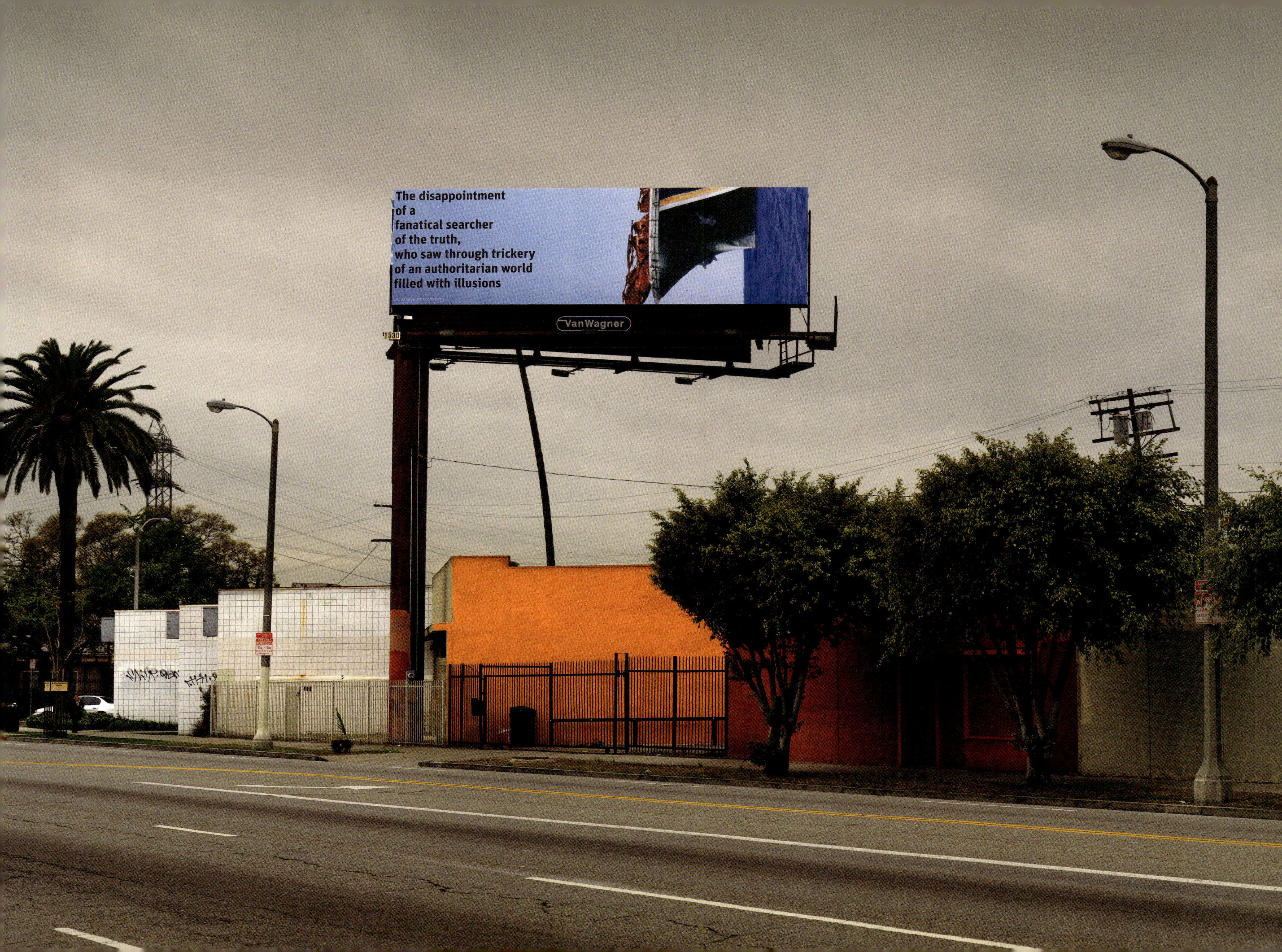
The disappointment
of a
fanatical searcher
of the truth,
who saw through trickery
of an authoritarian world
filled with illusions
VanWagner

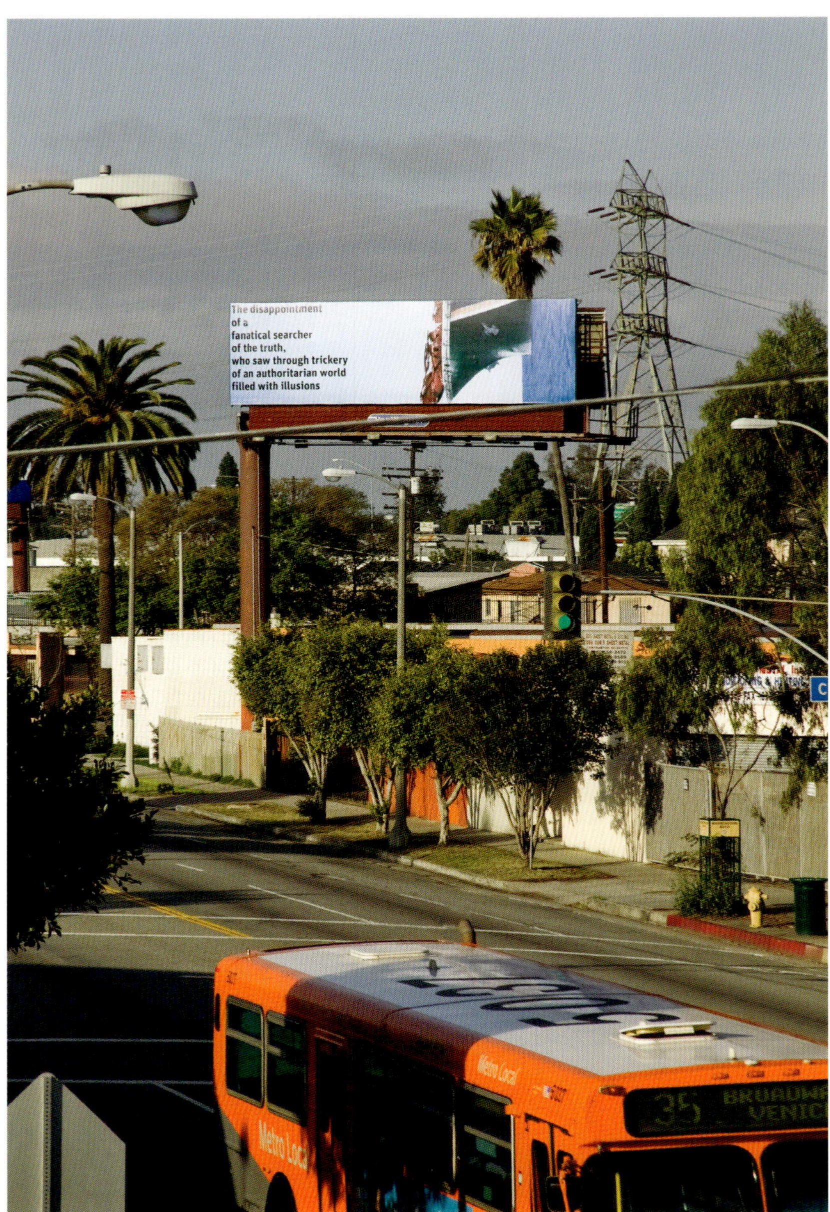
The disappointment
of a
fanatical searcher
of the truth,
who saw through trickery
of an authoritarian world
filled with illusions
Metro Local

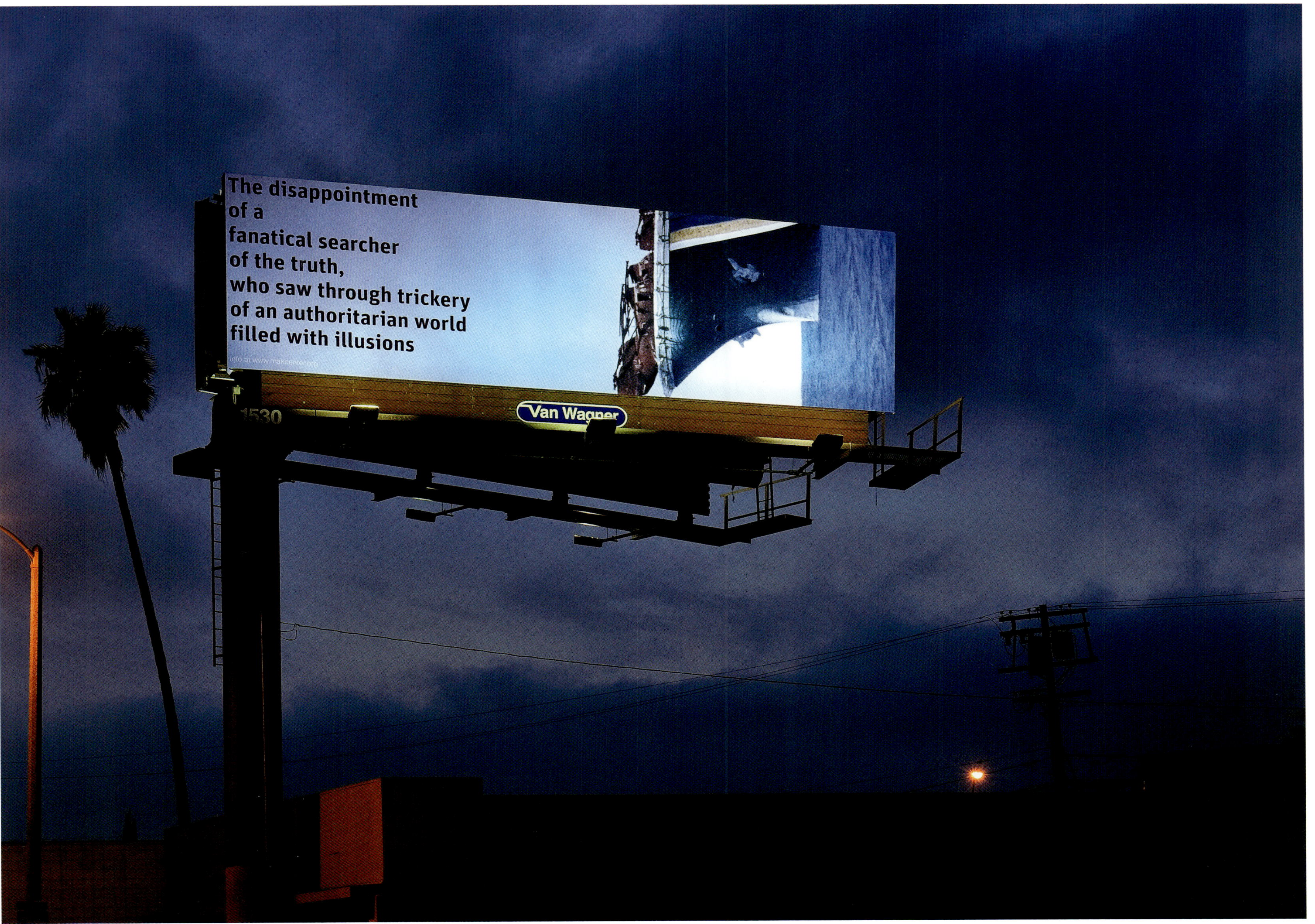
The disappointment
of a
fanatical searcher
of the truth,
who saw through trickery
of an authoritarian world
filled with illusions
1530
Van Wagner

KORI NEWKIRK

Folding double-entendres into his formal investigations, Kori Newkirk's semiotics of material play on literal and implied meaning. In his billboard image, the artist executes for the camera a bold gesture of ambiguous intent, distinguishing between what viewers see and what they can "read." Playing on the notion of self-portraiture at large, Newkirk's figure is captured at the center of the frame. A hint of shoulder muscle bulges with effort; his face is caught in a grimace. All the while an enormous snowball is stuck in his mouth. On the one hand, the viewer is called upon to play with the various implications of the image, with the caveat that to literalize the associations evoked by the colors, the materials, and the implications of their proper names would be to choke the artwork—pun intended. On the other hand, the denotation of the image oscillates between what may be pleasure, pain, or both—rendering unclear whether the object has been forced into the artist's mouth, or whether it represents an act of consent. Tension is thus set up between the two ways in which this image makes meaning, between reading it through its various symbolic implications or through the actions of its main protagonist. Its refusal of one single mode of interpretation connects directly to the artist's corporeal presence. His predicament here resists being over-determined. Still, a symbolic act of silencing exists, a sly play on the figure of speech "tongue-in-cheek," that nevertheless speaks volumes. Ball-in-cheek—the artist subjugates his own image to the desire/violence of the viewer's gaze. This gesture is amplified by the format of the billboard, in which the enormity of the image splays for public display the vulnerability of the moment in which the picture was taken. The gesture of extreme personal revelation, or literally exposure, is softened by the formal quality of the overall image. Originally recorded on a negative; the scanned and then enlarged photographic grain becomes as sensual as the body recorded.

BY NIZAN SHAKED

LOCATION: Wilshire Boulevard, west of Hoover Street, on the south side of the street, facing west.

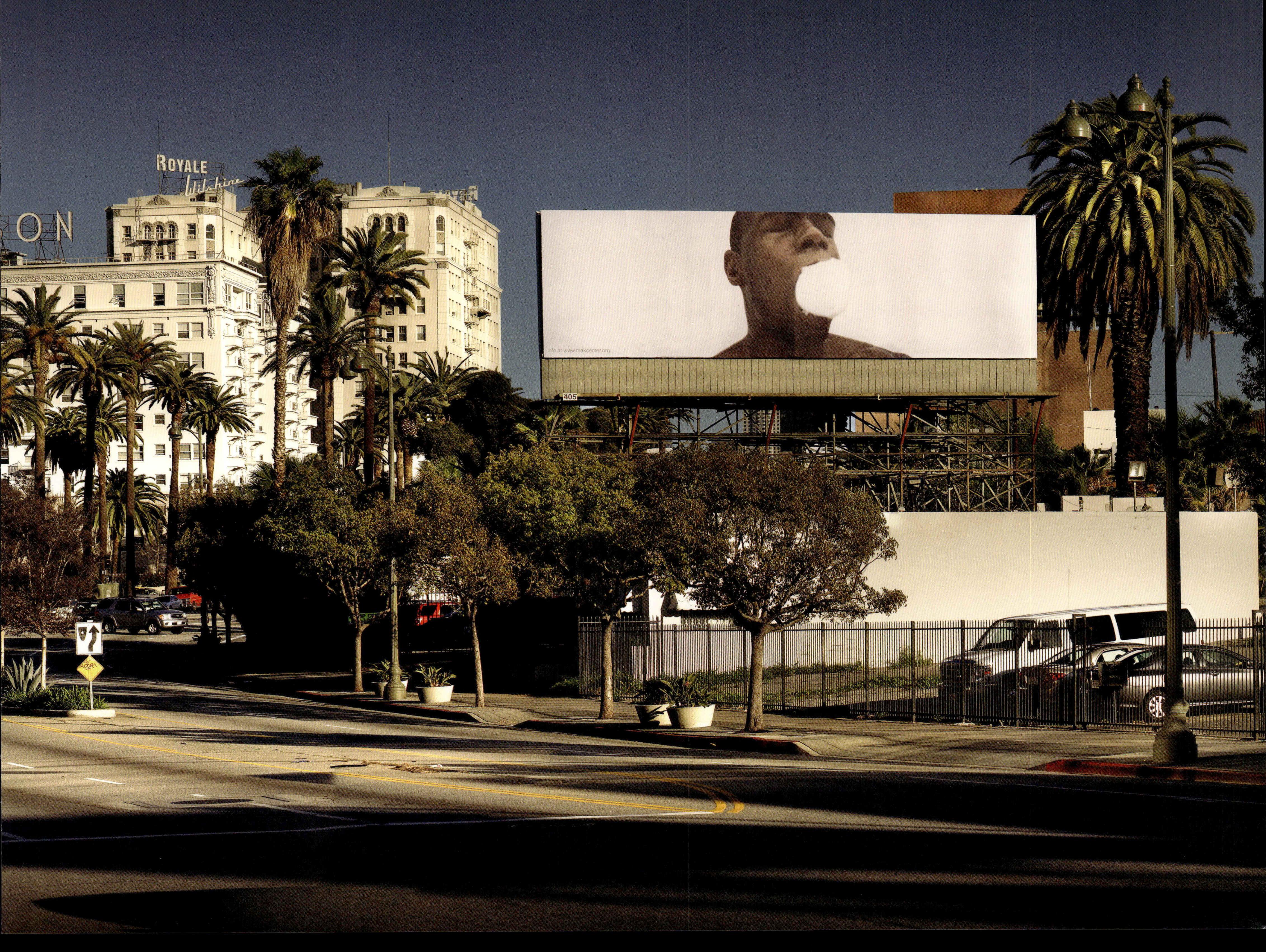
ROYALE
ON
info at www.makcenter.org
405

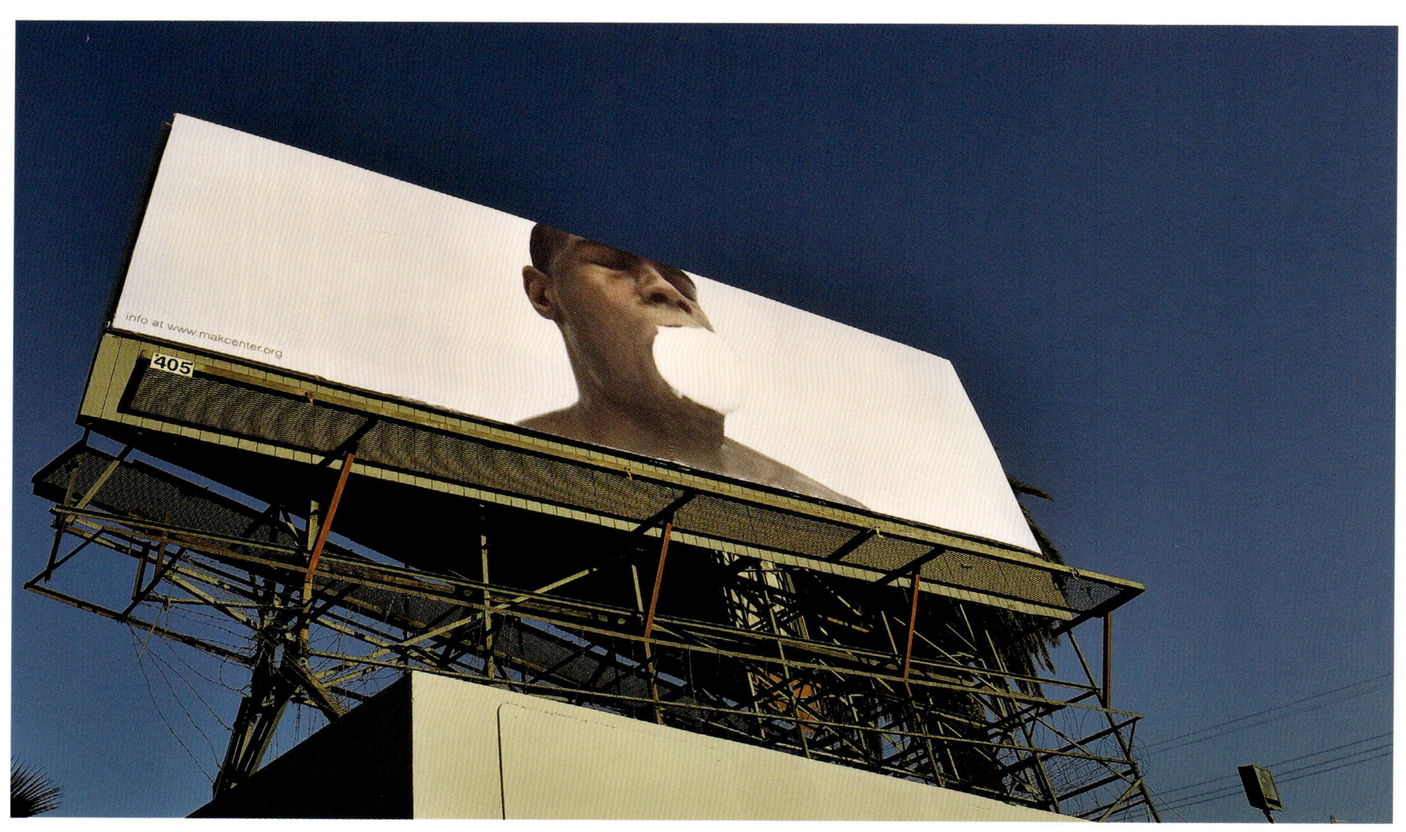
info at www.makcenter.org
405

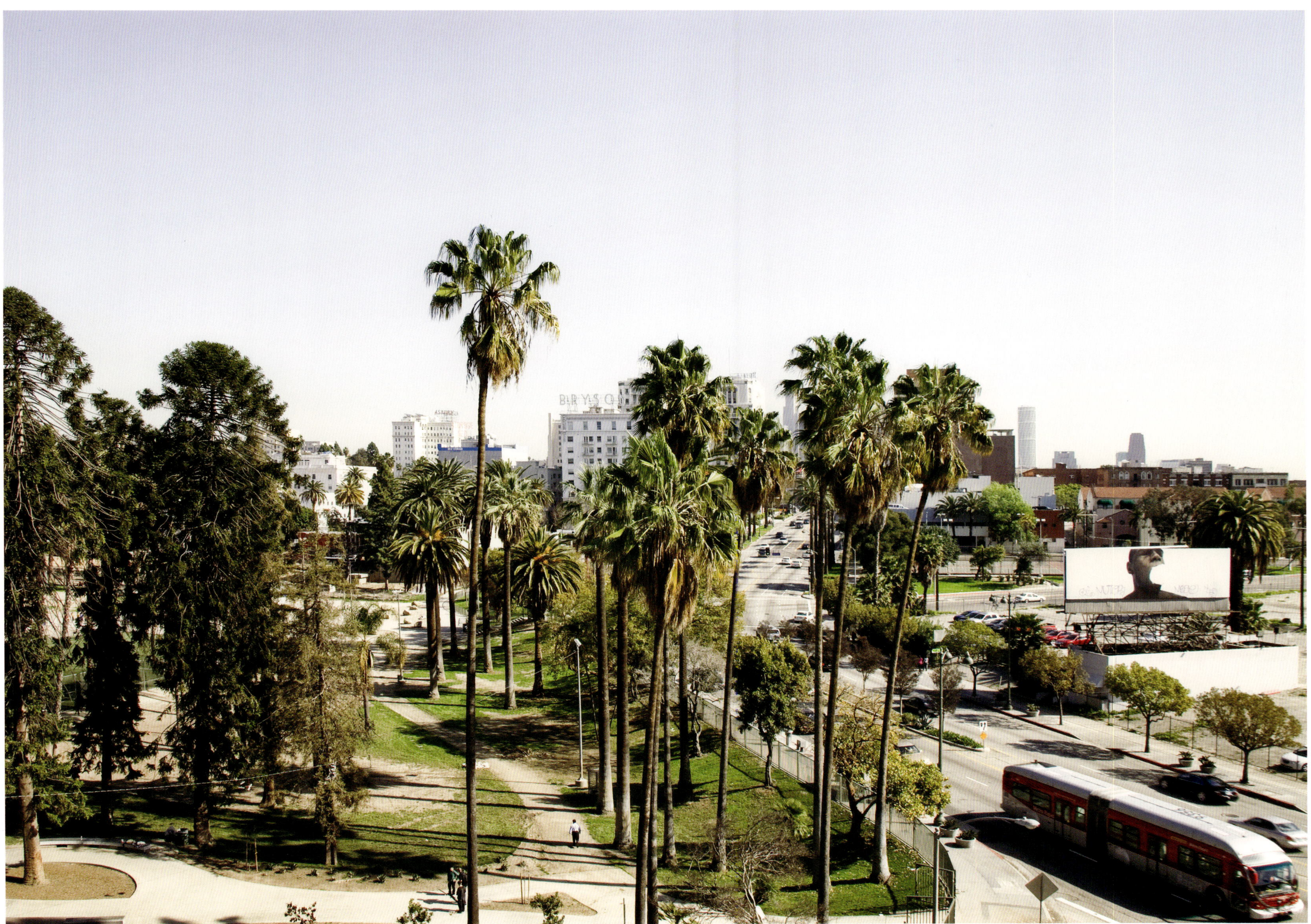
ASBURY

YVONNE RAINER

Yvonne Rainer's prodigious output over the past forty years crosses several spheres of art making. Her important work as both a choreographer and filmmaker radically infuses political and conceptual consciousness into the fields of dance and independent filmmaking. While these two trajectories of Rainer's practice follow distinct paths, both her dance compositions and films employ distancing strategies and disjunctive acts (such as fragmentation), and set up complex juxtapositions that interrupt the linear flow of narrative and time. Most notably, her dances and films eschew the grand gestures and excessive drama of modern dance and Abstract Expressionism, which dominated New York's art establishment when Rainer began her intermedia performances with Judson Church during the late 1950s and early 1960s. Instead, Rainer's work reflects the ordinary movements of everyday life, and her dance compositions dispel the distance between performer and audience by removing the proscenium stage. Rainer's *We Shall Run* (1963), for example, has non-professional dancers dressed in casual street clothes jogging for seven minutes. Her use of voiceover and intertitles in many of her films, along with appropriating whole texts (literary, cinematic, and philosophical) by other authors into her screenplays further distances her work from the illusionistic imperatives of traditional narrative filmmaking. In *The Man Who Envied Women* (1985) one of her most popular films, Rainer uses this technique of textual appropriation to deliver a comical and incisive account of artistic and intellectual pretension. Addressing themes of aging, menopause, and women's identity, *Privilege* (1990) is one of Rainer's more explicitly feminist films, representing the process by which women's bodies are coveted in youth but marginalized in older age.

For *How Many Billboards?*, Rainer plainly presents an enigmatic quote from a grand dame of Hollywood filmmaking, Marlene Dietrich. In an industry constantly churning out new talent, Dietrich's professional longevity was exceptional and is often attributed to her ability to constantly reinvent herself for both the camera and her public. Even in her self-imposed seclusion during the last decade of her life, Dietrich continued to captivate the public imagination. Despite her death in 1992, Dietrich's image remains ever present as a standard for glamour, which seems to corroborate the refrain "I look good" in Rainer's billboard text. By alluding to and defamiliarizing mass-media imagery, especially Hollywood movies, Rainer casts a critical light on various scenarios that contribute to women's oppression—social, political, and physical.

BY GLORIA SUTTON

LOCATION: Pico Boulevard, west of Fairfax Avenue, on the south side of the street, facing west.

"I look good, I know; I can't see, I can't hear, but I look good" was uttered by Marlene Dietrich in Maximillian Schell's 1984 documentary, Marlene. For some reason it has remained engraved in my memory ever since. - YVONNE RAINER

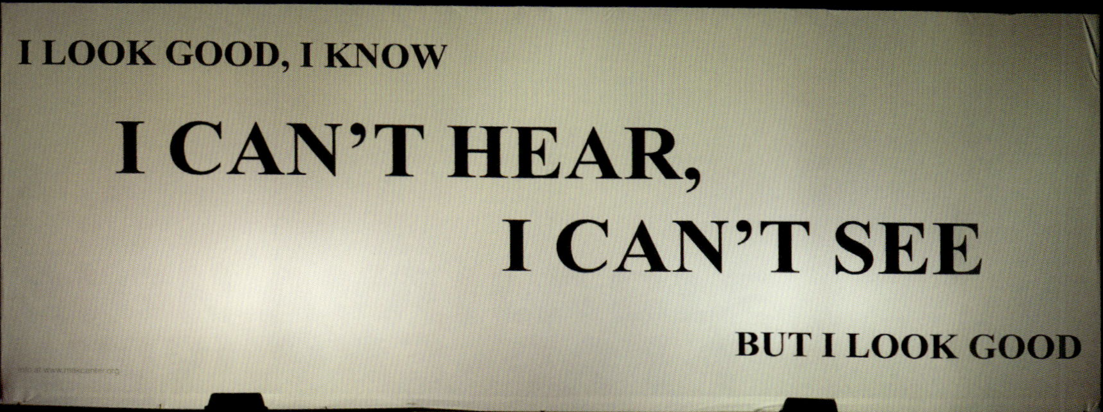
I LOOK GOOD, I KNOW
I CAN'T HEAR,
I CAN'T SEE
BUT I LOOK GOOD

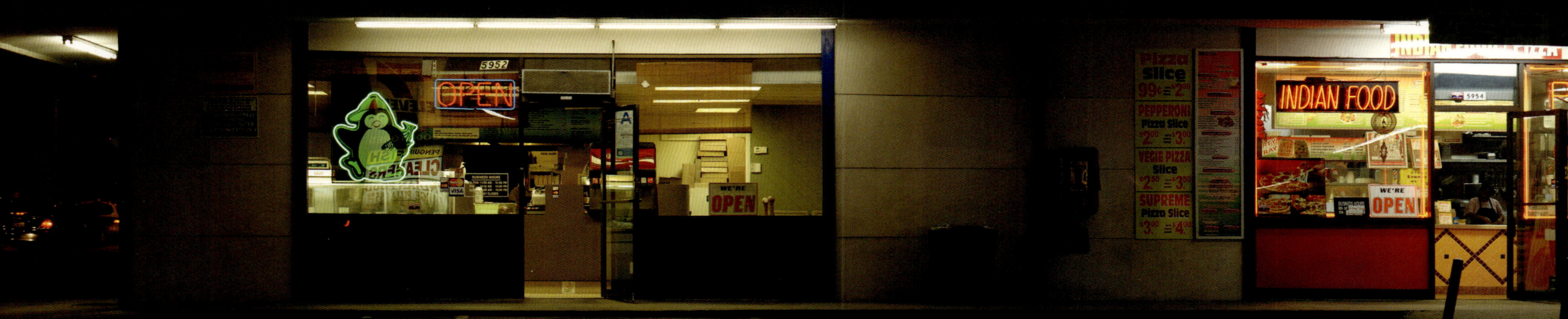
PENGUIN FISH & CHIPS
SEAFOOD
323-933-7661
GRILL REST
OPEN
INDIAN FOOD
WE'RE OPEN
WE'RE OPEN
Pizza Slice
PEPPERONI Pizza Slice
VEGIE PIZZA Slice
SUPREME Pizza Slice

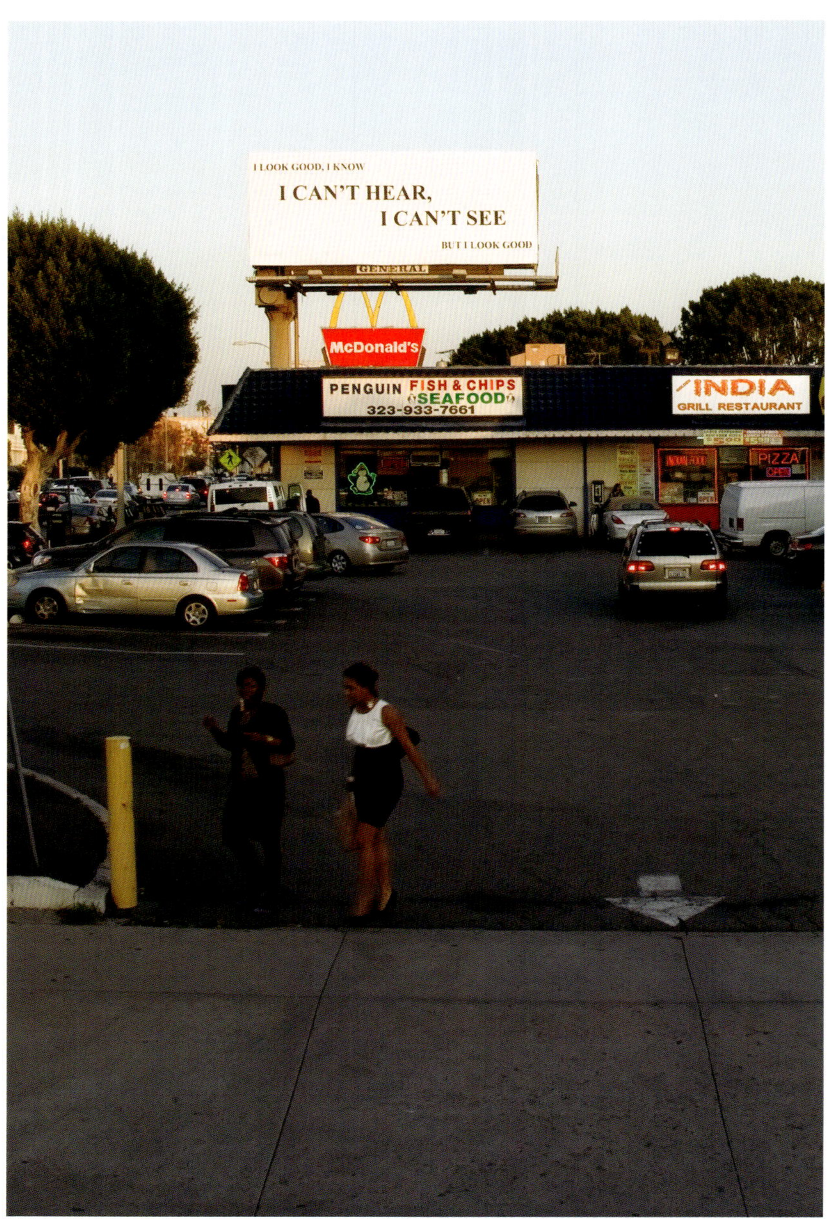
I LOOK GOOD, I KNOW
I CAN'T HEAR,
I CAN'T SEE
BUT I LOOK GOOD
GENERAL
McDonald's
PENGUIN FISH & CHIPS
SEAFOOD
323-933-7661
INDIA
GRILL RESTAURANT
PIZZA

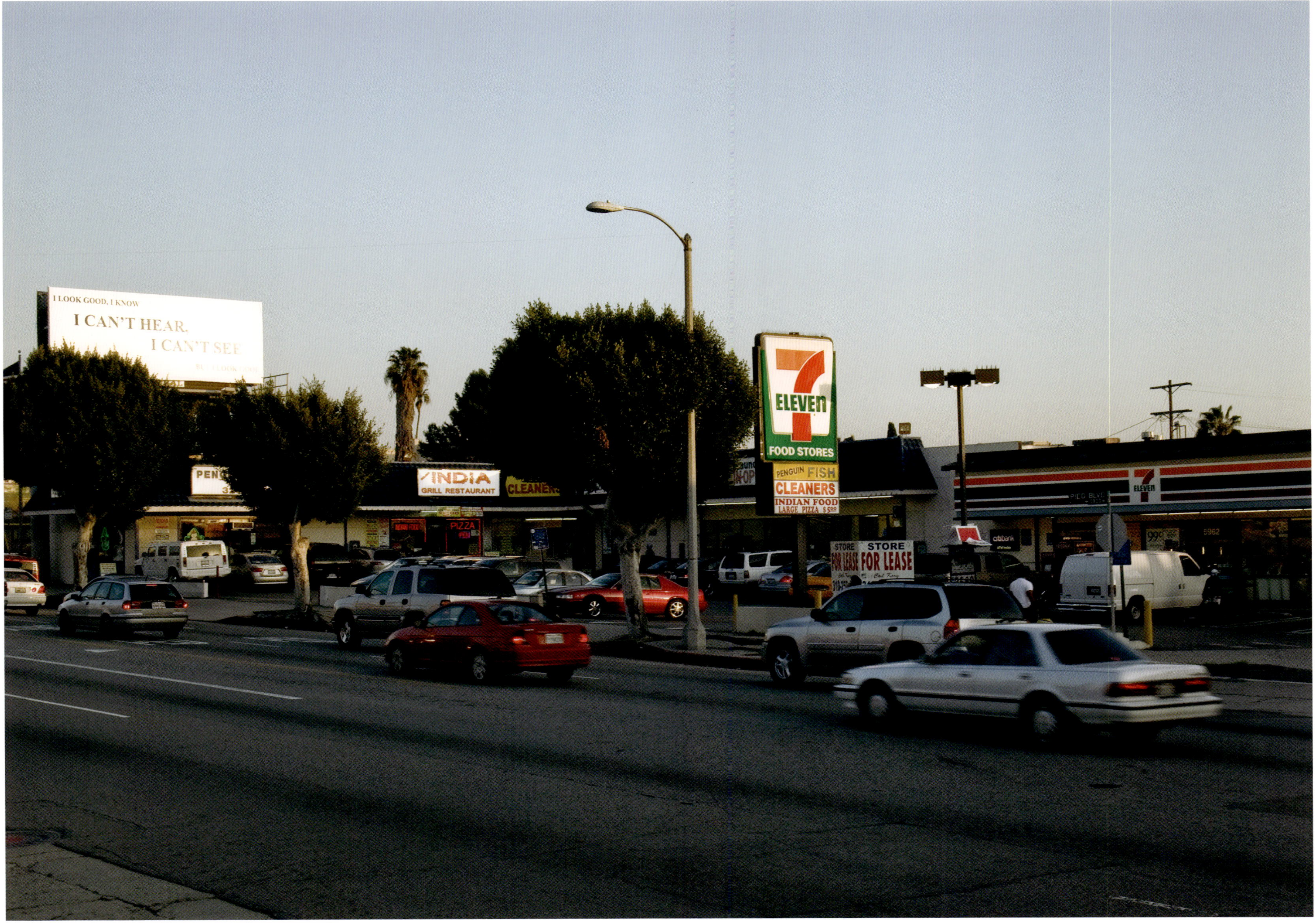
I LOOK GOOD, I KNOW
I CAN'T HEAR,
I CAN'T SEE
INDIA
GRILL RESTAURANT
CLEANERS
PIZZA
ELEVEN
FOOD STORES
PENGUIN FISH
CLEANERS
INDIAN FOOD
LARGE PIZZA $5.00
STORE FOR LEASE
STORE FOR LEASE
PICO BLVD
ELEVEN
5962

MARTHA ROSLER WITH JOSH NEUFELD

While conceptual artist and writer Martha Rosler works in a variety of media, her practice has been particularly important to the development of Conceptual photography. Rosler's approach to photography focuses equally on issues of gender, class, and American foreign policy, as well as the production, display, and dissemination of photographic images. Some of her most influential works in the medium consciously strive to reveal the power dynamics between subject and photographer. Her seminal photo series *The Bowery in Two Inadequate Descriptive Systems* (1974-1975) is a potent example of her persistent questioning of the unacknowledged complexities of photographing "the other" in American society under the guise of socially concerned or documentary photography.

For *How Many Billboards?*, Rosler uses the billboard as a site for social critique in addition to art making. In collaboration with graphic novelist Josh Neufeld, the artist emphasizes the desperate need for Americans to come together to address today's social inequities in order to secure our own future. Their references to California's "seismic shift" in the allocation of resources to prisons—as opposed to schools—and the unacknowledged power of corporations within the University of California system localize a national concern for Angelenos.

BY LISA HENRY

LOCATION: Sunset Boulevard, west of Cahuenga Boulevard, on the north side of the street, facing east.

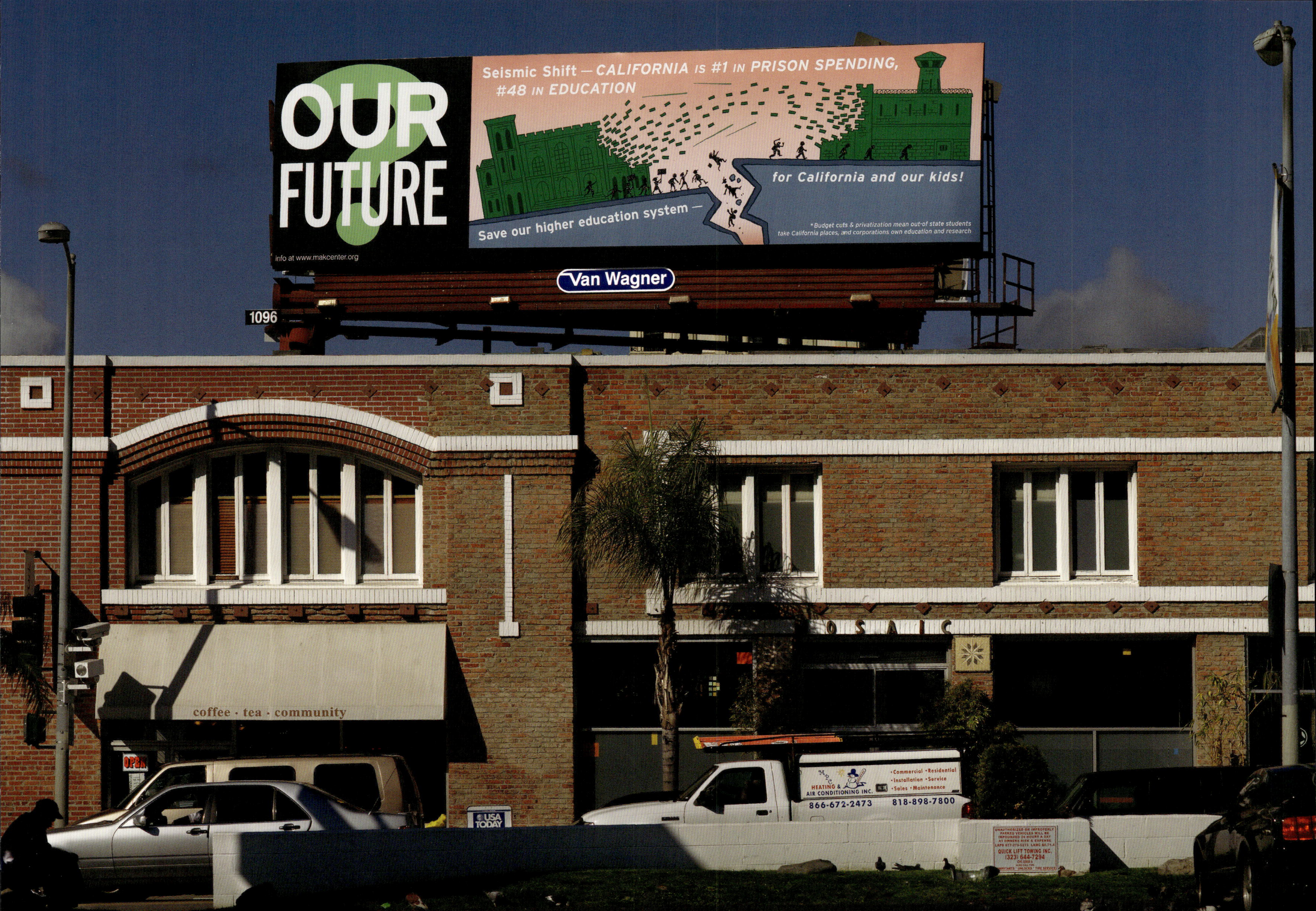

OUR FUTURE
Seismic Shift — CALIFORNIA IS #1 IN PRISON SPENDING, #48 IN EDUCATION
Save our higher education system —
for California and our kids!
*Budget cuts & privatization mean out-of state students take California places, and corporations own education and research
info at www.makcenter.org
Van Wagner
1096
coffee · tea · community
HEATING & AIR CONDITIONING INC.
•Commercial •Residential •Installation •Service •Sales •Maintenance
866-672-2473
818-898-7800
USA TODAY

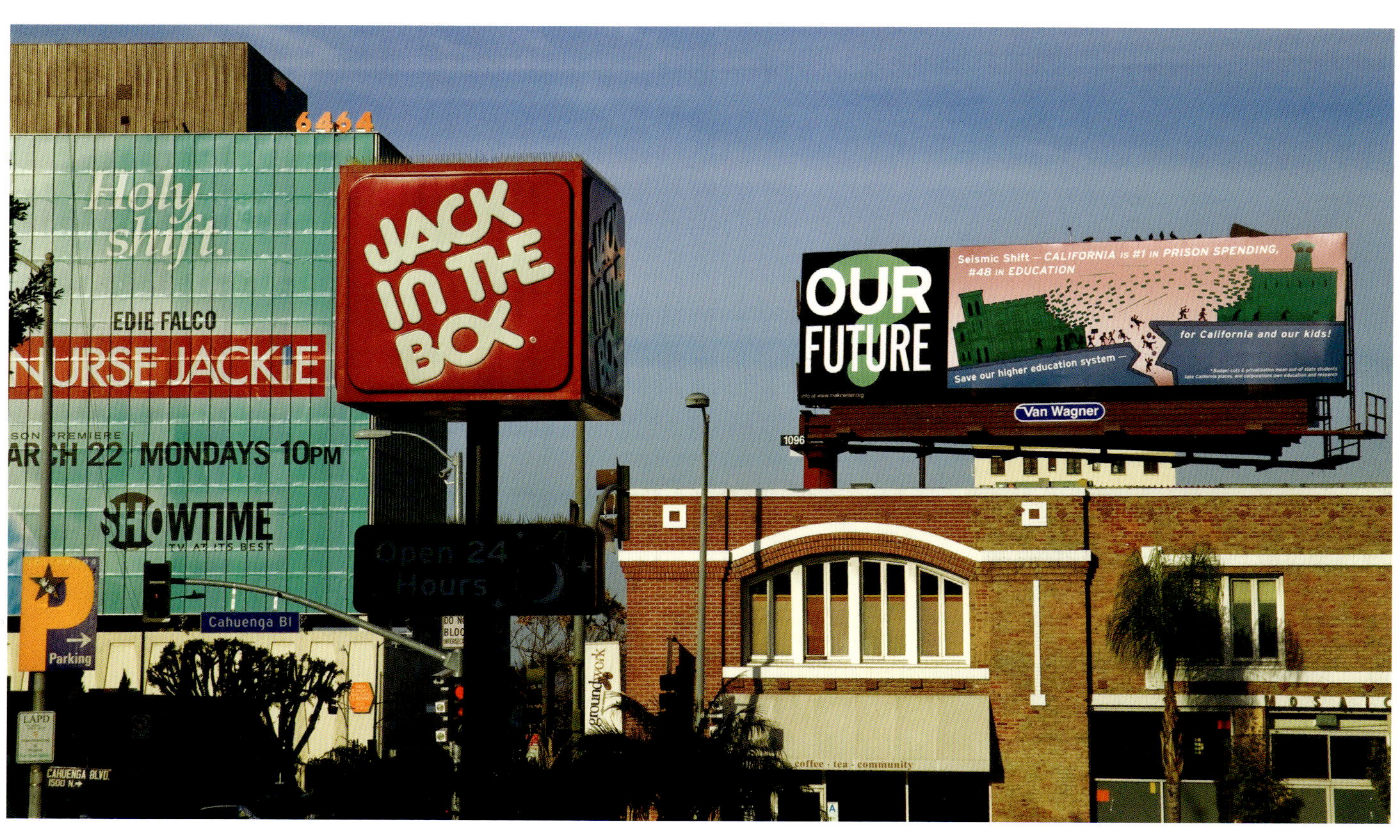
6464
Holy shift.
EDIE FALCO
NURSE JACKIE
ARCH 22 MONDAYS 10PM
SHOWTIME
JACK IN THE BOX
Open 24 Hours
OUR FUTURE
Seismic Shift — CALIFORNIA IS #1 IN PRISON SPENDING, #48 IN EDUCATION
Save our higher education system —
for California and our kids!
Van Wagner
1096
Cahuenga Bl
P
Parking
LAPD
CAHUENGA BLVD 1500 N.
coffee · tea · community

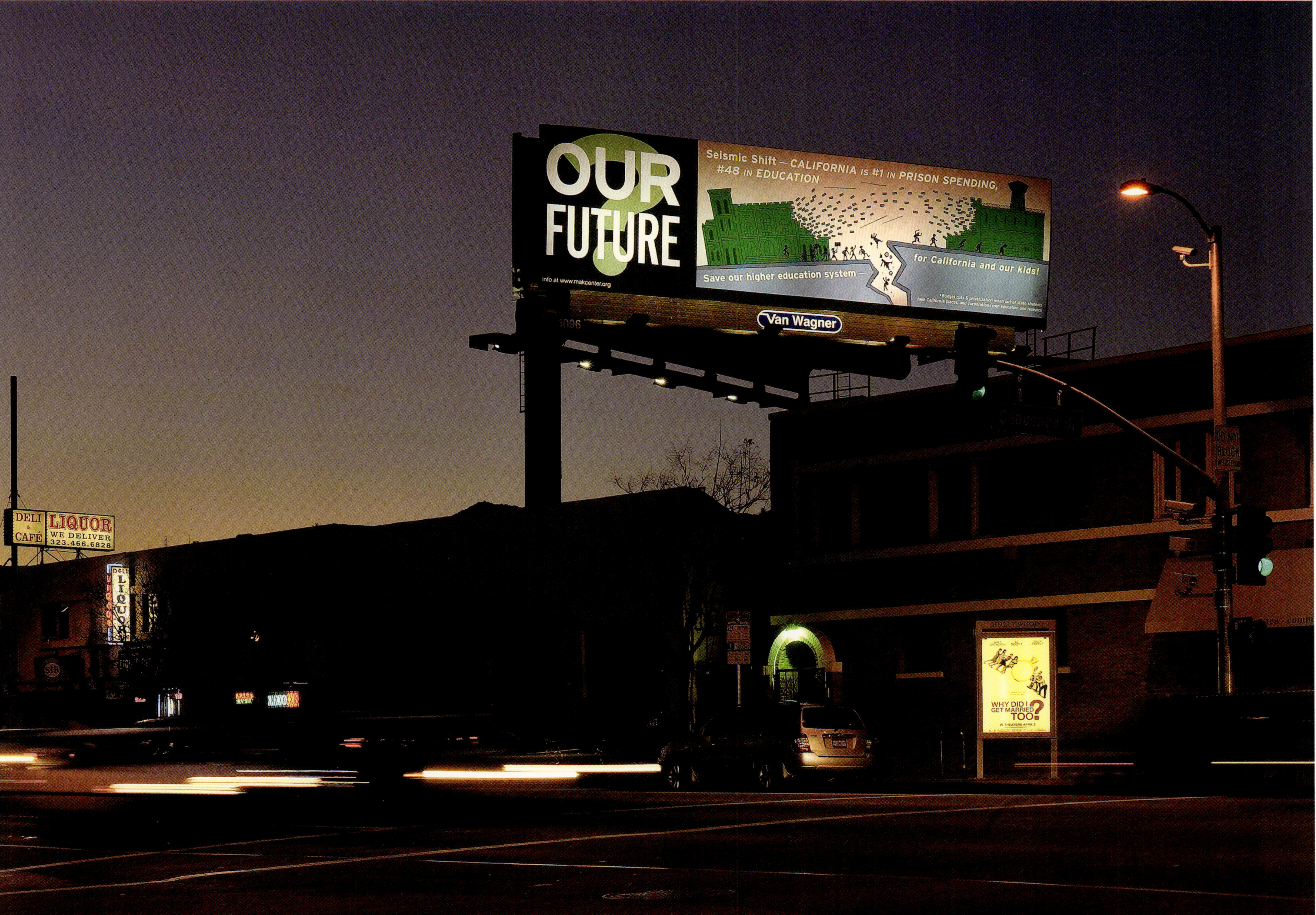
OUR FUTURE
info at www.makcenter.org
Seismic Shift — CALIFORNIA IS #1 IN PRISON SPENDING, #48 IN EDUCATION
Save our higher education system —
for California and our kids!
*Budget cuts & privatization mean out-of state students take California places, and corporations own education and research
Van Wagner
1096
DELI & CAFÉ
LIQUOR
WE DELIVER
323.466.6828
DO NOT BLOCK
WHY DID I GET MARRIED TOO?

ALLEN RUPPERSBERG

Allen Ruppersberg brings together his longstanding interests in books and posters in his billboard for this exhibition. Ruppersberg approaches the billboard at face value by asking, "What does a billboard do?" As an answer to this question, he creates an unsolicited advertisement for *Pacific Standard Time,* an upcoming project including exhibitions, performances, and publications. This massive undertaking, with leadership and funding from the Getty Foundation, will take place at numerous Southern California venues, and will focus on the history of postwar art in Los Angeles from 1945 to 1980. As an artist participating in *Pacific Standard Time*, and as a key figure in Los Angeles in the 1960s and '70s, Ruppersberg has both a professional and personal relationship to the exhibition project and the era it highlights.

The image of the book on the billboard is an alteration of the catalog *The Art and Technology Program, 1967—71*, which documents the Los Angeles County Museum of Art's well-known project that paired artists with high technology corporations. The cover of that publication features a grid of portraits of some of the artists, scientists, and corporate officials that participated in the program. For his unofficial, humorous advertisement for *Pacific Standard Time*, Ruppersberg inserted photographs drawn from his own personal archive and library of artists active in Los Angeles during the 1960s and '70s. In this way, he references the sweeping scale of both LACMA's *Art and Technology Program* and the Getty's *Pacific Standard Time* project, while interjecting his own history as a part of the larger cultural narrative.

BY KIMBERLI MEYER

LOCATION: Venice Boulevard, west of Midvale Avenue, on the north side of the street, facing east.

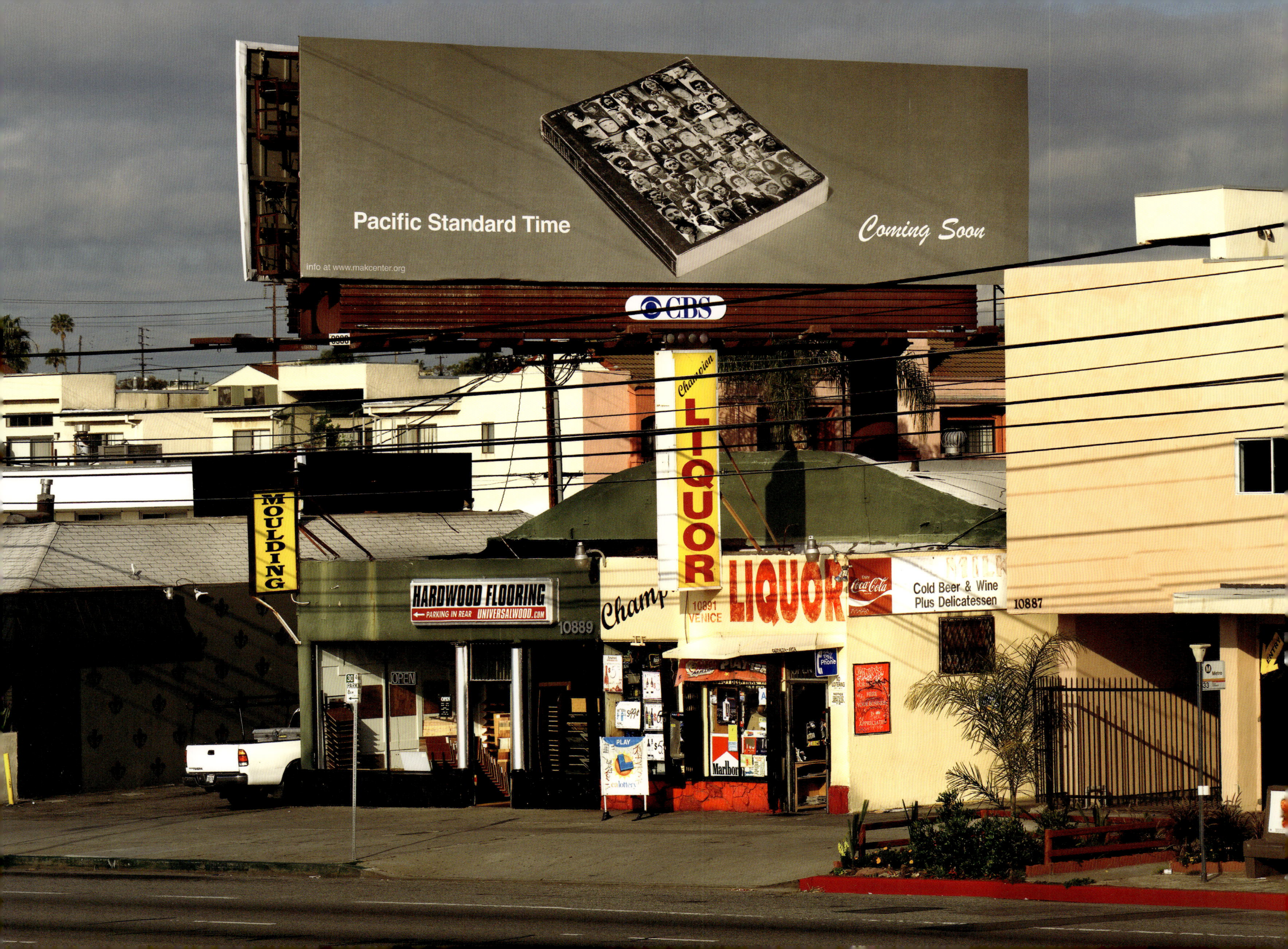
Pacific Standard Time
Coming Soon
info at www.makcenter.org
CBS
Champion
LIQUOR
MOULDING
HARDWOOD FLOORING
PARKING IN REAR UNIVERSALWOOD.COM
10889
OPEN
Champ
10891
VENICE
LIQUOR
Coca-Cola
Cold Beer & Wine
Plus Delicatessen
10887
PLAY
Marlboro
Metro

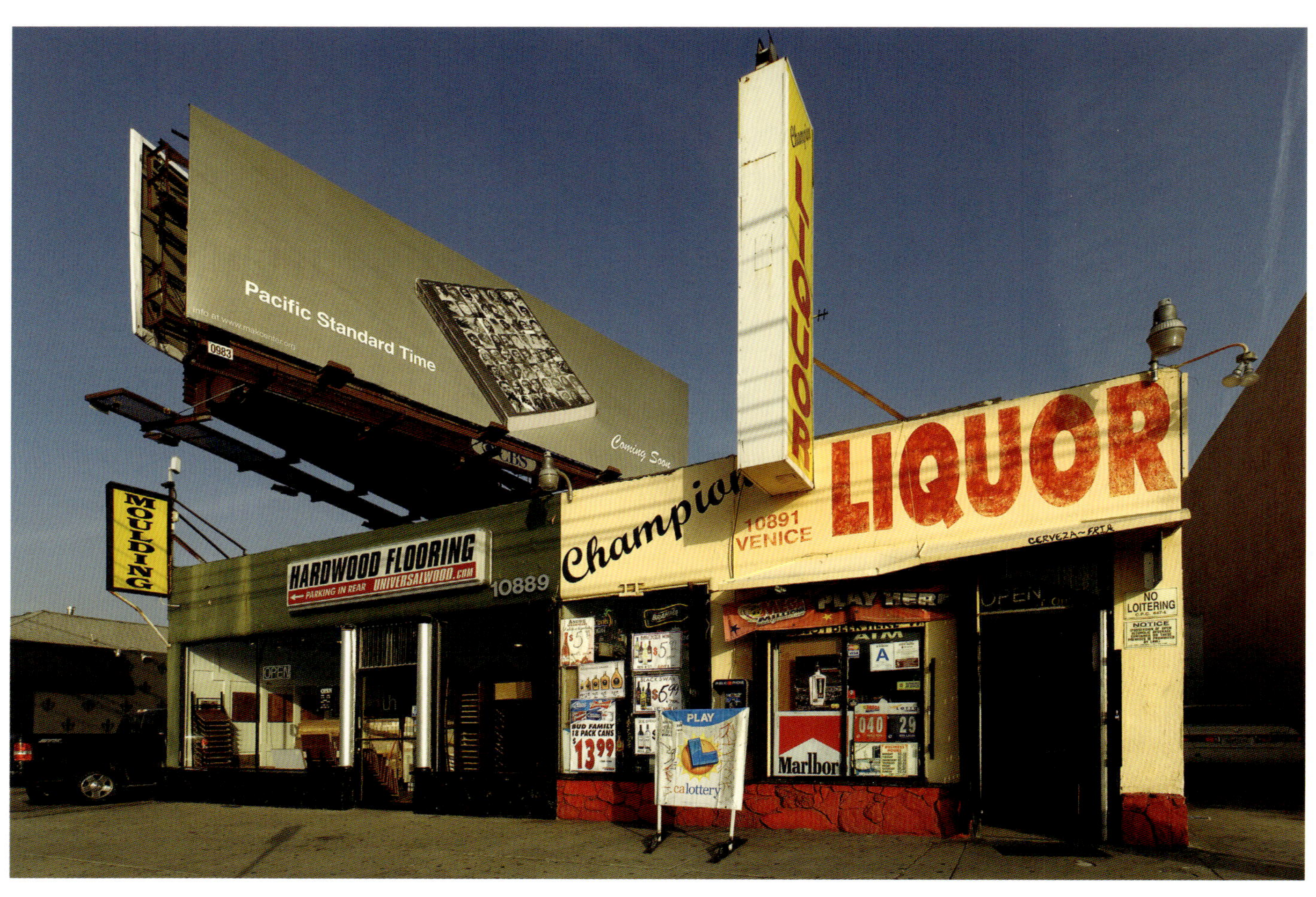
Pacific Standard Time
Coming Soon
LIQUOR
Champion
10891 VENICE
LIQUOR
HARDWOOD FLOORING
PARKING IN REAR UNIVERSALWOOD.com
10889
MOULDING
NO LOITERING
Marlboro
BUD FAMILY 18 PACK CANS
13.99
PLAY
calottery

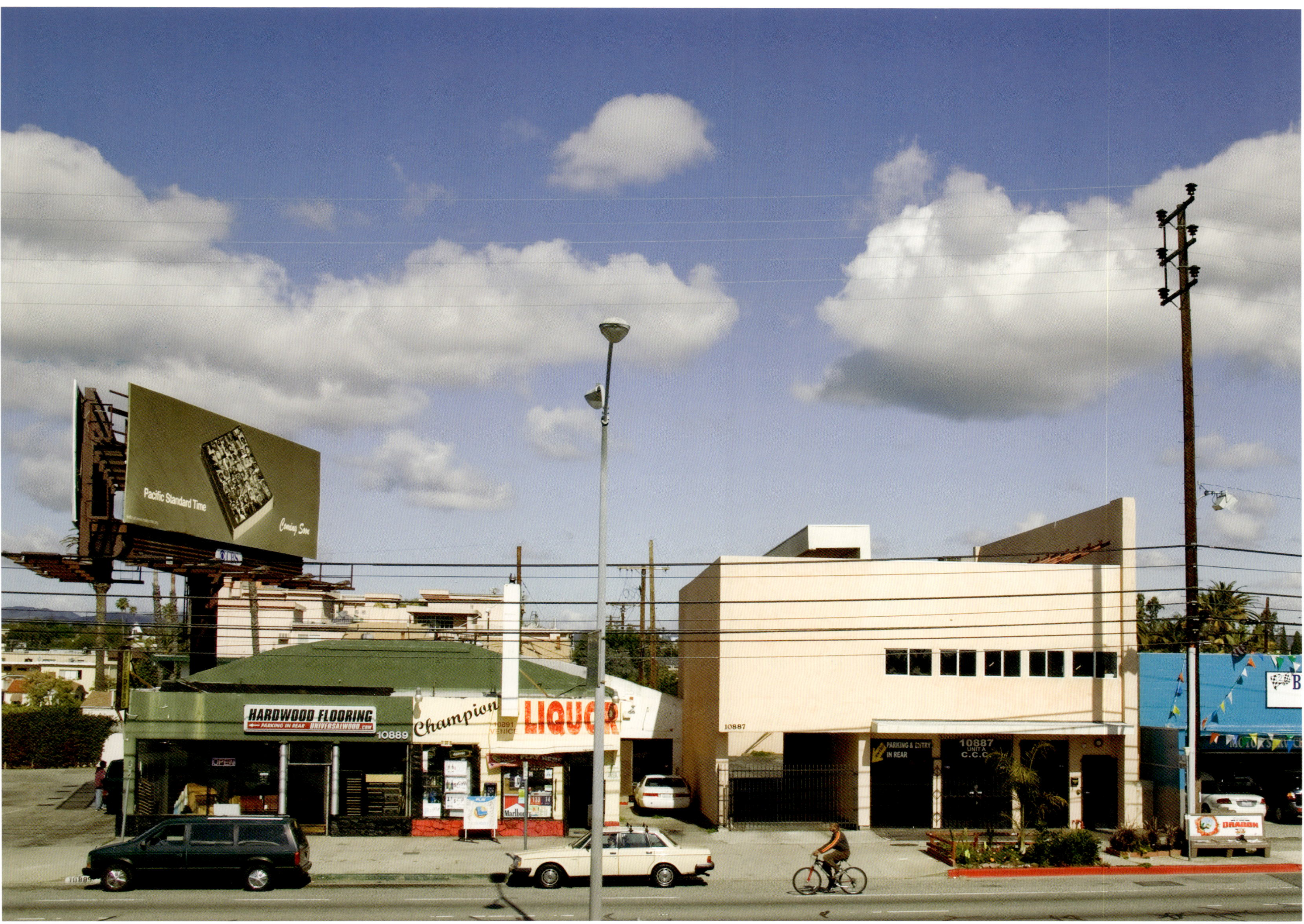

Pacific Standard Time
Coming Soon
HARDWOOD FLOORING
PARKING IN REAR UNIVERSALWOOD.com
10889
Champion
10887
PARKING & ENTRY IN REAR
10887 UNIT A C.C.C.

ALLAN SEKULA

Allan Sekula's impact as a Conceptual Artist, theoretician, and instructor shaped much of the postmodern photographic practice that developed in Southern California during the 1980s and 1990s. His work has long been focused on socio-political critique, manifested by a persistent interrogation of photography's long-standing claim to truth and evidence, and the photographic image's supposed ability to record essential cultural identities. His project for *How Many Billboards?* is in keeping with an ongoing series of image/text pieces that deal with the ramifications of unchecked capitalism and workers' rights.

For this exhibition, Sekula deploys an image previously exhibited at Documenta 12. A welder at a construction site holding a lit acetylene torch and crouching over his work takes a moment to look directly at the viewer. The words "The rich destroy the planet" are superimposed in Spanish over the photograph. The lettering, which looks as if it were cut letter by letter from old magazines, is slightly disjunctive in scale but chromatically balanced and ultimately aesthetically appealing. The message, however, is blunt and accusatory, and it functions succinctly for both English and Spanish speakers, since these words appear similar in both languages.

BY LISA HENRY

LOCATION: Olympic Boulevard, east of Robertson Boulevard, on the south side of the street, facing west. Originally located on Beverly Boulevard, east of Western Avenue, on the north side of the street, facing east.

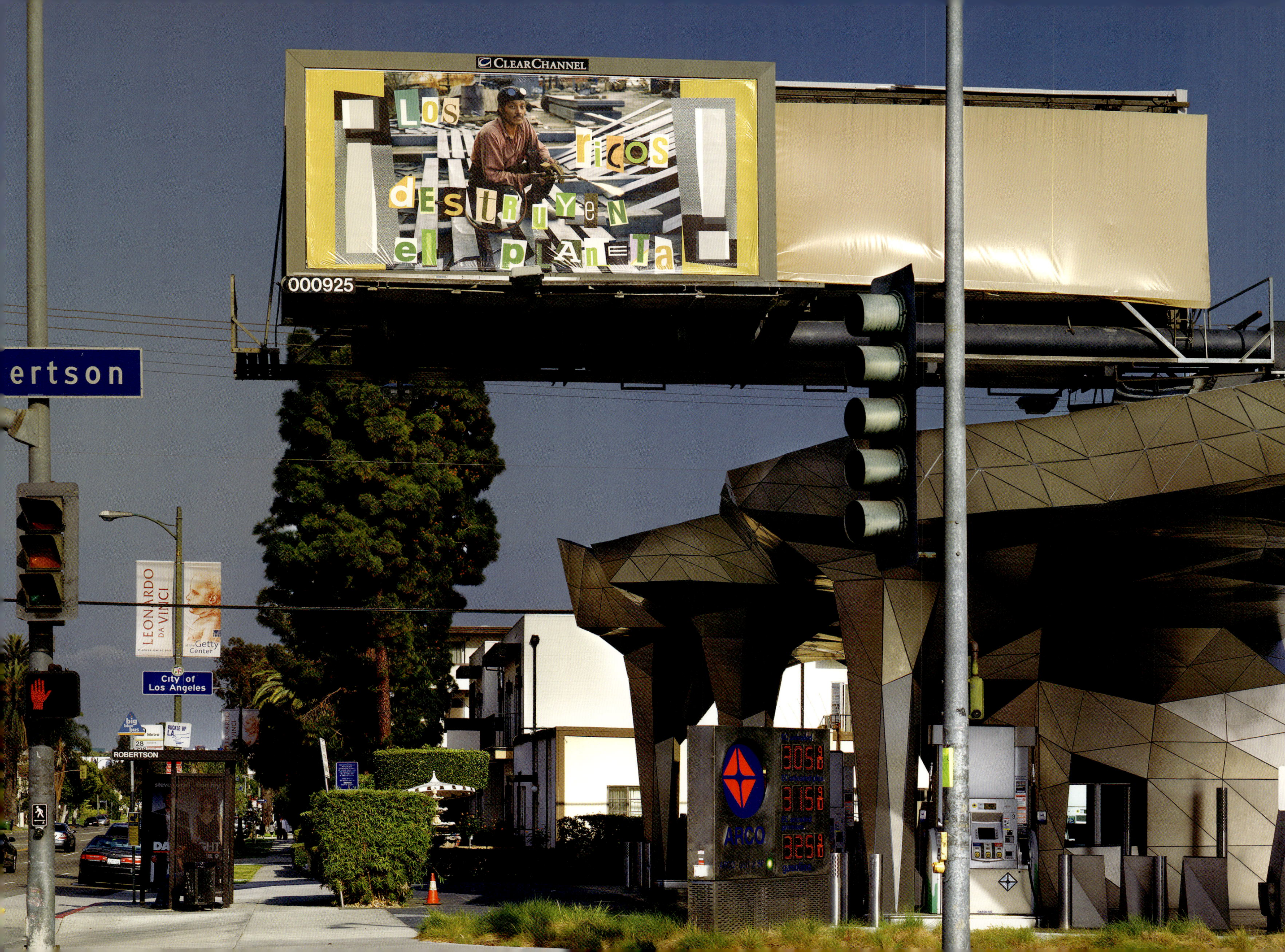

CLEARCHANNEL
Los ricos destruyen el planeta
000925
ertson
LEONARDO DA VINCI
Getty Center
City of Los Angeles
ROBERTSON
ARCO

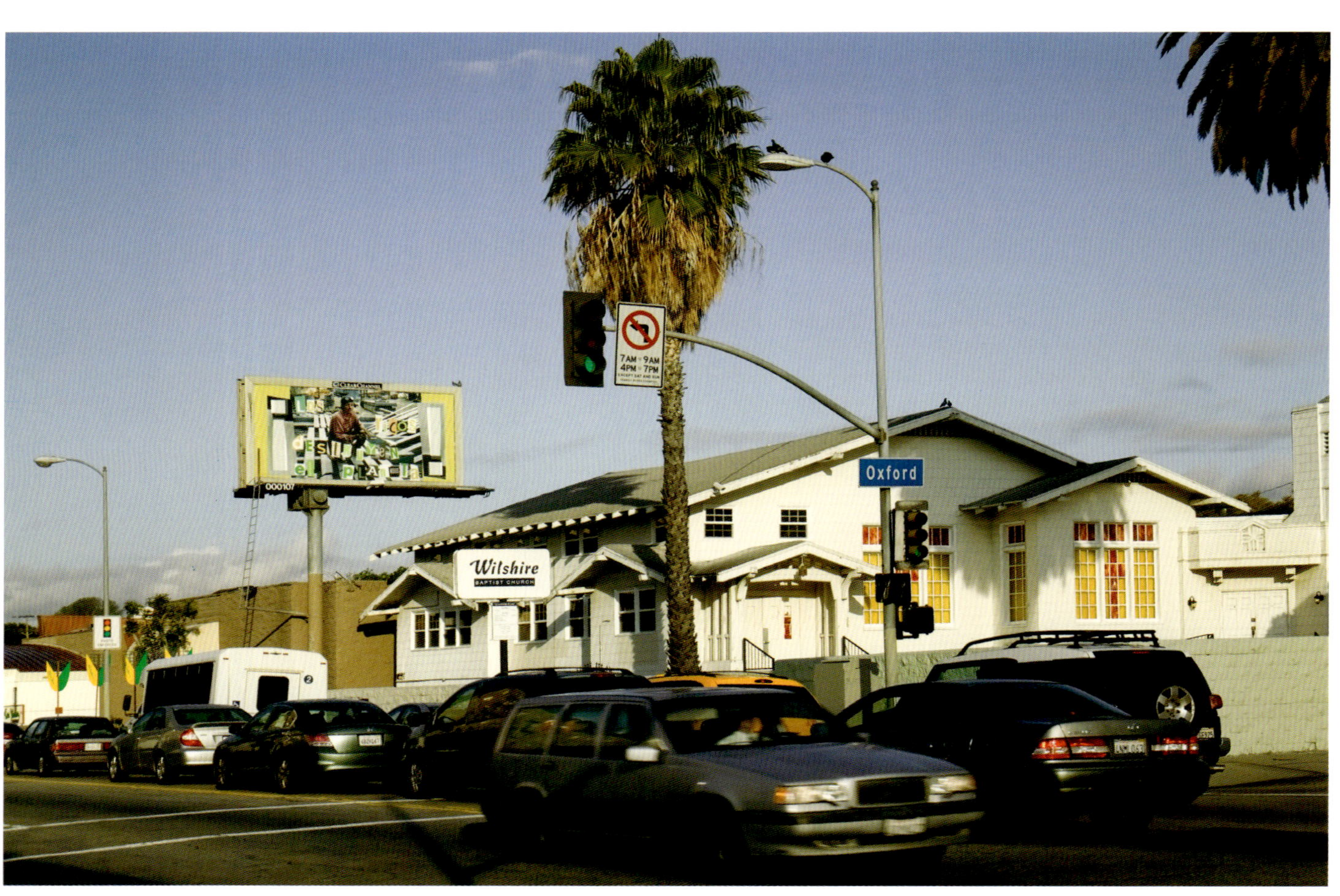
Oxford
Wilshire
BAPTIST CHURCH
7AM - 9AM
4PM - 7PM

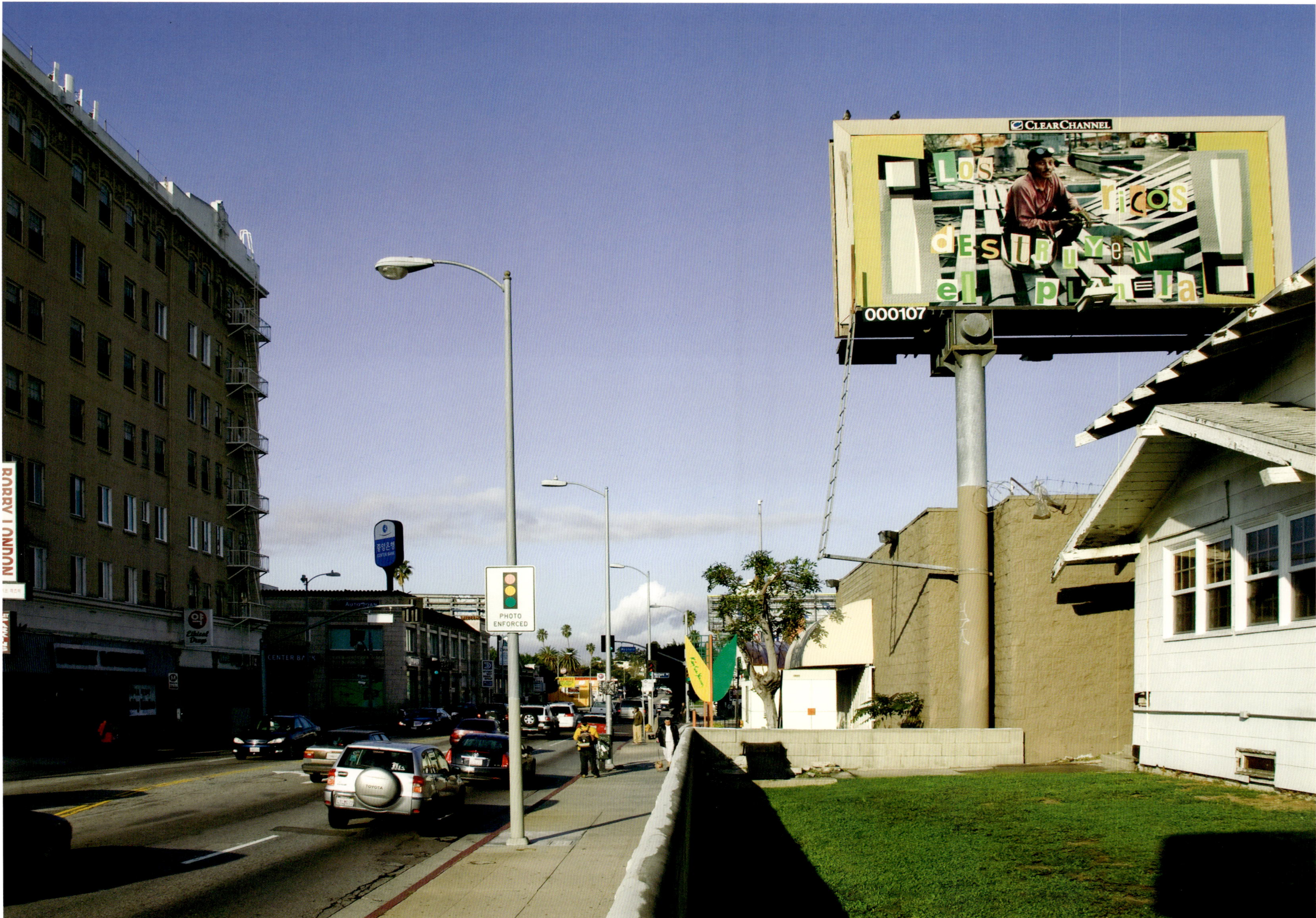
CLEARCHANNEL
¡Los ricos destruyen el planeta!
000107
PHOTO ENFORCED

SUSAN SILTON

Susan Silton's varied projects using photography, video, installation, and offset printing investigate both visual perception and the power of persuasion. Her images draw attention to the disorienting quality of motion and the desire for stasis in such a way that she is able to challenge viewers' assumptions about what they perceive and how they might categorize what they see. To do this, the artist uses blurring, distortion, repetition, and finely calibrated color combinations. Recently her investigations of the history and politics of stripes, with their varied associations ranging from military uniforms to minimalist paintings, have yielded a large series of printed works.

For *How Many Billboards?*, Silton has composed a dazzling array of colors within the regimented format of perfectly measured vertical stripes. This minimalist composition of thin bands of color, punctuated by repeated uses of bright yellow and blue, provides such an appealing chromatic display that the viewer may not at first see the large text that appears to float both behind and within the striped space. The phrase embedded within the candy-colored bars is "IF I SAY SO." Printed in all capital letters in a sans serif font, both the format and content of the text communicate the forceful presumption of an unseen speaker. "IF I SAY SO" is an excerpt from a 1961 telegram sent by artist Robert Rauschenberg. Rauschenberg had been invited to participate in an exhibition of portraits of gallerist Iris Clert. His contribution was a telegram that read: "This is a portrait of Iris Clert if I say so." Regardless of its specific source, Silton's text points to the persuasive power of the authoritative voice, especially when it utilizes the spectacular scale of the billboard.

BY LISA HENRY

LOCATION: La Cienega Boulevard, north of Rodeo Road, on the west side of the street, facing south.

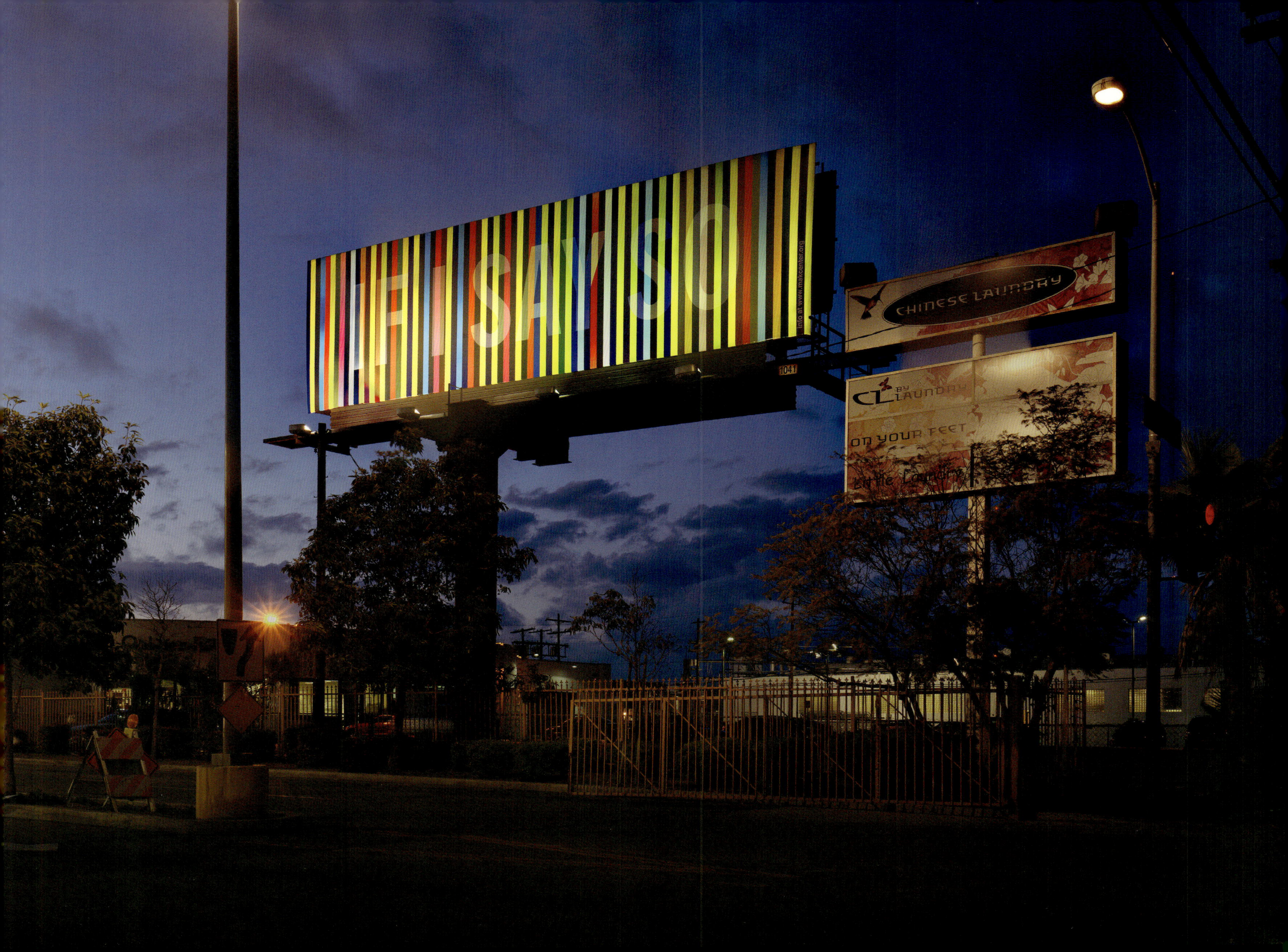
IF I SAY SO
info at www.makcenter.org
1041
CHINESE LAUNDRY
CL BY LAUNDRY
ON YOUR FEET

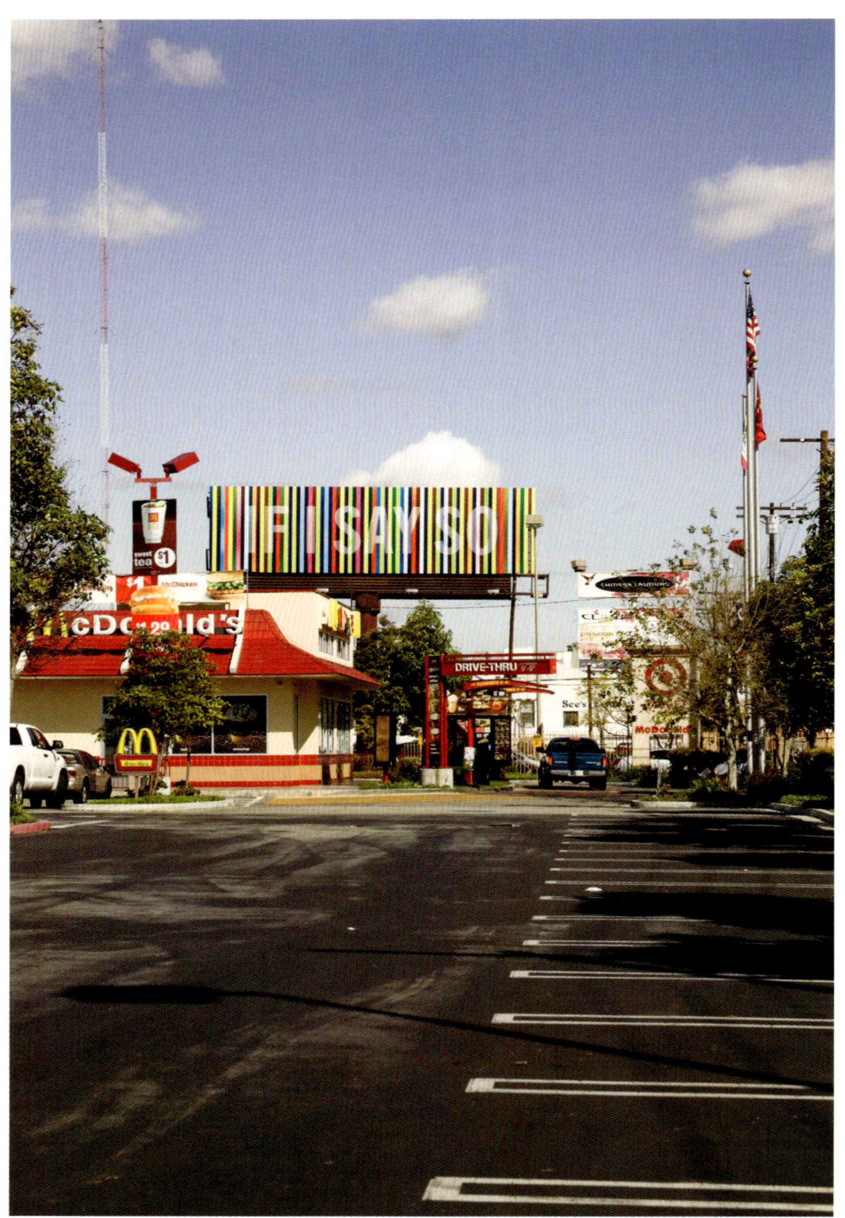
IF I SAY SO
DRIVE-THRU

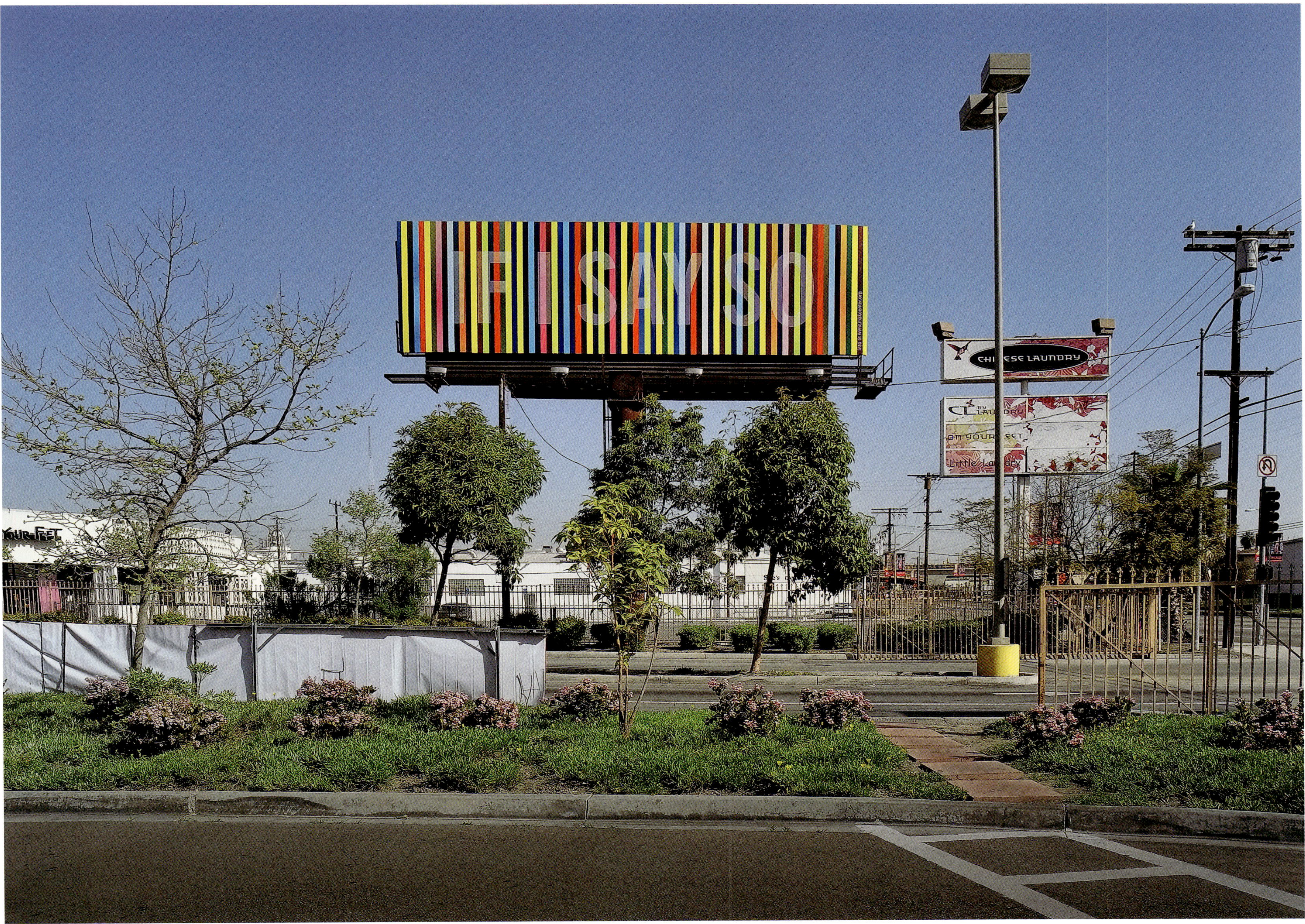
IF I SAY SO

KERRY TRIBE

Over the past decade, Kerry Tribe has mined themes of memory, identity, and coincidence, while calling attention to the theoretical and formal qualities that undergird film and video as artistic mediums. Most recently, Tribe's 16 mm film installation *H.M.* (2009) produces a type of mnemonic dissonance not unlike that experienced by the film's subject, an amnesiac who was only able to hold thoughts in his head for about 20 seconds.

Tribe's interests in questioning the formal tropes of media are represented by more quotidian forms as well. In *This too shall pass* (2002), she rendered the historical Hebrew inscription into a glaring neon sign. The innocuous space of a city-bus-bench ad in Hollywood was given the guise of a national historical marker in *Untitled (Historical Amnesia)* (2002-03). As a MFA student at UCLA, Tribe arranged and produced an audio CD of birdcalls whistled uncannily by her fellow artists *(A Birdsong Sampler,* 2001).

Tribe's billboard reflects the artist's interest in the problems associated with perception. Her abstraction of a darkening sky takes advantage of the proclivity to look up at billboards. Blending the site of the message with its airy backdrop, Tribe's image engages in a formal push and pull with perspective. Tribe's billboard transforms a space that typically directs one's attention outward (aiming the thoughts and desires of viewers toward a specific product) into a space of mental suspension, a hazy zone to lose one's thoughts within. Akin to her contemplative works, such as the abstract film *Northern Lights (Cambridge)* (2005), which uses low-tech optical effects to simulate aurorae (the luminous atmospheric phenomena that appear as curtains of colored light), Tribe's billboard gives the viewer a mental break from the onslaught of visual imagery to simply ponder what the image might be, and what purpose it may serve.

BY GLORIA SUTTON

LOCATION: La Brea Avenue, north of Venice Boulevard, on the east side of the street, facing north.

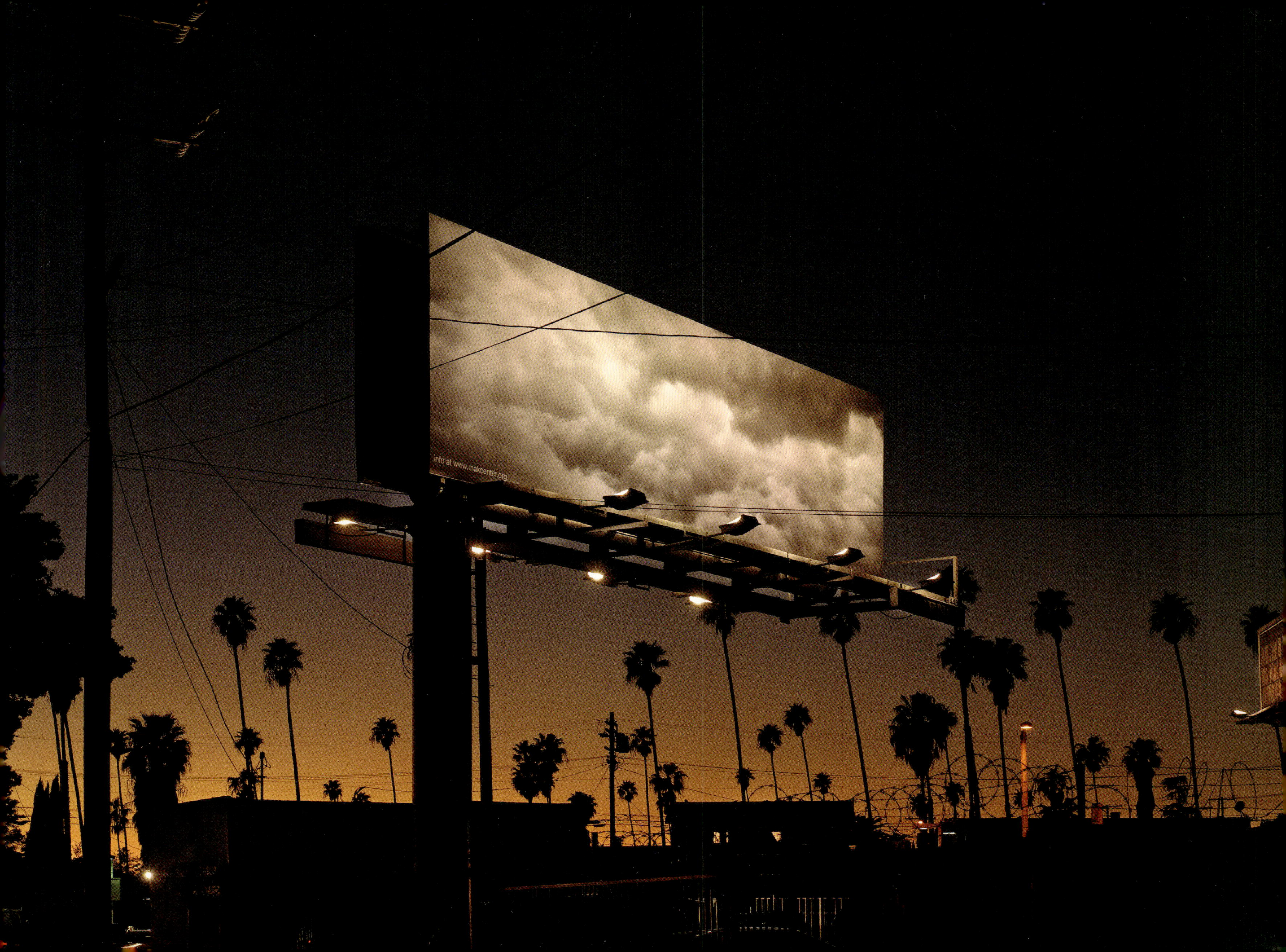
info at www.makcenter.org

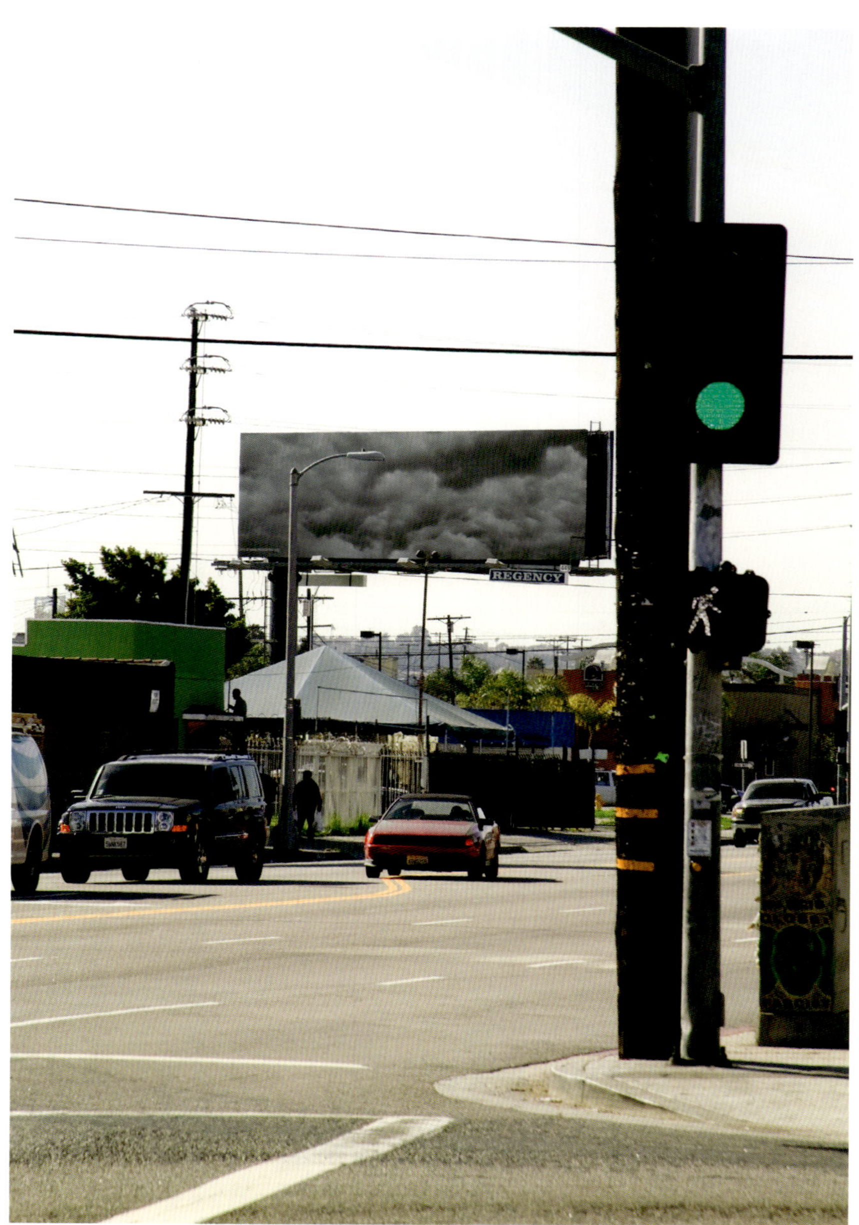
REGENCY

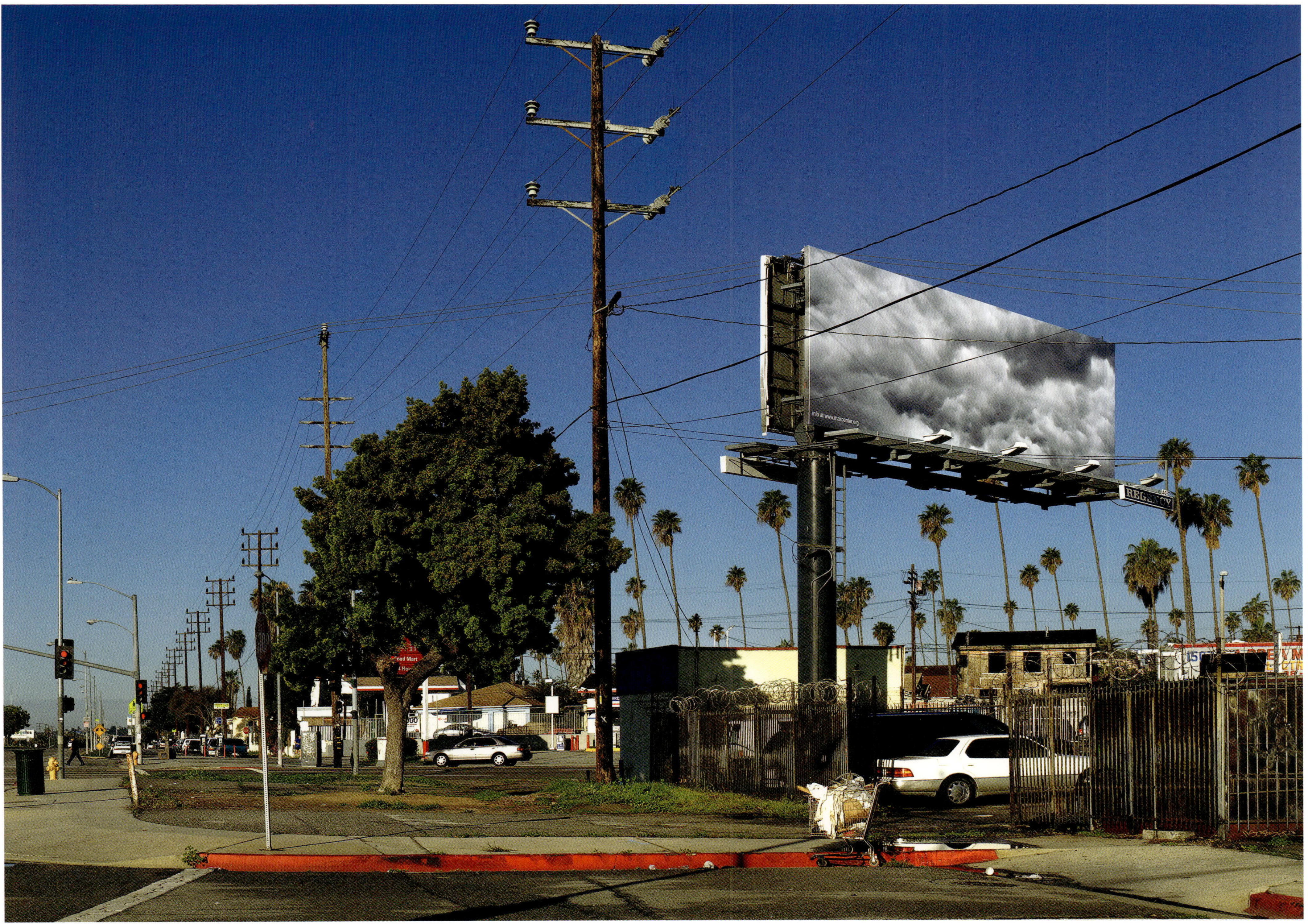
info at www.makcenter.org
REGENCY

JAMES WELLING

Photographer James Welling's varied body of work is driven by curiosity and experimentation with the photographic image. He has explored straight photography, landscape photography, and postmodern image making, including such unlikely subjects as crumpled tin foil. Welling sometimes combines Conceptualism, Minimalism, abstraction, and traditional photography. He has used unconventional cropping, super close-ups, repetition of forms, and color alteration in order to push both the conceptual and perceptual possibilities of the photograph. Welling has a deep, encyclopedic knowledge of the history of photography and is fascinated by the medium's most basic concepts, including the camera as a technical mechanism for capturing light, the importance of the photographic print, and how things are revealed photographically as opposed to how they appear to the human eye.

From the late 1990s to the present, Welling has alternated between abstracted representational photography, such as the *Glass House Series* (2006-2009), and the photogram, made using a darkroom technique that has gained renewed popularity through Welling's influence. For *How Many Billboards?,* Welling experiments further with photogram abstractions. His billboard image reveals rectangular shapes of deep blue with touches of brown slashing through a black background. Viewers are not meant to identify "what" the image is but rather to mentally slow down and think, prompting a self-conscious process of looking.

BY LISA HENRY

LOCATION: La Brea Avenue, south of the 10 Freeway, on the east side of the street, facing north.

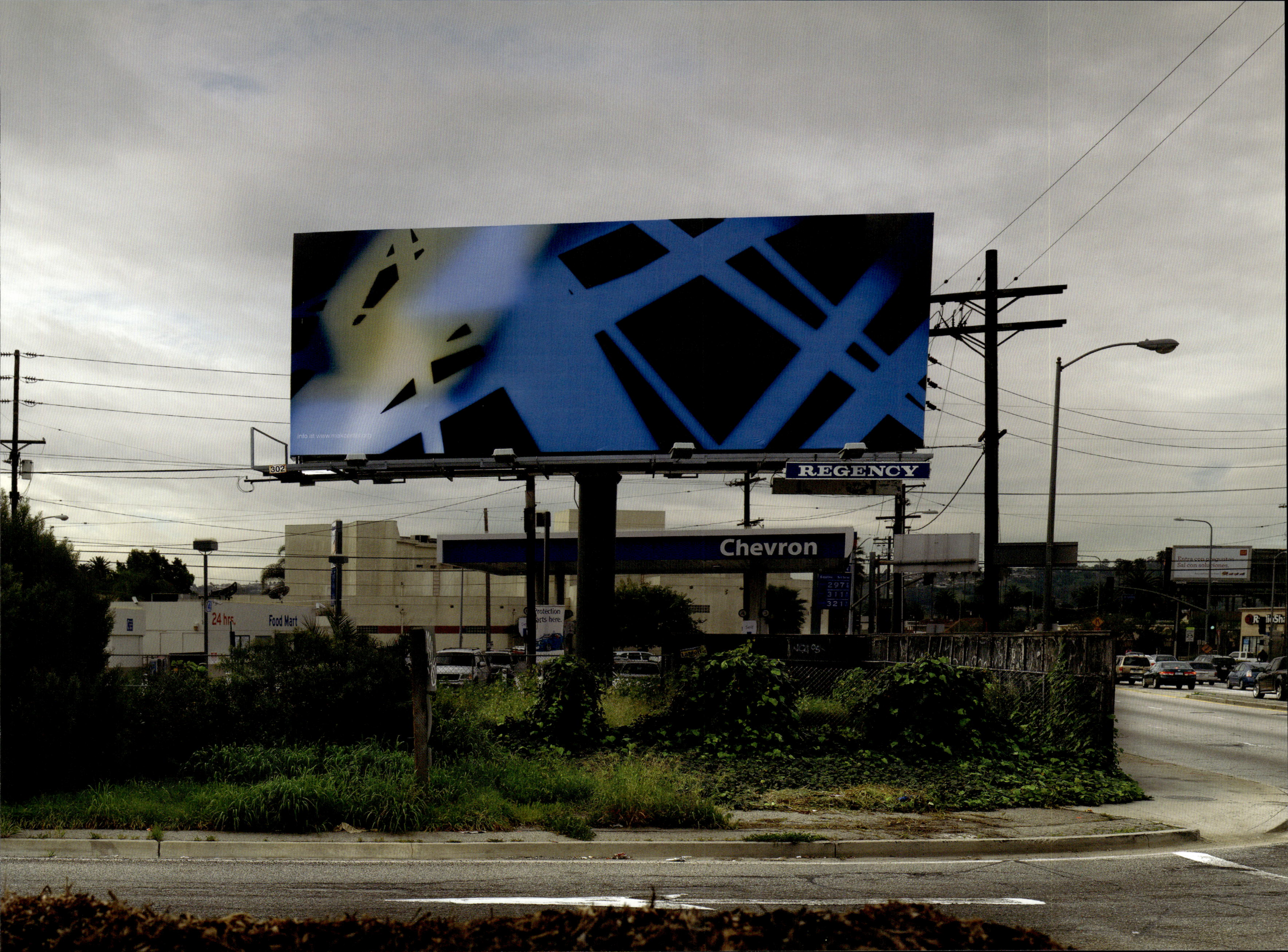
302
REGENCY
Chevron
24 hrs.
Food Mart

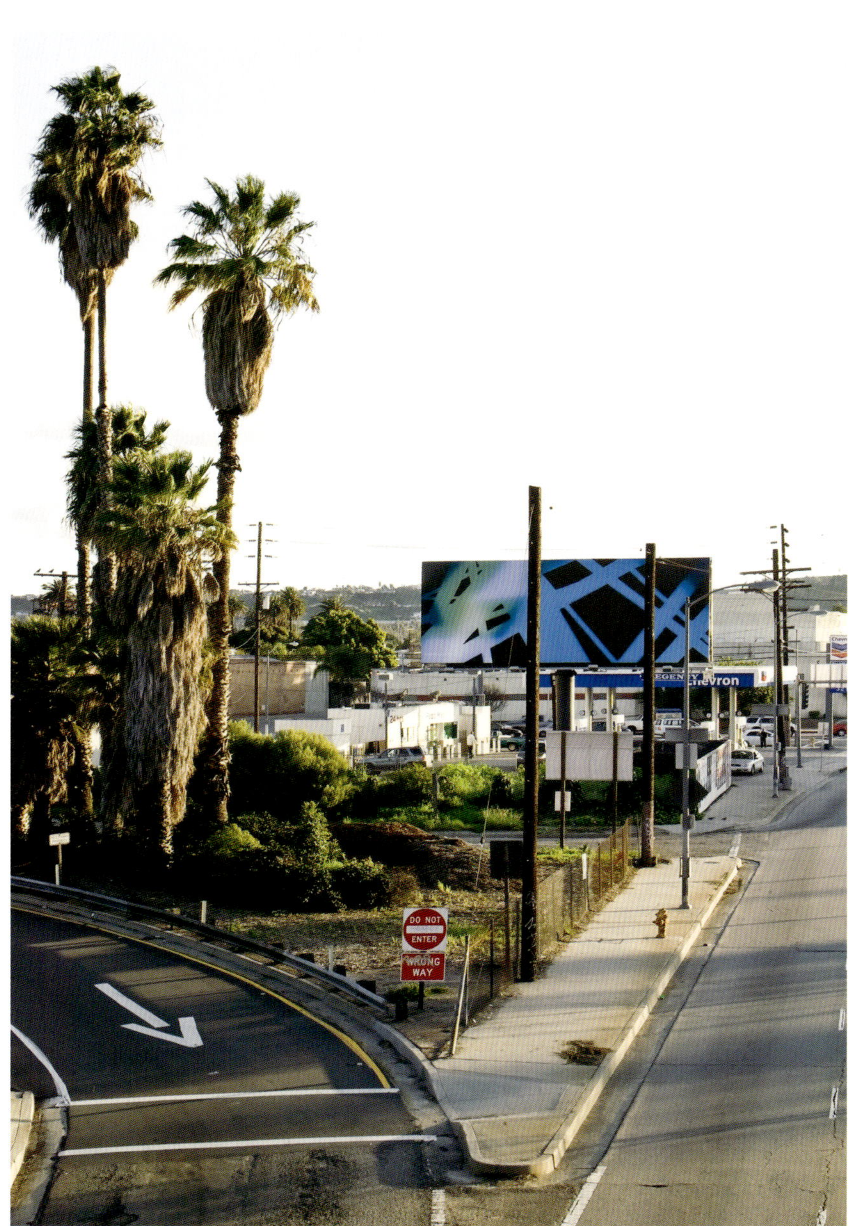
DO NOT ENTER
WRONG WAY

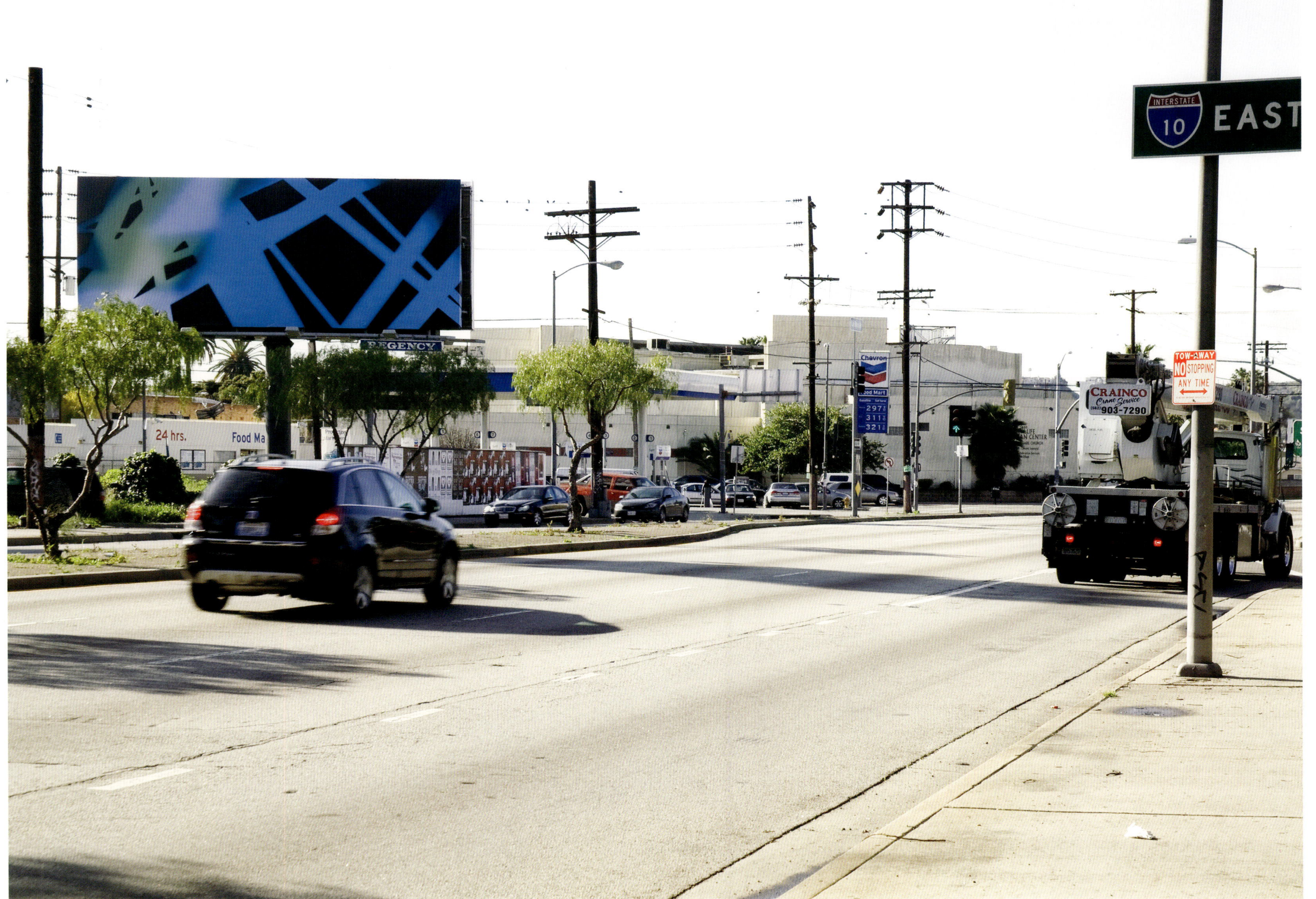
INTERSTATE
10
EAST
REGENCY
24 hrs.
Food Ma
Chevron
CRAINCO
Crane Service
903-7290
TOW-AWAY
NO STOPPING
ANY TIME

LAUREN WOODS

Cultural and collective memory, historical narratives, social psychology, and the politics of gender, class, race, and nationhood are some of the themes lauren woods frequently taps in her work. The text on her billboard is in Urdu; it is translated as follows:

As long as the earth and the sky last,
Smile like a flower in the garden of the world.

The lines are from a love poem by a prolific Urdu poet of the medieval period, Vali Dakhni, who is credited with inventing the poetic form ghazal, consisting of rhyming couplets and a refrain. Dakhni also inspired poets of Delhi to switch from writing in Persian, the language of the upper class, to writing in Urdu, which was the common language of the people. For many in Los Angeles, the image of the poem on the billboard does not transmit its meaning, because most of us read neither Arabic script nor the Urdu language. Language without legibility provides a kind of canvas upon which the viewer may project assumptions, passions, and fears. In post-9/11 America, this particular foreign language can appear both beautiful and vaguely threatening. Urdu is the national language of Pakistan, one of the most active hotspots for global tension. Woods presents this opportunity for mass projection as a chance for self-reflection. The work sets up a moment in which the viewer is prompted to observe her assumptions and possibly evaluate her prejudices. Woods's piece insists on seeing the beauty in distant cultures, especially when these cultures have been associated with enemies of our nation. It also plays with the idea of messaging, delivering a directive from a distant century, language, alphabet, and culture, yet one with an arguably universal meaning and contemporary relevance.
BY KIMBERLI MEYER

LOCATION: Fairfax Avenue, south of Melrose Avenue, west side of the street, facing north.

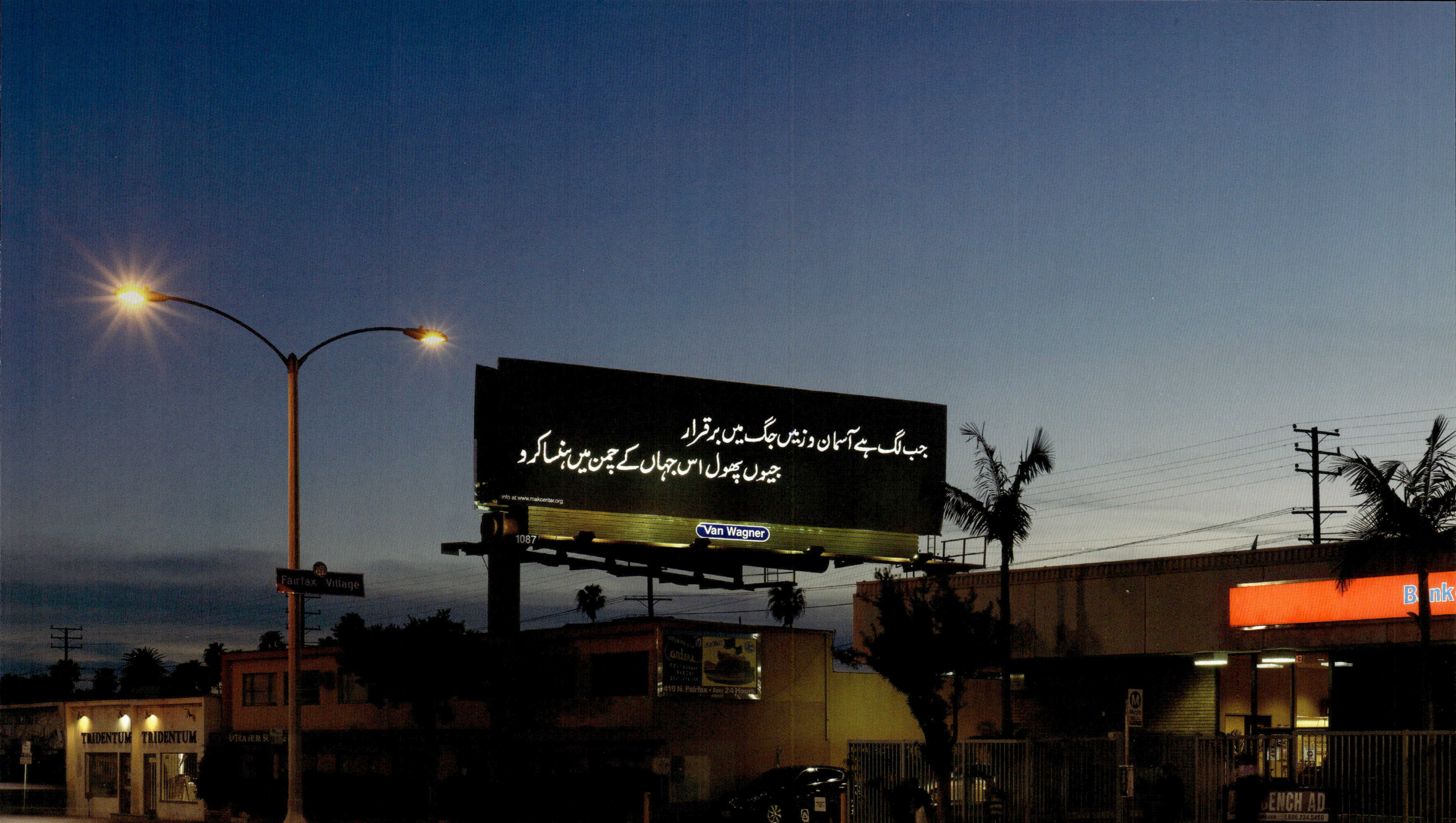
جب لگ ہے آسمان و زمیں جگ میں برقرار
جیوں پھول اس جہاں کے چمن میں ہنسا کرو
info at www.makcenter.org
Van Wagner
1087
Fairfax Village
TRIDENTUM
TRIDENTUM
Bank

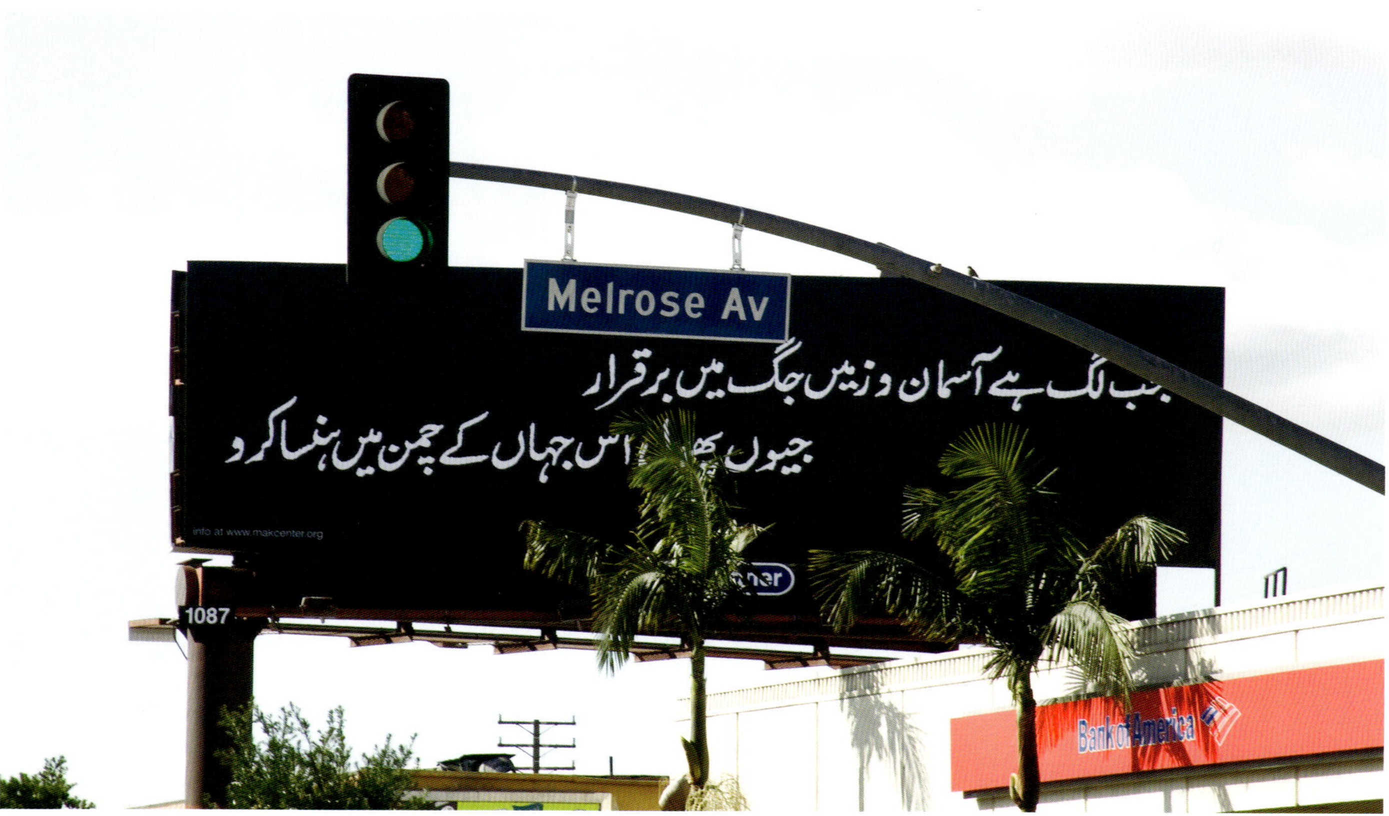
Melrose Av
لگ ہے آسمان و زمیں جگ میں برقرار
جیوں اس جہاں کے چمن میں ہنسا کرو
info at www.makcenter.org
1087
Bank of America

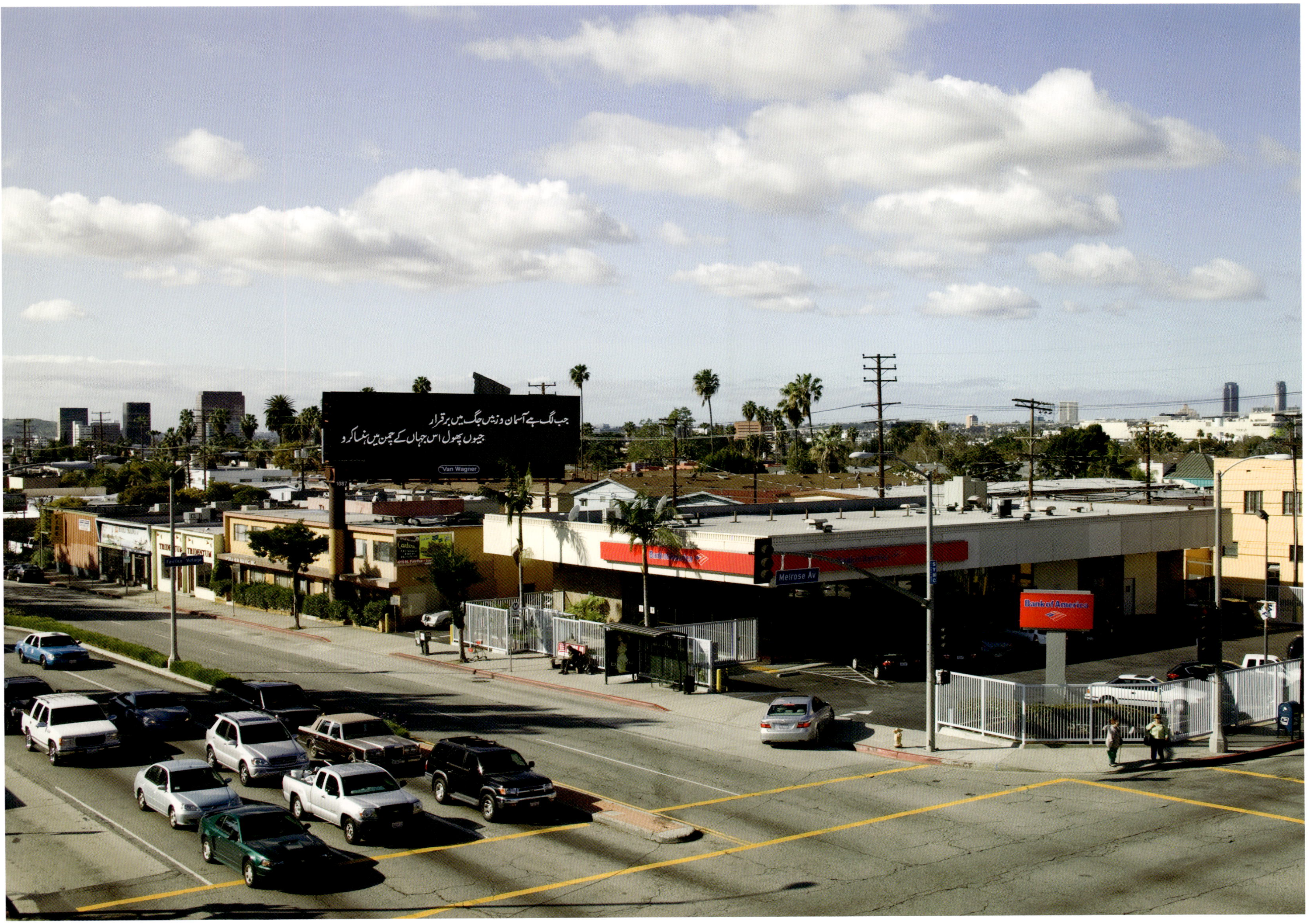
جب لگ ہے آسمان و زمیں جگ میں برقرار
جیوں پھول اس جہاں کے چمن میں ہنسا کرو
Van Wagner
1087
Bank of America
Melrose Av

THE PRESENCE OF LOS ANGELES: Prescription and Prediction

BY NIZAN SHAKED

It is artists—as much as museums or the market—who, in their very efforts to escape the institution of art, have driven its expansion.
Andrea Fraser

In Los Angeles an illusion of rationality or order has evolved through the use of designed displays in an otherwise boundaryless desertscape.
Kim Gordon

I hold that it is an excellent thing for a physician to practice forecasting.
Hippocrates

Democracy can be invigorated.
Cornel West

Much has been said about the current tendency to focus on the present moment. As opposed to previous generations' concern with the past, in the contemporary culture of constantly streaming media, multiple perspectives of the *now* increasingly preoccupy all walks of cultural activity. The concurrent scramble to define "The Contemporary" that has swept the art world and its academy reflects the urgent need for methodological clarity and disciplinary identity, as over the last forty-some years art has moved to function under new terms, within a global arena, and increasingly in relation to the logic of the market.[1] In panels, journals, and questionnaires, one finds practitioners who aim to sustain the politicized and philosophical core that has distinguished art as a critical practice since, at least, the development of the avant-garde, and who ask what it means to have a critical practice today. In these intellectual forums one often hears arguments against the dilution of art's criteria by market forces, as well as apprehension regarding the diminishing role of the intellectual.[2] In an era when so many major public museums have been displacing professional expertise with personal taste by mounting exhibitions showcasing works of single private collections, concern for our culture's future is justifiable.[3] However, it is also becoming clear that academic criteria that rely upon such distinctions as whether artworks are critical of—or complacent with—the establishment beg reassessment. Following the development of the politicized art of the 1960s and 1970s, many forms intended as subversive have been co-opted into the art market / exhibition complex, and the possibility of resisting or revolutionizing the system has come to be seen as a myth.

In this context, I see the exhibition *How Many Billboards? Art In Stead* contributing to the concerns of contemporary art by asking what it means to make critical art today. Many of the exhibiting artists re-examine the site of the political in art, and ask what it even means for an artist to be political today when critical distance is no longer considered a possible position to establish and maintain. Presented out of doors on billboards and thus widely available, *How Many Billboards?* does not assert that it is operating "outside" the system, or that subverting art's complacency with neoliberalism is even an option.[4] Instead, the intent is to test the possibility of producing critical art out of an ambivalent negotiation with a corporate-owned medium.

Los Angeles is a West Coast cultural center and a growing art capital where public space is dominated by corporate messaging. This context sets a parameter for the exhibition, which does not seek to establish any kind of stylistic or other regional unity, but rather serves as a test case. The exhibition's four curators cast a net of intellectual coordinates from Los Angeles outwards, inviting artists to respond to the phenomenon of the billboard in our urban and cultural landscape. Approaching the exhibition as a living history, *How Many Billboards?* was conceived by broadly rethinking the trajectories of West Coast Conceptualism and Institutional Critique, and examining their influences on current art practices. The resulting billboards offer a sample of the state of critical and political art today. As the show was mounted, the dominance of two major politicized artistic movements—Conceptualism and Identity Politics—came into focus, and it reflects the fact that the paths of the two movements have been crossing since the late 1960s.

In this essay, I propose using a broad definition of the term "prescription" to characterize operations used by artists and scholars because they are thought to produce the "correct" attitude in artwork-as-outcome. Based on historical models, such as Walter Benjamin's concept of art in the age of mechanical reproduction, subsequent principled equations aimed at ensuring art's criticality have yielded such major arguments as Conceptualism's rejection of artistic subjectivity, feminisms' competing viewpoints about essentialism, and Victor Burgin's politics of the signifier (elaborated upon by the editors of *October*). Yet, as important as these prescriptions have been to the ongoing project of art as analysis and intervention, to which I wholeheartedly subscribe, without constant revision these remedies can lose their potency.

In many respects, the outcome of *How Many Billboards?* reflects how legacies based on prescription, such as Conceptualism and Identity Politics, have revised their foundational postulations. By now, the term Identity Politics has come to encompass so much that it has all but lost its referent.[5] At various moments it has signaled a narrow definition of essentialist attitudes; the fragmenting force that Balkanized the Left; an over-determination of race, gender, and sexuality, resulting in reductive artistic practices; or a rejected political term.[6] Some of these assumptions have supported historical teleology, producing neat narratives such as that of feminism as an evolution from a naïve politic into a more critical one. Contrarily, it seems clear that since the late 1960s artists have been investigating the politics of identity as an analytic tool. Another common conception assigned to Identity Politics is a return to subjectivity and/or authenticity. Easily refuted today, it is clear to see how varying practices influenced by the politics of identity have been not antithetical to Conceptualism, but rather significantly intertwined with it.[7]

However, while many artists welcome an alliance with Conceptualism, for a variety of reasons the term Identity Politics is just barely beginning to overcome its status as "bad object," and is being examined for what it was and can be.[8] Susan Silton, one of the *How Many Billboards?* artists, identifies one of the reasons: "The institutional co-opting of Identity Politics in the late 1980s / early 1990s, and the constriction resulting from it, forever altered the way artists viewed the term and in turn positioned—or imagined positioning—their own work in relation to the term."[9] Silton emphasizes that artists consequently sought alternative strategies (formalist or Conceptual) to address similar concerns. A different perspective recently clarified by Greg Bordowitz underscores: "Rather than reject identity altogether, I wanted to explode it. I wanted to produce confusion about who I was. I thought the aim of Identity Politics was to destroy established identities, not to assert them."[10] Both interpretations imply that the term, and its history, are due for significant clarification.

How Many Billboards? triangulates prescription with "prediction," a prognostic impulse that revises the historic strategies of conceptually oriented practices against the horizon of the future. In contrast to the domination of a fluctuating art market—which is another form of foretelling—prediction shares with prescription a general aspiration for a cure. However, it replaces prescription's truth claims with a tentative approach, not to operate "against" a market, but rather to ask what kind of a market. Aiming at the widest audience possible, *How Many Billboards?* proclaims that to engage the public art need not be "populist." The term "populist" implies that art should be simplified for mass appeal, in order to counter the age-old accusation that art is elitist. While the term tends to be used pejoratively in most art circles, "populist" was recently employed by real estate magnate and philanthropist Eli Broad to describe his push for the selection of Jeffrey Deitch to direct The Museum of Contemporary Art in Los Angeles.[11] In contrast, *How Many Billboards?* acknowledges the intelligence of the public and emphasizes popular over populist. It follows the historical lessons of Pop Art, in which repurposed mass-media platforms can have vast impact without foregoing critical intervention.

In an unpublished artist's statement regarding his contribution to *How Many Billboards?,* John Knight points out that the exhibition still perpetuates two main conditions that post-avant-garde practices aimed to address: art as spectacle and viewership as passive cultural consumption. For the duration of *How Many Billboards?* Knight turned his billboard over to the Middle East Children's Alliance (MECA). In turn, MECA utilized the board to display a public relations ad for their MAIA project, which is developing water purification systems for Gaza schools.[12] Consistent with his forty-year career of dialoguing with Conceptual Art and Institutional Critique, Knight approached his contribution by first identifying the logic dictated by the project and then activating the media "without going to a position of pure negation—while implicating the apparatus, as well as my project, for the opportunistic use of its utility."[13] Knight presents a paradoxical condition where the ad functions both as art and as public service. As a result, the exhibition, the place of the artist within it, and MECA are all exposed as languages of the same order—not above, beyond, or outside a system that links, and often conflates, politics, media, and aesthetics. Installed on the Sunset Strip, the ad's content poses a jarring contrast to its affluent context, yet its fantastical image blends in with the artifice of a Gucci billboard across the street. The graphics of the MAIA ad—a large drop of water overlaying another stock photograph of a lush, green forest—are as distant from reality as the Sunset Strip is from Gaza. The image of water-richness bares zero relation to either of the deserts referenced in the ad's text: "From L.A. to Palestine Clean, Drinkable Water is a Human Right." Few would challenge this obvious truth and the organization's agenda to improve the lives of children. However, that is not the issue for the artist, who aims to emphasize the transaction and question where, consequently, meaning gets produced. As Jay Sanders observes of Knight's previous projects, they "...actively beg the question of their own existence and their status as objects—linked to whatever system brought them into being."[14] Thus, the cause is selected like an *objet trouvé*, not as a gesture of support or opposition, but because the cause is likely to produce the most intense response. In fact, one could argue that it is precisely its hot-button status that is put on display. Furthermore, Knight explains, "It is not my intent to replace the moment of the curatorial, rather to allow for the discursive possibility of a *real* politic and a discernible *public*." As such, the work extends the historical debate of the political in art in order to ask where—in the form, content, context, or structure—the politicized intervention can take place. Collapsing a politicized aesthetic operation with an outcome that spectacularizes politics, Knight's billboard isn't a synthesis, but rather an odd animal where the viewer cannot locate the "voice" of the artist. As such the site of the political in this ad is ultimately undecided: Is it in the transaction between the artist and the non-profit organization? Is it in giving voice to a philanthropic cause? Can it be found in the visual or textual aspect of the ad, its location, the possibility to mobilize on its behalf, and so on? There is no single answer. Instead,

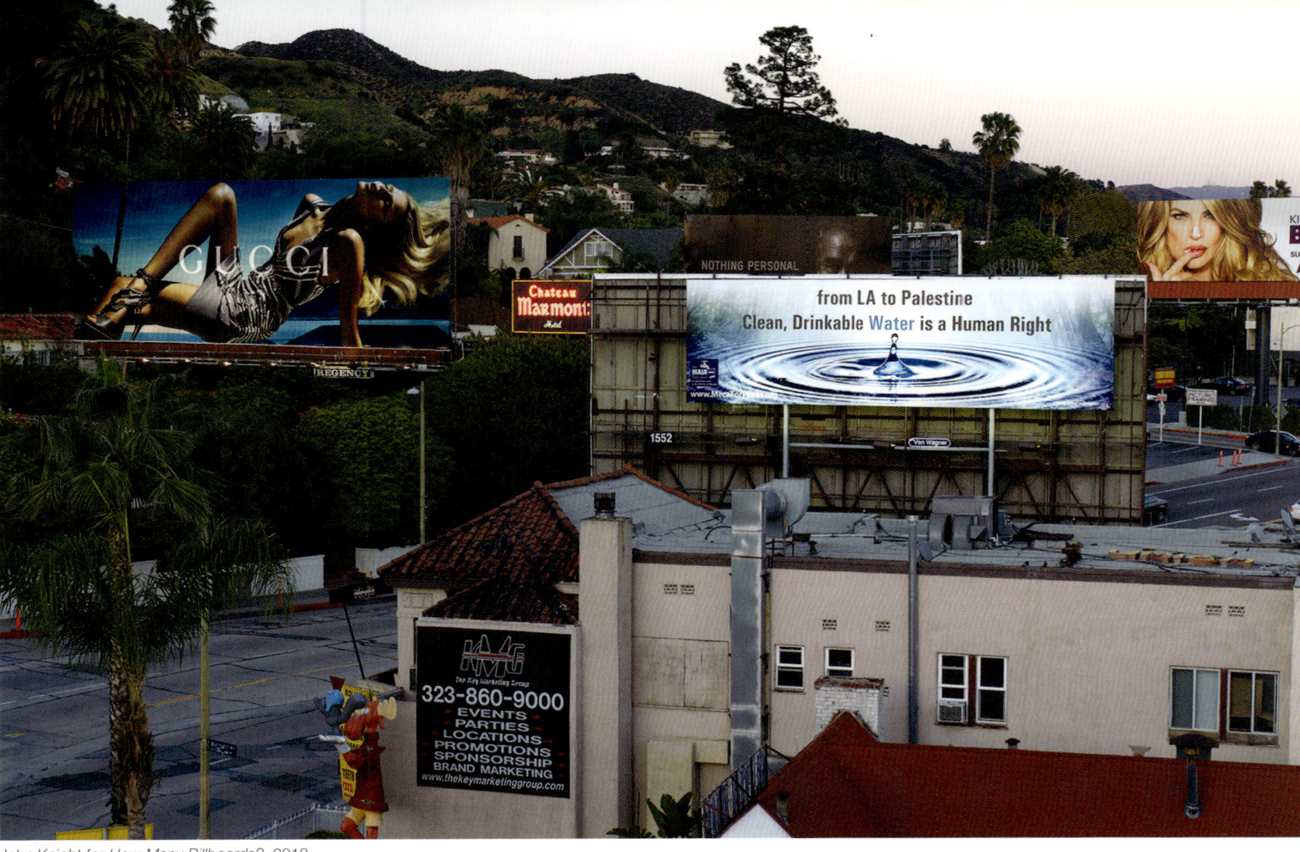

John Knight for *How Many Billboards?*, 2010.

the work displays not only its inability to address *realpolitik*, but how its condition as spectacle is the very *realpolitik* available for discussion.

In her article "The Third Citizen: On Models of Criticality in Contemporary Artistic Practices," Vered Maimon analyzes contemporary artistic approaches that have been informed by Conceptual Art. She asserts that because the new models "mobilize precisely what was often left out of these models [of Conceptualism], namely the imaginary and the fictional," they are better suited to address today's incarnations of sovereign power.[15] Maimon describes how, rather than attempt to unveil reality concealed by false consciousness, recent practices approach the imaginary as constitutive of experience. She analyses how Conceptualism's quest for truth—residues of which can be found in

Knight's summoning of "a discernible public"—is now reconfigured in recognizing reality as a form of spectacle (which Knight's project also does).[16] *How Many Billboards?*'s intervention is, in fact, based on the assumption that we cannot presume what constitutes the "public," or that a disciplinary method that can determine it as a coherent body exists.

Other theories have addressed the relationship of reality to the imaginary, mainly that of history to fiction in the work of the New History.[17] Joel Fineman's tentative introduction, "The History of the Anecdote: Fiction and Fiction," identifies what was at stake for the New History's focus on the craft of writing. He analyzes the unique function of the anecdote as an anomaly within historical narrative and its potential as an opening into the real.[18] Identifying anecdote as "the literary form that uniquely *lets history happen*," Fineman emphasizes how the formal dimension of writing history renders the past as a reality, drawing analogies, through Shakespeare, to how experience (desire) is derived from language, and never the other way around.[19] Fineman's characterization of the anecdote's undecided status reflects the various ways in which generations following Conceptualism enacted their ambivalence towards the movement's purposefulness. Correspondingly, *How Many Billboards?* demonstrates in broad strokes the ways in which political art has extended the approach of prescription (as faith in a reality yet to be discovered beyond false consciousness) into various incarnations of prediction (an acceptance of mediation as the condition of existence and not as lack of agency).

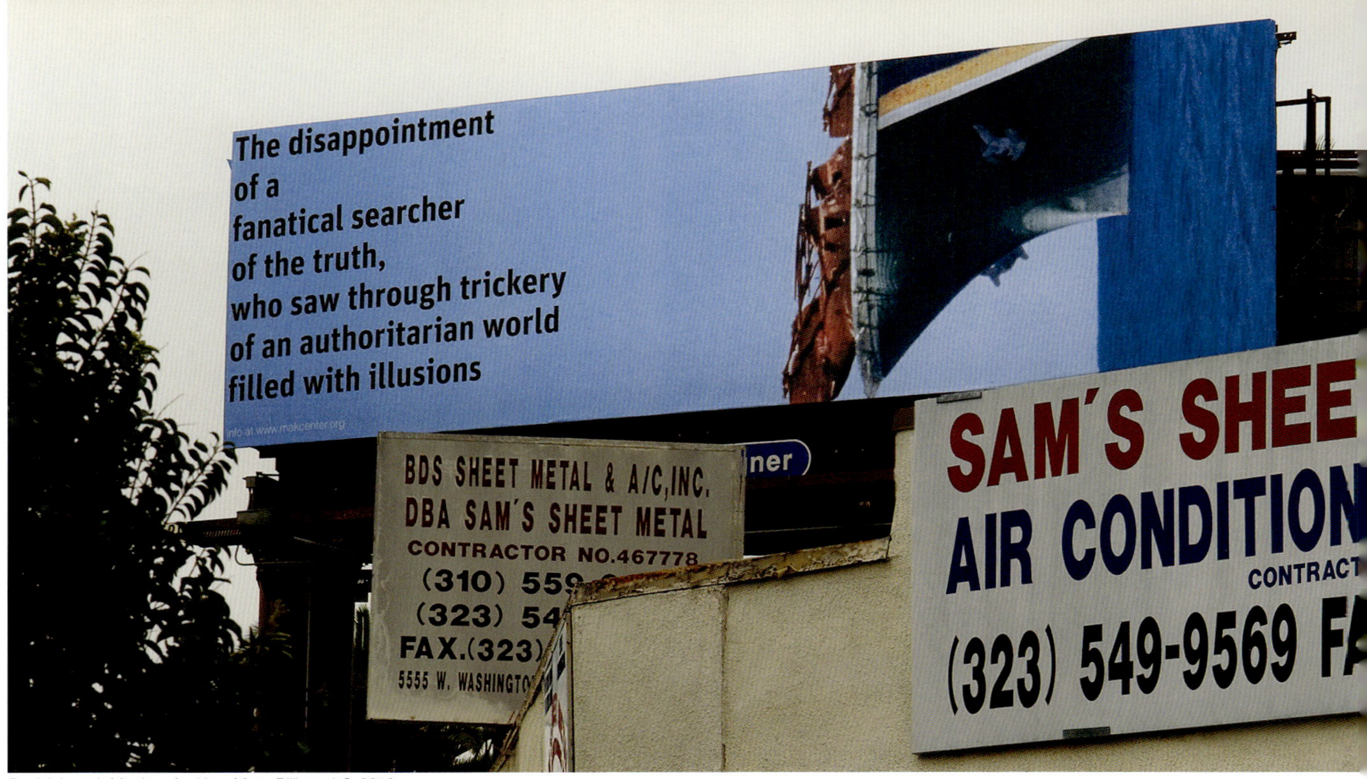

Daniel Joseph Martinez for *How Many Billboards?*, 2010.

Truth as specter is put on display in Daniel Joseph Martinez's billboard collage, where, in a world turned sideways, a military aircraft carrier is on the verge of dumping its fleet of Chinook helicopters into the ocean. The aircrafts are painted red, as if repurposed for environmental activism. The military/environmentalist amalgam is corroborated by the rainbow design painted on the ship's side, which is a reference to Greenpeace's Rainbow Warrior trawler. When agents of the French government sank the Rainbow Warrior in an Auckland harbor in 1985, Fernando Pereira, the ship's photographer, tragically died. Despite the fact that the agents pleaded guilty to charges of manslaughter and willful damage, they were released after serving fewer than two years. In a monument to inequality under the law, Martinez offsets the image with a text he composed: "The disappointment of a fanatical searcher of the truth, who saw through trickery of an authoritarian world filled with illusions." The implication that the searcher is fanatical, arriving from or belonging to an order of truth, is juxtaposed with the doctored image, aligning the two paradigms—prescription and prediction—on the same plane. Familiar means to organize signifiers are confused, rendering unclear to whom, or by whom, the various attributes are to be assigned, and how their relations should be configured. The peculiarity of the image evokes contradictory, paranoid analyses: the image of the warrior constructed to literally seem militant can be seen as propaganda to render Greenpeace as terroristic, or, conversely, a metaphor in support of their tactics and aptitude. Martinez's work highlights how organizations such as Greenpeace circulate in the media as imaginary or overinflated constructions, pointing to the gaps between event and reception, or event and consequence. Amplified by its placement on a billboard, the message seems to speak about the "authoritarian" and "illusionistic" medium that supports it.

Focused not on reality, but on the conventions and codes of realism, Allan Sekula's spin on historical, leftist strategies reevaluates prescription in light of feminism's embrace of narrative and storytelling. Sekula's utilization of the large-scale image as a monument to the proletariat and his critical use of realism—the rejected program of avant-garde political art—have been discussed at length elsewhere. [20] In Sekula's contribution to *How Many Billboards?*, the juxtaposition of image and text, which exhibits an affinity to socialist agitprop posters, activates the ways in which the billboard's speech can address multiple demographics at once. In the background image, an Ensenada-based shipyard welder is photographed not at work, but in repose, or rather, in a pose. The visible flame of his acetylene torch indicates that it has just been lit; the dramatic effect appears enacted for the camera and its eternal life as image. Refracted light on the subject's lifted goggles doubles as eyes; his piercing returned gaze crystallizes photography's potential impact. Collaged in ransom-note style, the billboard text reads: ¡Los Ricos Destruyen el Planeta! (The rich are destroying the planet!). Perceptually, at any given moment the viewer can either read the text or look at the image. The size, placement, and irregularity of the type determine that the viewer's eyes will dance back and forth between image and text, as opposed to reading one after the other, as many graphic layouts

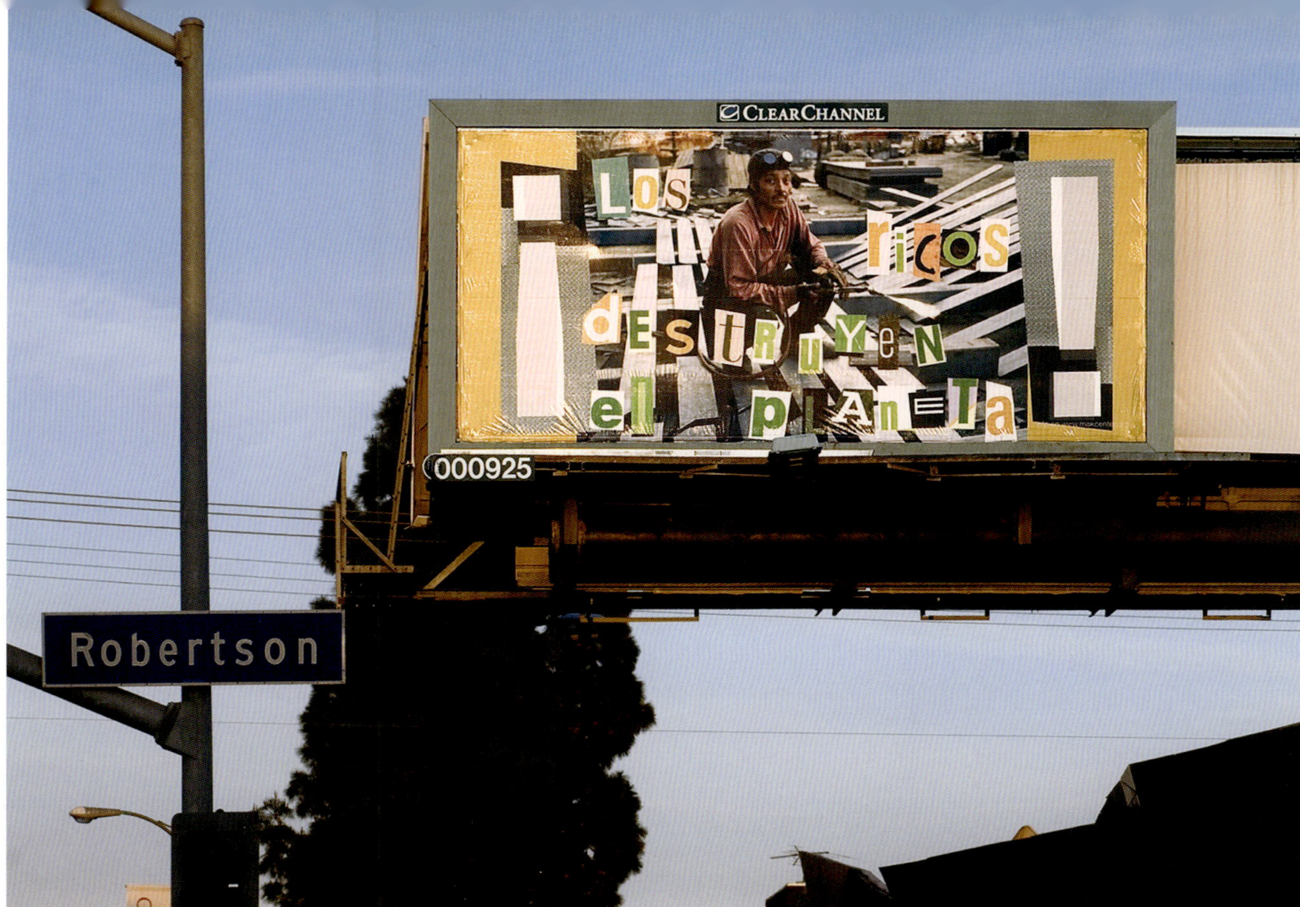

Allan Sekula for *How Many Billboards?*, 2010.

direct. The optical flicker turns the collage into a montage, destabilizing the potential identification with the image, which for some is with the figure of the laborer, for others with reality of their complicity, or both. In all cases, reality is represented as a coded and mediated condition.

At first glance, the panoramic seascape and graphics on Renée Green's billboard resemble a movie ad. Taken from the film portion of Green's installation *Endless Dreams and Water Between* (2009), five silhouetted figures line the horizon overlooking the wake of a ferry sailing away from San Francisco Bay. Sunrays seeping through an overcast sky follow the trajectory of single-point perspective, thus highlighting the still image's sense of motion. The mood seems to fuse 19th century

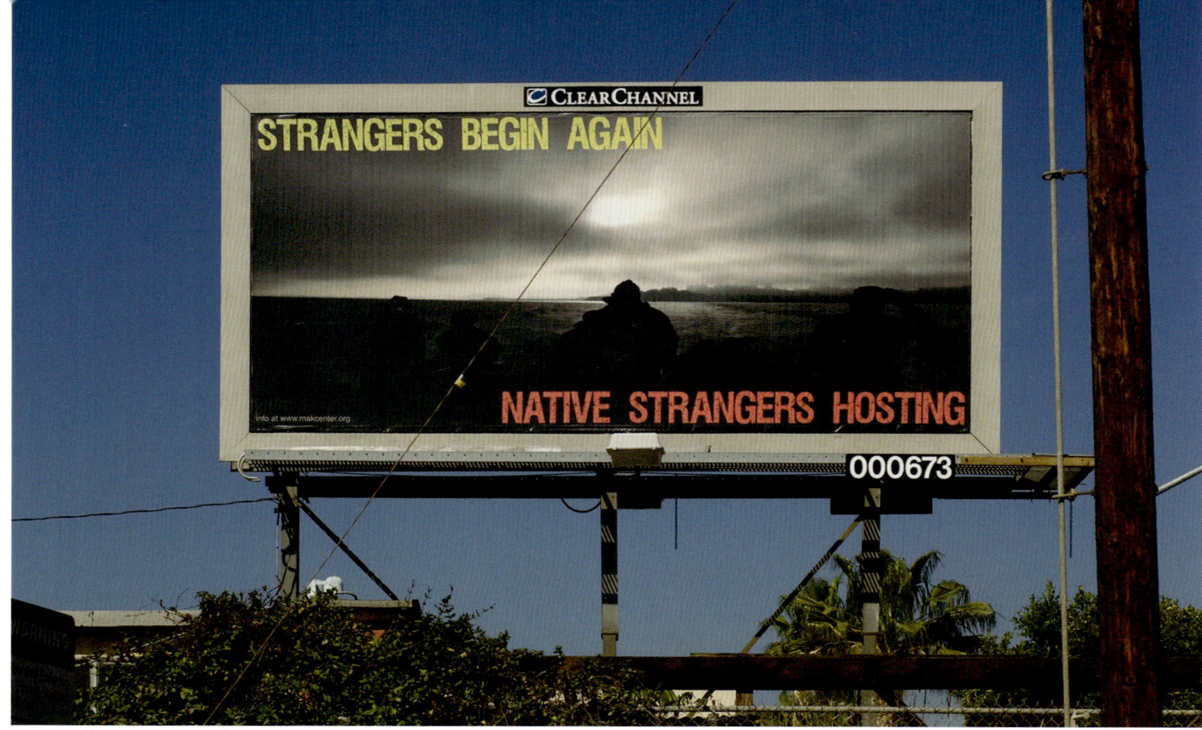

Strangers Begin Again. Native Strangers Hosting by Renée Green for *How Many Billboards?*, 2010.

romanticism with the apocalyptic visions of science fiction authors such as Philip K. Dick, Ursula Le Guin, and William Gibson. The sublime picture is annotated with a stylized sans-serif font, which proclaims "Strangers Begin Again" in yellow; "Native Strangers Hosting" frames the bottom in red. Deliberately open-ended, the terms refer obliquely to humanity's histories, which have always involved voluntary or coercive migration, conquest, and cultural exchange. Without clear referents, "native," "strangers," and "hosting" problematize how history is told (first there were natives, followed by strangers) by deliberately reconfiguring the order. As such, they highlight the ways in which history is narrativized and edited to play its role as a story. The billboard evokes quintessential themes of science fiction, such as the return of history and the displacement of populations (including the ambivalent, parasitic aspects of hosting). Green's aphorisms postulate the political agency of science fiction as a prophetic model, suggesting that the past be revised not in terms of the present, but of the future.

Ken Gonzalez-Day's *Untitled I (After Antico [Pier Jacopo Alari-Bonacolsi], Bust of a Young Man, 1520, and Francis Harwood, Bust of a Man, 1758)* animates the tension between two sculptures that eye each other across an expanse of gray. The sculptures, representing an African and a Caucasian man, both appear black in a photograph that minimizes the difference between bronze and black stone, and emphasizes the leveling effect of thrice-removed representation. Through photographic distanciation, racial formation appears as a discursive construction unhinged from an over-determined relation to the living body.[21] Succeeding the historical debates of representation, the work is positioned as a stage in a long history of depicting the human body. Tracing the development of Humanism into the concerns of the present, Gonzales-Day astutely positions his larger project *After* (from which the work is taken) against the horizon of the future:

"After" is about the legacies of the Enlightenment Project and asks, what, if anything, comes after race; after ideologies and their aesthetic manifestations have run their course. It is about the legacies of photography in shaping our understanding of the "real," in the digital age. It asks what comes after authorship, after language, after appropriation, and looks towards the future with all its unknowns intact—if unsettled.[22]

Like several other *How Many Billboards?* projects, Gonzales-Day's leap from past to future is strategic; it circumvents prescription's reliance on the present as a sufficient critical context. Just as putting the Enlightenment's righteousness into an historical framework reveals its foundational flaws, we require the future's perspective to speculate upon the now. Placed outdoors, the billboard also uses its erotic dimension to declare political urgency in defending the civil right to love.

A renewed urgency for Identity Politics, in its anti-essentialist incarnations that take identity not as a personal construct, but as an issue at large affecting not "my" rights but rights in general, is emerging. Disengaged from a particular referent (gender, race, or sexuality), it functions firstly to serve specific, complex, and in-between identities (including class) that are, and will increasingly be, the signs of our times; and secondly to function as a front for civil rights on a global scale. It is this vital insistence that will allow us to defend some of the most important principles of justice and equality that we have barely begun to achieve under democracy. Reporting on the inaugural Abu Dhabi Art Fair for *Artforum*'s online Diary, Lindsay Pollock commented: "Tony Shafrazi hung his '80s-themed stand with Basquiats, Warhols, and Harings."[23] Although Pollock was pointing out that the art that many dealers brought to the fair was "major," I cite this anecdote to remind us that not only are Warhol's flowers queer, but that without their queerness they are not "Warhols."[24] I congratulate Shafrazi's subversive act of selling works by two queer artists in a country where homosexuality is illegal. However, more importantly, the question formed against the horizon is not only do all newcomers to the scene recognize "the plague" that is contemporary art,[25] but do we have a clear vision of our own achievements, and what compromises we are willing to make for the sake of consensus. It is in this light that Douglas Crimp's urgent redress on the eve of the 21st century, when he asks whether we are "Getting the Warhol We Deserve," is persistently relevant.[26]

Susan Silton extends the question to ask if we are getting the Rauschenberg we deserve. Driving up La Cienega towards Silton's billboard, its colorful stripes shimmer, alternately concealing and revealing a translucent sentence proclaiming: "IF I SAY SO." The billboard references Rauschenberg's famous decree of 1961, when, in lieu of producing a portrait of his gallerist as requested, he sent a telegram, which read: "This is a portrait of Iris Clert if I say so." An anecdote about artistic authority is camouflaged within a formal field of colorful stripes. Silton's work with stripes has evolved from an earlier project documenting quintessential Los Angeles houses covered in striped tarps for fumigation. The artist references Michel Pastoureau's *The Devil's Cloth: A History of Stripes* (2003) in her use of the pattern as a mark of otherness, deviance, and transgression. The stripes' push and pull between figure and ground, as abstraction and reference vie for

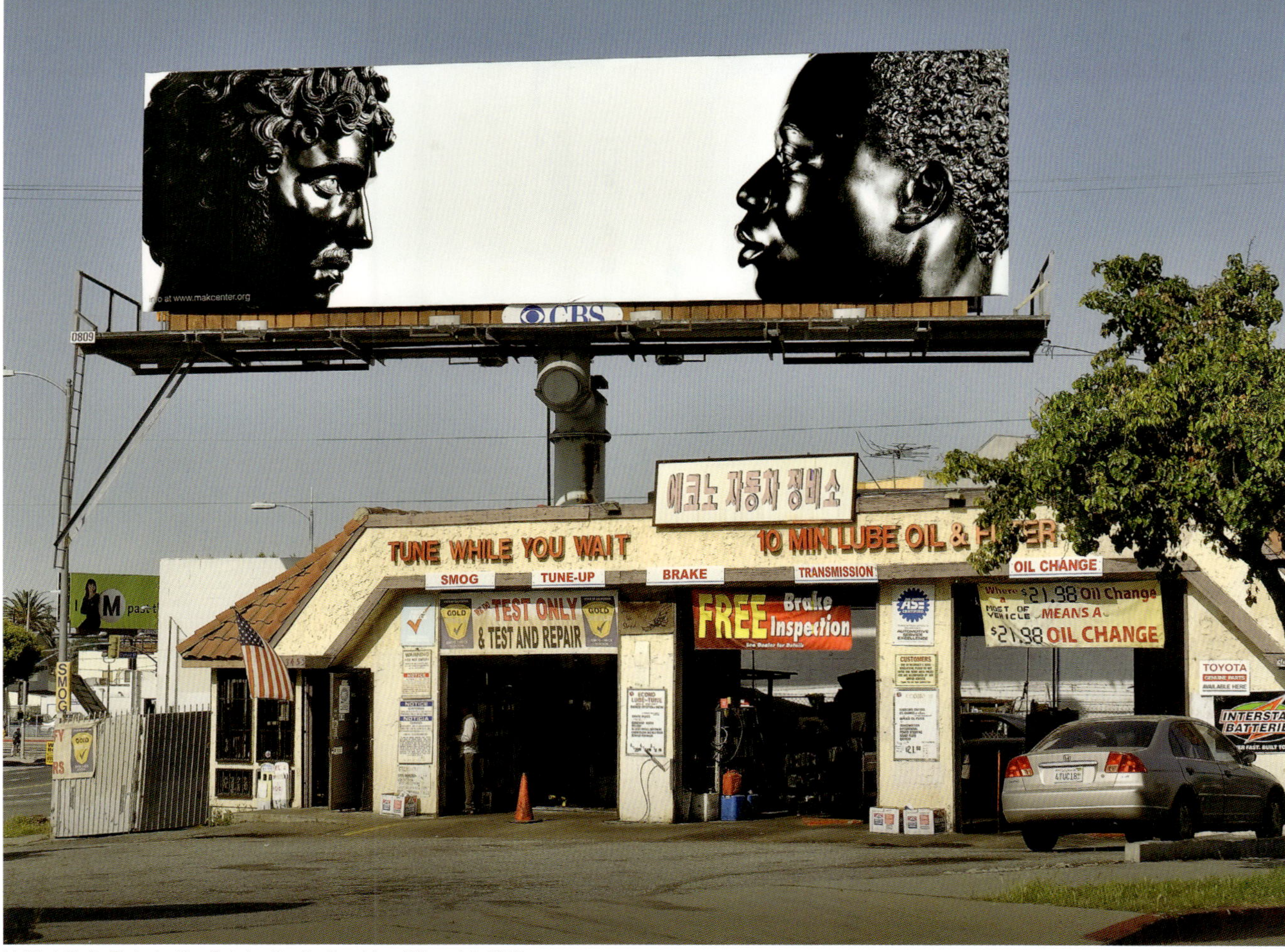

Untitled, Profile Series by Ken Golzales-Day for *How Many Billboards?*, 2010.

primacy in the billboard. The progressive, Duchampian/proto-conceptual gesture of stating, rather than creating, an artwork, with the historical import of Rauschenberg, is here contrasted with his insistence on remaining closeted long after the struggles for gay rights went public. Between the lines, the work also alludes to Daniel Buren's strategic bars and feminist artists' appropriation of pattern and decoration that examine the structure of conformity. Overlaying contradictory historical references, Silton's billboard foregrounds the uneasy marriage of Conceptualism and Identity Politics, not through its reconciliation in the 1990s, but by "outing" its inconsistencies and hybrid nature that has existed since the 1960s.

sYet if, as Silton argues, the problem arose with the "institutional co-opting of Identity Politics in the late 1980s / early 1990s," why not, as many have advised me, change the term or invent a new moniker to describe its critical strand? Aside from paying homage to the politics and continuity that the term represents, it is on the horizon of the art world's globalization (and its expansion as a market) that the importance of Identity Politics lies. Furthermore, artists worked to unhinge identity (as agency) from subjectivity or autobiography by examining how genres, forms, and constructs rendered political issues or the telling of history. As is manifest in so many of the exhibition participants' artistic oeuvres and/or billboards, Critical

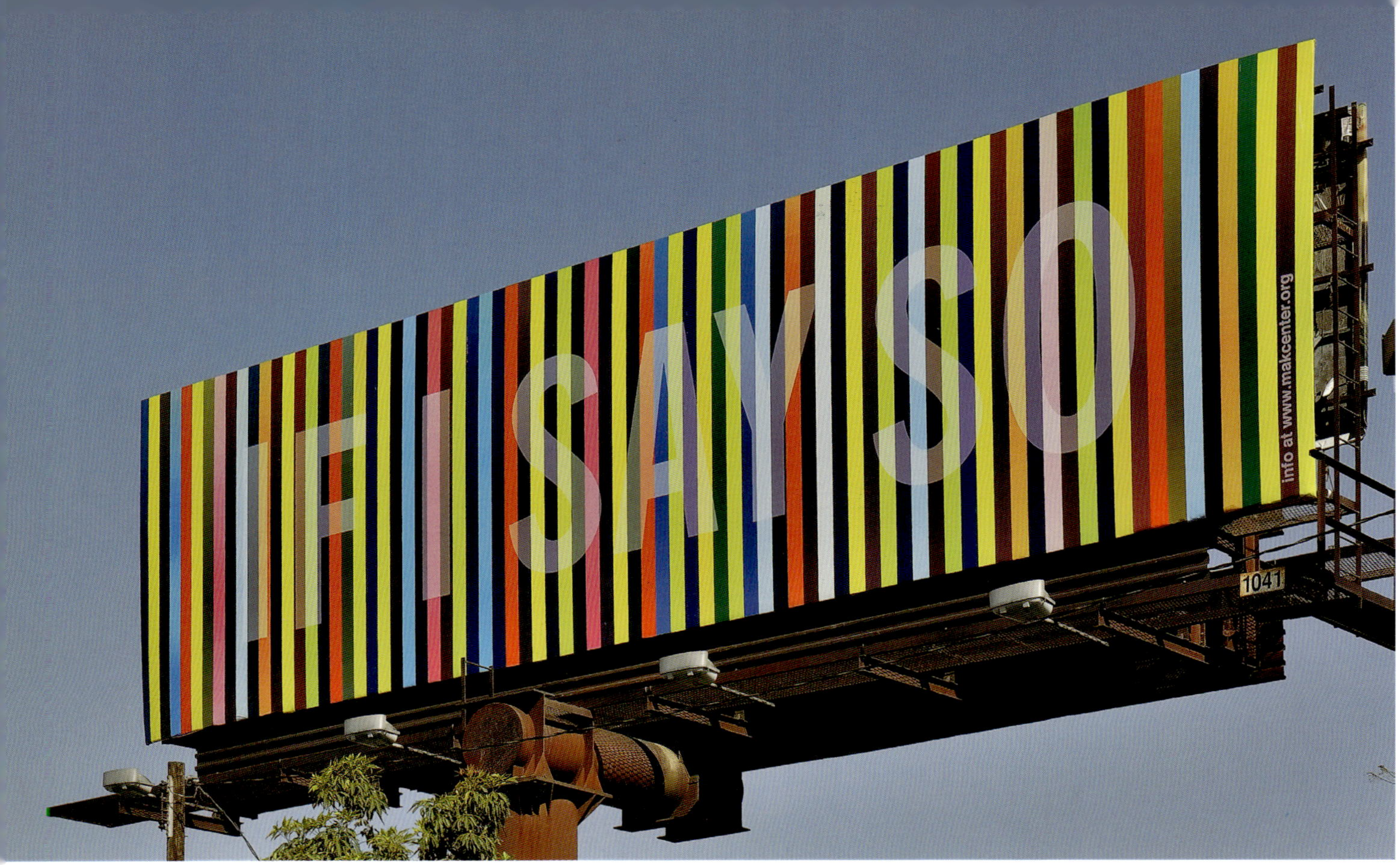

IF I SAY SO by Susan Silton for *How Many Billboards?*, 2010.

Identity Politics examines the relation of political agency to subject formation. Critical Identity Politics insists on the inseparability of identity, as the agent of politics (not of subjectivity), from conceptual inquiry. As the last century drew to a close and radical art movements became canonical, the terms and stakes of the political also changed. Today, with the unprecedented growth of the art world, previous assumptions simply cannot be made. In many countries on the global art circuit, democracy is not the rule; in some places it is not even an ideal. Thus what we may consider basic rights of equality or justice—principles fought for through the agency of the politics of identity—may not be of value at all to some. Thus we must put our local, recent history of art into the perspective of a globalizing artworld, in order to recognize where our most important

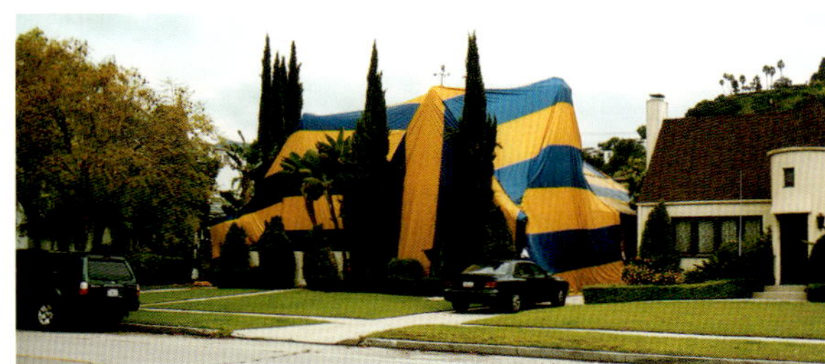

Susan Silton
#11, from *Infested*, 2006
Chromogenic print, 40 x 60 inches
Courtesy of the artist

achievements lie, and what principles need to be upheld on the horizon of the future.

It is important to emphasize that the redefinition of Identity Politics as the politics of difference and representation in the 1980s and 1990s was an elaboration upon materialist and ideological critique, or of a feminist read of psychoanalysis, in the context of a postcolonial, global, cultural exchange. This position was debated within the Left by a post-structuralist approach that sought the political in the forms and materials, rather than in the content, of the work. In this vein, Kori Newkirk boldly takes on forbidden tropes in direct reference to these debates of the 1990s. In spite of the oft-sounded critique of image consumption as spectacle, Newkirk boldly offers his own image for display. Newkirk steps out into public media with a self-portrait in which an enormous snowball is stuck in his mouth. Newkirk's image recalls another example of self-portrait as poetic self-censorship: Marcel Duchamp's visual / material / textual pun in *With my Tongue in my Cheek* (1959). While Newkirk's practice usually defers the referential for the formal, here the metaphors are shoved, as it were, into the viewer's face, pushing the monumentality of the media to its maximum capacity. As the viewer contemplates whether the grimacing figure is expressing pleasure or pain, the coherence of the image melts away; the blown-up photographic grain becomes

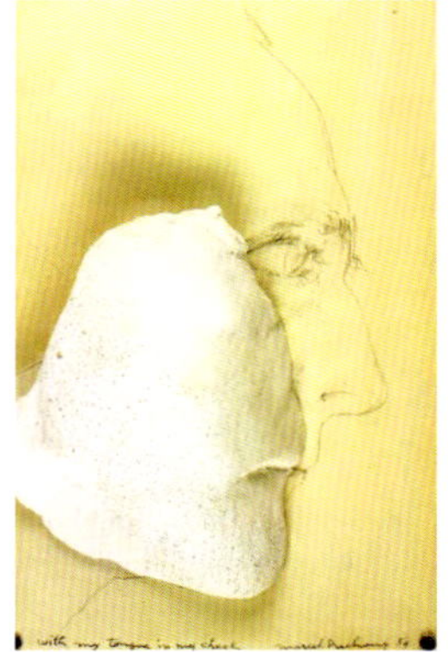
Marcel Duchamp
With my Tongue in my Cheek, 1959
Plaster, pencil on paper mounted on wood
Musee National d'Art Moderne, Centre Georges Pompidou, Paris, France
Courtesy of CNAC/MNAM/Dist. Réunion des Musées Nationaux/Art Resource, NY
© ARS, NY

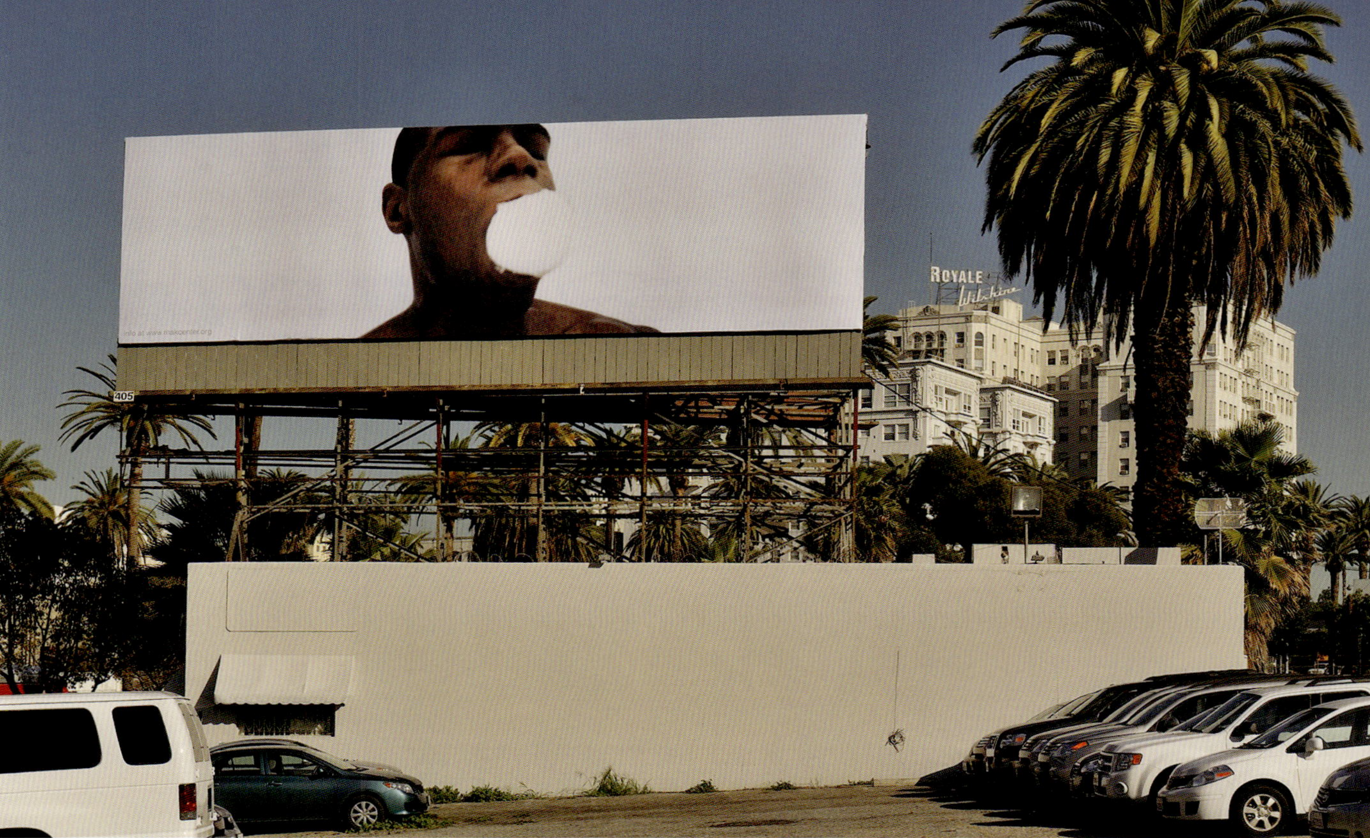

Kori Newkirk for *How Many Billboards?*, 2010.

increasingly dominant, swallowing the referent of the already over-determined image. By "advertising" himself as speechless, Newkirk sublimates the urge to "tell it like it is" (or to bite the hand that feeds). He exhibits instead the ambivalent position of the artist within the system, which thus brings us full circle to John Knight and the overall exhibition's negotiation with the billboard as one kind of system of exchange, a microcosm of a world order. But rather than speak against art's market, or through any other mode of binary opposition, *How Many Billboards?* sets up an alternative configuration, staging art in public as an attempt to speak through the media by questioning its, and art's, commitment to principles of civil liberties.

Although hanging by a hair, a distinction is still discernible between the creativity that drives art and universities, as opposed to that of sailing matches, car races, sports, fashion, and entertainment that directly support brand-based industries. This distinction is not made here to argue for the autonomy of art, but rather an appeal for intellectual independence from an end or a purpose, which is a foundational requisite for cultural development. If Western institutions such as museums and universities carry on their recent agendas of franchising in countries that lack foundations of civil liberties, and therefore disagree with one of the biggest messages that contemporary art has been concerned with, then they will inevitably undermine their authority to determine intellectual, and ultimately capital, value. Furthermore, art historically has carried the seeds of change that most of the conservative players in the global arena would fundamentally reject. That participants benefiting from the new markets for Western art aim to suppress this fact can yield one of two consequences. They will fail and the suppressed, subversive core of works by artists such as Warhol and Haring will posthumously erupt like so many time bombs, despite their new, conservative setting. Or, art measured against populist criteria will lose its ground and the entire platform of art-as-entertainment will collapse, leaving speculators around the globe with collections worth less than their monthly storage fees.

How Many Billboards? measures itself against the horizon of the globalizing future, while being critical of the apparent lack of prognostic vision exhibited by the expanding art world. *How Many Billboards?* also aims its contribution at its local context, and at the diminishing trust in the good faith of our own public institutions. Unable to distinguish the activity of collecting as consumption from curatorial expertise as production, the field of contemporary art is fraught with philanthropists imposing their taste.[27] The near-sighted leverage of capital power—whereby large individual or corporate gifts oblige museums into uninspired programming of limited scope—is arguably self-defeating. This will not only cost collectors dearly (as the grounds from which their collections draw their monetary value may collapse from under them, if it hasn't already), but will damage those institutions that have placed public cultural heritage in non-ordained hands.[28] Can it be that the foresight of cultural philanthropists is so narrow that they overlook how, by compromising museum standards, they expose our cultural institutions to attacks on their non-profit status, and thus, for example, the tax benefits that it supports?[29] The ethical guidelines of museums in the United States mandate that programs should be "founded on scholarship and marked by intellectual integrity." Clearly, a scholarly exhibition cannot be based on holdings from a single private collection that inherently represents a pool of work narrowed according to the personal taste of a layman.[30]

Moreover, collectors show their collections in museums not only for the prestige that it brings, but also for the automatic increase in value to any artwork that gets institutional recognition. It is not the role of museums to supply this service to their donors. If museums engage in such profit-oriented activities, it will be difficult for them to maintain that their "programs promote the public good rather than individual financial gain."[31] It is hence in the best interests of collectors to uphold the intellectual and scholarly framework of art's institutions, and, thus, their independence from private financial interests.

In light of the compromised practices by museums that have become increasingly ubiquitous, *How Many Billboards?* tests an alternative that can function within the system while practicing democratic principles. Positioned within—not against—the market, the exhibition instead asks what *kind* of a market. Of "market freedom," it asks what kind of freedom. Following the principle that democracy needs to be exercised consistently, the exhibition explores what a democratic praxis might be, and what it may mean to practice democracy regularly, if not experimentally.[32] Turning back to art's legacy of political engagement, *How Many Billboards?* explores how artists redefine the political after its previous, prescriptive terms. It thus brings Conceptualism's bequest into the present alongside its interlocutor, Critical Identity Politics, in order to make a claim for the significance of civil liberties and freedom of rights, for the work-in-progress called democracy.

1. A few examples include: Alexander Dumbadze and Suzanne Hudson, chairs, "What Is Contemporary Art History?" (Panel discussion, annual conference for the College Art Association, Los Angeles, CA, February 25-28, 2009); "What is Contemporary Art?," *E-flux Journal* 11 (December 2009) and *E-flux Journal* 12 (January 2009). http://www.e-flux.com/journal (accessed January 2010); and Hal Foster, et al., "Questionnaire on 'The Contemporary,'" *October* 130 (Fall 2009): 3-124.

2. See also "Roundtable: The Present Conditions of Art Criticism," in "Obsolescence," special issue, *October* 100 (Spring 2002): 200-228. The display of art has been increasingly professionalized since the 17th century. Consciousness of art's symbolic power has increased since the Enlightenment when art became a site of power struggles over who controls classification, criteria and value. In Modernism the role of the critic became central to interpreting and judging the work of art, which has increasingly been displaced by the dominance of the market. See also Isabelle Graw, *High Price: Art Between the Market and Celebrity Culture* (New York: Sternberg Press, 2009).

3. The New Museum, The Corcoran Gallery, and Los Angeles County Museum of Art are major institutions that are planning, or have recently mounted, exhibitions featuring works drawn from private collectors that have contributed to, or are otherwise associated with, the institution.

4. For a definition of the term "neoliberalism" see David Harvey, *A Brief History of Neoliberalism* (Chicago: University of Chicago Press, 2005).

5. The term clearly means so much more, and so much less, than the various referents assigned to it. It is my aim to develop a non-prescriptive approach in order to define it more accurately.

6. See my "Critical Identity Politics," *X-TRA* 11.1 (Fall 2008): 4-15.

7. The Identity Politics resurgence of the late 1980s and early 1990s was much more complicated than contemporaneous reception was able to detect.

8. See the excellent book by Darby English, *How to See a Work of Art in Total Darkness* (Cambridge, MA: MIT Press, 2007); and Jennifer A. González, *Subject to Display: Reframing Race in Contemporary Installation Art* (Cambridge, MA: MIT Press, 2008).

9. Susan Silton in e-mail correspondence with author, March 4, 2010. This position is also taken by Miwon Kwon in "The (Un)Siting of Community," *One Place after Another Site-Specific Art and Locational Identity* (Cambridge, MA: MIT Press, 2002), 138-155.

10. Rhea Anastas, Gregg Bordowitz, Andrea Fraser, Jutta Koether and Glenn Ligon, "The Artist Is a Currency," *Grey Room* 24 (Summer 2006): 114.

11. In his use of the term populist, Broad demonstrates how narrow is his scope of contemporary art and its history. "'We will find the right person,' Broad says, 'An unusual person who will create lots of involvement in the community and be a populist.'" Cited in Suzanne Muchnic,"???, The Next Director of The Museum of Contemporary Art," *Los Angeles Times Culture Monster Blog,* December 24, 2009, http://www.latimesblogs.latimes.com/culturemonster/2009/12/page/3/ (accessed March 14, 2010).

12. See http://www.mecaforpeace.org/section.php?id=65.

13. Shortly after the installation of his billboard, Knight was contacted by Boycott/Divestment/Sanction, who wished to seize upon the opportunity that the billboard presented to further mobilize a campaign to boycott Israeli-made products. Interested in the idea of opportunity, rather than the actual activity, the artist's response was simply: "It is there, you can do with it what you want," indicating that his role in the process was done. Cited from phone conversation with the artist on February 8, 2010.

14. Jay Sanders, "Jay Sanders Reads John Knight," *Parkett* 86, (November 2009): 6.

15. Vered Maimon, "The Third Citizen: On Models of Criticality in Contemporary Artistic Practice," *October* 129 (2009): 85.

16. Maimon's argument outlines the transforming conception of what constitutes a community. Her rhetoric traces an evolution between Hans Haacke's attempts to peel ideology and expose "reality," to Pierre Huyghe and Walid Raad's fictional constructions as modes of reality. My only objection to Maimon's temporal formulation is that rather than being a contemporary phenomenon, the "opening"

of Conceptualism has been taking place since the late 1960s / early 1970s in the practices of artists such as Adrian Piper, Mary Kelly, and David Hammons. Each of those artists' works served to complicate Conceptualism's truth claims, precisely by engaging its methods. Knight's practice has also consistently challenged many of Conceptual Art's certitudes since the 1970s.

17. Working through the theories of Jacques Rancière, Étienne Balibar, and Jean-Luc Nancy, Maimon identifies how virtualities came to be applied to contemporary artistic practice. I take a broader perspective that, following post-structuralist theory, virtuality is the episteme of our epoch. Central to my thinking here is Joel Fineman's "The History of the Anecdote: Fiction and Fiction," in *The Subjectivity Effect in Western Literary Tradition: Essays toward the Release of Shakespeare's Will* (Cambridge, MA: MIT Press, 1991). In addition to Fineman's work on Stephen Greenblatt, especially on the latter's seminal "Fiction and Friction" (Thomas C. Heller and Christine Brooke-Rose, *Reconstructing Individualism: Autonomy, Individuality, and the Self in Western Thought* (Stanford: Stanford University Press, 1986), I am here influenced also by the work of Hayden White and Stephen Bann.

18. It is beyond the scope of this essay to address in detail the remarkable contribution of Fineman, beyond hinting towards the accuracy of his insight.

19. Fineman, 72.

20. The majority of writing on Sekula's oeuvre, by himself and others, addresses his work as "critical realism." See, for example, Allan Sekula, *Dismal Science: Photo Works 1972-1996* (Bloomington: University Galleries, Illinois State University, 1999); and Allan Sekula and Benjamin H.D. Buchloh, *Fish Story* (Rotterdam: Witte de With, Center for Contemporary Art, 1995). Sekula credits feminism's return to storytelling as an influence: http://www.howmanybillboards.org/allan-sekula.html (accessed February 21, 2010). I am not arguing for a similarity between the idea of anecdote as an opening that lets reality happen, and realism as a code. What concerns me here is the sweeping recognition in the arts and humanities of the condition of mediation.

21. A common assumption underlying the concept of prescription was that practices influenced by the politics of identity, such as feminist performance or other identity-based formulations, assumed coherence through the somatic, and were hence inherently essentializing. It was never taken into consideration that most practitioners where not only aware of, but sought to highlight, the constructed nature of the somatic to begin with. Fineman compares the narrative nature of Hippocrates's medical histories to the biographic tendencies of the contemporaneous historian Thucydides. Contradicting the assumptions that take the somatic as "real," Fineman demonstrates, through the work of the New History, how descriptions of the organic are inevitably constructed like a story.

22. See http://www.kengonzalesday.com/projects/bonegrassboy/index.htm (accessed March 4, 2010).

23. See http://artforum.com/diary/archive=200911 (accessed December 14, 2009).

24. See Jennifer Doyle, Jonathan Flatley, and José Esteban Muñoz, ed., *Pop Out: Queer Warhol* (Durham: Duke University Press, 1996).

25. Upon arriving in the U.S., Freud famously remarked to Jung, "They don't realize we are bringing them the plague." In many countries and nations that have recently joined the international scene, personal freedom is non-existent. I am emphasizing the UAE because the acquisition of universities, and Western and contemporary art, is a government-led initiative there.

26. Crimp queers a question asked first by Hal Foster, emphasizing that to felicitously consider Warhol one must not repress his queer context and his inter-disciplinary production. Douglas Crimp, "Getting the Warhol We Deserve," *Social Text* 59 (1999): 49-66. About Rauschenberg's closeted homosexuality see Jonathan D. Katz, "Rauschenberg's Honeymoon," *Art/Text* 61. (May/June 1998): 44–47.

27. Beyond the institutions mentioned in footnote 3, the recent marriage arranged by Eli Broad for MOCA is a case in point. In vying for his art dealer, Jeffrey Deitch, to be named MOCA's new director, Broad jeopardized not only the institution's intellectual credibility but also several democratic principles. Beyond a forest of conflicts of interest, it seems that the process of selection itself was far from democratic. "Mr. Broad…ended up serving on the search committee. And people in the art world who were informed about the selection process, but spoke on condition of anonymity for fear of alienating Mr. Broad, said he was deeply involved, seeking the advice of dealers and auction house executives, as well as artists, in consultation with the museum's board and advisers." (Carol Vogel and Randy Kennedy, "Los Angeles Museum Taps Dealer as Director," *New York Times,* January 11, 2010). The fact that many of the interviewees around these events requested anonymity does not fair well for Broad. See Tom Christie, "Deitch's New Project MOCA's Big Gamble," *LA Weekly,* January 14, 2010, http://www.laweekly.com/content/printVersion/825590 (accessed January 15, 2010). Also see Mike Boehm, "L.A.'s MOCA Picks Art Dealer Jeffrey Deitch as Director," *Los Angeles Times,* January 12, 2010, http://articles.latimes.com/2010/jan/12/entertainment/la-et-deitch-moca12-2010jan12 (accessed January 19, 2010); and Jennifer Steinhauer, "Iron Checkbook Shapes Cultural Los Angeles," *New York Times,* February 7, 2010, http://www.nytimes.com/2010/02/08/arts/design/08broad.html (accessed February 8, 2010). In many respects his dictatorial choice structurally recalls another alarming failure in democracy, when Israeli Minister of Defense Ehud Barak exercised his authority to grant a college in the occupied territories the status of "University Center." The two events reflect authority misrecognizing its qualification, and consequently undermining institutional criteria and clout. Deitch's merit and intelligence are not questioned—he is a very qualified individual, just not for the job of museum director. The problem is that Broad does not understand the limits of his own, and Deitch's, expertise. Similarly, Ehud Barak does not comprehend what a university is and who is eligible to determine such status. As Professor Itzhak Galnoor, a former deputy chairman of Israel's Council of Higher Education (CHE), exclaimed: "We're in an anomalous situation, where a college outside the state's borders thinks it's possible to write its own rules. The defense minister would have done better to consult the CHE before exercising his authority over educational matters, about which he understands even less than CHE members understand about security issues." Cited in Or Kashti, "Barak Under Fire for Granting University Status to West Bank College," *Haaretz* http://www.haaretz.com/hasen/spages/1144116.html (accessed January 20, 2010).

28. See footnote no. 3.

29. The complicated and loophole-fraught relations between the profit and non-profit sectors of the arts have long been the targets of right-wing advocates. It will become increasingly difficult to defend the tax-exempt status of many of the field's transactions. Republican attacks on fractional or partial giving of art to institutions is one example.

30. It is clear to see that by exhibiting private collections museums have been compromising the ethical boundaries defined by the American Association of Museums. See http://www.aam-us.org/museumresources/ethics/coe.cfm (accessed March 2, 2010).

31. Ibid.

32. Artist and activist Linda Pollock makes this point through her extended praxis. See especially http://www.mydailyconstitution.org/.

ART ON OR AS BILLBOARDS

BY GLORIA SUTTON

The spectacle is not a collection of images; rather, it is a social relationship between people that is mediated by images.
Guy Debord

Artists do not work exclusively in the medium of billboards.
David Lamelas

By locating works of art *on* and *as* billboards, the exhibition *How Many Billboards?* makes a tacit statement not only about art's inability to remain autonomous within the broader media culture, but also that aesthetic experience is everywhere. Social space is completely saturated with the culture of the image. This condition is certainly not new; even by late 1967, when Guy Debord published *La société du spectacle,* his influential description of a "spectacular society" was already decades in the making. In the book (and in the 1973 film of the same title), Debord outlines a critique of spectacular modernity (essentially an urban modernity gone full tilt) in which streams of images not only operated as a form of distraction and illusion, but also came to define public space. Central to Debord's idea of a spectacular society is the transformation of culture into an all-enveloping "integrated spectacle." While the types of analogue image streams that typify modern experience date back to the 19th century, it is clear that contemporary digital media and their related networks have radically expedited these flows. Throughout the subsequent four decades, Debord's aphoristic prognosis has remained one of the most enduring descriptors of culture as a constantly shifting mediascape. Rising and falling with the market, "the cultural" is no longer limited to earlier, traditional, or even experimental forms but is consumed throughout daily life itself. By 2010, retreat or evasion hardly seems an option.

What does an exhibition mounted throughout a city infamous for its unrelenting and unregulated billboard spaces say about contemporary art's capacity to keep up with a constantly evolving spectacle without completely adhering to it? Conceptual Art's emphasis on communication, networks, and the staging of one's personality has certainly contributed to contemporary art's new value system. At the same time, Conceptual Art is historically bound up with the changing nature of the advertising, marketing, and public relations industries that were also developing in the late 1960s. Embedding an art exhibition within an existing advertising framework—one that is almost synonymous with modernity itself—raises myriad issues. The specific artists' billboards discussed in this essay register along two specific trajectories within the discourse of art history. The first can be thought of in terms of what art historians have decried as the "post-medium condition," in which much contemporary art production can be characterized as aiming to discredit the Modernist ideals of "progress" and formal innovation that buttress the borders erected between mediums and their concomitant disciplines or specializations. The second speaks to the contingent history of Conceptual Art, and the slippage between Conceptual Art as a proper term often used to denote a type of reductivism that pushes the art object toward a state of dematerialization on par with information developed in the wake of Minimalism, and "conceptualism," which represents a broader attitudinal expression frequently resulting in various designations such as "linguistic conceptualism."

While the artists selected for *How Many Billboards?* all operate under a rubric of Conceptual Art, the exhibition in no way makes a claim for a foundational lineage. In fact, *How Many Billboards?* can be read as an almost reactionary approach to what has become a type of Conceptual Art orthodoxy rooted in the practices established by European and New York-based artists during the late 1960s. At the same time, the exhibition's circumscribed West Coast focus should not be taken as a revisionist gesture. The aim is not to expand the history of Conceptual Art to include the practices of artists working in California. Rather, the emphasis is on reducing the scope of the exhibition and asking artists to respond to the billboard as a site of production. One of the results is that Conceptual Art's own sense of contingency is put on display.

Competing narratives of Conceptual Art's history are perhaps most visible in Allen Ruppersberg's billboard, which features the cover of an out-of-print publication that documents Los Angeles County Museum of Art's (LACMA) ambitious *Art and Technology Program* (1967-71).[1] The program paired artists with corporate sponsors such as IBM to support innovative projects, assist in the realization of previously unrealized proposals, and provide research residencies. In some cases, the collaborations operated under the express intent of not producing anything except dialogue and exchange. All of these experiments occurred under the auspices of a public museum in Los Angeles at a moment when critical attention was focused on the activities at select East Coast galleries. The LACMA report cover features a grid of black-and-white portraits of the participating engineers, scientists, and artists, including Richard Serra, Robert Smithson, Mark di Suvero, Andy Warhol, Öyvind Fahlstrom, Robert Irwin,

Robert Whitman, Claes Oldenburg, Sam Francis, and Jules Olitski. In this context, unexpected art historical associations form. Even if most never imagined Clement Greenberg's ideal Jules Olitski working with the American Cement Corporation, it is not the pairing of artists with engineers, or even corporate sponsorships, that raises an eyebrow. (Experiments in Art and Technology's event *Nine Evenings* had become a clear model for this type of collaboration in 1965.) Rather, it is the cross pollination of artists not typically associated with Conceptual Art all working under the framework of an art and technology program—in Los Angeles—that is remarkable. In Ruppersberg's reworking, he has repopulated the report's cover with 63 portraits of West-Coast-based artists such as Barbara T. Smith, Judy Fiskin, Mary Kelly, and Vija Celmins, who all practice their own particular strand of conceptualism, giving rise to a contested field of multiple and opposing practices that can all be thought of as Conceptual Art.

More notable is the fact that the more one attempts to trace shared formal strategies or critical leanings between the various artists commissioned to contribute to *How Many Billboards?,* the less useful or relevant those categories become in defining the term "conceptual." Increasingly, the work of these artists (many of whom have been regularly exhibiting since the late 1960s) demonstrates that Conceptual Art is not created in terms of geographical specificities or pedagogical affinities, but individual practices. As such, the history of Conceptual Art should be written to include those terms. Just as significant, is

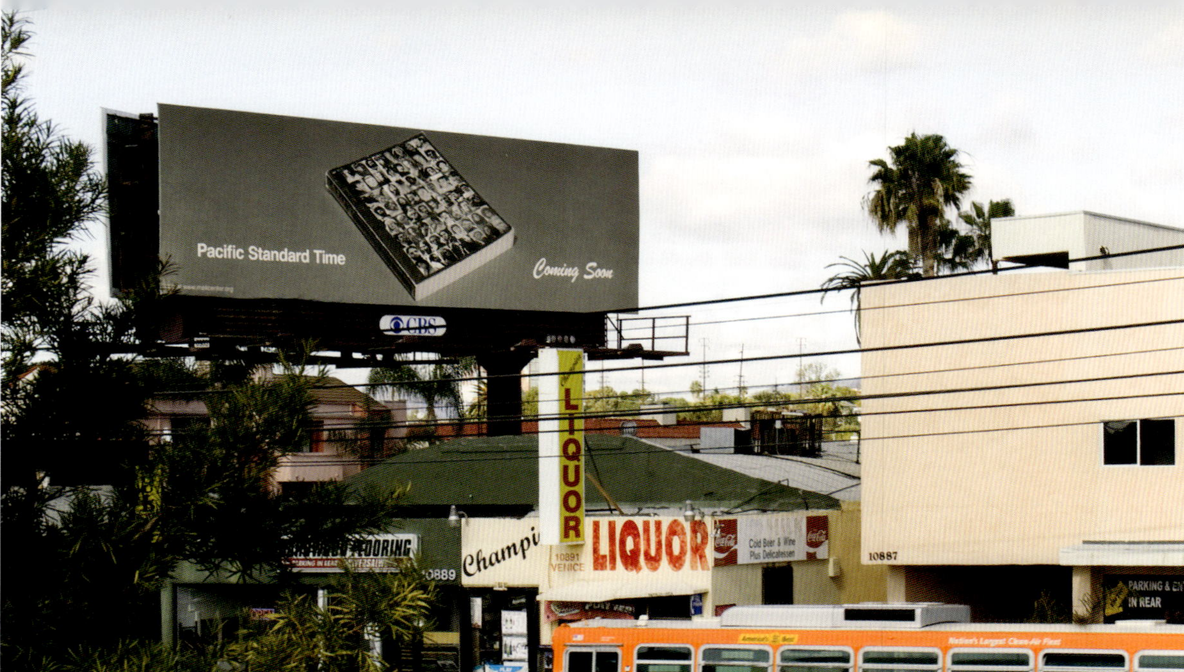

Allan Ruppersberg for *How Many Billboards?*, 2010.

the inclusion of artists who have also had an equal impact in the history of experimental film (such as Kenneth Anger, Yvonne Rainer, and David Lamelas), which complicates the designation of Conceptual Art as only an art historical term.

Visible on the street, through a car windshield, or bus window, each billboard included in the exhibition functions independently as a stand-alone encounter, relying on its own graphic profile to register against Los Angeles's dense field of signs and images. On the other hand, as reproduced in the exhibition catalogue and website, the billboards collectively operate as a type of series. Configured into the standard formats of outdoor billboards, the works of art circulate openly among the culturally familiar. Read one after another, each billboard redistributes the weight between not only what art historians refer to as the various "aesthetic theories or models of conceptualism,"[2] but also the categories that bind art and culture, often foregrounding what was once in the background and vice versa. Their images and texts figure passively against a mobile field, a permanent type of inconsistency that sometimes results in serendipitous associations. (Brandon Lattu's billboard advertising the private sale of a 1994 Cadillac Fleetwood, for example, appears squarely above an auto repair shop.) Formal coincidences also occur (such as the vividly colored vertical stripes of Susan Silton's board on La Cienega Boulevard appearing to enliven the red and white awning of the McDonald's it hovers above).[3] But mostly the billboards assemble and disassemble out of the corner of the eye, and under these conditions attention finds itself focused on the changing role of the image itself. If, for Debord, 20th century aesthetics were marked by mass image reproduction, the 21st century can be characterized as a moment of extreme image manipulation. Images are compressed, enlarged, downloaded, transferred, migrated, enhanced, and are not fixed by scale, form, or medium. A subsequent result of the unmooring of the image from its medium is the recognition that attention is still the discursive support of the current moment.

The billboard form itself can be read as an index of the transformation of the image. Within the specific terrain of *How Many Billboards?,* we see a shuttling back and forth between analogue and digital forms (from wheat paste and newsprint to 400 by 1400 pixel screens and moving images). Fixed rectilinear formats appear next to amorphous supergraphics that envelop high-rise facades and stretch around the bulbous surfaces of buses. Within Los Angeles' billboard ecology it becomes evident that the introduction of new digital forms does not make older techniques obsolete or even outmoded. The temporary, paste-up poster still holds our attention while we wait for the light to change. In fact, a wide-ranging sampling of irritations happens when these forms (old, new, and newer) rub up next to one another, sometimes even at the same intersection. Akin to what Fredric Jameson aptly calls "intensification," a heightening upwards or downwards of perceptual experience occurs, which accentuates the very condition (rather than the technology) of media and its ability to produce sense experience.[4]

In order to avoid general allusions, and attain some clarity or precision about the formal operations of the billboards, I specifically address the projects contributed by Kerry Tribe, Jennifer Bornstein, David Lamelas, Yvonne Rainer, and Kenneth Anger in terms of a type of spatial proliferation of the image. These projects can be looked at in terms of staging or representing the transformation of media, which is not intrinsically representable in its own right.

Let's begin then by reconsidering the causal relationship art historians have drawn between the rise of Conceptual Art and the waning of medium specificity in the last half of the twentieth century. In her influential book *A Voyage on the North Sea*, Rosalind Krauss uses Marcel Broodthaers's visual riddle "FIN ARTS," printed on the cover of the October 1974 issue of *Studio International,* to generate a complex and highly nuanced rebus of her own. Krauss deftly rearranges the tropes of Modernist painting to spell out how Conceptual Art's "transcendence of the particular," as exemplified by Broodthaers's *Museum of Modern Art, Department of Eagles* (1968–1971), signaled not the end of art, but the end of medium specificity in art.[5] Rather than a permanent collection tied to a specific locale, the project foregrounded the apparatus of collecting and was organized around what Broodthaers referred to as "sections" devoted to reproductions of works of art, inscriptions, texts, film, and other ephemera that all carried the sign or motif of an eagle. As an "emblem of Conceptual Art," Krauss posits that Broodthaers's eagle points to this shift by "enacting the *form* that this loss of specificity" takes on.[6] For Krauss these "forms" take the shape of a variety of material supports from those widely referred to as media (film and video) to more discursive notions of medium including language, the readymade, and various "sites," including the pages of art magazines, gallery spaces, museums, and trade fairs. To this list, I would add billboards. In Krauss's formulation, the resulting intermedia rebus reads as a dismal leveling, or the folding of multiple forms into a "system of pure equivalency by the homogenizing principle of commodification."[7] But what happens if we change some of the terms in the puzzle, scramble the references, and make some slight alterations to the set of images Krauss uses to spell out the end of medium specificity? The assumed sustainability of conventions like "media" and "site" generate a false sense of stability for which any complication or challenge to their durability registers as a loss. Instead of asking what happens *after* medium specificity is no longer a guiding criteria, the focus should be on what *parallel* typologies become recognizable during this process. A viable example is thinking of a medium not as a stable condition, but as a particular type of apparatus that functions as a means or place for interaction: an interface.

The term "interface" was introduced in 1967 by Marshall McLuhan in *The Medium is the Massage: An Inventory of Effects*.[8] Published the same year as Debord's critique of spectacle culture, McLuhan's graphically illustrated text conveys the English scholar's argument about the power of communication media (an amalgam of both analogue and electronic forms—moveable type to television) and its subsequent homogenizing effects on art and culture. Referred to as "a collide-oscope of interfaced situations," McLuhan's treatise outlines how the introduction of communication technology led to the automation of perceptual habits and the shaping of contemporary social interactions.[9] An interface is an apparatus designed to connect two different or distinct systems so they can be operated jointly. The connection process is both an automatic and an automatistic function innate to interfaces, which thus generates a point of commonality, interaction, and exchange. That is to say, interfaces depend upon the mechanics of their structures (computer code, the format of a book, a billboard) in a manner that is automatic, almost reflexive.

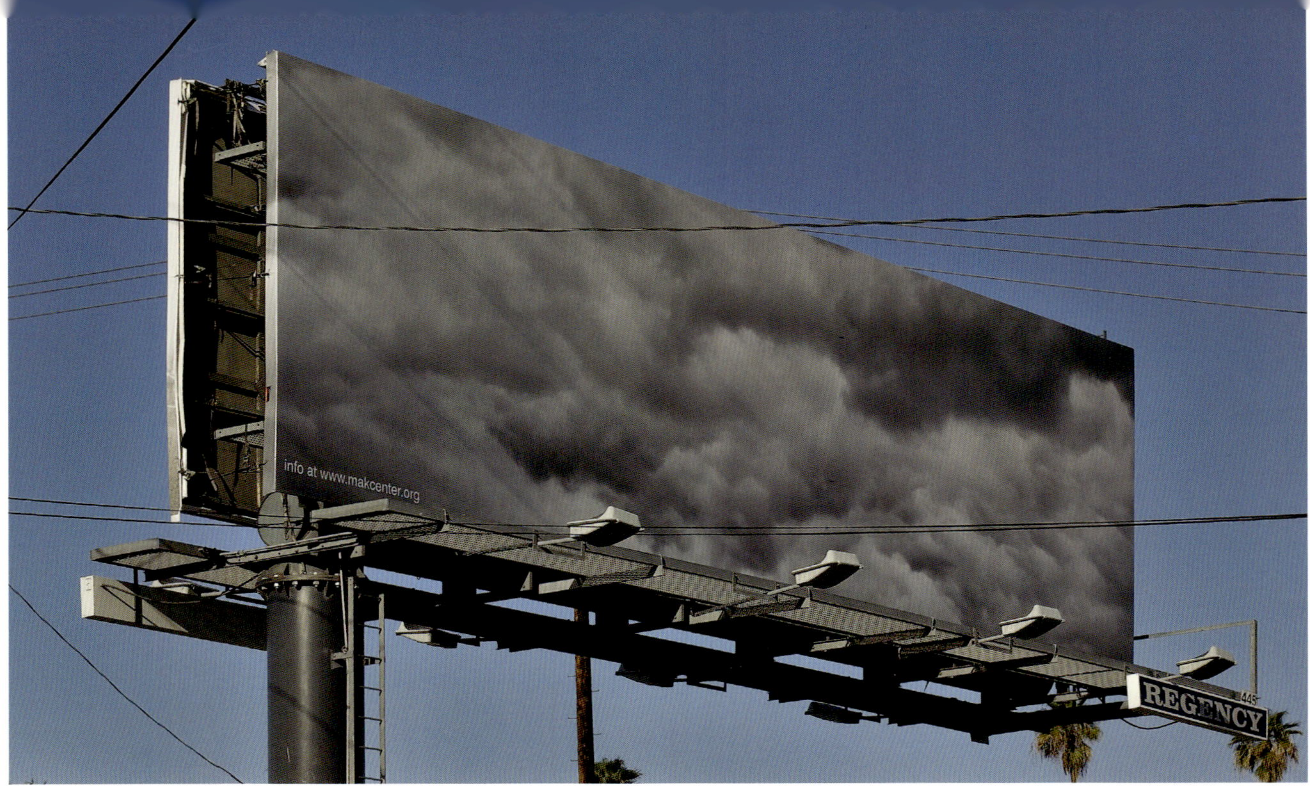

Kerry Tribe for *How Many Billboards?*, 2010.

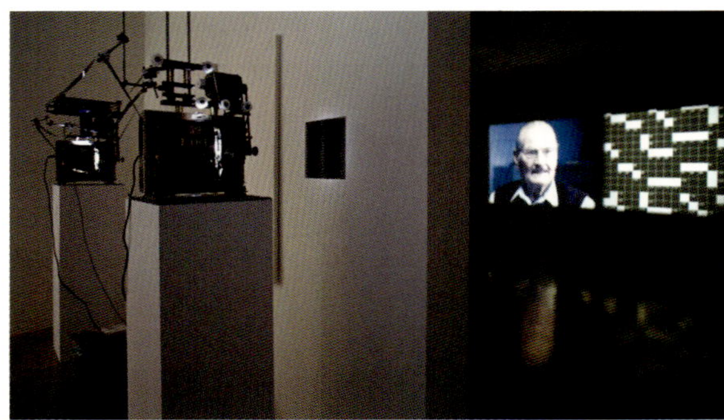
Kerry Tribe
H.M. (Installation view), 2009
Courtesy of the artist and 1301PE.
Photograph by Fredrik Nilsen

We unconsciously follow the established procedures of each interface: clicking icons, turning the page of a book once we reach the bottom, and glancing up distractedly to a message positioned off an armature, building, or other structure while we navigate traffic. More germane to my argument, thinking in terms of interfaces over mediums shifts the emphasis toward an operational mode of art production, which reflects a sense of activism (both in the functional and political sense of the term). While interfaces may be more attuned to the arguments that surround television and computing, their application to the reconsideration of Conceptual Art practices has yet to be fully considered. A possible result of employing the logic of an interface is that "post-medium" artworks do not default to an enigmatic riddle of images, but may in fact produce new forms of mutuality: relations between viewers and systems of meaning.

Kerry Tribe's contribution to *How Many Billboards?* optimizes the automatic response innate to interfaces. Reflecting the artist's ongoing investigation into the problems associated with perception and memory, Tribe's billboard transforms a medium that typically directs one's attention toward a specific product or service into a space of cognitive suspension. Tribe's darkening, stormy sky plays on the viewer's proclivity to look up at billboards. Her image initiates a formal push and pull between the site of the message and its outdoor backdrop. Located above a scattershot section of La Brea Avenue near Venice Boulevard, Tribe's cloudscape prods the abstracted forms of the surrounding power lines and palm trees into relief. In this context, Tribe's image of the sky operates in a manner that the hazy sky of Los Angeles often fails to do. This subtly disjunctive gesture, splitting the image from the real, also calls attention to the theoretical and formal qualities that support the reception of photography, film, and video as aesthetic mediums, issues that Tribe consistently mines in her practice.

For example, Tribe's installation *H.M.* (2009) collapses the time-based operations of film with cinema's narrative forms to produce a type of mnemonic dissonance in the viewer not unlike that experienced by the film's subject, an amnesiac who was only able to hold thoughts in his head for about 20 seconds. A series of photographs, letterpress prints, and drawings all relate to a 16 mm film installation, in which a single strip of celluloid runs through two adjacent film projectors. As a result, viewers see side-by-side projections of two different parts of the same film reel. A custom-built looper moderates the film's speed and weight—allowing for the literal suspension of time in space between the projectors, so that a 20-second delay is generated between the two images. Like Tribe's cloud billboard, the installation's formal fissure creates a strange sense of spatial and temporal deferment. The film's subject is an unremarkable looking, older, white man known to the world only by his initials; the film's form is structured around his unforgettable contribution to neuroscience. The five-decades-long study of H.M.'s short-term memory loss (suffered after undergoing experimental brain surgery to alleviate his epilepsy) forms the cornerstone of modern scientific understanding of memory and, more notably, its related disorders. With H.M.'s passing in 2008, just as Tribe was finishing production of the piece, his identity as Henry Molaison was publicly released. The subsequent dissection and digital scanning of Molaison's brain this year by researchers at the University of California, San Diego, adds a strange rejoinder about memory and identity to the project.

Jennifer Bornstein has consistently mined the mutability of identity and its relation to seriality through serialized images that she has produced in a variety of media, including photography and 16 mm film, since the early 1990s. The mimetic functions of these two media in particular lend themselves to the artist's interest in co-mingling the formal protocols of documentary studies with the casualness of a tourist. Bornstein does not only stand behind the lens, she often positions herself alongside her subjects, subtly aping their physical attributes. The color photographs that comprise the series *Public Libraries and Basketball Courts* (1996-1997), for example, depict the artist on a Los Angeles neighborhood court. With lank posture and ill-fitting shorts, she easily passes for a teenage boy. As a whole, the series creates a situation in which the artist is able to hide in plain sight by drawing on her own flexible presence, rather than any elaborate disguise, in order to question not only the certainties of gender and age, but also photography's complicity with image manipulation.

While doing research for a film project in 2003, Bornstein became interested in an even older means of serial image making. Pouring over various 19th-century periodicals, she became especially intrigued by their engraved illustrations. Bornstein began the arduous task of learning the techniques of incising and copperplate printing in order to generate intaglio prints that were then used as studies for films. Bornstein's choice to contrast the labor-intensive process of this antiquated form of image making against the so-called immediacy of film or photography agitates the formal expectations with which we imbue various types of media. Her conscious use of copperplate etching, which requires hours of practice and remains entirely dependent on the expertise of the hand, offers a counterpoint to the narrative of photographic de-skilling often associated with West Coast Conceptual Art. Bornstein's diminutive, black-and-white etchings shakily record her observations in rough, thin lines, showing friends and strangers alike engaging in mundane activities such as riding the bus or waiting for a mud mask to dry. Anthropological conflations are more directly seen in the tightly framed renderings of famed researchers Margaret Meade and Ruth Benedict (*Study*

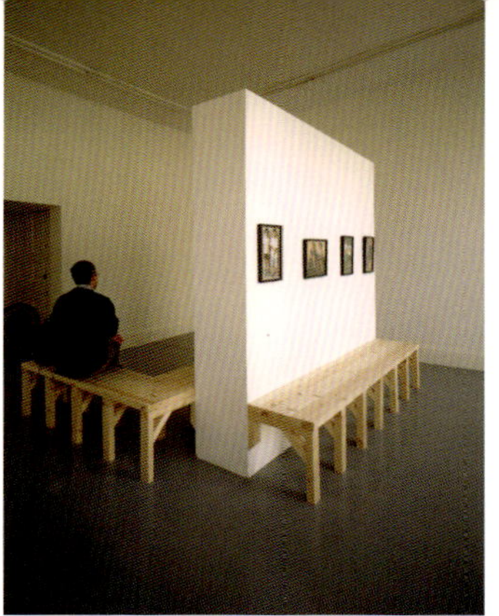

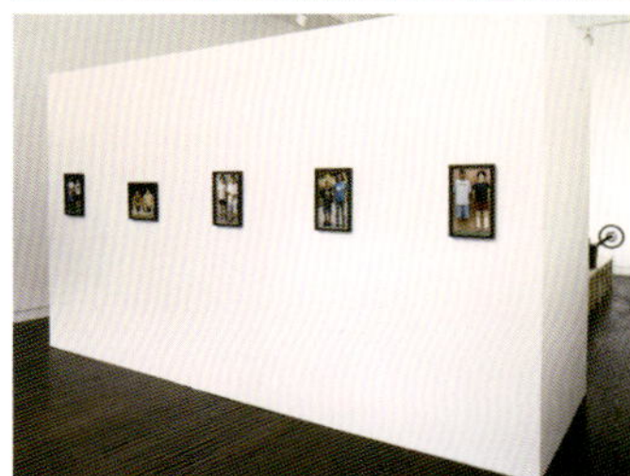

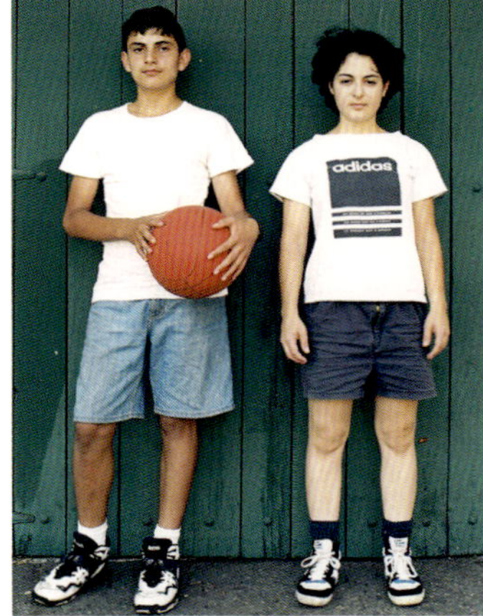

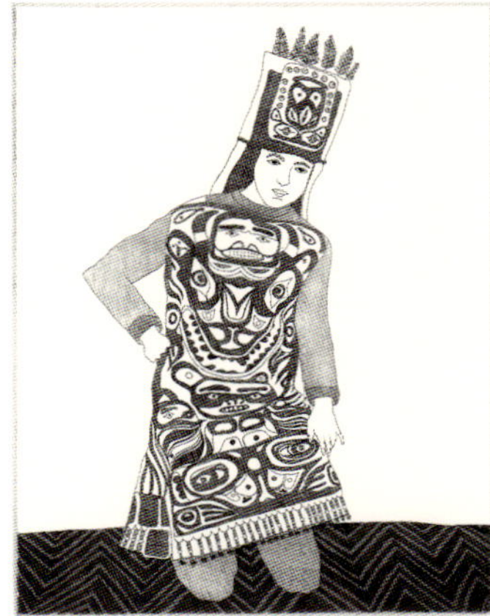

Jennifer Bornstein
Photographs / 16 mm film
January 17 - February 23, 1998
Greengrassi, London
Courtesy of the artist and Blum & Poe, Los Angeles, and Greengrassi, London

Jennifer Bornstein
Photographs / 16 mm film
January 17 - February 23, 1998
Greengrassi, London
Courtesy of the artist and Blum & Poe, Los Angeles, and Greengrassi, London

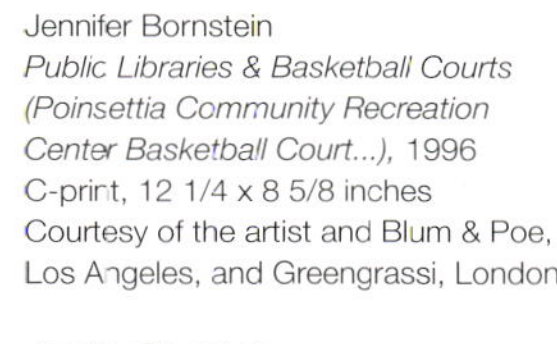

Jennifer Bornstein
Public Libraries & Basketball Courts (Poinsettia Community Recreation Center Basketball Court...), 1996
C-print, 12 1/4 x 8 5/8 inches
Courtesy of the artist and Blum & Poe, Los Angeles, and Greengrassi, London

Jennifer Bornstein
Study for 16 mm Film (Ruth Benedict, Lover and Mentor of Margaret Mead, Kneeling on a Handwoven Navajo Blanket), 2005
Copperplate etching, 14 x 12 inches (14 1/4 x 12 inches framed)
Courtesy of the artist and Blum & Poe, Los Angeles, and Greengrassi, London

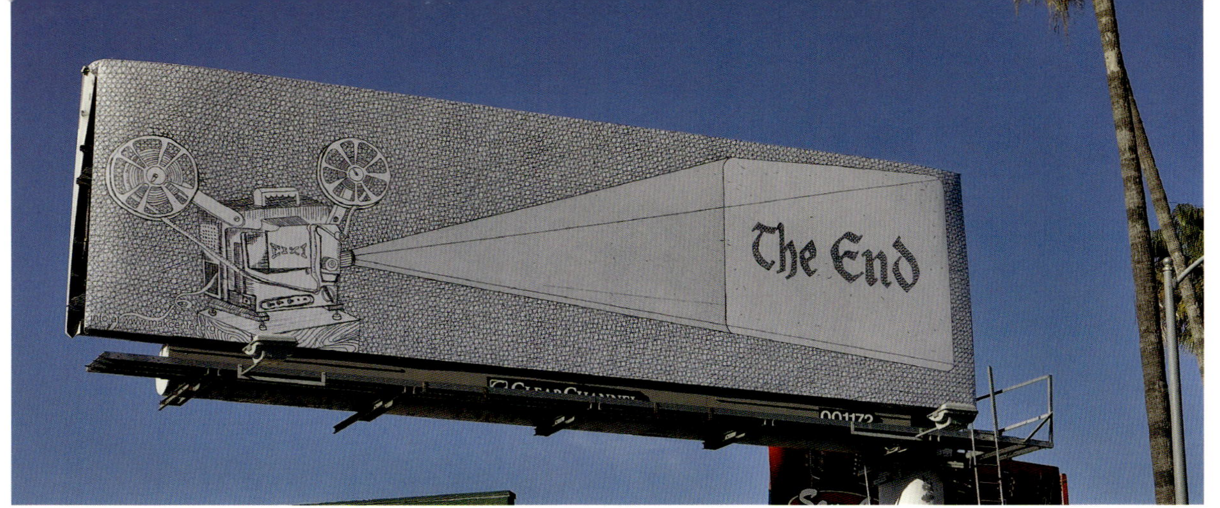

The End by Jennifer Bornstein for *How Many Billboards?*, 2010.

for 16 mm Film [Ruth Benedict, Lover and Mentor of Margaret Meade], 2005). Some of the portraits are composed as if Bornstein's subjects are posing for a camera, further reflecting her interest in eroding the distinctions between fact and fiction.

Featuring an etching of an Eiki 16 mm film projector, Bornstein's billboard anachronistically layers several forms of image making. Her subject is the entire cinematic apparatus. Here the medium of film is not only the celluloid strip, the camera, the projector, and the beam of light, but all of these elements taken together, including the audience's position caught between the source of the light behind it and the image projected onto a screen in front. Her etching of the crate that props up the projector shows the lines and knots of pine, which are reminiscent of the planks that Bornstein uses to build the benches, risers, and flooring that she often exhibits alongside her photographs and films. These objects are intended to, in Bornstein's words, "masquerade as ordinary fixtures" in the room.[10] As such they function less as sculptures and more as interfaces to the images, encouraging groups of people to sit together, or directing access to the photographs. Bornstein uses the lumbering frame of a huge outdoor billboard, an "old" analogue medium that refuses to disappear, in a similar way to interface with the public on the street. The projected image is the fragmentary words "The End"; the gothic type not only transcribes

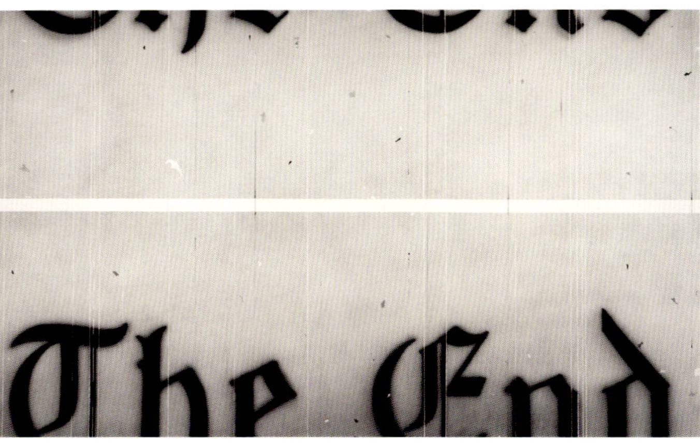

Ed Ruscha
The End, 1991
Acrylic on canvas
70 x 112 inches
Courtesy of the artist

the imminent demise of celluloid in today's digital environment, but also refers to the history of Conceptual Art. In Ed Ruscha's painting *The End* (1991), which shows the same phrase, the bottom register is cut off and the words are repeated at the top, mimicking film's movement in frames. This image is emblematic of Ruscha's storied ability to generate metaphorical meaning from words and type. Using the same words and type, Bornstein generates a picture of media obsolescence not as a smooth sequence predicated on technical advancements in image refinement, but more of a co-mingling of stubborn forms.

If Bornstein's etchings direct our attention to the formal incongruities that result from comparing systems of representation, then David Lamelas's billboard moves the discussion of the slippage from medium to media squarely into the realm of celebrity and stardom. For *How Many Billboards?*, Lamelas gives the character of an archetypal, aging rock star the public attention he craves. Best known for the structuralist films and media installations he produced in London and Los Angeles during the late 1960s and early 1970s, Lamelas tests the efficacy of art as a means of direct communication, while questioning its capacity to create self-awareness.

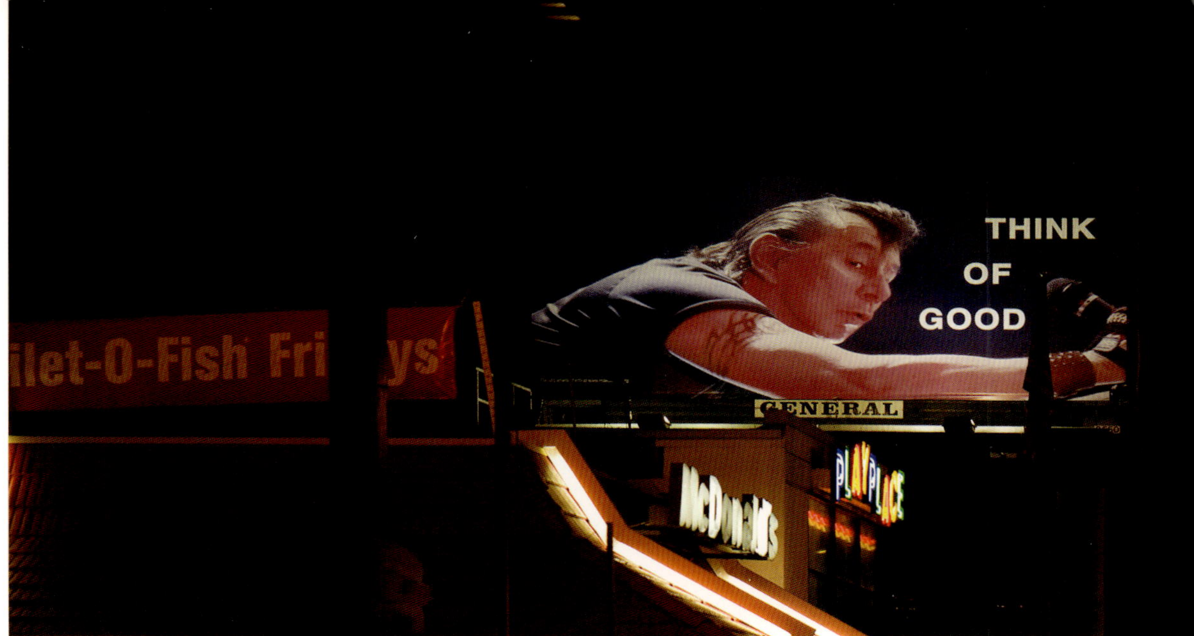

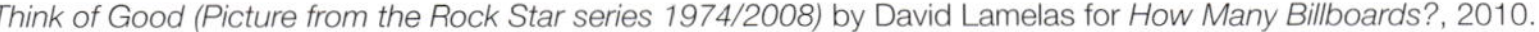
Think of Good (Picture from the Rock Star series 1974/2008) by David Lamelas for *How Many Billboards?*, 2010.

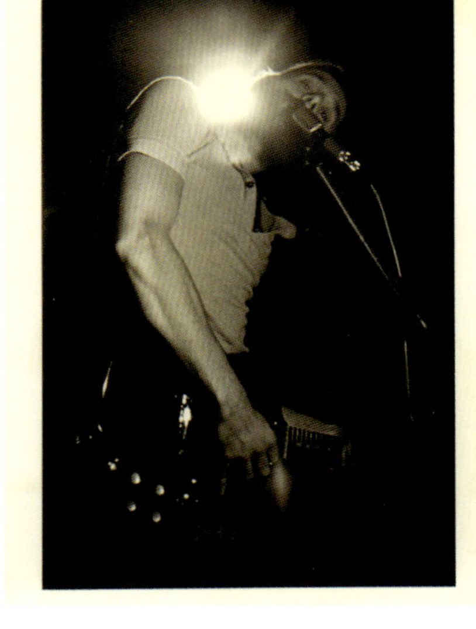
David Lamelas
Rock Star (Character Appropriation), 1974
Seven black-and-white photographs
12 x 16 inches
Courtesy of the artist and Galerie Jan Mot

Lamelas's photographs, films, sculptures, and drawings convey his ongoing interest in redirecting techniques and systems used within the film and television industry toward the burgeoning discourse on public space and media technology. His 1968 installation *Office of Information about the Vietnam War*, for example, helped establish the practice of bringing real-time information (news reports and television footage) into the space of the gallery not as abstracted material, but as actual news intended as a political provocation to the audience. In this sense, Lamelas uses media not only to put information on display in lieu of an object, but also to point attention to the various systems of display that disseminate information and convey social stature. Lamelas's billboard image documents the artist adopting the role of a lead singer in a band. The referent is not specific to a particular singer or act; rather Lamelas seems to be implicating the persistence of "types" and photography's imbrications with publicity. His black hair is slicked back in a pseudo-retro sweep and a rolled-up black t-shirt reveals generic "tribal" tattoos on his arms. The resulting image is less a reference to "photo-conceptualism," (an exploration of the intelligibility of linguistic and visual codes) than a pastiche of photographic styles. The electric pink cast and the exaggerated pose of his body add to the overall distortion of the image and demonstrate how Lamelas is not only engaged in the act of staging a photograph, but also staging the body for a photograph, which has been a primary concern for artists since photography's invention. The words "Think of Good" are stacked like bricks one on top of another, but they do not seem to add up to a singular statement. It is not clear if the message is directed at the rock star or the audience.

Lamelas's insertion of himself into this lead role is itself an act of appropriation; it refers to his earlier project entitled *Rock Star (Character Appropriation)*, executed in 1974. The suite of seven black-and-white self-portraits depicts Lamelas miming in the distinctive rock aesthetic of the period—loose, long hair and skintight jeans—and are taken from the angle of a fan gazing up at the stage. The terms Lamelas uses to describe both the billboard and the earlier rock star incarnation have little to do with acting or role-play, but rather with what he astutely labels character appropriation. Lamelas's billboard image points to two seemingly contradictory tendencies within Conceptual Art's critique of representation: the aspiration for a type of self-criticality (emancipation from the art world's dependency on cult or star status), and a full-scale assimilation of the technologies of both media and spectacle culture.

While Lamelas's billboard offers an image of an anonymous yet instantly recognizable figure, Yvonne Rainer presents an unattributed quote from one of film's most enduring icons, Marlene Dietrich, a German-born actress who became a Hollywood legend. Rainer's prodigious output over the past forty years crosses several spheres of art making. Her important work as both a choreographer and filmmaker radically infuses political consciousness into the fields of dance and independent filmmaking. Positioned back-to-back on Pico Boulevard, Lamelas's and Rainer's billboards are set in a recto-verso relationship, inviting comparisons on the use of image and language in Conceptual Art. On Rainer's billboard, the statement "I look good, I know / I can't hear, / I can't see / But I look good," is plainly printed. The black text against

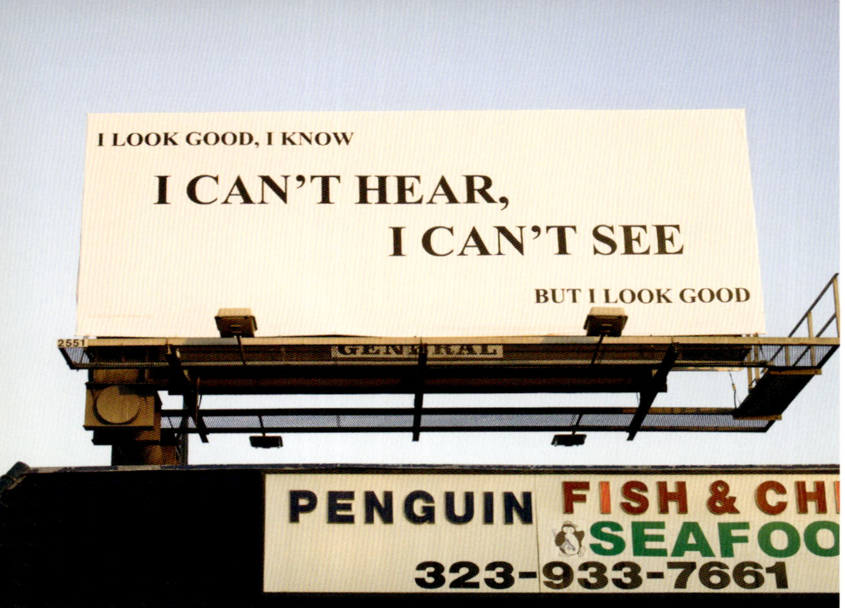

Looking Good by Yvonne Rainer for *How Many Billboards?*, 2010.

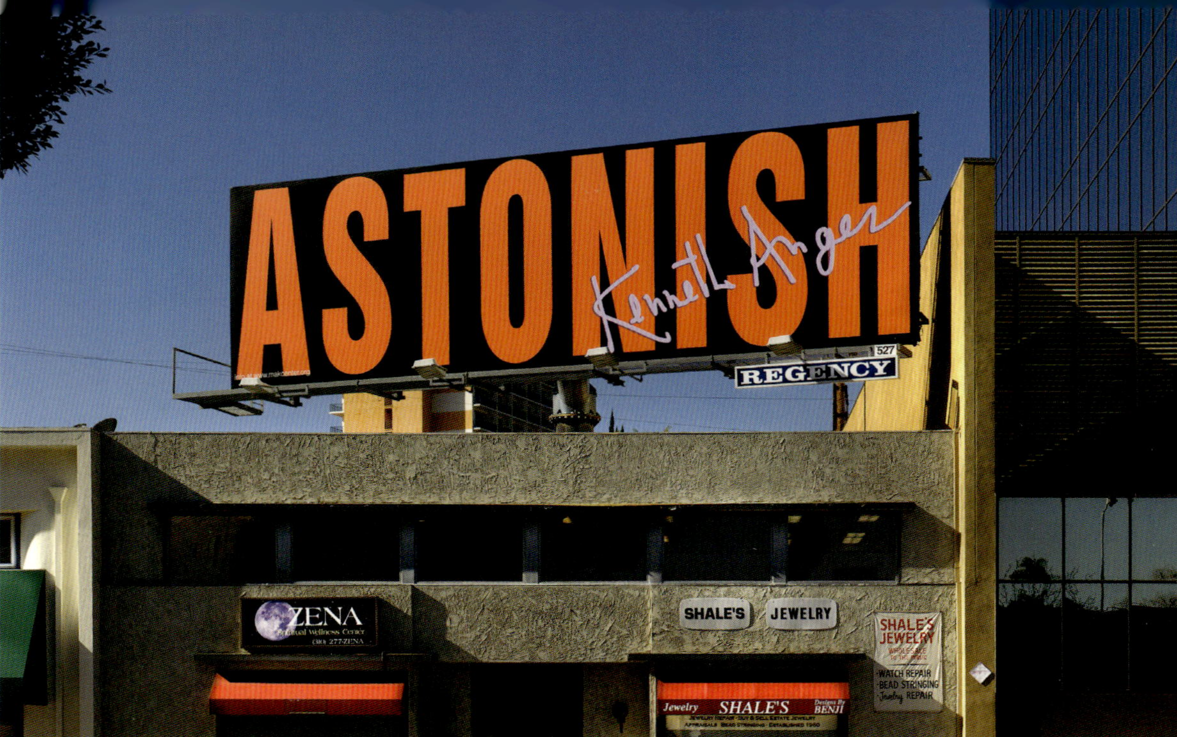

Kenneth Anger for *How Many Billboards?*, 2010.

a white background formally conveys a sense of "neutrality," which resists not only the hyperbole of design associated with advertising and publicity, but also the domination of images. I also think that her billboard suggests a new kind of reception in which the sensory experience is co-mingled with the theoretical. Rainer demonstrates that the specificity of art lies in its confrontation with the commodity form, albeit resisting its essential reification. However, using Dietrich's quote provides an injection of humor that allows Rainer to discreetly participate in another debate about image culture and the female body. In an industry constantly churning for new talent, Dietrich's enduring presence was exceptional and is often attributed to her ability to constantly reinvent herself both on screen and in the public's consciousness as an actress, entertainer, and an American patriot during World War II. Even during the last decade of her life, Dietrich continued to captivate the public imagination as the world's most fascinating recluse.

Rainer's quotation of Dietrich reflects the artist's longstanding use of voiceover and inter-titles in many of her films, and her appropriation of whole texts (literary, cinematic, and philosophical) by other authors into her screenplays as ways of further distancing her work from the illusionistic imperatives of traditional narrative filmmaking. *The Man Who Envied Women* (1985), one of Rainer's most popular films, maximizes this technique of textual appropriation to deliver an incisive account of artistic and intellectual pretension that invites the audience to find the humor in acts of self-importance. Foregrounding society's avoidance of the subject of menopause, *Privilege* (1990) is one of Rainer's more explicitly feminist films; it addresses the process by which women's bodies are coveted in youth but marginalized in older age. This very process seems to be reinforced by the Dietrich quote on Rainer's billboard. The female body's failure to hear or see does not matter as long as it continues to look good.

Kenneth Anger has trafficked in the collective mythology of Hollywood cinema and the theme of ritual transformation that is particular to American culture since his debut film *Fireworks* (1947), a pre-Stonewall examination of homosexuality, violence, and American youth. Anger's work has been vital to the radical invention of filmmaking as an avant-garde art practice that produces rather than consumes film, and remains conscious of the ideological issues surrounding self-representation within an industry designed to manufacture myth. For instance, his films *Scorpio Rising* (1963) and *Kustom Kar Kommandos* (1965) feature gay motorcycle and customized car subcultures in a manner that short-circuits sexual codes from both mainstream and underground filmmaking. In Anger's indelible films, hyperbolic images of masculinity function not only as visual icons or indices of desire but also as affective strobes designed to mesmerize the viewer while destabilizing sexual identity. Anger's filmic representations of leather clad men also mine the cultural potency of rock and roll, appropriating the sexual doubleness of performers such as Mick Jagger (no doubt just the "type" of male performer that Lamelas also had in mind). At the same time, Anger uses the established rhythms of popular rock music in his soundtracks to drive much of the film's energy, so that there is a constant tension between the subversive or "exotic" imagery depicted on film and the familiar refrains of conventional popular culture.

Anger's studied ability to simultaneously celebrate and satirize is used to full effect in *How Many Billboards?* Anger blows up the word "ASTONISH" to fill the horizontal expanse of his billboard; a sober, sans serif font mitigates its flashy, neon orange hue. The meaning of "astonish" remains ambiguous and polyvalent. It echoes Anger's filmic strategy of using fast paced montage sequences to annunciate what cannot be fully or completely articulated (desire, for example). The speed of the edits generates a type of flash effect that keeps the audience on edge. In this case, the word narrates the action that is taking place while the viewer reads the billboard, collapsing conventional art historical distinctions between affect and critical distance. Even as Anger's cinema proposes itself as a subversive alternative to mainstream Hollywood fare, the two are intrinsically linked through a shared sense of duplicity. Perhaps more than any other underground film, *Scorpio Rising* has experienced wide circulation and become a pop culture icon itself, responsible for the growth of the motorcycle film genre in the sixties (as exemplified by *Easy Rider* [1969]). "ASTONISH" also recognizes film's ability to astound, both in terms of the mercurial pace of celebrity culture and media's power over the public. Anger's lavender signature, which hovers diagonally across the lower right corner, only heightens this sense of duality. Commonly standing in for presence, Anger's signature plays on the Modernist gesture of signing an artwork—proof of the artwork's authenticity—and the notion of the celebrity autograph. Blown-up and illuminated by spotlights at night, the scale and retail function of billboards amplify the process of commoditization and reflect the larger cultural transaction that has taken place.

In *How Many Billboards?* viewers contend with being part of an atomized, dispersed audience and in the process new forms of mutuality occur. This practice attempts to mitigate—or at least triangulate—the reductive dichotomy between the "art market" and "the academy" as the only two designated spheres of aesthetic discourse in the current moment. Forty years after Debord's prophetic account of the autocratic reign of the market (which by 1967 was already forty years in the making), art critics and historians still seem to be describing the critical reception of their work in terms of a waning sense of power. But when was criticality the dominant mode? One element common to all of the billboard projects is that through interfacing via an unknown public, artists no longer rely on the Duchampian maneuver in which the audience "completes" the work of art (nor do they depend on any of the other Modernist antecedents often used to frame Conceptual Art). By mounting artworks *on* and *as* billboards, meaning is produced through the breaks or gaps in the perceptual system of late capitalism. Their reception is consummated by a collectivity in a constant state of distraction.

Like many of the individual projects included in the exhibition, *How Many Billboards?* attempts to move beyond the rhetoric of subversion as the only maneuver for art in the current moment. Mounting artworks on and as billboards is clearly not a new gesture, nor are the resulting billboards for the most part aiming towards a radical position resisting commoditization. The artwork is not extractable from its market or communicative contexts. Instead of conceptualizing the current spectacle culture in terms of encroachment—a measurable tide of images—it is the ecology we operate within. What has changed in the past forty years is that media saturation is no longer an external condition. For this reason, McLuhan's notion of an interface as a means of interaction becomes not only intriguing, but also a critically viable way of rethinking the terms of medium specificity and media overload. The viewer's tendency to scan rather than read is not limited to the news or the Internet; all forms are now subject to what has become an instinctive response to the visual environment. The attenuating work for critics and historians is to mine the subtler ways in which subjectivity conceptually reflects our changing information systems. Within the framework of *How Many Billboards?* it is about the mutability of images and media, or more precisely, images as media.

1. *A Report on the Art and Technology Program of the Los Angeles County Museum of Art, 1967–1971*, organized by Maurice Tuchman (Los Angeles: Los Angeles County Museum of Art, 1971). The entire catalog has been reproduced for LACMA's online reading room, which presents out-of-print material. Available at http://www.lacma.org/art/collections.aspx.

2. Alexander Alberro, ed., "Reconsidering Conceptual Art, 1966–1977," *Conceptual Art: A Critical Anthology* (Cambridge, MA: MIT Press, 1999), xvii.

3. Silton's thin vertical stripes alternately conceal and reveal her billboard's underlying text: "If I Say So." This quote is attributed to a 1961 telegram in which Robert Rauschenberg stated, "This is a portrait of Iris Clert if I say so."

4. Fredric Jameson, *The Cultural Turn: Selected Writings on the Postmodern, 1983-1998* (London: Verso, 1998), 112.

5. Krauss maintains that the linguistic form of Joseph Kosuth's analytical propositions "would merely signal the transcendence of the particular, sensuous content of a given art, like painting or photography, and the subsumption of each by that higher aesthetic unity—Art itself—of which any one is only a partial embodiment." Rosalind Krauss, *"Voyage on the North Sea": Art in the Age of the Post-Medium Condition* (London: Thames and Hudson, 1999), 10.

6. Ibid., 12. Emphasis mine.

7. Ibid., 15.

8. The *Oxford English Dictionary* cites Marshall McLuhan's *The Medium is the Massage: An Inventory of Effects* (1967) as the source for defining the term "interface" in relation to interaction.

9. Marshall McLuhan and Quentin Fiore, *The Medium is the Massage: An Inventory of Effects* (New York: Bantam Books, 1967), 10. Written by McLuhan, the book's signature graphic presentation was designed by Quentin Fiore and coordinated by Jerome Agel.

10. Bornstein, as quoted in Ann Goldstein, "Between Bodies and Objects," *Jennifer Bornstein* (Los Angeles: Museum of Contemporary Art, 2005), 55.

THIS MUST BE THE PLACE

BY LISA HENRY

When I moved from New York City to Los Angeles in 1995, I discovered that some of the clichés about Los Angeles really are true—the light is different and so many sunny days occur in a row that people forget what season they are in. At the same time, the city truly is sprawling and full of billboards. As revealed in aerial photographs of the city—from Ed Ruscha's *Parking Lots* (1967) to David Maisel's recent *Oblivion* series (2004)—Los Angeles is a horizontal, car-centric expanse that appears to stretch out forever in all directions. However, while one is bombarded by a lot of corporate advertising, the buildings, homes, and storefronts are so low that one can always see lots of sky above.

The overarching goal for *How Many Billboards? Art In Stead* was to have commissioned artworks displace corporate ads on billboards. We hoped that the new billboards would act as portals into the artists' visions, and give drivers and pedestrians a chance to pause and consider the visual information that is constantly vying for their attention. The artists' billboards are viewable 24 hours a day, seven days a week. They are bathed in sunlight—or haze—during the day, and dramatically illuminated at night.

Because of the ubiquity of corporate billboards in Los Angeles, the works in the exhibition are sometimes hard to identify. The bold and simple design of Kenneth Anger's billboard, for example, achieves the slickness of a teaser ad intended to pique the public's curiosity about a new product or fashion accessory. In contrast, works by Allan Sekula and collaborators Martha Rosler and Josh Neufeld disarm the viewer with their striking political messages. Sekula's "Los Ricos Destruyen el Planeta" (The rich destroy the planet), and Rosler and Neufeld's critique of state spending on prisons in comparison to public schools, each come out of the artists' longstanding critical practices. Eileen Cowin's combination of image and text alludes to the undercurrents of human relationships. The Arabic text on lauren woods's billboard is beautifully scripted, yet the words are mute to the majority of viewers, who cannot read the language. Billboards by Christina Fernandez and Kira Lynn Harris invite viewers to consider Los Angeles as a site—as a landscape and an urban community. The contributions of James Welling and Kerry Tribe draw attention to the light and space that is unique to Southern California. Tribe's elegiac photograph of gathering storm clouds presents a dramatic contrast to the myth of sunny California, while Welling's graphic abstraction invokes the glamour of Hollywood spotlights.

The participating artists share various institutional links. Many attended the same art schools and some of the billboard artists, including Sekula, Welling, and Michael Asher, are members of the faculty where several of the younger artists in the exhibition completed their training. The unique dynamism of art education in California—which has helped to shape a significant body of artworks and made Los Angeles a key destination for art students, as well as practicing artists—offers a useful lens through which to view the artworks in the exhibition.

For the last 40 years or more, California art programs have cultivated an environment for Conceptual Art that has its own distinct character, yet continually renews itself. Artist/instructors such as John Baldessari and Asher initiated the groundbreaking, "post-studio" approach to teaching art at the graduate level at California Institute for the Arts (CalArts) in Valencia, and the University of California, Los Angeles (UCLA). Over the years, MFA programs throughout the University of California and California State University systems, as well as private universities and art schools including Otis College of Art and Design, University of Southern California, and Art Center, have hired artists who are interested in new media, found objects, and unconventional methods of display. Much of the work produced by faculty and students associated with these schools can be seen as a distinctive type of West Coast Conceptualism that mixes Pop Art, humor, experimentation, and art theory. By downplaying grades and treating students like peers, these California schools attract faculty and students who question assumptions about art and academia. In addition, many of these artist/instructors and students are as invested in political struggles for social justice as they are in creating new forms of art.

A number of seminal figures in contemporary art, including Baldessari, Robert Heineken, Betye Saar, who taught at Otis, and Larry Sultan, are (or were) based in California. Looking at their work in the region as teachers brings insight to works produced by their students and colleagues. *How Many Billboards?* contributor James Welling participated in this experimental form of education at an early stage as one of Baldessari's students at CalArts. Perhaps partly as a result of his experiences there, Welling embraces chance and experimentation, and continually pushes the boundaries of what a photograph can be. Welling now teaches photography at UCLA, and extends these principles to upcoming generations of artists. Heineken, who designed the photography curriculum at UCLA in 1961, was one of the artist/instructors who

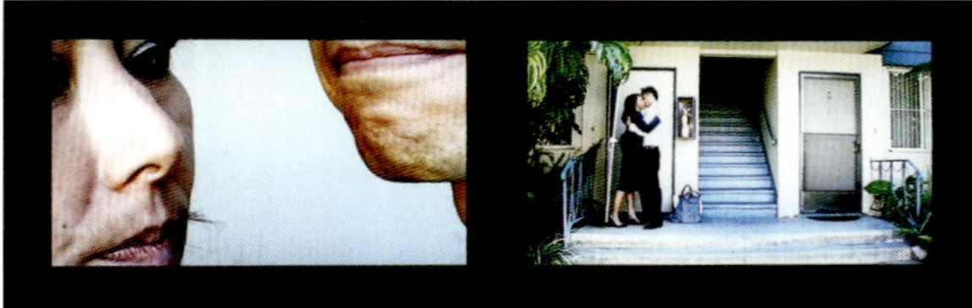

Eileen Cowin
Video still from *When the Sky is Falling I want to think about love*, 2008
Two-channel video
Courtesy of the artist

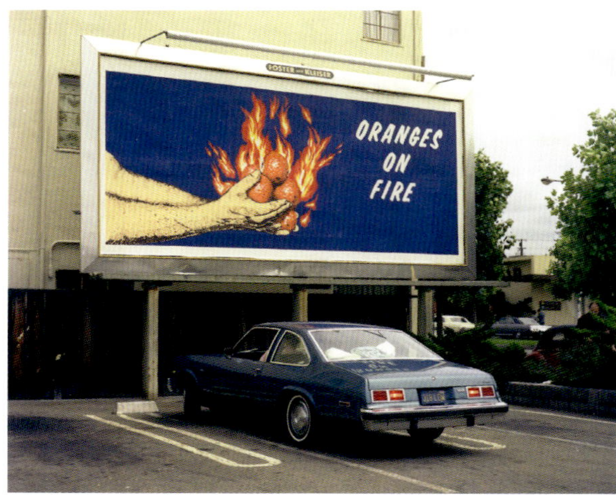

Larry Sultan and Mike Mandel
Oranges on Fire, Billboard installed in San Francisco, CA, 1976
Courtesy of Mike Mandel and the Estate of Larry Sultan.

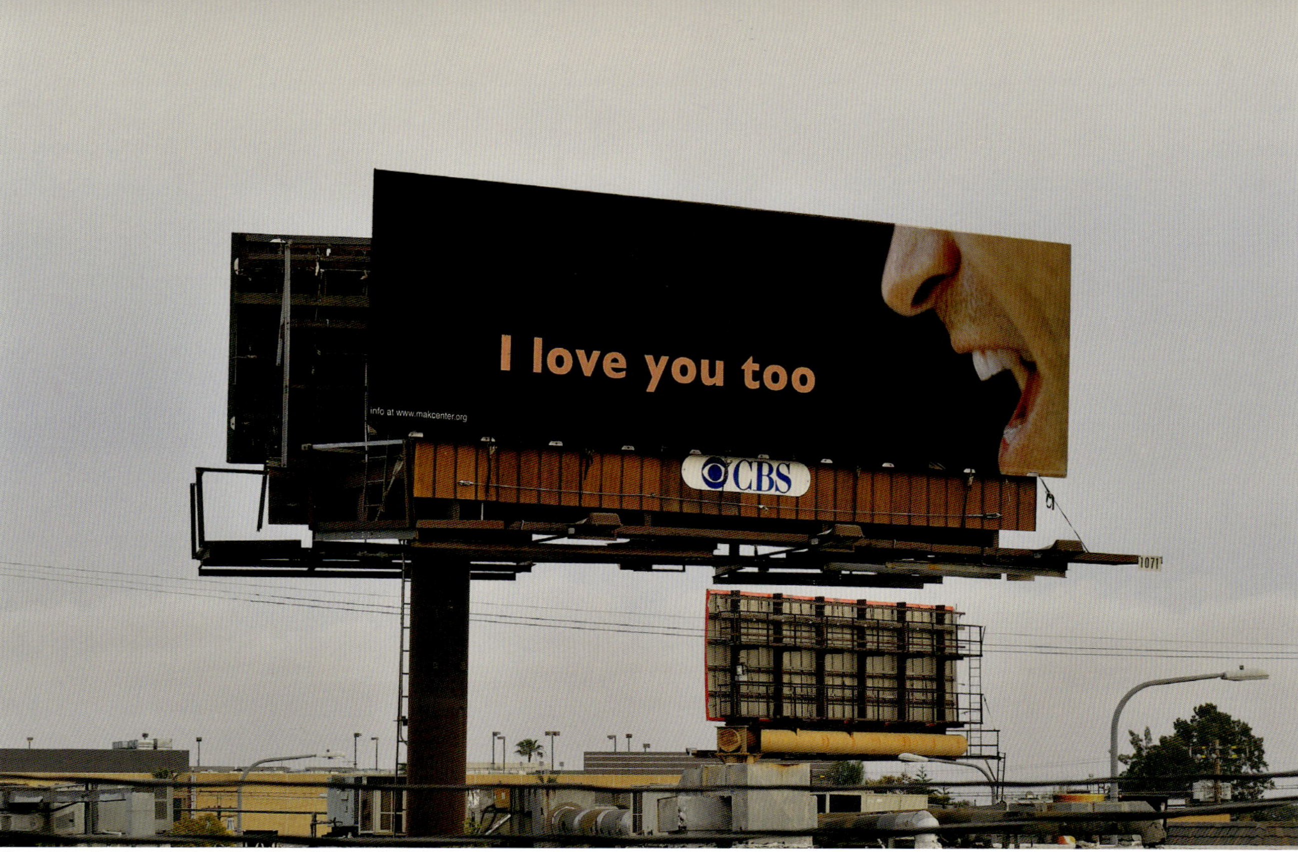

I love you too by Eileen Cowin for *How Many Billboards?*, 2010.

were instrumental to the development of West Coast Conceptualism in the 1970s and 1980s. Heineken is widely known for his manipulated photographs that incorporate magazine images and double exposures.

Sultan, who taught at the California College of the Arts until his death in 2009, was considered an important professor in the Bay Area. In collaboration with Mike Mandel, Sultan made the photographic book *Evidence* (1977). Consisting of found and reassembled photographs culled from public institutions and corporations, *Evidence* struck a powerful cord for artists using photography. Sultan and Mandel also collaborated on influential billboards during the mid-1970s that critiqued California's image of itself during a time of national uncertainty and skepticism. In the 1980s, Sultan embarked on a number of projects focusing on his family, including *Film Stills from the Sultan Family Home Movies, 1943-72,* (printed by the artist in 1985) and his well-known *Pictures from Home* (1982-92). Combining family photographs and video with his portraits of his retired parents, Sultan chronicled their suburban California existence. Sultan was a close colleague of many Southern California artist/instructors, including *How Many Billboards?* artist Eileen Cowin. Cowin remarks, "He produced a number of highly influential bodies of work. As an instructor I always showed his work to my students."[1]

While to my knowledge he has not taught at any of the region's art schools, Ed Ruscha's singular presence in Los Angeles since the 1960s has rendered him a permanent touchstone for West Coast Conceptual Artists. His influence on *How Many Billboards?* is palpable. For example, Jennifer Bornstein's billboard features an etching of a larger-than-life film projector presenting the words: "The End." Her image nods to Ruscha's painting *The End* (1991), which shows the same phrase in a similar, Gothic font. Ruscha's deadpan photographs and commercial art techniques have been jumping off points for succeeding generations of L.A.-based artists. The exhibition, like much of Ruscha's works, observes and quantifies the vernacular signage of a city built for cars.

The opportunity to "take back" some of the commercial spaces reserved for corporate ads and replace them with art came with challenges. The artists and curators struggled with the importance of making room for individual creative voices, and not simply supplanting corporate advertising with "ads for art." As a strategy for differentiating her project from advertising, lauren woods eliminated all traces of figurative representation and concentrated on the billboard as text. The artist

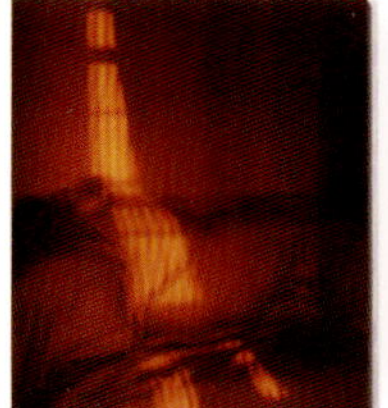
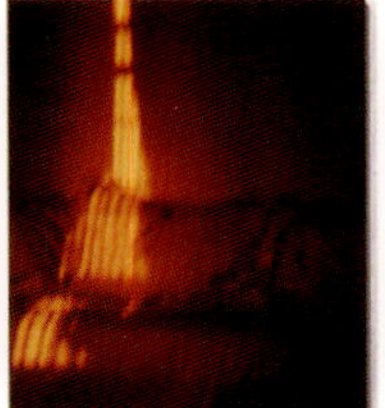
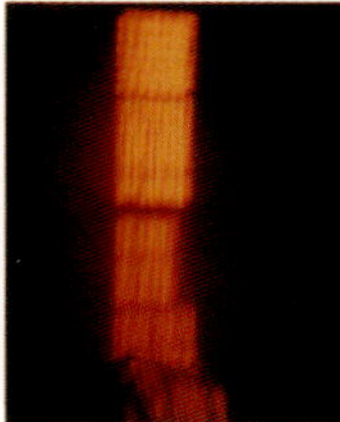

Kira Lynn Harris
Sunrise, Harlem (Installation view), 2003
Series of digital C-prints
20 inches x 20 inches (each)
Courtesy of the artist

is particularly sensitive to what she sees as the pitfalls of sounding like the voice of God in the name of Art, and of making yet another artful ad. Woods cites the powerful and persuasive works of Barbara Kruger, an influential artist and professor at UCLA, which borrow the language of advertising to make provocative social statements. But woods felt uncomfortable using the authoritative tone of advertising to make an artistic statement, even for a message that she felt passionate about. Her clearly wrought yet complex solution was to quote an Urdu poem by Vali Dakhni using Arabic text. With her use of a foreign language, woods captures the attention of viewers, including a segment of the population who fears Middle-Eastern cultures as a threat to America. It is the artist's hope that viewers will be curious enough to seek out what the words mean. (As with all of the works, an address for the exhibition's website is printed at the bottom of her billboard; an English translation of the poem can be found there.) Many viewers, regardless of their political views, would likely be sympathetic to the sentiment and universal themes alluded to in Dakhni's two-line verse:

As long as the earth and the sky last,
Smile like a flower in the garden of the world.

Woods's use of text as image refers back to a long tradition in Conceptual Art. At the same time, the meaning of the poem shares an affinity with a history of American optimism currently symbolized by President Obama.

Taking a different tack, Eileen Cowin's billboard combines figure with text. She pares both elements down to the point where their juxtaposition is jarring. The text of Cowin's piece—"I love you too"—is presented clearly using a simple typeface. Yet, a white man shown in cropped profile appears to be yelling the words. As a result, the familiar phrase suddenly sounds ambiguous and unsettling. Like her billboard text, Cowin's two-channel video *When The Sky is Falling, I Want to Think about Love* (2008), at first appears to convey a gentle sentiment, but the visual tableaux soon reveal the awkwardness of human interaction and the universal problem of miscommunication:

In my artistic practice I shift between photography, installation and video. One of the definitions of shift "is to change gears in a motor vehicle" and I like to think of myself as changing gears and using underhanded methods."[2]

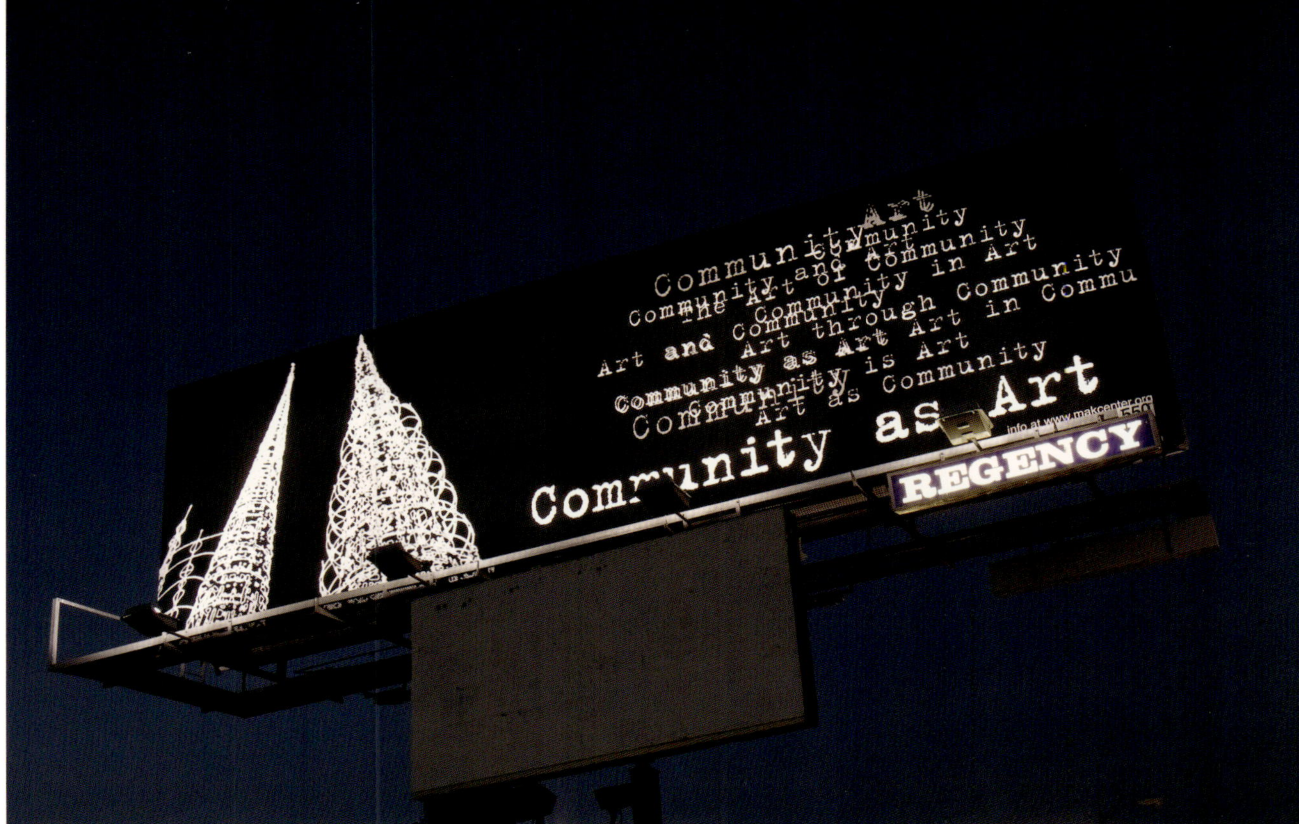

Untitled (The Towers) by Kira Lynn Harris for *How Many Billboards?*, 2010.

In this case, Cowin's subversiveness lies in combining tender words with an image that bristles with hostility. Both her billboard and video comment on the fragility of romantic relationships, while walking a fine line between "real emotion," lived memory, and photographic construction. Cowin meets the challenge of creating a captivating billboard by simplifying her text and imagery. She uses ambiguity to connect with the driver or pedestrian who might suddenly look up and have an encounter with her work.

The importance of tone and reception are also key elements of Kira Lynn Harris's text-and-image billboard. Many of her earlier photo-based works are striking in their use of lush color and glowing light to symbolize a sense of place and subtly refute the notion that the urban environment is gritty, as opposed to beautiful.[3] Harris, who now lives in New York, studied at CalArts

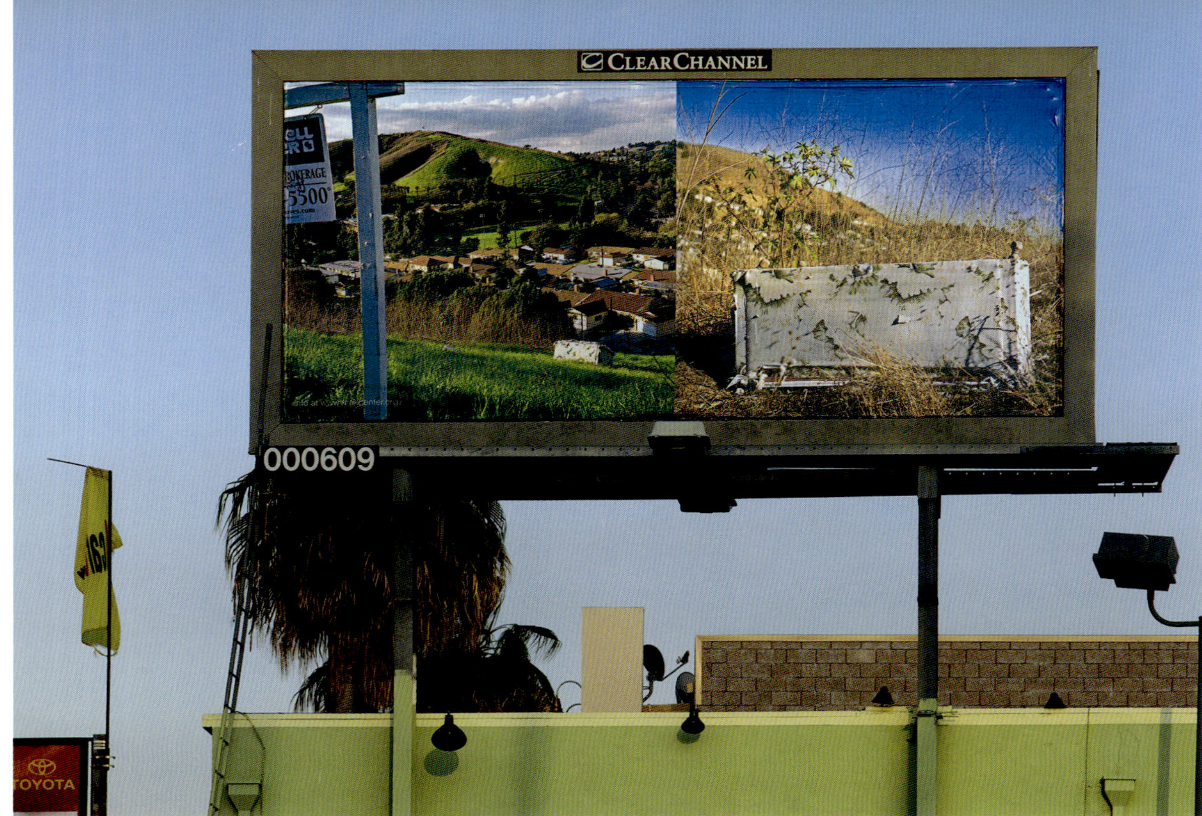

Coldwell Couch by Christina Fernandez for *How Many Billboards?*, 2010.

with Conceptual Artist Charles Gaines. For her contribution to *How Many Billboards?*, Harris embraced the opportunity to design a billboard in her native Los Angeles as if it were an ad for art.

In her depiction of the Watts Towers, Harris's billboard emphasizes the concept that combining art and community can not only create masterpieces, it can also form a foundation for personal expression and social activism:

I liked the idea of using the billboard as advertising for a value, or set of values, rather than a product. I also liked the idea of re-calling the viewer's attention to a very positive aspect of the Watts community. In talking with Rosie Lee Hooks, the Executive Director [of the Watts Towers Art Center], and with Edgar Arceneaux of the Watts House Project, I realized that focusing attention on the towers (and surrounding community) could be a good thing. And now I've just learned that Watts Towers Art Center is being threatened with closure because of the state and city budget crises.[4]

Harris's white text, rendered in an antiquated typewriter font, repeats and recombines the words "art," "through," "of," "as," and "community." The phrases slightly overlap in a fashion that mimics the delicate tracery of three Rodia spires pictured on the left side of the billboard. The resulting statements advocate "Community in Art," "Art through Community" and most vividly, "Community as Art."

While the billboards of woods, Cowin, and Harris rely on text and notions of "voice," photographer Christina Fernandez jettisons words all together for her contribution to the exhibition. Fernandez, who attended CalArts and UCLA, explores the political and visual aspects of landscape photography. Since the mid-1990s, she has developed a unique vision that integrates the documentary style of the New

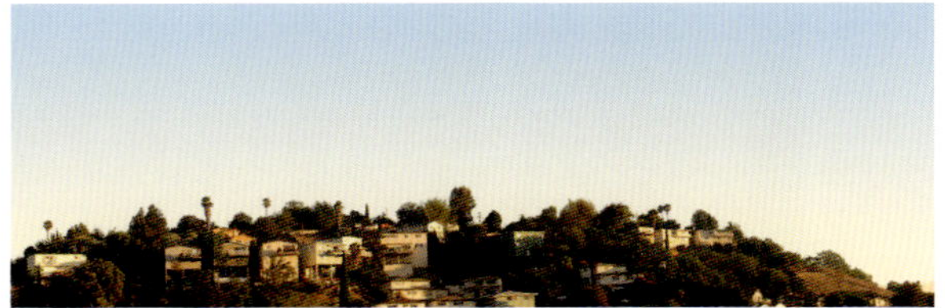

Christina Fernandez
View From My House Facing South, from Hilltops of El Sereno, 2010
Courtesy of the artist

Topographics photographers of the 1970s with ethnicity, class, and gender issues. With her widely known series *Lavanderia* (2002-03), Fernandez reveals links between the personal and historical in underrepresented neighborhoods of East Los Angeles.

Fernandez's billboard, titled *Coldwell Couch,* consists of two square-format photographs that view the geography of her El Sereno neighborhood from distinct vantage points. The horizon lines of the two images align perfectly, which at first glance makes the board appear to be a continuous panorama. However, after a moment the viewer becomes aware that the two photographs, though recording the same site, were shot from different angles at different times of the year. Fernandez uses clean, frontal images that evoke the signature style of Lewis Baltz, a photographer associated with the New Topographics movement who has taught at CalArts and a number of campuses within the UC system. Fernandez considers Baltz a major influence, yet she expands on his deadpan picture-making style to include visual dialogues between her working-class identity and the topography of Los Angeles, while being mindful not to objectify her subjects. Fernandez cites Baltz's series *San Quentin Point* (1982-1983) and *New Industrial Parks* (1974) as touchstones: "Lewis's work in San Quentin always juxtaposes the far apart and the near…but my work starts from my roots and it comes from my place as a Californian, my family's immigrant history, and [my role] as a mother."[5] Fernandez's billboard uses a battered and abandoned couch on a vacant lot to reflect upon her own neighborhood, and to comment on the continuing housing crisis and recession that is happening across the country.

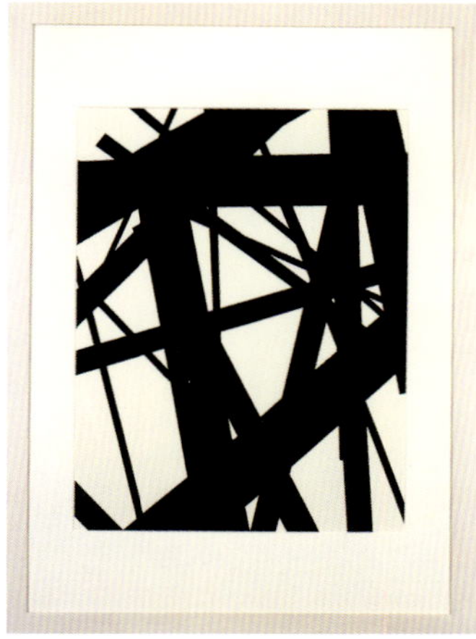

James Welling
Untitled #1A (New Abstraction), 1998
Gelatin silver print
35 x 27 inches, Ed. of 3
Courtesy of Regen Projects, Los Angeles
© James Welling

James Welling's billboard also relies on an image alone. Expanding on his current photogram series, the abstract image is strikingly evocative. A horizontal black space is shot through with blue and greenish-yellow diagonal lines of varying widths. The crisscrossing shards echo the klieg lights that symbolize Hollywood film premieres. Welling's photograph recalls *Large Trademark with Eight Spotlights* (1962), Ruscha's famous rendering of the 20th Century Fox logo surrounded by intersecting spotlights. Coincidentally, Welling's billboard is placed right above a Chevron gas station, and the artist's graphic image meshes perfectly with the blue and white of Chevron's corporate marquee. Though the billboard locations were not known in advance, the serendipitous placement of Welling's piece for me also evokes Ruscha's seminal photography book *26 Gasoline Stations* (1962).

Welling has a comprehensive knowledge of photo history and a unique ability to find points of interest in works as disparate as those by 19th century French photographer Gustave LeGray and the photographs associated with New Topographics. Welling's work reveals longstanding interests in abstraction, subjectivity, and recording the built environment. L.A.-based photographer Mark Wyse sums it up well:

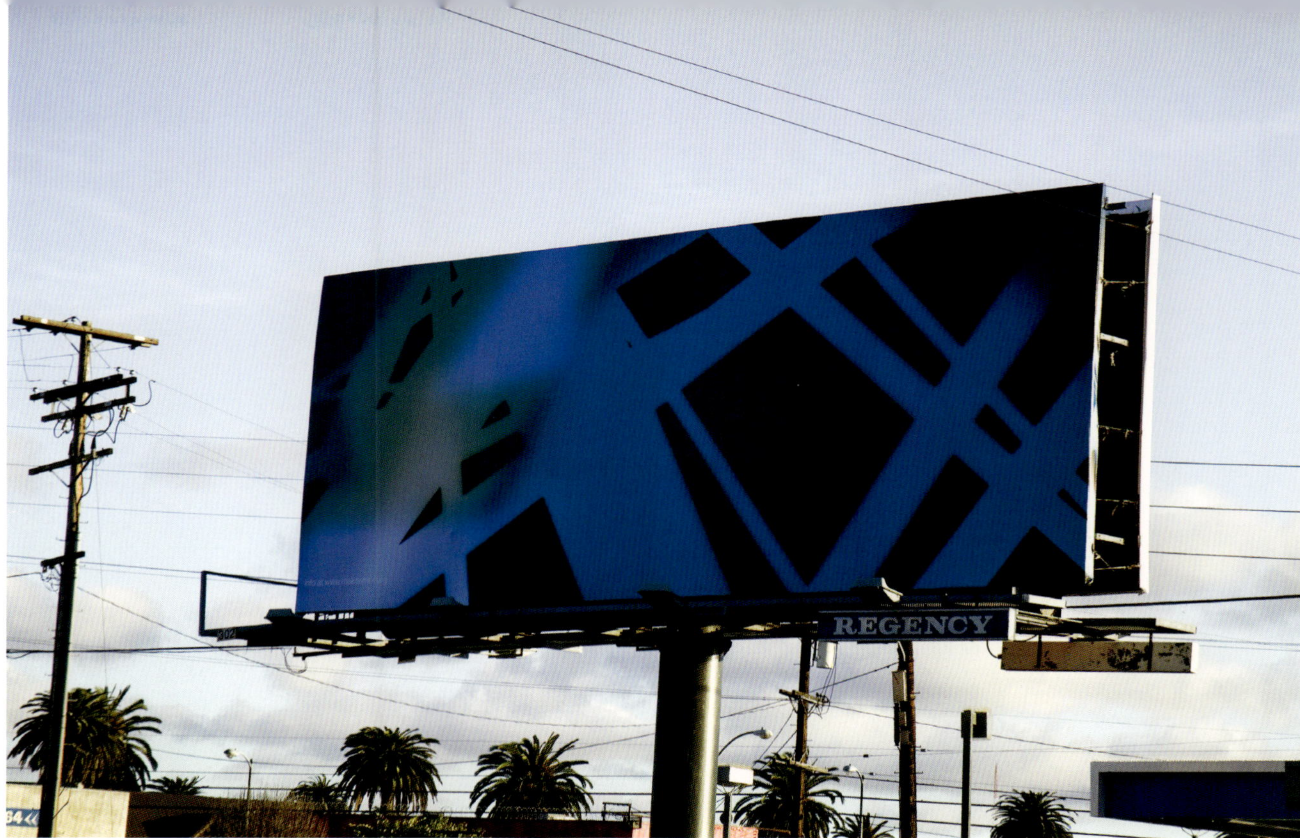

Minima Moralia by James Welling for *How Many Billboards?*, 2010.

Jim has a system that includes everything. Chance, accidents, and the whole history of photography.[6]

Welling discovered fine art photography near the end of his studies at CalArts. After happening upon a group of exceptional photogravures from the 1940s made in Mexico by Modernist master Paul Strand, Welling's art practice is said to have radically shifted. Since that time, he has made photographs that are often as elegant and technically skilled as any 20th century master, while simultaneously working to detach his images from a recognizable object and disassociate them from any particular moment in time.[7] This approach gives his work a highly polished appearance that is open to multiple interpretations. In this case, Welling's billboard signals diverse references—Ruscha's Conceptual Art, glamorous Hollywood spotlights, an ominous set of searchlights, and even Ocean Pacific Surfwear.[8]

The wide-ranging works in *How Many Billboards?* introduce emerging and historical figures of West Coast Conceptual Art to a broader public. Each billboard offers viewers an opportunity to pause and reflect on the act of looking in the midst of Los Angeles's ever-growing mediascape.

1. Conversation with Eileen Cowin, March 11, 2010.

2. Ibid.

3. Sandra Rowe, "From the Curator," *Urban Aesthetics*, exhibition brochure, California African American Museum, Los Angeles, 2003, unpaginated.

4. Email correspondence with Kira Lynn Harris, March 23, 2010. At the time of publication, a groundswell of community response in Los Angeles is rallying to keep the Watts Towers Art Center open.

5. Conversation with Christina Fernandez, January 21, 2010.

6. Conversation with Mark Wyse, March 16, 2010.

7. Douglas Eklund, *The Pictures Generation, 1974-1984* (New York: Metropolitan Museum of Art; New Haven and London: Yale University Press, 2009), 223.

8. From an observation by Gloria Sutton on James Welling's work, during a *How Many Billboards?* curatorial meeting, July 2009.

VISIBLE PROGRESS: Short Stories of Billboards and Los Angeles

BY JANET OWEN DRIGGS

I have some land on a major highway and wanted to use some wasted space for a billboard placement.
Message board post, Real Estate Investing Club, February 8, 2006

On the one hand, the history of billboards is a heroic tale in which technology and commerce advance the conjoined states of prosperity and democracy. This story starts circa 1450, when Guttenberg's invention of movable type launched "advertising in the modern sense…in the form of the handbill."[1] It continues with the invention of lithography, which made sophisticated illustration possible, and the advent of purpose-built roadside display boards. The bills were freed from their small scale in 1835 when posters of fifty square feet were achieved, and released from their local focus in 1900, when the billboard industry adopted standardized hoardings that encouraged nationwide campaigns.

As billboards spread across the country, City Beautiful proponents condemned willy-nilly erection as a threat to public virtue, lawsuits arose when billboards toppled, and public health concerns hovered around the hidden spaces behind.[2] The billboard industry's well-organized, professional body successfully resisted external regulation, however, by meeting in court all attempts at control with allegations that landowners were being unconstitutionally deprived of their private property rights. At the same time, outdoor advertisers were urged to secure goodwill by pursuing design excellence, "voluntary censorship," and active cooperation with "civic representatives and local officials."[3]

On the other hand, if one considers the forces that built and continue to shape Los Angeles, billboards can tell a rather more compelling story. For lurking behind the hoardings that now line our streets, one finds the far-reaching tentacles of a railroad, the growth of an orange industry and, in the shadowy back, the westward momentum of Manifest Destiny.

***

She saw…the galloping terror of steam and steel… its single eye, cyclopean, red, shooting from horizon to horizon…with tentacles of steel…the Octopus.[4]

While a murderous land dispute inspired these words about the Southern Pacific Rail Road (SPRR), "the Octopus," as it was known, rarely erupted into open violence. Instead, the railway's grip was maintained by thousands of instances of corruption, collusion, and litigation. For example, when California denied the railways certain tax rights that were bestowed on individuals, SPRR refused to pay taxes. The ensuing legal case wound up in the Supreme Court in 1886, when the judges, who included a close friend of SPRR owner Leland Stanford, found in favor of the railroad.[5, 6]

But for a headnote (a legal interpretation) written by a Court Reporter who had himself once owned a railroad, the 1886 case might have been forgotten.[7] The interpretation states that corporations enjoy the same rights as natural persons. SPRR's litigation consequently laid the foundation for advertisers to resist external control by citing First Amendment rights that were designed to protect human beings. In 1981, for instance, *Metromedia Inc. vs. San Diego* found a billboard ban in San Diego to be unconstitutional. Although subsequent judicial decisions have contradicted the case, it "remains the central First Amendment billboard authority,"[8] and it currently influences the billboard industry's relationship with Los Angeles. As a case in point, fear of litigation based on the *Metromedia* precedent underpins Los Angeles' 2002 moratorium on new billboards.[9] The moratorium is intended to give city officials "time to crack down on the forest of 10,000 billboards."[10]

In effect however, the moratorium continues to delay regulatory action while simultaneously protecting such industry giants as Clear Channel and CBS Outdoor from their smaller rivals. Further, the moratorium has neither prevented the installation of approximately 900 digital signs ("oil wells in the sky"[11]), nor prompted the removal of 4,000 illegal hoardings. Suggesting that there may be a new Octopus in town, Los Angeles' civic representatives, including Mayor Antonio Villaraigosa and at least thirteen of the city's fifteen council

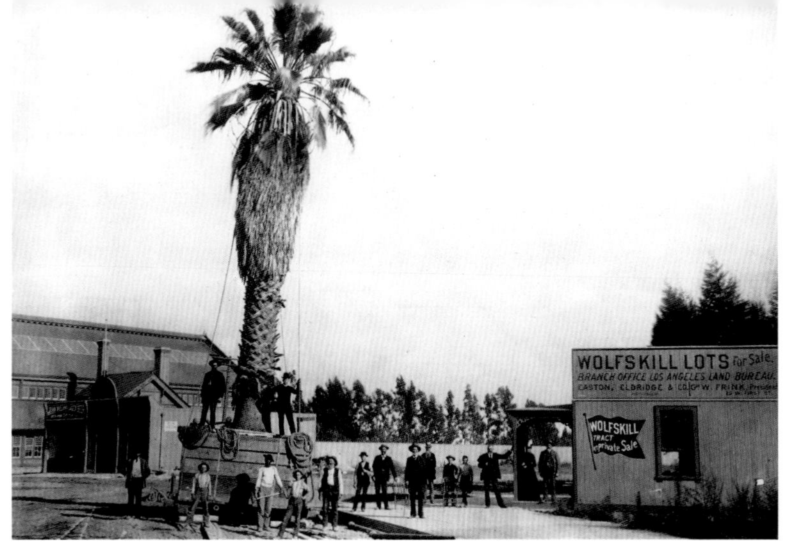

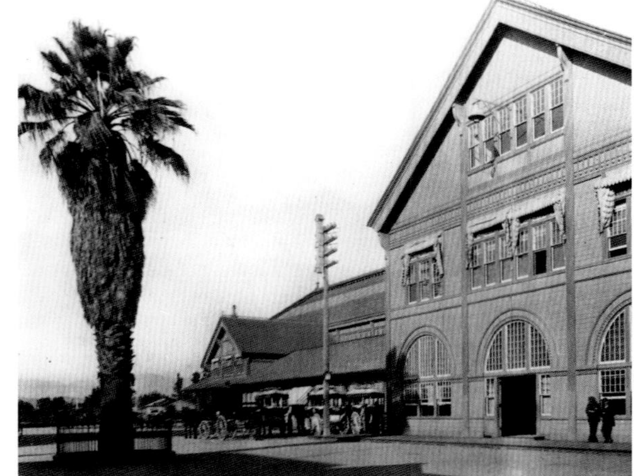

Far left: San Pedro palm being brought to Fifth Street and Central Avenue for depot, 1889
Courtesy of University of Southern California, on behalf of the USC Special Collections

Left: Pierce, C.C. (Charles C.), 1861-1946
Southern Pacific Arcade Station on Alameda Street between Fourth Street and Sixth Street
ca.1895-1900
Courtesy of University of Southern California, on behalf of the USC Special Collections

members, have "accepted campaign funds from the industry they have failed to regulate."[12]

***

The primary drivers of Los Angeles' late-19th-century growth are present in a photograph from 1889. Leaning toward the image center, a boxed palm tree dwarfs both the workers posing at its base and a building in the bottom right corner, where a rooftop billboard reads: "WOLFSKILL LOTS For Sale."[13] In 2010, this site is the Fifth Street and Central Avenue intersection in Downtown Los Angeles, but shortly before the picture was taken the land supported two thousand citrus trees planted by William Wolfskill, originator of the Valencia orange. The orchard was cleared when the Wolfskill family donated part of their land for a new SPRR passenger station and subdivided the rest for sale. Intended to substantiate the "Semi-Tropic California"[14] propaganda that was luring visitors to Los Angeles, the palm tree was the first thing that passengers saw as they stepped into the city.

***

In 1887, SPRR brought 120,000 visitors to Los Angeles and property values doubled. One billion acres of public land had been gifted to rail corporations during the construction of America's railroads and SPRR, which owned ten million acres of California, consequently had a vested interest in promoting Los Angeles' growth. Unfortunately for the corporation, however, by 1889 the real estate bubble had burst.

In response, SPRR engaged in the conjuring that Kevin Starr describes as "studied self-invention and exotic possibilities."[15] In its own magazines and others', at World's Fairs, in trams, on trains, on billboards, and on orange crates, SPRR and its citrus-growing partners portrayed Southern California as an Eden where the "climate for health and wealth"[16] nurtured the edible essence of life-giving sunshine itself—the orange. Forty million crates of Californian oranges were sold in 1900, by which time Los Angeles' population had doubled. But the city that "needed the adrenaline of boosterism to make the future seem plausible"[17] could not stop conjuring. With growers' cooperative Sunkist taking up the booster baton from SPRR, advertising for Southern California continued through the boom/bust cycles of the twentieth century.

***

Los Angeles is indebted to billboards in at least two ways. First, they were among the arsenal of advertising tools that turned Los Angeles into "America's Eden."

Second, in a car-centric city of now almost four million people, billboards might well be described as the tools by which Los Angeles propagandized itself to itself, and conjured the future into being.

Advertising arouses desire by promising redemption—the restoration of an imagined state of grace (health, wealth, virility, etc.). For 19th-century Americans, the concept of Manifest Destiny conflated the moral imperative of a post-lapsarian return to Eden's grace with the physical thrust of westward expansion. In the 21st century, both spiritual and literal journeys are conflated with the process of consumption. In this context, each act of consumption is a step toward grace. Yet, of course, we can never arrive. Instead, advertising reawakens desire and the attempt to achieve grace must be made again, and again, and so on.

Working to arouse desire, billboards turn otherwise unused walls, skies, and alleyways into agents of redemption. Tirelessly activating such apparently idle spaces as memory, imagination, and the peripheral vision of passers-by, and "so placed that everyone must absorb the advertiser's lesson, willingly or unwillingly,"[18] billboards turn the visual field into real estate and colonize the senses. Regardless of their content, the ongoing proliferation of billboards must beg the question: What kind of future are we conjuring?

1. Outdoor Advertising Association of America, http://www.oaaa.org/about/historyofoutdoor.aspx (accessed February 26, 2010).

2. Cason v. City of Ottumwa, Iowa, 1897, found the city liable for injury from a falling billboard.

3. Michelle H. Bogart, *Artists, Advertising and the Borders of Art* (Chicago: University of Chicago Press, 1995).

4. Frank Norris, *The Octopus: A California Story* (New York: Doubleday, Page & Co., 1903), 180.

5. *Santa Clara County v. Southern Pacific Railroad Company*, 118 U.S. 394 (1886). Notably, Justice Stephen J. Field was a crony of SPRR owner and former Governor of California Leland Stanford; Judge Lorenzo Sawyer had received his first judgeship from Stanford and remained a firm friend.

6. Richard Rayner, *The Associates: Four Capitalists Who Created California* (New York: W. W. Norton, 2008), 146, 164.

7. "The court does not wish to hear argument on the question whether the provision in the Fourteenth Amendment to the Constitution, which forbids a State to deny any person within its jurisdiction the equal protection of the laws, applies to these corporations. We are all of the opinion that it does." Headnote quoted in Doug Hammerstrom, "The Hijacking of the Fourteenth Amendment," *ReclaimDemocracy.org*, 2002, http://www.reclaimdemocracy.org/ (accessed February 25, 2010).

8. First Amendment Center, http://www.firstamendmentcenter.org (accessed April 2, 2010).

9. Because the city cannot find language to distinguish between commercial and artistic intent, the ban is also extended to murals. Information about this ongoing situation is available at: http://www.savelamurals.org.

10. Christine Pelisek, "Why L.A.'s Latest Billboard Fix Won't Work," *LA Weekly* C.ity News Blog, January 12, 2009, http://blogs.laweekly.com/ladaily/city-news/will-las-new-billboard-ordinan/ (accessed April 2, 2010).

11. Ibid. As comparatively profitable as an oil well, each digital billboard generates $128,000 per month for its owner.

12. Coalition to Ban Billboard Blight keeps an eye on illegal billboards and Los Angeles politician/billboard industry alliances. See http://banbillboardblight.org/.

13. Strictly speaking, billboards advertize goods and services that are available some distance away, while signs mark places at which the goods and services are actually available. It could be argued therefore that this is a sign, because land can be bought in the office concerned. However, because the land being sold is not inside but at some distance from the office, I have chosen to call it a billboard.

14. "In 1874, Major Ben C. Truman, who would go on to head the literary bureau of the Southern Pacific, called the region 'Semi-Tropical California.' A magazine called *Semi-Tropic California* pictured a verdant landscape of palms." Douglas Cazaux Sackman, *Orange Empire* (London and Berkeley: University of California Press, 2005), 29.

15. Kevin Starr, *Inventing the Dream: California through the Progressive Era* (New York: Oxford University Press, 1985).

16. Sackman, 37.

17. Starr, *Material Dreams: Southern California through the 1920s* (New York: Oxford University Press, 1990), 104.

18. Sackman, 97.

FAIR USE: Legal Issues Involving Speech and Copyright for Artists Using Outdoor Media

Interview with Christine Steiner Conducted by Joshua Decter

EDITED BY SARA DALEIDEN
INTRODUCTION BY JOSHUA DECTER
CONDUCTED IN-PERSON AT THE SCHINDLER HOUSE

The utilization of outdoor media platforms—whether based in analogue or digital technology—as "sites" for the articulation and/or display of artworks is not a new phenomenon. It has, in a sense, become a genre of curatorial practice in the public realm. One might even look back at Robert Venturi and Denise Scott-Brown's architectural tract, *Learning from Las Vegas* (1972), as an influence upon the development of curatorial and artistic strategies that re-appropriate and critically inflect (with permission/institutional sanction, or perhaps without) the manmade environment of roadside commercial advertising. To evoke Reyner Banham, perhaps the *How Many Billboards?* exhibition can only really be experienced through the rearview mirror (or, more precisely, through any available car window); i.e. a project that functions to re-mobilize and re-map our vision of Los Angeles, the city of flows. Here, a constellation of art projects developed for billboards (each a distinct, location-specific node) distributed across multiple urban territories might be imagined to operate as an urban acupuncture that re-activates—and engenders interconnectivities within—the discontinuous, hyper-spatialized enclaves of Los Angeles In the interview with attorney and legal scholar Christine Steiner that follows, however, the focus is upon matters that are not necessarily visible at street-level: the complex legal issues that both underpin, and are generated by, this type of exhibition.

Joshua Decter: Within the context of a project like the MAK Center's *How Many Billboards?*, what is the relationship between artistic and commercial speech?

Christine Steiner: Commerce and art speak the same language; they can inhabit the same place; they can use the same codes visually and textually. Commercial speech and artistic speech live in the same category as far as the law is concerned, which means that they can be regulated, but they can only be regulated for certain legitimate purposes. Commercial speech can be symbolic, and we regularly see advertising employing artistic strategies to sell a product. For example, if Yoko Ono takes out a full page ad in the *New York Times* saying "Imagine Peace," that is a very different kind of speech than if the army uses the phrase as a recruitment campaign, or if Blackwater uses it as the cover of its annual report. Generally speaking, it doesn't matter what the message is, the important consideration is the context. Context includes both speaker and place. The question is: Whose speech is it and where does the speech occur?

The law is concerned with property. It can be tangible,

such as land or personal goods, or intangible, that is intellectual property, such as copyrights. The First Amendment is concerned with both speech and property, and it protects expression, press, religion, assembly, and other categories for the public good. Within the category of speech, of which artistic speech is part, there is an interesting spectrum. There is pure speech, which protects opinions, politics, ideology, et cetera. There is symbolic speech, which includes actions, conduct, images, music, or anything that is a visual expression, and for our focus, it includes commercial speech as well. There is unprotected speech, which includes obscenity, child pornography, defamation, and the like, because the law says these fall outside the public good. So why does the law protect some speech over other speech, and how?

JD: If one of the artworks contains obscenity, are the artist's rights protected?

CS: Obscenity is never protected. However, pornography, lewd speech, and vulgar speech are protected. Obscenity is a narrow category of the law that says for public purposes, something is so far beyond what we as a society deem legitimate standards of decency that we are not going to give it *any* protection. In contrast, artists legitimately use lewd and vulgar speech as pure expressive speech, and that is deserving of protection. If the artist is relaying an opinion or a political view with that lewd and vulgar speech, it can be deemed legally expressive.

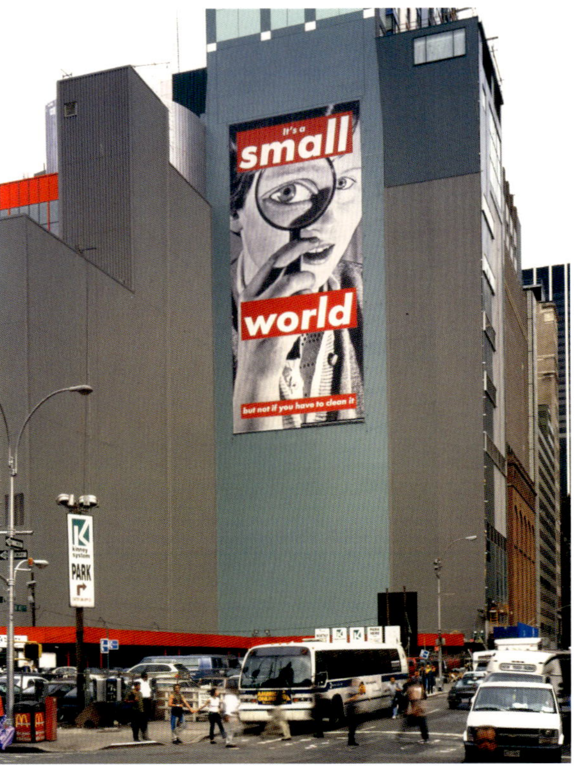

Barbara Kruger
Untitled (It's a small world but not if you have to clean it), 1990
Photographic silkscreen on vinyl
143 x 103 inches
Installed at the Hilton Times Square Hotel, New York City
Collection of The Museum of Contemporary Art, Los Angeles
Purchased with funds provided by the National Endowment for the Arts, a Federal agency, and Douglas S. Cramer
Courtesy of the artist

JD: What constitutes a clear copyright infringement? How is "fair use" a means of protecting the rights of artists in terms of questions of appropriation and copyright of images?

CS: Copyright is a property right like any other and it can be sold, leased, lent, or licensed. One infringes copyright of another when one uses the work without permission (a license) or without a legitimate defense. That's what fair use is, a legitimate defense to taking the property of another without permission. Fair use is akin to the First Amendment because it is in service of the public good on the theory that new work builds on old work. People cannot claim a right in something that is beyond their own creative expression. When a copyright infringement suit is filed, the courts look at four factors, known as the "fair use test" to assess the defense:

1) What is the purpose and character of the use?
2) What is the nature of the copyrighted work?
3) What is the amount and substantiality of the portion you use in relation to the whole?
4) What is the economic impact on the existing or potential market for the copyrighted work?

The pivotal factor for this discussion is the purpose of the use, what is called the transformative use. If you take someone else's work and you so transform it such that it is a new work, for a different purpose, to a different audience, in a new manner of expression, generally the courts are going to find that your new use is transformative and deny the copyright infringement claim. This means you are allowed to trespass over that property for your own purposes. The test is always a case-by-case test. Each time, you must evaluate those criteria against your purpose and context to determine whether your use is appropriate.

JD: What are legal precedents within art that have tested fair use and the First Amendment as they relate to provocative artistic speech?

CS: There was a significant case involving Barbara Kruger's work *It's a Small World But Not If You Have to Clean It* (1990). Kruger used a photograph published in the 1960s in a German magazine. She took the image, cropped it, enlarged it, and added her signature bold text. The work was in Kruger's exhibition that opened here in Los Angeles at The Museum of Contemporary Art (MOCA). When the exhibition traveled to the Whitney Museum in New York, the museum advertised the show with a multi-story reproduction of the image on a building wall. Not surprisingly, it drew the attention of the photographer and the subject of the photograph, both of whom lived in New York. They filed suit against Kruger, the Whitney, MOCA, WNET (which had a thumbnail sketch of the image on its website), MIT (the catalog publisher), Kruger's gallery, and a whole host of others as contributory infringers. The court found ultimately in favor of the artist (and the other defendants), concluding that "Kruger's composite itself is pure First Amendment speech in the form of artistic expression with [sufficient transformative elements] and deserves full protection." The court protected appropriation as speech when the new work sufficiently indicated a different purpose to a different audience. This decision was important because it provided guidance on copyright claims involving works of art.

Another well-known case involved Jeff Koons's *String of Puppies* (1988). There, Koons created a life-size sculpture of a couple with their puppies based on a photographic postcard copyrighted by plaintiff Ed Rogers. The court found that Koons's use was not protected because the court did not see a social purpose in Koons's use of Roger's work without asking his permission (i.e., a fair use). Koons asserted that the work was a parody of Roger's photograph, but the court didn't think Koons "parodied" Rogers. The court stated that the underlying work itself had to be the object of the parody and Koons's wasn't accomplishing this. In a subsequent case involving a work by Koons in the early 2000s, he was sued by another photographer whose work he appropriated. In this case, Koons prevailed, not on parody, but on transformative grounds. The court used the four-factor fair use analysis to declare that Koons had a "genuine creative rationale" for borrowing the photographer's work.

So, the case law is becoming clearer and stronger for protecting uses of appropriation for transformative purposes.

JD: How would you characterize the distinctions, on legal terms, between the legal protections afforded artists working in so-called public spaces, and those working in so-called private contexts?

CS: Public space, public money, public commissions all imply public choice and comment. And the public, as we know, may be different "publics" with different notions of where to draw those lines. It is a difficult task because government regulators, whether they are courts, the NEA, Congress, municipalities, or any other entity, have to impart some degree of objectivity to art, which is inherently subjective. These government regulators are not necessarily the best ones to make objective decisions, which is why courts are often overruled, why the culture wars happened in the late 1980s and early 1990s, and why controversies continue to arise. It is also the reason the laws go back and forth on these issues.

The private sphere does not have such challenges. Private commissions, and the commercial marketplace, for that matter, are generally free of public comment. Here, laws are concerned with matters of fairness in business transactions, but not with content restriction.

JD: Where and how does the law enter into a situation when artists engage in acts of guerrilla expression in public space, without tacit institutional support?

CS: In terms of permission, context is always the issue. Art itself can never be illegal. Where it is placed can make it illegal. This returns us to the discussion about property. Art can be illegal if it is placed in an impermissible context. It could, for example, violate trespass laws or be considered vandalism. Based on this, our city suppresses graffiti across the board, even though it has symbolic speech protection.

I find it fascinating that in Los Angeles we have clear, strong ordinances against graffiti that can be enforced criminally and civilly, but we don't have a strong system of zoning. Some municipal jurisdictions enforce zoning in better ways than others, which can lead to a more aesthetically pleasing environment. The city is full of commercial visual clutter. Some of the clutter is on the vulgar and lewd side of the speech spectrum, some of it entirely tasteful, but most of it is mediocre in the pursuit of commerce. The clutter is not at all enforced. Even though it is difficult to enforce aesthetics, it is possible to make subjectivity objective.

JD: Are there any artworks as part of *How Many Billboards?* that you think trigger any of the legal issues we've discussed in terms of artistic

speech, copyright infringement, or obscenity?

CS: The MAK Center's billboard exhibition places art in traditionally commercial spaces. While this exhibition is an elegant solution to visual blight, what's interesting for me, legally, is that the exhibition is no stranger to our understandings of property law. The billboards are either leased or licensed, the artists are selected pursuant to curatorial norms, and the artists were engaged pursuant to a commission agreement.

One legally interesting issue was Michael Asher's use of the Volkswagen Beetle advertisement from the 1960s. The ad, like any other, had a series of rightsholders—the auto company, the advertising company, perhaps others in the creative process. Of course, Asher is using the ad for a different purpose, a transformative purpose, so a taking without permission would trigger the case-by-case fair use test. And I expect he would prevail in this analysis and the use would be deemed fair. In the end, though, Asher sought and received permission from Volkswagen to utilize the ad because he needed the best, most faithful reproduction. So he went to the source.

One other legal issue involves lauren woods's work, which includes a line of poetry in Urdu that, as best as I can determine, is quoted without attribution. Now, my Urdu is not what it should be, and I assume I am not alone here. So, is it an infringement if most viewers do not know what they are seeing? In this case, of course, I expect fair use would permit the short quotation, but I do not know the length of the original work, or its other features.

Some of the non-legal issues we have discussed, the privatizing of public space and the public's right to comment, come into play. For example, some works use billboards for the conventional purpose—to sell

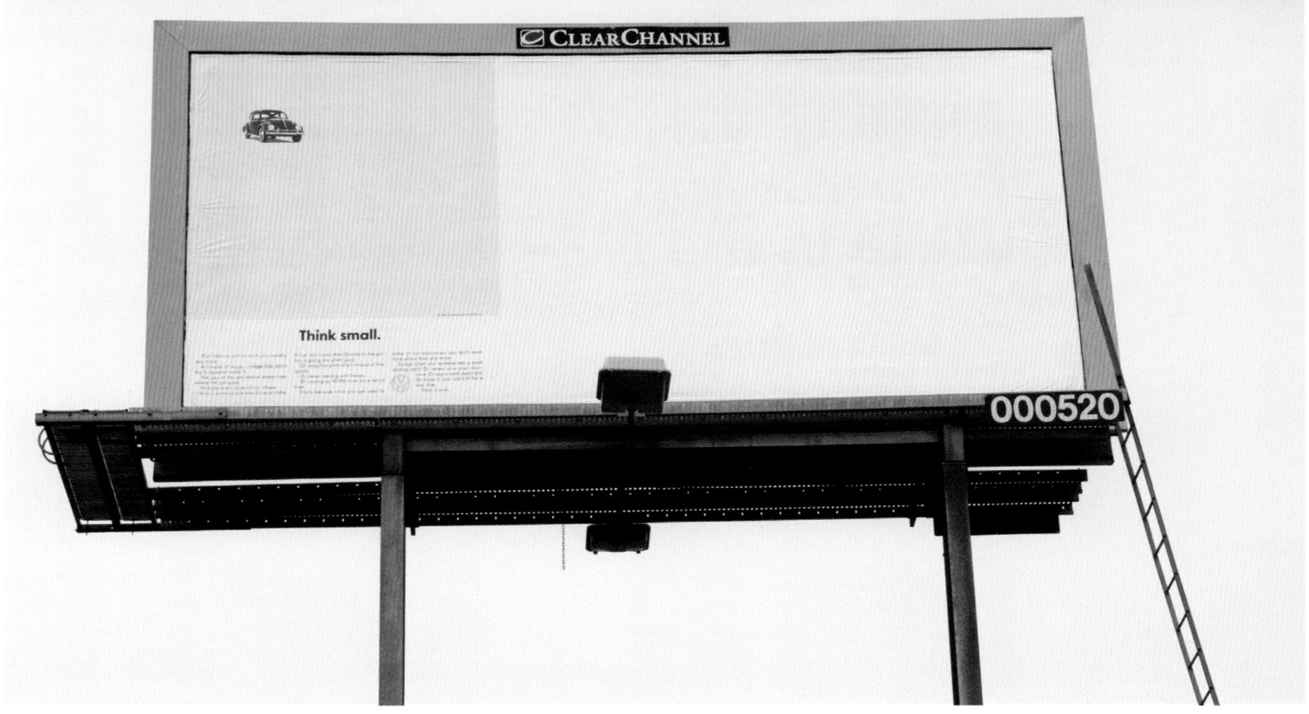

Michael Asher for *How Many Billboards?*, 2010.

something, to raise social or political awareness, to advertise an upcoming art exhibition, and the like. These messages subvert these traditional purposes, but allow the public to ask, "Is it art?"

I would like to make one final point about copyright. A party that commissions a work, such as the MAK Center for this exhibition, could be potentially liable for copyright infringement if an artist used the copyrighted work of another without permission or a favorable fair use analysis performed in advance. Copyright infringement asks who is responsible and how that liability is sorted out, and the speaker is generally liable. The artist is the speaker, but where the MAK Center commissioned the artwork, it is also the speaker. Copyright infringement runs both upstream and downstream; everyone in the line is potentially liable, either as a direct or a contributory infringer. So the MAK Center would certainly be responsible for resolving a question of copyright infringement before endorsing and displaying a work: Is it infringing, is it free speech, or is it fair use?

JD: The law and art: not such strange bedfellows after all. Thanks, Christine, for your trenchant insights into these complex issues.

The First Amendment to the U.S. Constitution

Congress shall make no law respecting an establishment of religion, or prohibiting the free exercise thereof; or abridging the freedom of speech, or of the press; or the right of the people peaceably to assemble, and to petition the Government for a redress of grievances.

Source: First Amendment Center,
http://www.firstamendmentcenter.org/about.aspx?item=about_firstamd
(accessed March 13, 2010)

Copyright Law of the United States of America in Title 17 of the United States Code Section 107.

Limitations on exclusive rights: Fair use—
Notwithstanding the provisions of sections 106 and 106A, the fair use of a copyrighted work, including such use by reproduction in copies or phonorecords or by any other means specified by that section, for purposes such as criticism, comment, news reporting, teaching (including multiple copies for classroom use), scholarship, or research, is not an infringement of copyright. In determining whether the use made of a work in any particular case is a fair use the factors to be considered shall include:

1) the purpose and character of the use, including whether such use is of a commercial nature or is for nonprofit educational purposes;
2) the nature of the copyrighted work;
3) the amount and substantiality of the portion used in relation to the copyrighted work as a whole; and
4) the effect of the use upon the potential market for or value of the copyrighted work.

The fact that a work is unpublished shall not itself bar a finding of fair use if such finding is made upon consideration of all the above factors.

Source: U.S. Copyright Office,
http://www.copyright.gov/title17/92chap1.html#107
(accessed March 29, 2010)

VISUAL RELIEF IN A BLANK BILLBOARD

Interview with Anne Bray
Conducted and edited by Sara Daleiden

CONDUCTED IN-PERSON AT FREEWAVES IN HOLLYWOOD

I know we live in a mass culture so I want to approach viewers personally. I know we operate in a commercial arena, so I want to exchange with them without a price tag. I know we exist in a society that is alienating in both its specialization and its conformity, so I want to encourage dialogue and inclusion. I want to offer challenges at low risk in a milieu which usually associates change with fear. Most importantly, I want to activate people's imaginations and critical sense simultaneously.
Anne Bray, *Art Paper* 7, 1988

Since the 1980s, Anne Bray has been a seminal producer of media art in public space. In addition to being an artist, Bray is the founding director of Freewaves, which sponsors new media festivals in Los Angeles that showcase experimental videos, films, and media art from around the world. In 2008, the 11th Freewaves Festival turned Hollywood Boulevard into a multi-layered screening room, contrasting perceptions of "Hollywood" as mega-entertainment industry against the actual, multi-faceted neighborhood of Hollywood. Entitled *Hollywould*..., the five-day festival perpetuated the organization's objective of inserting the alternative messages of experimental media artworks into mainstream commercial sites in order to question our relationship to culture and the built environment.

As panel series curator for *How Many Billboards?*, Bray organized and moderated two panels: *Visual Rights to the City* and *The Visual Ecology of Advertising and Architecture*. Bray designed both panels to encourage public discussion amongst lawyers, city planners, media corporations, journalists, scholars, activists, architects, artists, and audience members about current political debates surrounding billboards in Los Angeles. The following interview explores Bray's view of the dominant presence of outdoor commercial media and public art's potential to offer another form of speech.

Sara Daleiden: How would you describe Los Angeles' relationship with billboards?

Anne Bray: Did Los Angeles have billboards before housing? They came, they staked it with an ad, and then they settled into homesteading afterwards.

I think of billboards as the largest in a family of ads within the streetscape. Billboards, along with development in this city, are indicative of the high priority Los Angeles has given to commercialism. Land development is more important than community. Advertising is more important than visual environment. It has been this way since the city was formed—over 150 years of commercial priorities.

In 2007, several major billboard companies reached a settlement with the City of Los Angeles, which allowed them to begin legally converting over 850 static traditional billboards into the upgraded technology of digital LED billboards throughout the city. This was in the face of a ban on new billboards that has been in place since 2002. Los Angeles already has an extensive issue with billboards because an alarming number of billboards are erected illegally. In 2008, *LA Weekly* reported that at least 4,000 of the over 10,000 billboards in the city aren't permitted. There are only three sign inspectors at the City of Los Angeles and the process of removing an illegal billboard based on an inspector's citation can be arduous and time-consuming. Neighbors to the LED billboards protested loudly to the city about the distracting brightness and motion of the LED boards. There was a public outcry and political disputes surrounding billboards; the city issued a moratorium on all off-site, supergraphic, and digital billboards until they could develop new signage ordinance language. Concurrent to this signage moratorium, there has also been a ban on new public murals, which are a long-standing visual tradition in Los Angeles. One challenge in defining signage and mural ordinance language is establishing clear guidelines for the production of visuals in the city to avoid visual pollution. That to me is a very interesting task because the differentiation between art and advertising plays a large role in the definition of culture for a city. The city's lawyers and staff have been working on the signage ordinance for more than a year and still don't have a resolution.

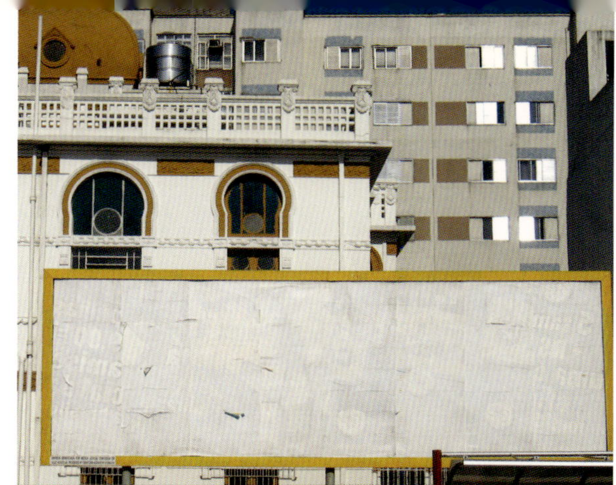

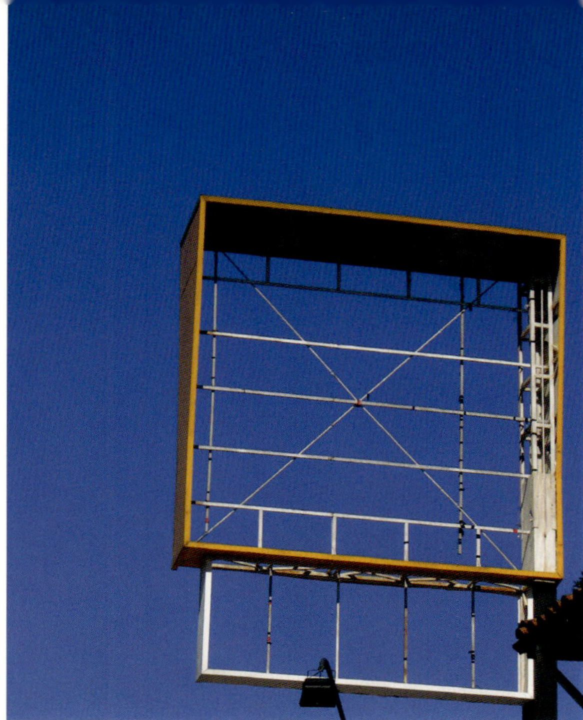

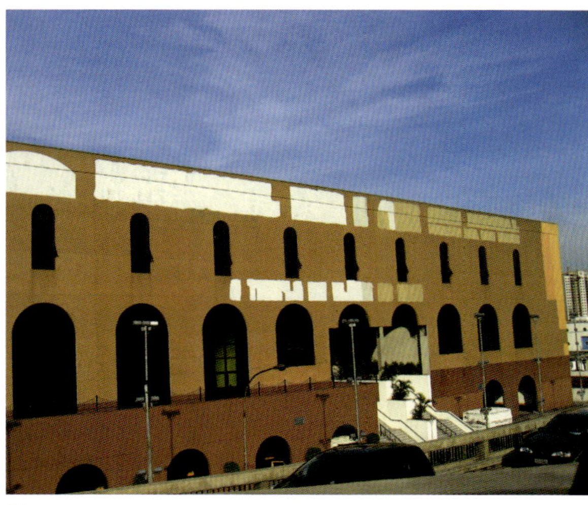

This page:
Tony de Marco
São Paulo No Logo, 2007
Courtesy of the artist.

Each city responds to this question of differentiation according to its own priorities through zoning laws. Zoning laws here in Los Angeles have produced the huge difference in the advertising spaces of neighborhoods such as West Hollywood in contrast to Beverly Hills. Currently, numerous lawsuits issued by billboard companies are pending against the City of Los Angeles regarding who can place outdoor media where in the city. They are trying to determine why one neighborhood protects free speech in advertising while another neighborhood does not.

The outdoor advertising industry makes up $7 billion of the $300 billion a year overall advertising industry in the United States. On average, we each absorb 5,000 ads a day into our subconscious. It is amazing that we can possibly form our own opinions. Advertising sets the agenda for what we should be thinking about. Ads seem to tag the city by marking buses, benches, fences, and every other possible surface with imagery and text. They create so much visual clutter that it reaches the point where our eyes have trouble differentiating.

Ads either dangle a carrot of desire in front of us, or they threaten a knife to our back. They relay messages that "you are ugly, stupid, and lazy," or "you will be beautiful, smart, and rich if you buy what the ad is promoting." We are always placed between this dichotomy in a dizzying consumer role.

While teaching media literacy, I have seen students quickly transition from "I don't even think about that" to "Oh, I get it." In all age groups. But if no one teaches them media literacy, they go through their teens and twenties as prime advertising targets, being bombarded and manipulated unconsciously. Commercial interests form many of their ideas about who they are, what they want to become, and what society is. All of Stuart Ewen's books, and Adam Curtis's documentary *The Century of the Self,* are excellent resources for understanding the effects of all-consuming advertising on views of self and democracy, and questioning whose interests are involved. Kids can be taught to deconstruct advertising pretty fast, but it takes strong, habit-bending efforts on their part to consistently counterbalance advertising's seductions. Saskia Sassen links these issues with free speech, public space, and personal and collective empowerment. She recommends generating public space that she calls "urbanizing open sources."

SD: What is your opinion of the 2007 action led by Mayor Gilberto Kassab in São Paulo, Brazil? With his "Clean City Law," he pledged to remove visual pollution via billboards, thus making the world's fourth-largest metropolis essentially advertising-free?

AB: That's my idea of heaven on earth. I daydream of moving there because visual interruption isn't the norm

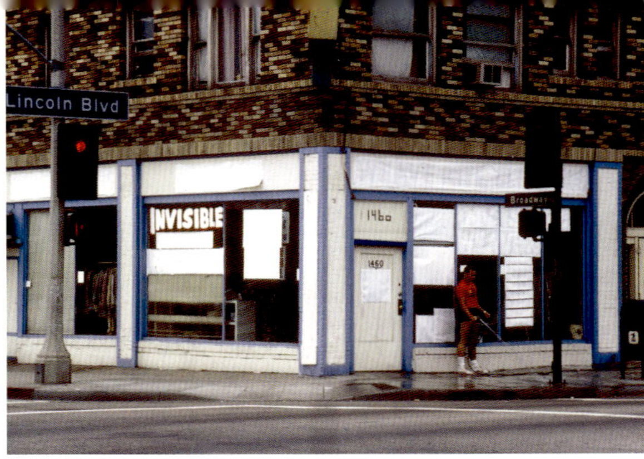

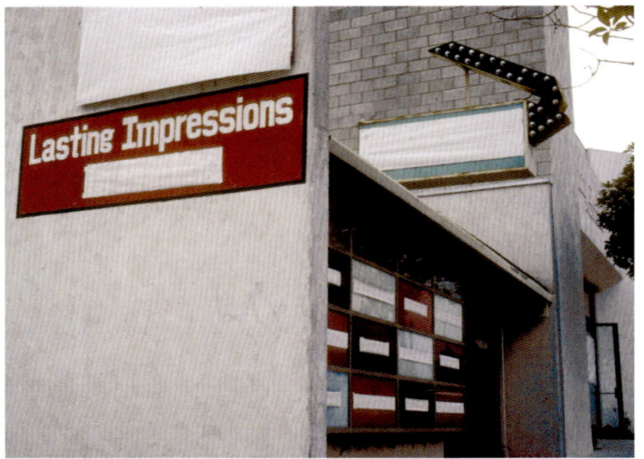

Top and Bottom:
Anne Bray
White Out, 1985
Intersection of Lincoln and Broadway, Santa Monica, California
Courtesy of the artist.

and my eyes wouldn't be seduced to avert regularly. Without outdoor advertising, public space is not dominated by an imperative voice issuing commands to buy, spend, look, and capture.

I don't think it is politically possible for Los Angeles to do what São Paulo did. I am very concerned that Los Angeles is a city that could be used as a national model regarding signage ordinances for LED billboards. If we set a precedent, we directly influence the Ninth Circuit Court, and this could then affect a national ruling. I think as a city we should be careful.

As a regional issue, I do think the city government should re-examine Los Angeles the way that São Paulo has done. The mayor of São Paulo is the one who determined and enforced the elimination of all the billboards. It has drastically changed the whole city.

SD: With *White Out* (1985), you created an earlier, local version of what happened in São Paulo at the intersection of Lincoln Boulevard and Broadway Street in Santa Monica. What was your experience in advocating for a day without signage?

AB: It was a visual and social experiment. Making art visible in a very commercial environment like Los Angeles is already a "belly of the beast" challenge. The project took place at an intersection on a busy commercial street, and it went one block in every direction from that corner. We used white paper to cover up 500 ads that were between the sizes of a Visa sticker in a storefront window to a rooftop billboard.

I went door-to-door for six weeks getting permission from every store, mostly through joking. Only half of the shop owners asked me why I was doing the project. I called it a visual experiment, instead of art. What if we had no ads? Everyone could relate to wanting to know that answer.

Every TV station in Los Angeles showed up to document the project. They interviewed the shop owners, the pedestrians, and me, and they reported on the project on television that night. In their voiceovers the reporters were saying sarcastic things about the project, but the images they showed clearly read as a "white out" of advertising. People could interpret it however they wanted to, but it was very clear and simple.

The main impression I felt while standing at the intersection once all the paper was in place was calm. An elderly man walked down the street, as he did every morning. But on this day, he said, "Where am I?" He was lost, disoriented by not having any signage.

SD: Since you boldly claim that you would prefer a version of Los Angeles that abolished billboards, what would you suggest the visual field of the city could communicate? How would temporary art projects in public space play a role?

AB: I saw a beautiful book the other day from Spain entitled *Textura: Valencia Street Art,* by Luz A. Martin. It featured graffiti from that city, including stencils, paint, and spray paint. This type of graffiti is not like name-based tagging, which I don't appreciate. It's gorgeous visuals by a variety of people who create an exciting discourse on the street. While it does create visual clutter, which is one of my objections to advertising, it also expresses what people living in the city see and want. I can see street art becoming a really common form of public language. Because these street artists' cover each other's pieces relatively quickly, the result is an ongoing, shifting visual dialogue in the city. If we say that advertising is legal and graffiti is illegal, we are giving corporations permission to be in charge of our world and our thought processes.

As we have commercial zones, we could have free speech zones. Every time our society is trying to make a shift in our values and policies, we need to publicly address messaging. I find it ironic that we call our legal right "free speech." It is actually very expensive speech, often too expensive for alternative visions. Perhaps it would be a better use of LED billboards to take advantage of their rotating messages to allow for a greater diversity of voices.

The question *How Many Billboards?* brings up for Los Angeles is "What could be the relationship between public art and billboards?" This question has been asked by a number of contemporary art organizations in Los Angeles during the last thirty years including Freewaves, Los Angeles Contemporary Exhibitions (LACE), Clockshop, West of Rome, and LA><ART. As billboard photography gets replaced with video, our eyes will be even further seduced by the imagery in the streetscape, because we are biologically trained to look at the points of contrast between light and dark in moving imagery. I encourage art to exist in these advertising spaces because, unlike advertising, art tends to ask provocative questions and encourage new consciousness, often in contrast to the environment around it. I want a city that is open to discussion for us collectively. I think that many of the artists' projects in *How Many Billboards?* address the idea of spectacle in a new way. Many of them are still big, loud images, but they are countering the mainstream spectacle to create a layer of questioning about media's role in the city.

BIBLIOGRAPHY

Bray, Anne. "Going Before the Public: Responses to a Questionnaire on Public Art." *Art Paper*, 7. 9 (May 1988).

The Century of the Self. DVD. Directed by Adam Curtis. United Kingdom: British Broadcasting Corporation, 2002.

Ewen, Stuart. *Captains of Consciousness: Advertising and the Social Roots of the Consumer Culture.* New York: McGraw-Hill, 1976.

Harris, David Evan. "São Paolo: A City Without Ads." *Adbusters* 73, August 3, 2007. https://www.adbusters.org/magazine/73/Sao_Paulo_A_City_Without_Ads.html (accessed February 13, 2010).

Johnson, Caitlin A. "Cutting Through Advertising Clutter: The Average Person May See 5,000 Ads a Day." CBS Sunday Morning, September 17, 2006. http://www.cbsnews.com/stories/2006/09/17/sunday/main2015684.shtml (accessed April 2, 2010).

Martin, Luz A. *Textura: Valencia Street Art*. New York: Mark Batty Publisher, 2009.

Outdoor Advertising Association of America, Inc. "FAQ: What are the revenue numbers of outdoor advertising?" http://www.oaaa.org/about/faq.aspx (accessed April 2, 2010).

Pelisek, Christine. "Billboards Gone Wild: 4,000 Illegal Billboards Choke L.A.'s Neighborhoods. Is City Hall Corrupt, or Just Inept?" *LA Weekly*, April 24, 2008.

Sassen, Saskia. "Public Interventions: The Shifting Meaning of the Urban Condition." *Hybrid Space* 11 (2006), 18-26.

Pegi Christiansen; Dennis Hathaway, President, Coalition to Ban Billboard Blight; Joshua G. Stein; and Jane Usher, Special Assistant City Attorney, City of Los Angeles provided editorial input.

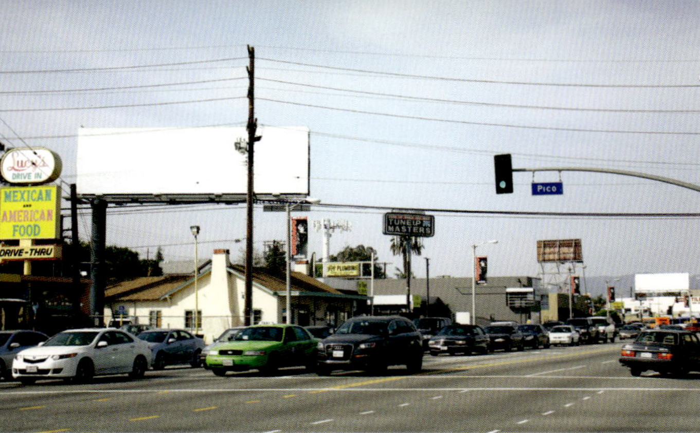

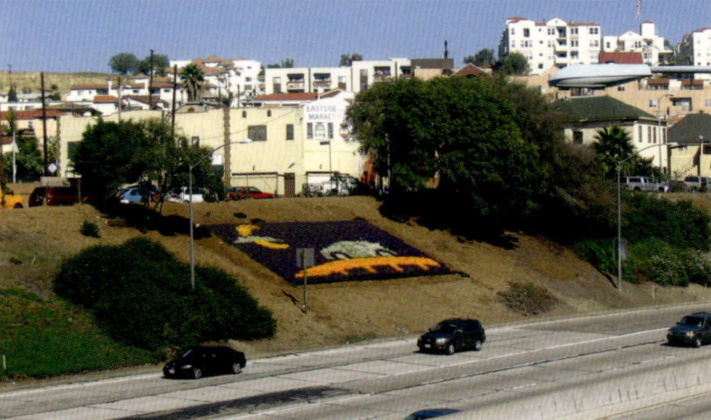

Top: Intersection of La Brea Avenue and Pico Boulevard. Outdoor media corporations have less to say in these recession-charged days. With the infamous Hollywood sign in the distance, two blank billboards pop-out against a sea of signage lining the major north-south corridor of La Brea Avenue. Is Los Angeles starting to prefer white space in the streetscape, following São Paolo's lead?

Bottom: 110 Freeway at Cesar E Chavez Avenue. An unfortunate casualty of a 2002 municipal moratorium on new outdoor media has been a parallel moratorium on Los Angeles' historic public tradition of community murals. Skirting the moratorium's definition of a mural, California's Department of Transportation has invented a creative, vegetative solution for enlivening the driving experience. Rectangular floral murals composed of colorful annuals portray romantic, moonlit drives along the peripheral landscapes of the highly used 110 Freeway.

TIMELINE: A Summary of Recent Political History of L.A. Billboards

1972 The Florida Department of Transportation obtains an inventory list from billboard companies, which is necessary before activists, neighbors and inspectors can identify and dispute illegal billboards. (Over time, inventories are sought in cities such as Houston, Texas; Philadelphia, Pennsylvania; and San Francisco, California.)

1980 The city of Houston bans billboards after local newspaper articles dub it the "Ugliest City in America," thanks to its sea of 10,000 billboards.

1980s Los Angeles City Councilman Marvin Braude and his aide Cindy Miscikowski try to ban new billboard construction; however, they are unsuccessful. Construction unions complain that the ban would lead to unemployment in their industry. At the same time, with historically high rates of murder and street crime, billboard clutter is barely on other city leaders' radar.

1984 Architect Ted Wu helps the city council pass a law preventing billboards from appearing within 600 feet of each other.

1987 Residents in Jacksonville, Florida, vote to ban new billboards. Twenty years later, the city has 1,000 fewer boards than it had in 1987.

1990s Gerry Silver, a professor of business administration at Long Beach City College, and Ted Wu are ordered by the Los Angeles City Council, via City Attorney James Hahn, and with the support of major billboard firms, to halt their efforts to have height regulations imposed on towering new billboards being placed atop Los Angeles buildings.

1997 Los Angeles Department of Building and Safety general manager Andrew Adelman employs just two inspectors to police billboards across 469 square miles of territory.

1999 In an initial effort, Adelman orders inspectors to survey the legal and illegal billboard inventory on a single stretch of Pico Boulevard. Inspector David Keim later admits that the city is incapable of tracking violations.

2001 Councilman Jack Weiss calls for a yearly billboard inspection fee on billboard owners, which would finance an inventory of the signs. The fee was contested through lawsuits filed by the outdoor media companies.

Outdoor media owners donate billboard space valued at more than $400,000 to tout "Rocky Delgadillo for City Attorney." Delgadillo's campaign is successful.

2002 In a landslide vote, San Francisco citizens approve Proposition G, which bans all new billboards and requires outdoor media companies to hand over their inventory lists.

The city of Los Angeles establishes a ban on new billboards and supergraphics (large-scale advertising that covers the façades of buildings). Department of Building and Safety officials don't enforce the inspection fee on either legal or illegal billboards.

2005 Vista Outdoor admits they are "unable to locate" permits for 500 smaller billboards in Los Angeles and agrees to take them down. In 2008, building officials openly admit that they have no clue whether they have been removed.

2006 Dennis Hathaway, Ted Wu, and Gerry Silver form the Coalition to Ban Billboard Blight.

Los Angeles City Attorney Rocky Delgadillo and the city council meet privately to work out a settlement with outdoor advertising companies that have sued the city in response to the inspection fee. They agree to the following: certain billboard companies have six years to take down ninety-eight boards of their choice (3% of their inventory); the inspection fee is reduced to $186 per structure; illegal boards built before 1986 are grandfathered in; and 877 boards are approved for modernization (replacing the existing board with LED displays). The companies are required to turn over an inventory list; they file lawsuits claiming the lists are trade secrets.

2007 A crew of workers for L.A. Outdoor Advertising pours a concrete foundation next to the Harbor Freeway and erects an illegal billboard atop an equally illegal ten-ton superstructure that can be removed only with a wrecker. Work is done in full view of the offices of Los Angeles city billboard inspectors.

2008 Large companies continue to resist releasing their inventory lists.

On April 22, the city council votes to let Clear Channel erect two large billboards along the 10 Freeway, setting a precedent for advertising on the freeway. The city of Los Angeles faces lawsuits from other, smaller billboard companies for the right to build digital billboards in the city. Under pressure from citizens, the city approves a three-month moratorium on new digital billboards.
A federal injunction, issued by U.S. District Judge Audrey Collins, stops the city from enforcing the three-

month moratorium and the 2002 ban. The injunction cites preferential treatment in the 2006 settlement towards certain companies. An increase of super-graphics on buildings around the city results. In response, the city adopts a new ban on all new outdoor advertising and, in a related moratorium, outdoor art murals are banned.

2009 No new structures go up, but existing legal and illegal billboards, supergraphics, and digital signs continue to operate. Residents of buildings covered by supergraphics, such as Dr. David Allen of West Los Angeles, begin to protest, and the *Los Angeles Times* writes an editorial asking Mayor Antonio Villaraigosa to do something about the supergraphics, since the "witless" city council and city attorney's office have not.

2010 Los Angeles City Attorney Carmen Trutanich seeks fines for illegal signage of up to $10,000, and files lawsuits alleging that supergraphics were unlawfully installed on 12 buildings throughout the city, in violation of the city ban on new such signage. Billboard companies claim that the move violates the 2008 federal injunction. Four days later, Kayvan Setareh, a businessman from Pacific Palisades, is arrested at his home, accused of posting illegal supergraphics on a building at the intersection of Hollywood Boulevard and Highland Avenue. He is held on $1,000,000.00 bail, but that is reduced to $100,000 after he agrees to remove the advertisement within 24 hours of his release. In the weeks that follow, several more supergraphics are removed.

BIBLIOGRAPHY

This timeline was culled and paraphrased from the following sources. Special thanks go to Jane Usher for her clarifications on the contemporary legal situation.

"Council votes to ban digital billboards," KABC-TV/DT Los Angeles, http://abclocal.go.com/kabc/story?section=news/local/los_angeles&id=6954682, August 7, 2009.

"L.A.'s Supergraphics Plight," *Los Angeles Times*, January 26, 2009.

Pelisek, Christine. "Billboards Gone Wild: 4,000 Illegal Billboards Choke L.A.'s Neighborhoods. Is City Hall Corrupt, or Just Inept?" *LA Weekly*, April 24, 2008.

Pelisek, Christine. "West LA Doctor's Website Targets Super-Graphics" *LA Weekly*, http://blogs.laweekly.com/ladaily/city-news/westwood-doctors-website-targe/, January 27, 2009.

Powell, Amy. "Hollywood Supergraphic Battle May Be Over," KABC-TV/DT Los Angeles, http://abclocal.go.com/kabc/story?section=news/local/los_angeles&id=7306833, March 1, 2010.

Zahniser, David. "Businessman jailed for allegedly posting supergraphic at Hollywood intersection," *Los Angeles Times*, February 28, 2010.

Zahniser, David. "L.A. city attorney files lawsuit against supergraphic sign companies," *Los Angeles Times*, February 23, 2010.

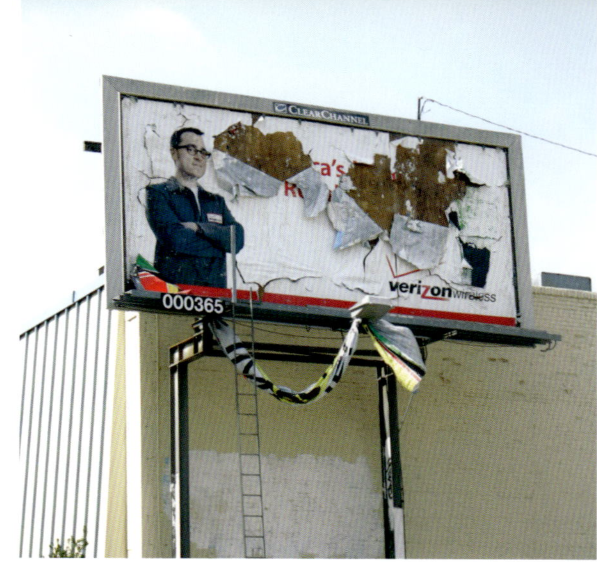

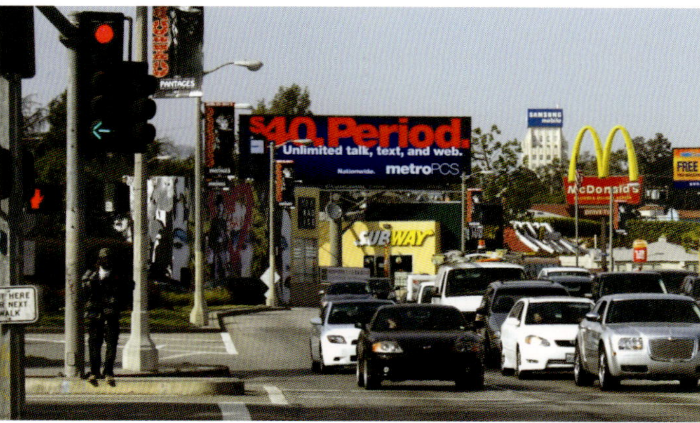

Top: Intersection of 11th Street and Hill Street. Are printed billboards a dying breed? Clear Channel's forgotten offspring is a palimpsest of aging outdoor media, with multiple layers of falling and failing imagery.

Bottom: Intersection of La Brea Avenue and San Vicente Boulevard. New LED digital billboards change images every eight seconds to maximize consumer suggestion. Despite the moratorium, LED billboards were grandfathered in last year due to a settlement between the City of Los Angeles and outdoor media corporations. Public debate surrounding these frenetic billboards involves varying expert opinions about whether their brightness and motion constitute traffic hazards.

THE MAKING OF *HOW MANY BILLBOARDS?* A "Public Art" Perspective

BY SARA DALEIDEN

In accepting the challenge of serving as a consultant to the MAK Center's *How Many Billboards? Art In Stead*, I consciously added the term "public art" to my title. I was operating out of an awareness that *How Many Billboards?* would not be presented as a public art project, but rather as an "urban exhibition presented on billboards in Los Angeles."[1] Within a contemporary art dialogue, responses to the term "public art" lie on a continuum between impatient eye rolling and vigilant allegiance, depending on one's professional position. The MAK Center engaged me to co-produce the billboard project along with a curatorial team, knowing my interest in exploring contemporary art production that looked at the intersections between museum and public art commissioning efforts. Regardless of whether it manifests as an extension of—or a rebellion against—the protection and emphasis of a contemporary art museum, I'm convinced of the effective power of art that is interwoven into the city. I am an advocate for wrestling with the term "public art" in order to investigate the political nature of placing art in quotidian spaces of the city, and I believe that public art has a critical role to play in the cultural identity-building agendas of public and private agencies that form a city.

The initial working title of the MAK Center's large-scale, outdoor media project was *Gladys Glover*, referencing the memorable heroine in the 1954 film *It Should Happen to You.*[2] Gladys was a working-class girl who had a bold ambition to make a name for herself. To do so, she rented a billboard in the middle of Manhattan and emblazoned it with her name. When fame arrived fast and furious, Gladys found herself enjoying the attention. But she eventually came to question the meaning of her new identity that the billboard had facilitated.[3] Referencing Gladys, public art historian Harriet Senie relays: "Earnest but naïve Gladys knew instinctively, billboards seduce. In the hands of sophisticated artists, they may have the power to transform."[4] Senie's quote is from a catalogue for the survey *Billboard Art on the Road* (1999) at the Massachusetts Museum of Contemporary Art (MASS MoCA), which was an influential source for our project in Los Angeles.

With Gladys's trajectory as a poetic prompt, the MAK Center project serves as a platform for facilitating artists to work on billboards as they borrow the strategies of advertising, explore popular culture stereotypes, consider billboards as a cultural site, and engage discussions of meaning in public messages. As Senie elucidates, artists' billboards "ask implicitly if artists are capable of communicating directly with a general public, if art today is able to create even temporary disturbances in the fields of mammon."[5] The coded messages of advertising and art share the "power to inform, instruct, arouse, and divert."[6] However, potential differences lie in the fact that art can prompt thoughts about civic participation and responsibility, as opposed to ads' primary focus on consumption.[7]

Art historical connections have periodically highlighted artists' usurpation of commercial language to explore popular culture's growing relationship to media, as exemplified in the Des Moines Art Center's seminal comparison of outdoor media and Pop Art in the exhibition series *Signs of the Times* (1963).[8] *How Many Billboards?* further develops an art historical view of artists' investigations of commercial media by following the interaction of Pop Art and Conceptual Art as it has been cultivated in California since the 1960s.

In its distinct position as a Viennese museum's exotic Los Angeles satellite, the MAK Center approaches its curatorial efforts from the perspective of acknowledged standards of contemporary art and architecture history that stem from American and European ideals. Within the progressive cultural landscape of Los Angeles, the MAK Center is considered a crucial alternative space, in comparison to the city's large museums, and is known for initiatives that consider the context of Los Angeles and impact the city through art and architecture experiments. Part of the MAK Center's mission is the preservation of three residences built by the innovative Modern Architect Rudolf M. Schindler, as well as a popular, annual tour of Modern Architecture in the city. By programming the Schindler sites, the center animates important historical structures of Los Angeles and brings attention to the fact that the Modern Architecture movement was one of the decisive factors that brought global recognition of Los Angeles as a cultural hub,[9] despite the city's infamous tendency to consider its architecture disposable. In appreciation of Schindler's provocative legacy, *How Many Billboards?* extends the cultural production values of the MAK Center beyond its current sites. The exhibition emerges as a temporary intervention that explores media structures in the urban landscape. The MAK Center produces culture in these permanent and temporary forms as advocacy for experimental visions for the development of Los Angeles. MAK Center Director Kimberli Meyer, initiator and co-curator of the project, states: "In *How Many Billboards?*, the streets of Los Angeles become the walls of the exhibition, and the city itself becomes a large museum."[10]

In its contemporary American usage, the term "public art" refers to a phenomenon that can be traced back to the first ordinance that mandated that a percentage of building costs be devoted to art, which was approved in Philadelphia in 1959.[11] The idea reflects urban planning agendas seeking to affect the aesthetics of cities after the influx of Modern Architecture and public plazas. Art and urban planning began to find camaraderie under activities described as "redevelopment," "rehabilitation," and "renewal." Depending on the governing body defining percent-for-art ordinances nationwide, both civic and private developers with construction projects of various scales were suddenly pressed to consider art in an integral, if minor, fashion. Historically, this newly dedicated funding stream opened up opportunities for artists to explore production processes, scale, location, and audience within particular urban contexts. Museum and gallery exhibitions and markets remained prominent, but another significant cultural producer formed. The funding stream was large enough to attract prominent curators and artists, though over time the public art market would find itself segregated from the dominant art market of museums and galleries. In the form of public art agencies, consultants, and artists, this new cultural producer came to favor a vein of art production that explored what "public" meant in relation to how culture could be formed within a city.

Even though the exhibition was meant to occur in urban public space, *How Many Billboards?* was never intended to be financially supported by percent-for-art funds. In addition to looking at MASS MoCA's *Billboard Art on the Road,* we investigated local models for producing artists' billboards, including those developed by Clockshop, Freewaves, LA><ART, Los Angeles Contemporary Exhibitions (LACE), and West of Rome. Pioneering organizations such as the New York City-based Public Art Fund and Creative Time were crucial for showing us a history of provocative content on artists' billboards since the 1980s, which existed despite what Senie refers to as "the pervasive stupefying effects of the media."[12] In response to this research, we spent several years testing urban exhibition models from a variety of proposal angles, with national art funders in mind.[13] A successful combination was reached with a primary funder, the Emily Hall Tremaine Foundation. We proposed to use the art historical premise of California's Conceptual Art and Pop Art movements from the 1960s to the present as the underpinning of new works commissioned for billboards. Other sources of support were also secured, but while the overall funding base was impressive for a small, ambitious nonprofit (and larger than any previous project produced by the MAK Center) the project could only be feasible if one crucial factor was met: the billboard space was donated.

Monthly billboard rental fees in Los Angeles generally range from $5,000 to $50,000, depending on the location.[14] With the MAK Center's goal to generate at least 20 billboards, this key production cost was prohibitive. As a public art consultant for progressive cultural nonprofits and practitioners, I strategize and implement numerous aspects of project development, site analysis, and public relations. From my perspective, the artwork isn't complete or publicly relevant until funding, location, and audience are determined. My role as public art consultant to *How Many Billboards?* specifically required that I, in collaboration with the MAK Center, discover the magical key to convincing major outdoor media companies to donate precious advertising space at major intersections radiating out from MAK Center's base at the Schindler House in West Hollywood. Through a series of informational interviews with government agencies, advertising firms, real estate developers, arts organizations, and artists with experience engaging public space, including via billboards (many of whom would eventually join our advisory board[15]), we miraculously found Rick Robinson of MacDonald Media.

With over 23 years of working for outdoor advertising as a creative director and media buyer, Robinson has operated as a public face for the influential Outdoor Advertising Association of America. He is frank about the creative opportunities, the economic structure, and the political debate surrounding outdoor media in Los Angeles and beyond. For our agenda, the remarkable synergy we found in Robinson revolved around his extensive outdoor media network in combination with his history of supporting billboards by artists such as guerrilla poster-maker Robbie Conal. Robinson promptly exhibited a remarkable willingness to collaborate on an outdoor media occupation that was extensive by art world standards, though minor compared to one of his major clients such as Nike. Through charismatic cajoling, Robinson took advantage of his longstanding business relationships with outdoor media corporations working in international markets to convince the major local players to donate in-kind support. Instead of relegating our artists' billboards to the public service announcement billboard space that is often located on side streets or less visible B-sides, Robinson helped us to occupy outdoor media at major intersections in the dense commercial and residential areas from the Westside to downtown, and from Hollywood to the 10 Freeway.

While we had been thinking about artists' billboards for years, when it came to producing the project in 2009, we quickly discovered that our timing coincided with a sensitive political and economic moment in Los Angeles surrounding outdoor media.[16] This debate often framed outdoor media companies as culprits. Since the widespread use of billboards at the beginning of the twentieth century, California has cyclically addressed public debate about the value of outdoor media. For example, in the 1960s Governor Pat Brown "compared a billboard blocking a view to littering highways with refuse."[17] Also relevant to our circumstances, and to the current round of political negotiations over outdoor media, is the fact that the United States is still experiencing a significant economic recession. The impact of that recession on the outdoor media industry can be seen in the number of blank, out-of-date, and decaying billboards present throughout the metropolitan area. Because of the recession and the political atmosphere, many local outdoor media corporations had billboard space ready to receive a fresh new image in terms of public relations and physical presence.

In response to the public debates locally and internationally, billboard companies are advocating that their visual presence in the city is synonymous with culture. In the wake of a shocking and potent ban on outdoor media in São Paulo, Brazil, in 2007, major media companies, including Clear Channel Communications, are inflamed by the loss of sources of revenue. As noted in an article in *Adbusters*, "Weeks before the ban took effect, Clear Channel launched a counter-campaign in support of outdoor ads, with desperate slogans that failed to resonate with the masses: 'There's a new movie on all the billboards—what billboards? Outdoor media is culture.'"[18] *How Many Billboards?* used the device of an outdoor media campaign to offer a unique cultural product that could adroitly question the distinctions between advertising and art.

In soliciting projects for the exhibition, the MAK Center did not engage the type of public evaluation process prevalent in public art production. Instead, we relied heavily on a contemporary art curatorial vetting process with artists who were primarily accustomed to working in museum and gallery settings. The curators sought artists who would take a strategic and critical approach to the billboard as a potential site of cultural dialogue. In complement to this vetting process, we generated an advisory board to assess the artists' proposals and to support us publicly in terms of networking, but also should our artists' billboards generate public outcry.

In addition to the artworks' contents, a powerful factor influencing the public experience of the billboards was their physical siting, which resulted in interesting spatial and conceptual connections between image and context. The donated billboard space was volatile in terms of geography, since the outdoor media corporations frequently wouldn't commit to exact locations until the last minute. The MAK Center was required to make decisions about where to place artists' works quickly, right before installation. The results were often spontaneously compelling. For example, Kira Lynn Harris's *Community as Art* billboard offers a high contrast skeleton of the Watts Towers. The billboard, which faces south toward the unique cultural outpost, is located along the 10 Freeway, one of the main boundaries between the lower income neighborhoods of South Los Angeles and affluent neighborhoods to the north. David Lamelas's and Yvonne Rainer's were placed back-to-back near a McDonald's, and both billboards emphasized the term "good" to question the production of style and identity. Kenneth Anger's would-be fashion ad, which elicits name brand marketing and our popular hunger for spectacle, is located a stone's throw from legendary Rodeo Drive. Jennifer Bornstein's carefully etched image of an old-fashioned film projector claiming "The End" on Sunset Boulevard in Hollywood offers a double entendre for the death of certain obsolete image-making techniques, both in film and outdoor media. Contrasted against the dominant red, white, and blue motif of the Bank of America, lauren woods's Urdu poem in Arabic script insinuates that overlapping symbols of American and Middle Eastern culture can be read in a poetic light. With all these situations, passers-by are provided healthy leeway to assess: "Ad or Art?," as well to consider the intended audience indicated by each billboard's location.

Collaborations with public and private partners were crucial to building awareness of *How Many Billboards?*'s broad geographic purview, experimental artistic concepts, and political examinations. We were particularly focused on reaching viewers unversed in contemporary art, as well as those already alert to it. Thus far, public response via press and public programs has been positive. Contentious public reactions to the artists' billboards have been mild, including a few unsurprising occasions of graffiti on tempting white spaces, despite potentially inflammatory subjects such as human rights, class, race, sexuality, identity, and the military.

With *How Many Billboards?,* the MAK Center serves as a liaison between the contemporary art world and outdoor media companies to explore what cultural production could mean in a city like Los Angeles. Vito Acconci, an artist known for his seminal Conceptual Art performances and installations in the 1970s, as well as his decades of public space projects, proffers that "the establishment of certain space in the city as 'public' is a reminder, a warning, that the rest of the city isn't public."[19] Acconci believes that contemporary public space is becoming a "composite of privates."[20] His critique of the private consumption of public space can be applied to Los Angeles's prolific billboards as a diagrammatic metaphor for the viral assertion of commercial messaging over civic decision making. Acconci stresses that public space occurs where people have a right to gather by legal definition, but also where they don't have a right and turn private space into public through sheer desire and force.[21] Acconci is concerned that public space must be asserted in a time where we are bombarded with the speed and information density of our digital culture. As a case

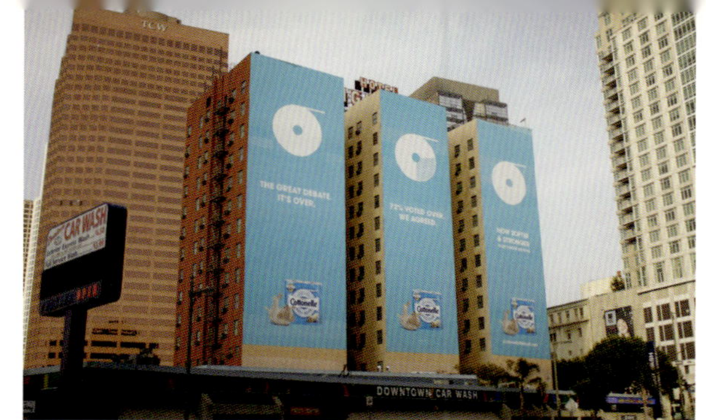

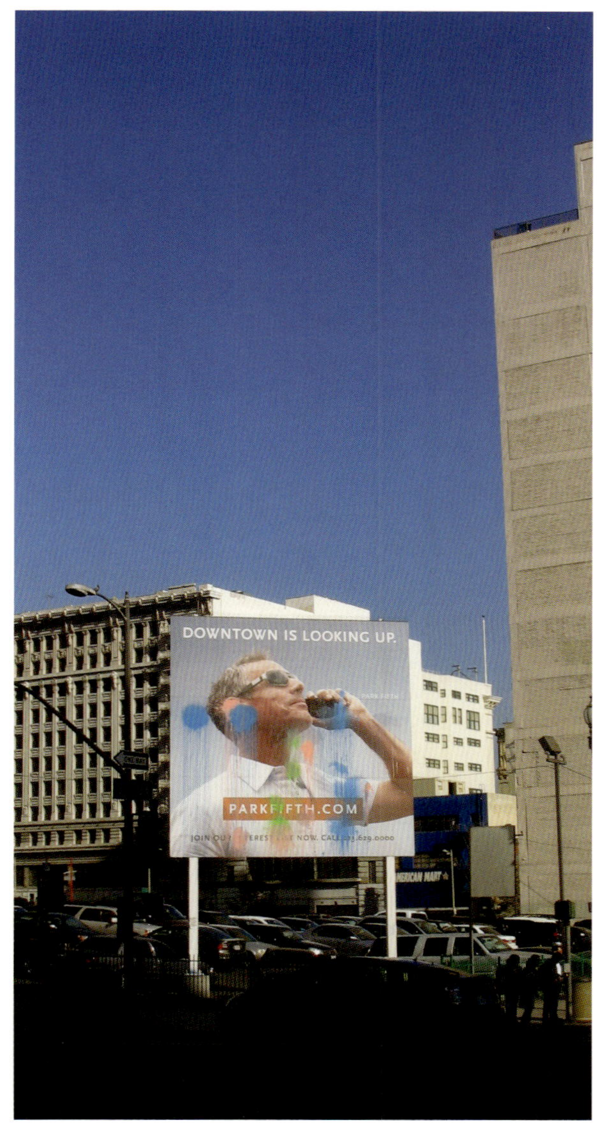

Top: Intersection of Figueroa Avenue and Olympic Boulevard, Los Angeles. A tall-wall triad consumes the side façade of the historic Figueroa Hotel, visually dominating the 1980s peach and beige redevelopment aesthetic of the downtown skyline. The Cottonelle baby-blue toilet paper ad suggests softer and stronger urban comfort is possible by claiming: "The Great Debate. It's Over." Are they predicting the city's acquiescence to—or removal of—supergraphics like these?

Bottom: Intersection of 5th Street and Olive Street, Los Angeles. Selling hopeful and hip redevelopment of Downtown Los Angeles, this billboard encourages a look upward to imagine construction yet to come. Covered with spectacular peach and blue paintball splotches, was this yuppie attacked by guerrilla billboard commentary, or is this a sign of advertising's usurpation of the subcultural deconstruction of imagery?

in point, witness the proliferation of rapidly shifting LED billboards around Los Angeles. Another quote by Acconci offers a resource for reading *How Many Billboards?* as a public art project that addresses the role of media in our city and encourages us to clarify what public voice we want primarily visible:

Public art comes in through the back door like a second-class citizen. Instead of bemoaning this, public art can use this marginal position to its advantage: public art can present itself as the voice of marginal cultures, as the minority report, as the opposition party. Public art exists to thicken the plot.[22]

Acconci's words serve as a prompt. In discussing the visual field of the streetscape, we can consider the entire city as a space for the public's free speech, instead of reinforcing the commercial speech supremacy of private landowners.

In closing, I propose that *How Many Billboards?* serves as a model for how a multi-pronged action can offer opportunities to investigate our relationship with public space. Occupying a threshold of private and public interests, billboards are intrinsically ambiguous. To understand the potency of *How Many Billboards?* as a cultural production relevant to political dialogue, I emphasize the symbiotic state of the inspired billboard image solutions produced by artists and the organizational synthesis that determined the economic, physical, and social definitions of the production—through financial support, siting, and distribution of the project. Typical curatorial methods of contemporary art focus on the artist's image as the main cultural product; decisions about display and production are frequently secondary. The production specifics of *How Many Billboards?* serve as emblems for reconsidering how art is defined and made relevant in a city. As an experimental foray by the MAK Center, *How Many Billboards?* offers a playground for public-art-centric and museum-centric contemporary art dialogues to merge, in light of civic dialogue about the role of billboards and other outdoor media in our vision.

1. See the *How Many Billboards?* full press release, http://www.howmanybillboards.org/HMB_PressRelease.pdf, (accessed April 14, 2010).

2. *It Should Happen to You*, DVD, directed by George Cukor (1954, Columbia Pictures; RCA/Columbia Pictures Home Video, 2004).

3. "It Should Happen to You (1954) - full review!" Classic Film Guide, http://www.classicfilmguide.com/index.php?s=other_reviews&item=128 (accessed April 14, 2010).

4. Harriet Senie, "Disturbances in the Fields of Mammon: Towards a History of Artists' Billboards," *Billboard Art on the Road: A Retrospective Exhibition of Artists' Billboards of the Last 30 Years,* ed. Laura Steward Heon, Peggy Diggs, and Joseph Thompson (Cambridge, MA: MIT Press, 1999), 26. The MASS MoCA survey is an important American predecessor for a large-scale artists' billboard exhibition because it built an important partnership with outdoor media companies and advocacy agencies to commission new work by regional artists, reprint and site a selection of historically important billboards, and catalogue the history of artists' billboards from an East Coast focus.

5. Ibid., 15.

6. Ibid., 16. Senie is referencing William H. Wilson's "The Billboard: Bane of the City Beautiful," *Journal of Urban History* 12. 4 (1987): 89-119.

7. Ibid., 20.

8. Ibid., 19. As referenced by Senie, *Signs of the Times* drew connections between commercial graphic production and Pop Art's commentary on and use of commercial visual and semantic strategies. The exhibition series subtitles were *Trade Signs and Symbols of the Nineteenth Century, Poster and Billboard Art of the Nineteenth and Early Twentieth Centuries*, and *Work by Twelve Contemporary Pop Artists.*

9. See "Overview," p.8.

10. See *How Many Billboards?* press release, http://www.howmanybillboards.org/HMB_PressRelease.pdf (accessed April 14, 2010).

11. John Wetenhall, "A Brief History of Percent-for-Art in America," Forecast Public Art, http://forecastpublicart.org/anthology-downloads/wetenhall.pdf (accessed April 14, 2010). Published in *Public Art Review* 9 (1993).

12. Senie, 20.

13. I initially undertook to strategize about the idea of artists' billboards from a public art perspective during my graduate coursework at the University of Southern California's Master of Public Art Studies program (MPAS). My mentor, public art consultant Jessica Cusick, was influential in directing my attention to the community relationship-building that supported production of this scale of project. The MPAS program at USC is one of the oldest in a growing number of public art, public practice, and social practice graduate programs in the United States. Under Joshua Decter, director of the program since 2007, the program is currently undergoing a name change to "Art/Curatorial Practices in the Public Sphere," which broaches theoretical questions about how to refer to art produced in public spaces and purviews. See "About the MPAS Program," Master of Public Art Studies Program at the University of Southern California Roski School of Fine Arts, http://roski.usc.edu/pas/ (accessed April 15, 2010) and Joshua Decter's interview with Christine Steiner, pp. 137-141.

14. As noted in conversations with Rick Robinson of MacDonald Media, the media buyer who acquired donated billboard space for *How Many Billboards?*, July 2009-April 2010.

15. For a list of advisors to *How Many Billboards?* see "Overview," p. 9.

16 .For an overview, see "Timeline: A Summary of Recent Political History of L.A. Billboards," pp. 146-147.

17. Senie, 19.

18. David Evan Harris, "São Paolo: A City Without Ads," *Adbusters* 73, August 3, 2007, https://www.adbusters.org/magazine/73/Sao_Paulo_A_City_Without_Ads.html (accessed February 13, 2010).

19. Vito Acconci, "Public Space in a Private Time," *Critical Inquiry* 16. 4 (1990): 901.

20. Ibid., 914.

21. Ibid., 904.

22. Ibid., 918.

Unrealized Proposals. A number of artists presented multiple proposals that the curators liked but for external reasons were un-realizable. A selection of mock-ups are shown here. One factor that we considered was that billboard companies are loath to take on potentially controversial material and will pull any board that causes a public outcry. To avoid a disruption in the show, we opted to vet the proposals with our media buyer well ahead of production. Another factor was the legal ramifications, revolving around the question of fair use and rights to images. Since the MAK Center has no fund for litigation, we attempted to stay away from projects that required a legal opinion and that could eventually be contested in court.

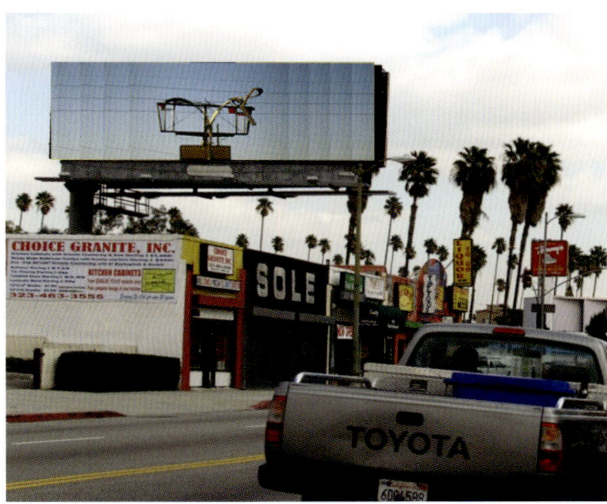

lauren woods, *Empire #1*, Proposal for *How Many Billboards?*, 2010
Courtesy of the artist

This work features a photograph of a mangled McDonald's sign in New Orleans, after Hurricane Katrina. McDonald's is one of the biggest advertising clients in the country, and no outdoor media company wants to alienate it. Though the curators loved the work, there was a strong likelihood of it being pulled, so this project was not produced.

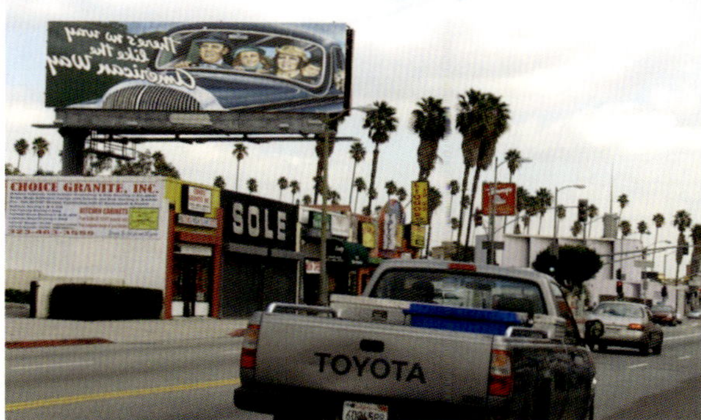

lauren woods, *There's no way...*, Proposal for *How Many Billboards?*, 2010
Courtesy of the artist

This proposed billboard image is appropriated from a photo by Margaret Bourke-White from 1937. The original photo shows a line of predominantly African-Americans waiting for bread in front of a billboard that proclaims: "WORLD'S HIGHEST STANDARD OF LIVING" and "There's no way like the American Way." The National Association of Manufacturers produced the billboard in the 1930s in an attempt to quell potential unrest among the working class and poor. The association still exists and we were concerned that they would claim copyright infringement.

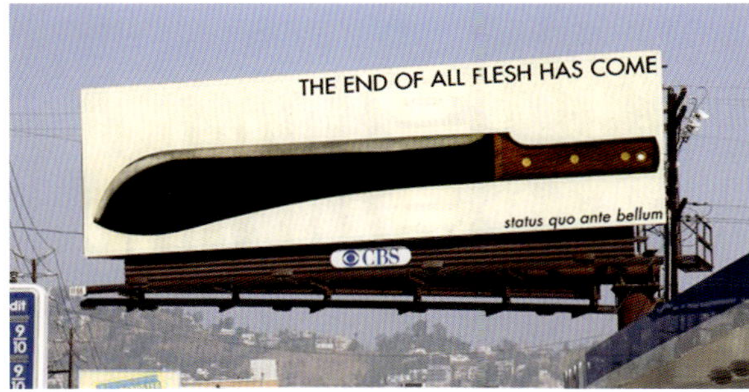

Daniel Joseph Martinez, No title, Not realized, Proposal for *How Many Billboards?*, 2010, Courtesy of the artist and Simon Preston Gallery

This proposal did not pass the vetting process with our media buyer. The violent connotation of the machete combined with the words "status quo ante bellum" was deemed too controversial to mount.

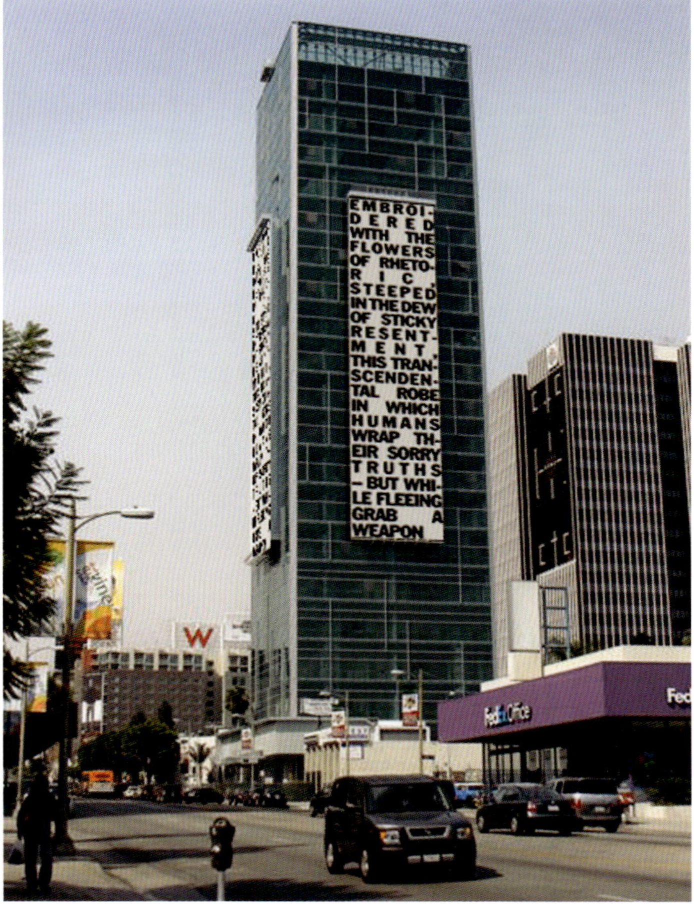

Daniel Joseph Martinez, No title, Not realized, Proposal for *How Many Billboards?*, 2010, Courtesy of the artist and Simon Preston Gallery

The text in the proposal is an alteration of language in Karl Marx's *Das Kapital*. The billboard site is owned by Sky Tag, notorious in Los Angeles for putting up building-sized images of the Statue of Liberty. The company initially calls them art, then later transforms the space into advertising. Although Sky Tag initially indicated that it was open to considering a proposal from the MAK Center at that location, it declined to move forward with this piece.

PUBLIC PROGRAMS

The MAK Center produced the following series of public programs, including film screenings, discussions, and bus tours, in order to investigate *How Many Billboards? Art In Stead* in relation to the visual field of the city.

TOURS
Saturday, February 27
Saturday, March 6
Bus Tours: Guided by exhibition curators and public art consultant

Sunday, March 7
Bike Tours: The MAK Center offered a 12-mile bike tour

Bus Tours on Metro: All works were located near public bus lines. The MAK Center partnered with the Metropolitan Transit Authority (Metro) to encourage public transit bus ridership as a way of viewing the exhibition.

ARTIST DISCUSSIONS

Panel Discussions with *How Many Billboards?* Curators and Artists
Sunday, February 28

Messaging in the City
Moderated by Kimberli Meyer
Participating artists:
Kira Lynn Harris
David Lamelas
Brandon Lattu
Martha Rosler
lauren woods

Public Speech and the Possibility of Political Art
Moderated by Nizan Shaked
Participating artists:
Daniel Joseph Martinez
Kori Newkirk
Allan Sekula
Susan Silton
Kerry Tribe

Lecture: Artist Renée Green
Tuesday, April 6

Co-presented with the Master of Public Art Studies Program: Art / Curatorial Practices in the Public Sphere, University of Southern California Roski School of Fine Arts in Los Angeles.

FILM AND VIDEO SCREENINGS

Co-presented with The Museum of Contemporary Art, Los Angeles (MOCA).

Thursday, March 11
David Lamelas, *The Desert People* (1977)
Kerry Tribe, *Northern Lights (Cambridge)* (2005)
Eileen Cowin, *Studio Visit* (2009)
Allan Sekula, *A Short Film of Laos* (2006)

Thursday, April 8
Renée Green, *Endless Dreams and Water Between* (2009)
Jennifer Bornstein, *Phantom Limb* (2009)
Allan Sekula, *Lottery of the Sea* (short version), (2006)

Panel Series on the Current State of Billboards in Los Angeles
Curated by Anne Bray

Visual Rights to the City
Wednesday, March 24

Co-presented with Library Foundation of Los Angeles and California Lawyers for the Arts.

As part of ALOUD at Central Library, this panel of outdoor media professionals and legal experts focused on the city's recent debate surrounding LED billboards and illegal signage, and examined free speech rights as they relate to images on the streets.

Moderated by Anne Bray
Participating panelists:
Toby Miller, Professor of Media and Cultural Studies, University of California, Riverside
Rick Robinson, General Manager, MacDonald Media
Christine Pelisek, Journalist, *LA Weekly*
John Tehranian, Attorney and Partner, One LLP

The Visual Ecology of Advertising and Architecture
Thursday, April 15

Co-presented with the Southern California Institute of Architecture (SCI-Arc) and the Goethe-Institut, Los Angeles.

Held at SCI-Arc, this panel of outdoor media, art, architecture, and planning experts focused on current architectural signage and surface strategies to review the city's relationship between consumer ads and urban structures.

Moderated by Anne Bray
Participating panelists:
Bill Roschen, Principal, Roschen van Cleve Architects
Mirjam Struppek, President, International Urban Screens Association
Alan Bell, Senior City Planner, City of Los Angeles
Dennis Hathaway, President, Coalition to Ban Billboard Blight

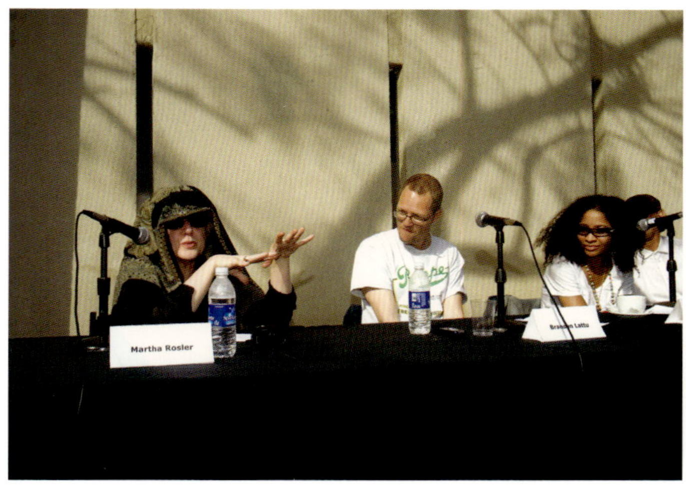

Martha Rosler, Brandon Lattu, and lauren woods on an artists' panel at the Schindler House.

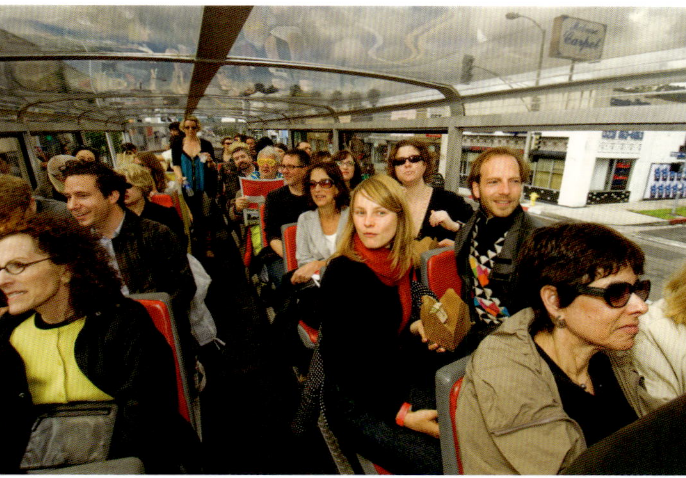

Touring the exhibition on a clear-acrylic-topped, double-decker bus.

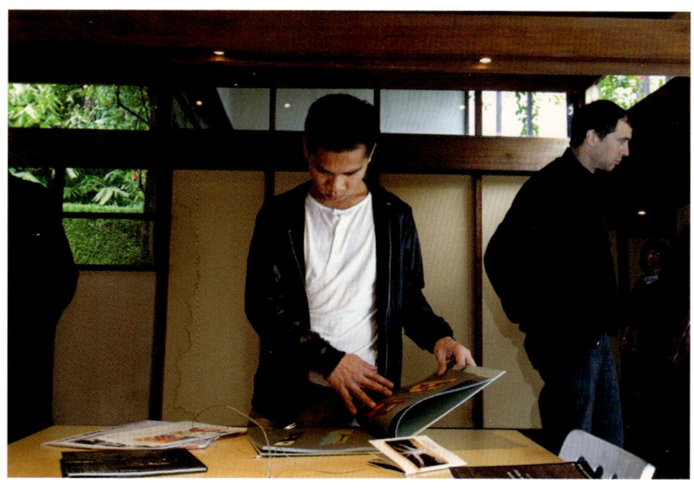

Reading tables in the *How Many Billboards?* exhibition at the Schindler House

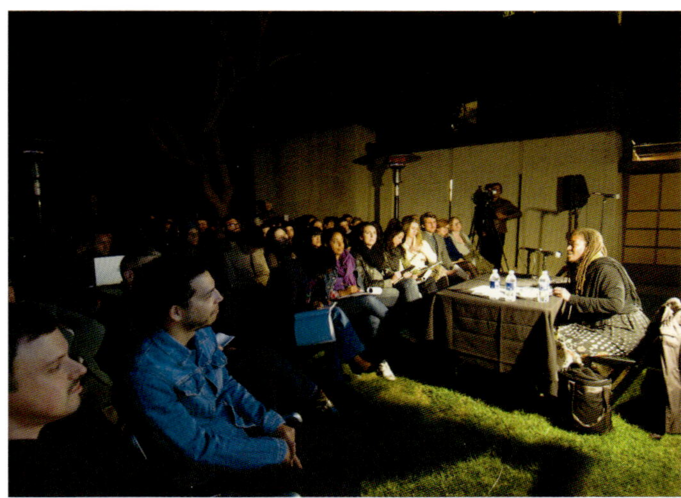

Lecture by Renée Green at the Schindler House.

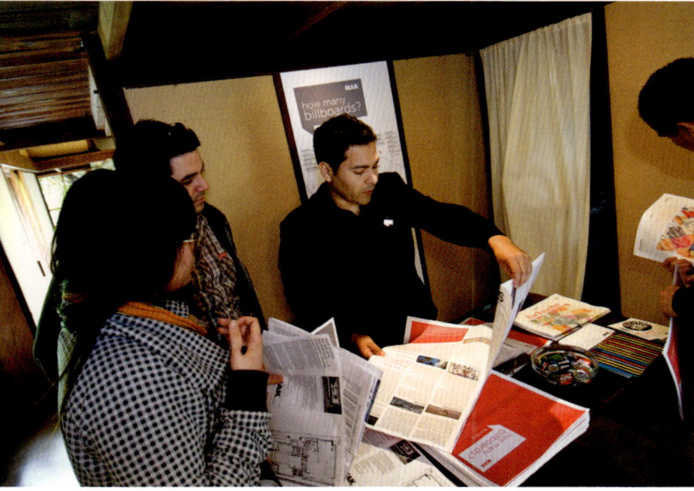

Maps and didactic material at the Schindler House.

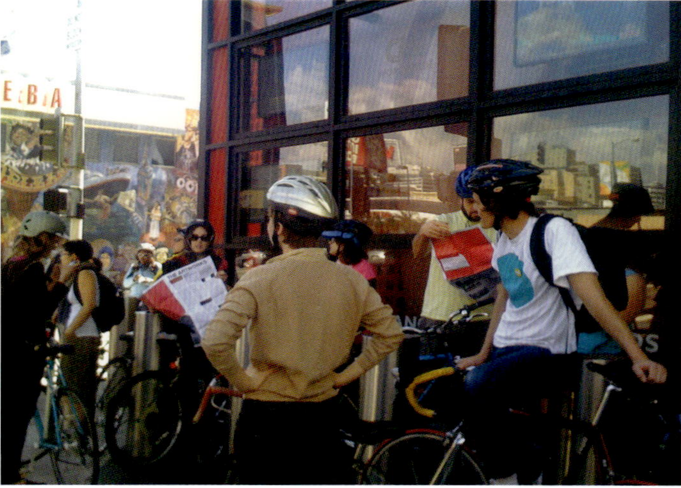

Taking a break near the Rosler/Neufeld billboard during a bicycle tour of the exhibition.

ARTIST BIOS

KENNETH ANGER (B. 1927)
Kenneth Anger has been making films since 1947, and is internationally recognized as an influential force in avant-garde cinema. His films function as radical critiques of Hollywood film, often evoking pop culture icons within occult settings and depicting youth counterculture engaged in scenes of violence and eroticism. Through his work, Anger explores themes of ritualistic transformation, utilizing heightened sensuality as well as exaggerated colors and imagery. He was recently the subject of a retrospective at P.S.1 Contemporary Art Center, New York (2009).

MICHAEL ASHER (B. 1943)
A lifelong Angeleno, Michael Asher is one of the pioneering figures of Conceptual Art in California. His influence derives from his subtly provocative installations in museums, including the Kunstverein, Hamburg; Centre Pompidou, Paris; Museum of Modern Art, New York; and most recently, the Santa Monica Museum of Art (2008), as well as through his engagement with students in "post-studio" courses at California Institute of the Arts beginning in the early 1970s. Asher's works have become touchstones for contemporary artists and the discourse of "institutional critique." His practice is not based on the creation of collectible or displayable objects, but rather elides the conventions of viewing and display, making the museum and gallery his medium.

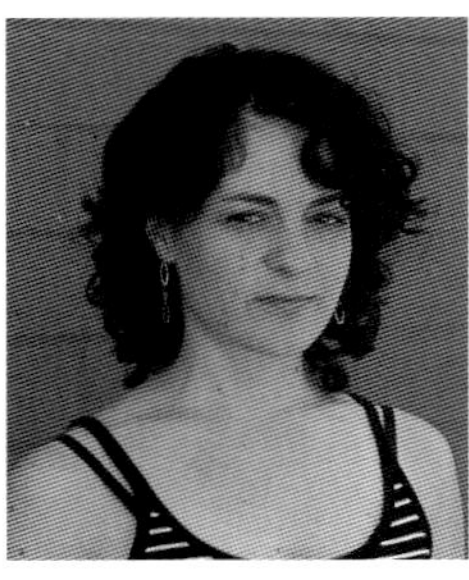

JENNIFER BORNSTEIN (B. 1970)
Based in Los Angeles, Jennifer Bornstein received her MFA from University of California, Los Angeles. Her work explores the possibility of setting up physical and conceptual interactions between people, and between bodies and objects, heightening the viewer's awareness of the relationship between spectator and performer. A filmmaker, Bornstein is equally well known for her small, detailed etchings and her evocative studies for films that she may or may not make. She has had solo exhibitions at Blum & Poe, Los Angeles; greengrassi, London; Gavin Brown, New York; Studio Guenzani, Milan; Färgfabriken, Stockholm; and The Museum of Contemporary Art, Los Angeles.

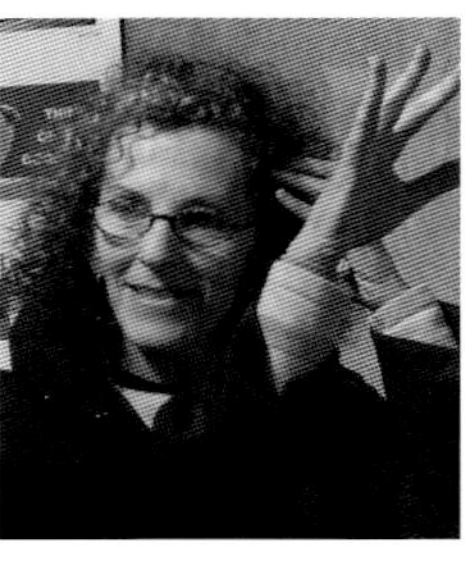

EILEEN COWIN (B. 1947)
Eileen Cowin's photographs and videos investigate the relationship between image and text. Cowin's works have been featured in numerous exhibitions throughout Europe, Japan, and the United States, including Los Angeles County Museum of Art; Museum of Modern Art, New York; and San Francisco Museum of Modern Art. She studied with Aaron Siskind and Arthur Siegel at the Institute of Design, Illinois Institute of Technology, Chicago, where she earned an MS in photography.

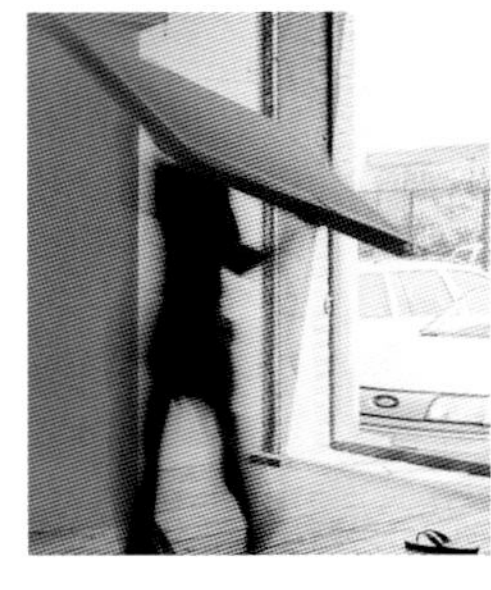

CHRISTINA FERNANDEZ (B. 1965)
Christina Fernandez is a photographer/artist and educator who lives and works in Los Angeles. Fernandez earned an MFA. from California Institute of the Arts. Fernandez's work examines the intersections between private and public space, personal and historical narratives, ex-urban and city spaces, and the cultural border and historical relationships between the United States and Mexico. Fernandez's photographic works often utilize text or other methods of narration in which the more-than-personal narrative is of primary importance. Fernandez's work was shown in recent group exhibitions including *Phantom Sightings: Art after the Chicano Movement*, Los Angeles County Museum of Art (traveling); *This Side of Paradise: Body and Landscape in Los Angeles Photographs*, Huntington Memorial Library and Gardens, San Marino (traveling); and *Index: Conceptualism in California*, The Museum of Contemporary Art, Los Angeles. She is an associate professor of photography at Cerritos College.

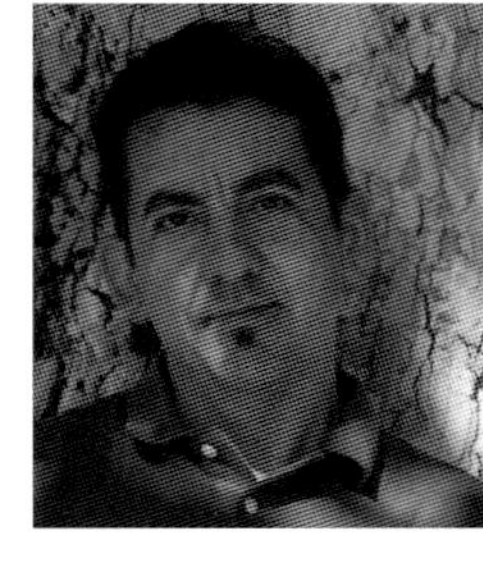

KEN GONZALES-DAY (B. 1964)
Ken Gonzales-Day is a Los Angeles-based artist and writer. He studied painting and art history at the Pratt Institute before receiving his MFA in photography from University of California, Irvine. His practice often takes a conceptual lens to historically charged imagery,

investigating the often violent and disruptive social and political past of the United States. His book, *Lynching in the West: 1850-1935*, was published by Duke University Press in 2006. Gonzales-Day is currently a professor at Scripps College.

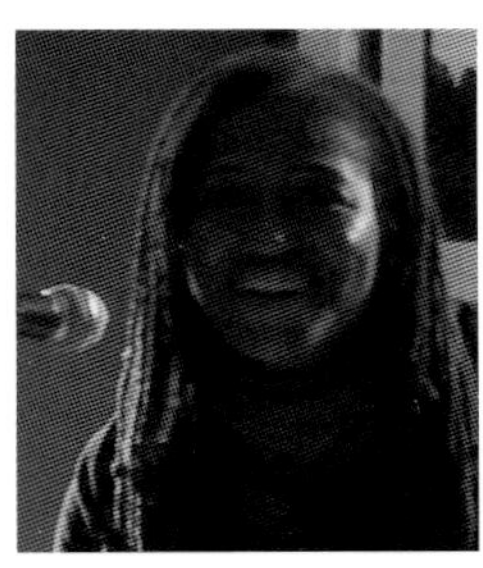

RENÉE GREEN (B. 1959)
Renée Green is an artist, filmmaker, and writer who lives and works in San Francisco and New York. A survey of 20 years of her work was organized in 2009 by the Musée Cantonal des Beaux-Arts, Lausanne. In 2008, the Galerie Nationale du Jeu de Paume, Paris, organized a retrospective of her films. Selected solo exhibition venues include the Museum of Contemporary Art, Los Angeles; Dallas Museum of Art; De Appel Foundation, Amsterdam; Vienna Secession; Fundació Antoni Tàpies, Barcelona; Contemporary Arts Center, Cincinnati; and National Maritime Museum, Greenwich, London. Her work has been included in many group exhibitions including Museum Ludwig, Cologne; Museu d'Art Contemporani de Barcelona; Centre Pompidou, Paris; and International Center of Photography, New York. Her work has also been present at the Whitney, Venice, Johannesburg, Kwangju, Berlin, Sevilla and Istanbul Biennials, as well as in Documenta 11. She has published essays in *Transition, October, Frieze, Flash Art, Texte zur Kunst, Spex,* and *Sarai Reader*, among other magazines and journals.

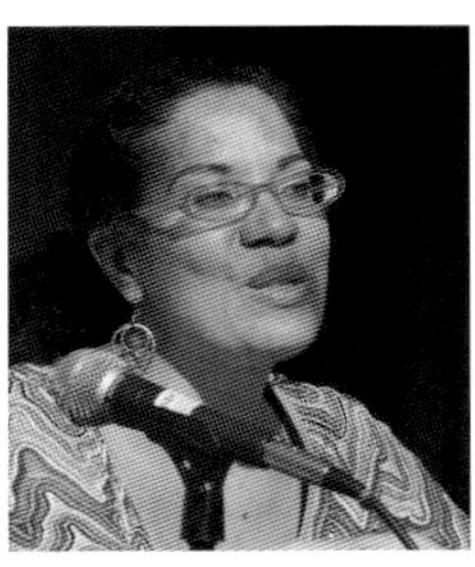

KIRA LYNN HARRIS (B. 1963)
Born in Los Angeles, Kira Lynn Harris lives and works in New York. She received her MFA from California Institute of the Arts. Often creating architectural and environmental interventions, the goal of her work is to provide a disorienting encounter for the viewer, which destabilizes and reorients the subject. Besides large-scale installations, Harris also creates conceptual photography that investigates phenomenological discourse, space, and perception. Her work has been exhibited in museums and galleries throughout the United States and internationally, including CUE Art Foundation and P.S.1 MoMA, New York, and Delaware Center for the Contemporary Arts.

JOHN KNIGHT (B. 1945)
Since the late 1960s, the project of John Knight has managed to negate easy categorization by establishing a critical distance from the overly generalized label of Conceptual Art. Instead, Knight assumes a more singular position, by re-employing object/subjects within the vernacular, beyond the simple reinterpretation of the readymade or simulacra. Recent projects include shows at Richard Telles Fine Art, Los Angeles (2009); Museu d'Art Contemporani de Barcelona (2009); Hamburger Bahnhof Museum, Berlin (2009); Galerie Rüdiger Schöttle, Munich (2008); and Espai d'Art Contemporani de Castelló (2008).

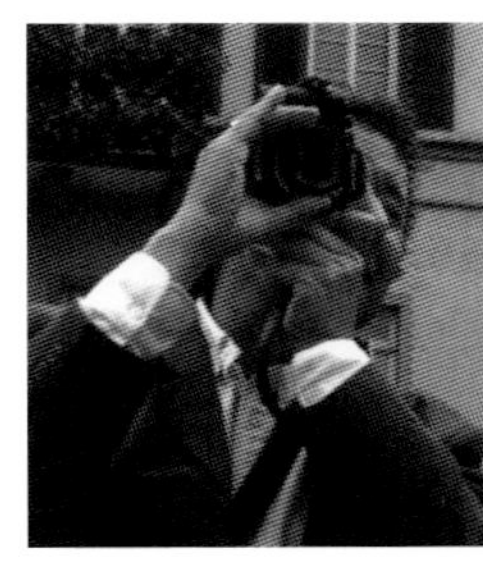

DAVID LAMELAS (B. 1946)
Born in Argentina, David Lamelas lived in London before he moved to Los Angeles in 1976. Since the 1960s, Lamelas has been among the most important proponents of a conceptual approach to art. His early structuralist films and media installations, made in the '60s and '70s, display a highly individual treatment of time and space. In his projects, Lamelas deals with the question of the limits of art's temporality, and its potential for creating alternative processes of communication and cognition. Recent solo exhibitions include Museum für Gegenwartskunst, Basel (2008); Wien Secession, Vienna (2006); and Museo Nacional Centro de Arte Reina Sofia, Madrid (2005). He was part of the group exhibition ***The Quick and the Dead*** at the Walker Arts Center, Minneapolis (2009).

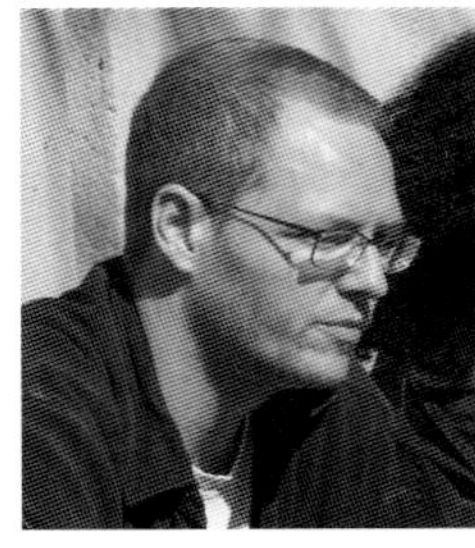

BRANDON LATTU (B. 1970)
Brandon Lattu received his MFA from University of California, Los Angeles in 1998, and lives in Los Angeles. His work utilizes photography, sculpture, and video to investigate the state of representation today in order to push beyond the conventional empiricism that pictures of the world have traditionally invoked. Lattu is Assistant Professor of Art at the University of California, Riverside. Most recently, his work has been included in *Walker Evans and the Barn* at the Stedelijk Museum Bureau, Amsterdam; *Tractatus Logico-Catalogicus*, curated

by Klaus Scherubel at the Vox Centre de L'image Contemporaine, Montreal; and *The Movement of Images* at the Centre Pompidou, Paris. Lattu was the subject of a survey exhibition held at the Bielefelder Kunstverein in 2007, which was accompanied by an artist's book titled *Office Gray Case*. Upcoming solo exhibitions are scheduled at Leo Koenig Inc., New York and Monte Clark Gallery, Vancouver.

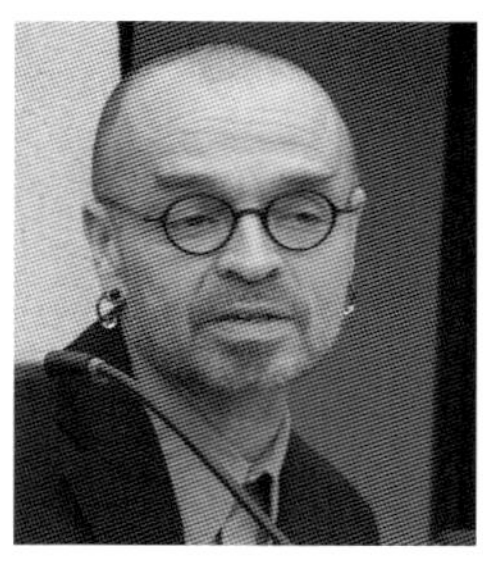

DANIEL JOSEPH MARTINEZ (B. 1957)
Over the thirty years of his art practice, Daniel Joseph Martinez has investigated social, political, and cultural mores using a complex artistic vocabulary of text, sculpture, installation, painting, video, and photography. His work seeks to address historical and current geopolitical realities, exposing their complicated dynamics and destabilizing them in myriad ways. Martinez has exhibited in the United States and internationally since 1978, including the 1993 and 2008 Whitney Biennials. He had a one-person exhibition at Museo de Arte Carrillo Gil, Mexico (2001) and in 2006 he represented the United States at the 10th Cairo International Biennale (Museum of Fine Arts, Houston). Hatje Cantz recently produced the monograph *Daniel Joseph Martinez: A Life of Disobedience*. Martinez teaches at the University of California, Irvine, where he has been a professor of theory, practice, and mediation of contemporary art since 1990.

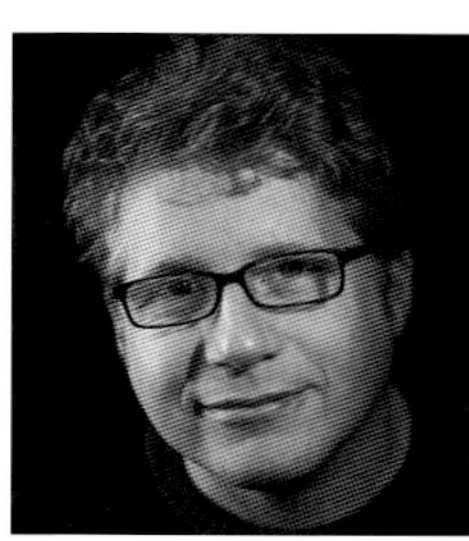

JOSH NEUFELD (B. 1967)
Josh Neufeld is a Brooklyn-based writer and artist. His works include *A.D: New Orleans After the Deluge* (Pantheon Books, 2009), a nonfiction graphic novel about Hurricane Katrina, and the graphic travelogue *A Few Perfect Hours (and Other Stories from Southeast Asia & Central Europe)* (Alternative Comics, 2004). His work has been featured in *The Vagabonds, Keyhole,* and *Titans of Finance,* as well as in numerous comics anthologies, newspapers, magazines, and literary journals. He is a longtime artist for Harvey Pekar's *American Splendor*, and his art has been in gallery and museum exhibits in the United States and Europe. For *How Many Billboards?* he collaborated with Martha Rosler.

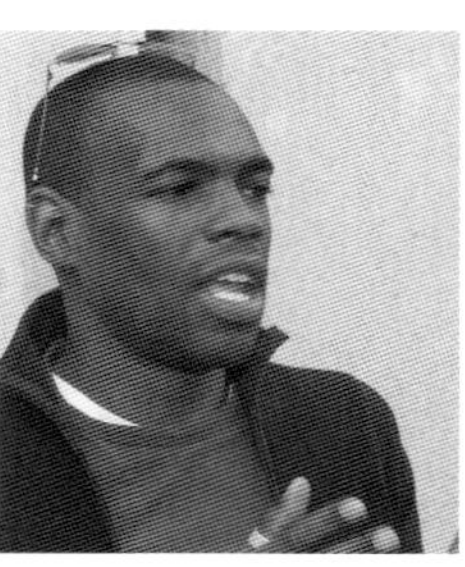

KORI NEWKIRK (B. 1970)
Kori Newkirk lives and works in Los Angeles and received his MFA from the University of California, Irvine, in 1997. Newkirk makes multimedia paintings, sculptural installations, and photographs that explore the formal properties of materials, the politics of identity, and the artist's personal history. Newkirk has had solo exhibitions at the Studio Museum in Harlem, New York (2008); Pasadena Museum of California Art (2008); LA><Art, Los Angeles (2008); Project, New York (2006); MC, Los Angeles (2006); Museum of Contemporary Art, San Diego (2005); and Locust Projects, Miami (2005).

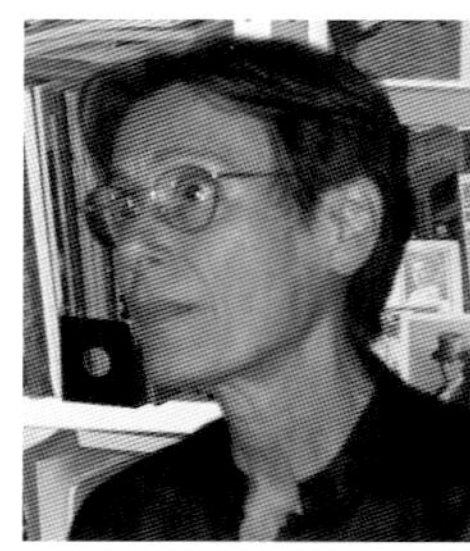

YVONNE RAINER (B. 1934)
Yvonne Rainer made a transition to filmmaking following a 15-year career as a choreographer/dancer (1960–1975). After making seven experimental feature films—*Lives of Performers* (1972), *Privilege* (1990), *MURDER and murder* (1996), among others—she returned to dance in 2000 via a commission from the Baryshnikov Dance Foundation for the White Oak Dance Project. Her most recent dances are "AG Indexical, with a little help from H.M.," a re-vision of Balanchine's "Agon"; "RoS Indexical," a re-vision of Nijinsky's "The Rite of Spring" and a Performa07 commission; and "Spiraling Down," a meditation on soccer, aging, and war. Her dances have been performed in New York, Vienna, Helsinki, Kassel, Berlin, Sao Paolo, and, in June 2009, at REDCAT, Los Angeles. A memoir, *Feelings Are Facts: A Life*, was published by MIT Press in 2006. Rainer is currently a Distinguished Professor of Studio Art at the University of California, Irvine.

MARTHA ROSLER (B. 1943)
Martha Rosler works in multiple media, including photography, sculpture, video, and installation. Her work on the public sphere centers on war but also on everyday life and the media, often with an eye to women's experience. Investigating landscapes of the everyday, she has produced works on the uses of space, including architecture and housing, as well as systems of airplane, automobile, and subway travel. Her project *The Martha Rosler Library* toured the U.S. and Europe from 2005 through December 2009. She currently is a professor at Rutgers University in New Brunswick, New Jersey. For *How Many Billboards?*, she collaborated with graphic novelist Josh Neufeld.

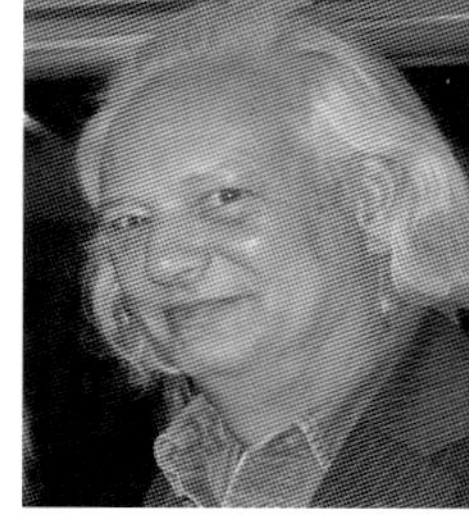

ALLEN RUPPERSBERG (B. 1944)
Allen Ruppersberg is from Cleveland, Ohio, and has been working in Los Angeles and New York since the late 1960s. Focusing on a mixture of text and image in his drawings, prints, photographs, installations, and artist books, Ruppersberg has fashioned an artistic practice that continually calls for viewer participation, from ordering one of many unique

dishes at *Al's Café* (1969) or renting a room in *Al's Grand Hotel* (1971) to being given free pages in *Art, and therefore, Ourselves* at the Santa Monica Museum (2009) and *The Never-ending Book Part 1* (2007). He is represented in major collections, including Museum of Modern Art, New York; Los Angeles County Museum of Art; Art Institute of Chicago; and Whitney Museum of America Art, New York.

ALLAN SEKULA (B.1951)
Allan Sekula is a photographer, writer, and filmmaker based in Los Angeles, where he teaches in the program in photography and media at the California Institute of the Arts. He has explored an experimental social documentary practice since the early 1970s. His books include *Photography Against the Grain, Fish Story, Geography Lesson: Canadian Notes, Performance under Working Conditions, and TITANIC's wake*. His work was presented in Documenta 11 in 2002, and in Documenta 12 in 2007. For Documenta 12, Sekula presented a large-scale, outdoor billboard piece, *Shipwreck and Workers,* consisting of multiple photographic images and graphic panels installed on a floating raft and on a steep hillside in the baroque Bergpark inKassel, Germany.

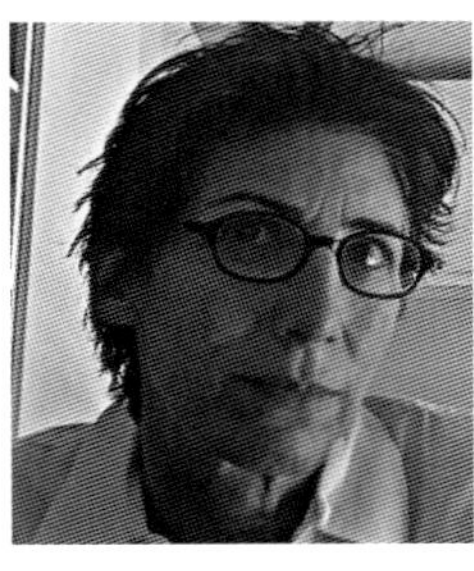

SUSAN SILTON (B. 1956)
Susan Silton is a Los Angeles-based, multidisciplinary artist whose work has been exhibited in solo and group exhibitions internationally, including at SolwayJones, Los Angeles; SITE Santa Fe; Australian Centre for Contemporary Art, Melbourne; and Allanz Zeignierderiassung, Berlin. Her work investigates how perception is shaped and distorted by spin, consumerism, and the weight of history, identity, and information overload. She incorporates photographic-based processes, video, installation, performative works, and offset lithography, collectively and variously, to reconsider, complicate, and subvert interpretation, especially as it relates to subjectivity.

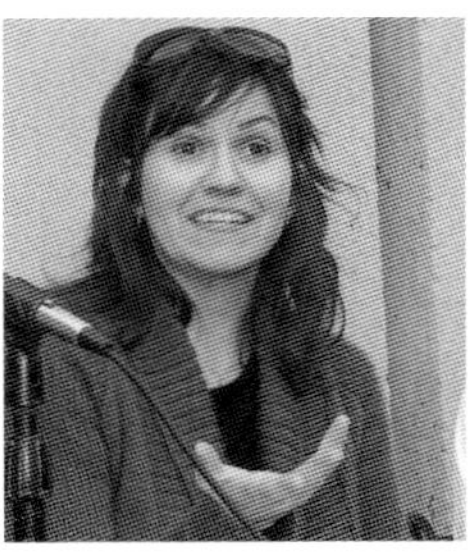

KERRY TRIBE (B. 1973)
Kerry Tribe's rigorously crafted, large-scale projects form an ongoing investigation into memory, subjectivity, and doubt. She regularly invites actors, crew members, and technical specialists to participate in her work, producing ludic philosophical inquiries through structurally rigorous forms. Tribe's work has been exhibited at the Whitney Museum of American Art and New Museum of Contemporary Art, New York; Hirshhorn Museum and Sculpture Garden, Washington, DC; Generali Foundation, Vienna; Kunst-Werke, Berlin; and Stedelijk Museum voor Actuele Kunst, Gent. Tribe currently splits her time between Los Angeles and Berlin.

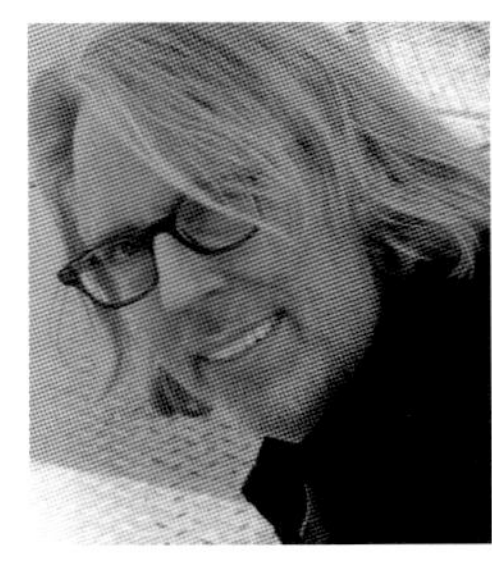

JAMES WELLING (B. 1951)
James Welling received his MFA from the California Institute of the Arts, where he worked primarily in video, studying with Wolfgang Storechle and John Baldessari. In the late 1970s, Welling emerged as an artist for whom photographic norms are not a given but rather a field of contest between different formal languages. His recent museum shows include *The Pictures Generation* at the Metropolitan Museum of Art (2009), the 2008 Whitney Biennial, and a 25-year survey of his work at The Museum of Contemporary Art, Los Angeles. Welling exhibits at Regen Projects, Los Angeles; David Zwirner, New York; Donald Young, Chicago; Galerie Nelson-Freeman, Paris; Maureen Paley, London; Galerie Nächt St. Stephan Rosmarie Schwarzwälder, Vienna; and Wako Works of Art, Tokyo. He is on the faculty of the University of California, Los Angeles, in the department of art.

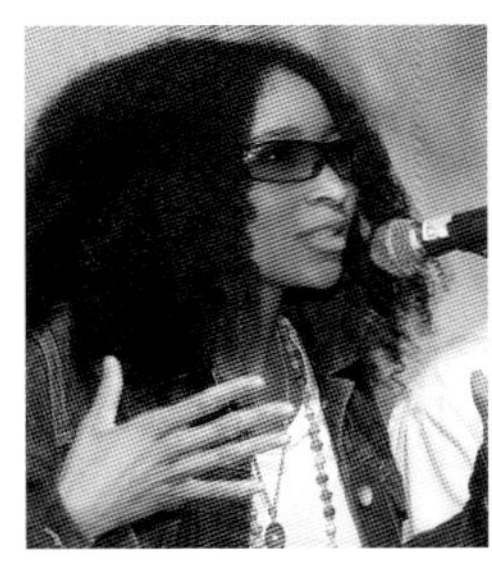

lauren woods (b. 1979)
lauren woods is a multimedia artist based in the Bay Area of California. Her hybrid media projects—film, video and sound installations, interventions, and site-specific work—engage history while contemplating the socio-politics of the present. Challenging the tradition of documentary/ethnography as objective, she creates ethno-fictive documents that investigate invisible dynamics in society, remix memory, and imagine other possibilities. In 2006, she received her MFA from the San Francisco Art Institute. Her work has been exhibited throughout the United States and internationally, including Washington, DC, San Francisco, Los Angeles, New York, Dallas, and Miami, as well as Puerto Rico, China, Taiwan, South Korea, Japan, Mali, and France.

CONTRIBUTOR BIOS

Anne Bray is an artist, teacher, and director of FREEWAVES, a grassroots yet global media arts organization in Los Angeles connecting innovative, relevant, independent new media from around the world (www.freewaves.org). She developed the concept of the multicultural network of media artists and venues in 1989, and has continued to see the organization through the technological, social, and aesthetic changes of the 1990s to now. As an artist she exhibits her work as temporary installations in art venues and public sites. Her projects combine personal and social positions via video, audio, slides, and 3-D screens at gas stations, malls, movie theaters, department stores, billboards, and on TV; now she wants art to be everywhere. She teaches public art and multimedia at Claremont Graduate University and University of Southern California.

Sara Daleiden is an artist, curator, and organizer who focuses on participant experience through the creation of identity systems and interventions within the city. She works as a consultant in conceptual strategies, organizational development, and project coordination with clients including the MAK Center for Art and Architecture, Suzanne Lacy, Freewaves, Marc Pally, Cliff Garten Studio, and the Community Redevelopment Agency of Los Angeles. She received her Master of Public Art Studies from the University of Southern California (USC), is a core member of the collective, the Los Angeles Urban Rangers, and serves on the board of the Los Angeles Forum of Architecture and Urban Design. She has taught at USC, Woodbury University, and the Milwaukee Institute of Art & Design.

Joshua Decter has been a critic and curator since the late 1980s. He is a regular contributor to *Artforum*, *Afterall*, and other periodicals. Decter has organized exhibitions at PS1, New York; Center for Curatorial Studies / Hessel Museum of Art at Bard College; Apex Art, New York; Kunsthalle Vienna; and Santa Monica Museum of Art. He has contributed essays to numerous exhibition catalogues and books over the past 20 years. Decter has taught at Bard College, New York; The School of Visual Arts, New York; University of California, Los Angeles; Art Center College of Design, Pasadena; and is currently the director of the Master of Public Art Studies Program: Art/Curatorial Practices in the Public Sphere at the University of Southern California Roski School of Fine Arts in Los Angeles.

Janet Owen Driggs is a writer, artist and curator. She has exhibited internationally, including in the United States, Europe, Scandinavia, and Brazil. She has curated exhibitions and screening programs in the United Kingdom, United States, People's Republic of China, and Mexico. In February 2010, she co-curated (with Matthew Driggs) the touring exhibition *Performing Public Space*, which debuted at Tijuana's Casa del Tunel. Her writings have been published most recently in *Hammer Projects 1999-2009*, *Heike Baranowsky: Kolibri*, and *Art Review*. A member of the Metabolic Studio team, Owen Driggs also teaches at the University of Southern California Roski School of Fine Arts in Los Angeles.

Lisa Henry is an independent curator based in Los Angeles. She received an MA in Critical and Curatorial Studies from the University of California, Los Angeles, and a BA in American Studies from Brown University. She is the curator of the exhibitions *Off the Grid* and *Americans: Contemporary Portraits by Keliy Anderson Staley* at the California Museum of Photography at University of California, Riverside; *Connections,* Jenkins Johnson Gallery, New York; *Saturday Night/Sunday Morning*, Leica Gallery, New York; *Horace Bristol's California Photographs*, J. Paul Getty Museum, Los Angeles; and *I'm Thinking of a Place*, UCLA Hammer Museum, Los Angeles. Her essays on photography have appeared in *Fotophile, Nueva Luz, Dodge & Burn,* and *Exposure*: *The Journal of the Society for Photographic Education.* Her essay "Sheila Pree Bright and the Construction of a Portrait Series" appears in *Young Americans: Photographs by Sheila Pree Bright,* published jointly by the Wadsworth Atheneum and the High Museum of Art (2008). Forthcoming publications include "Artists in the Archive" in conjunction with the upcoming exhibition *Digging Deeper* at the Atheneum; "Love, Landscape, and Los Angeles: Glynnis Reed's Urban Environments" (*Exposure),* and a profile of Bay Area photographer Stela Kalaw for *En Foco online*.

Nizan Shaked is an Assistant Professor of Contemporary Art History, Museum, and Curatorial

Studies at California State University, Long Beach. She received her PhD in cultural studies with an emphasis in museum studies from Claremont Graduate University, where she wrote her dissertation "The Paradox of Identity Politics as an Agent in Critical Art: 1970s to the 1990s." Shaked holds an MA in Critical and Curatorial Studies from the University of California, Los Angeles, and an MFA from Otis College of Art and Design. Shaked has contributed texts to monographs on artists including Judie Bamber, Todd Gray, Kendell Carter, Kianga Ford, and Liat Yossifor. She has written reviews for academic and art publications, including an article-review of the exhibition *Phantom Sightings: Art after the Chicano Movement* for *American Quarterly: The Journal of American Studies,* and has three entries currently under review for the *Oxford University Press Encyclopedia of Art*: "Los Angeles," "Institutional Critique," and "Laylah Ali." Shaked is a regular contributor and a member of the editorial board for the Los Angeles-based contemporary art quarterly *X-TRA.*

Christine Steiner is an experienced attorney whose practice emphasizes visual arts law, intellectual property, publishing, and general business transactions. Her prior positions include Secretary and General Counsel, J. Paul Getty Trust; Assistant General Counsel, Smithsonian Institution; and Assistant Attorney General of Maryland for state colleges and universities. She is also an adjunct professor at Loyola Law School, where she teaches visual arts law, and has served as a visiting professor of international art law in Florence, Italy, and Cambridge, England. Her writings include *Model Agreement for Public Art Commissions* (Public Art Network, Americans for the Arts, 2005), *Primer on Copyright for Visual Artists* (Public Knowledge, 2005), *A Museum Guide to Copyright and Trademark* (American Association of Museums, 1999), and the chapter on copyright for the recently published *Museum Registration Methods* (American Association of Museums, 2010), among other publications. She was a member of the U.S. Conference on Fair Use (CONFU), formerly chaired the Visual Arts Section of the American Bar Association, and serves on the Editorial Board of the Copyright Society of the United States.

Gloria Sutton received her PhD in Contemporary Art History at the University of California, Los Angeles, in 2009; her research focused on the history of media art. She has been a fellow at the Whitney Museum of American Art's Independent Study Program and the Getty Research Institute. Her scholarship on expanded cinema is featured in *Future Cinema: The Cinematic Imaginary after Film* (2003) and *Mainframe Experimentalism: Early Digital Computing and the Experimental Arts,* forthcoming from UC Press. Her criticism appears in the exhibition catalogs *Renée Green: Ongoing Becomings, 1989-2009* (Musée cantonal des Beaux-Arts Lausanne, 2009), *Laura Owens* (Kunsthalle Zurich, 2007), *Ice Cream: Contemporary Art in Culture* (Phaidon, 2007), *Vitamin Ph: New Perspectives in Photography* (Phaidon, 2006), *Kerry Tribe Recent History* (American Academy in Berlin, 2006), and *Ecstasy: In and About Altered States* (Museum of Contemporary Art, 2006). As Ahmanson Curatorial Fellow at The Museum of Contemporary Art, Los Angeles, she co-curated *MOCA Focus: Karl Haendel* (2006). Sutton is currently working on a book on the American artist Stan VanDerBeek and expanded cinema practices of the 1960s.

MAK CENTER FOR ART AND ARCHITECTURE, LOS ANGELES, AT THE SCHINDLER HOUSE

Acting as a "think tank," the MAK Center for Art and Architecture encourages the exploration of experimental, theoretical, and practical trajectories of contemporary art, architecture, urbanism, design, and international discourse. Offering a year-round schedule of exhibitions, lectures, symposia, and concerts, the MAK Center presents programming that challenges conventional notions of architectural space and relationships between the creative arts, thereby making a unique contribution to the artistic and cultural landscape of Los Angeles.

Peter Noever, CEO and Artistic Director of the MAK Vienna (Austrian Museum of Applied Arts / Contemporary Art), founded the MAK Center Los Angeles in 1994 as a satellite of MAK Vienna in cooperation with the Friends of the Schindler House. The MAK Center is partially funded by the Federal Ministry of Education, Arts, and Culture of the Republic of Austria. The MAK Center's activities are based in three of the most important houses designed by Austrian-American architect Rudolph M. Schindler (1887-1953) in West Hollywood and Los Angeles.

The Schindler House, R. M. Schindler's own live-work space built on Kings Road in 1921-22, serves as the public forum for MAK Center activities. A social idealist and experimental architect, Schindler developed a unique approach to design made possible by the moderate California climate. Schindler's ideas about space and the interplay between architecture and landscape were precursors to a new, distinctly Californian conception of architecture. Schindler and his wife Pauline regularly hosted artists, musicians, poets, writers, and actors, turning their West Hollywood home into an axis for avant-garde art and ideas. Today, the Schindler House remains a site for progressive cultural inquiry. It is one of the most beloved architectural and cultural landmarks in Los Angeles. The MAK Center seeks to promote the house and its grounds, as well as its legacy, by working in partnership with the Friends of the Schindler House, a nonprofit organization whose mission is to conserve and maintain the Kings Road house.

Built by Schindler in 1939, the Pearl M. Mackey Apartments were secured by the Republic of Austria in 1994. Soon thereafter, they were established as the location of the first permanent arts residency scholarship program for Austrian artists and architecture students outside of the country. Since then, the Mackey Apartments have become the vibrant base of the MAK Center Artists and Architects in Residence Program, today one of the most sought-after international scholarships today.

The Fitzpatrick-Leland House, built by Schindler in 1936, is an exemplary modern residence located in Los Angeles at the crest of Laurel Canyon Boulevard and Mulholland Drive. The house was donated to the MAK Center by Russ Leland in 2008. Recognizing that the home's light-filled spaces and expansive grounds provide an ideal setting for a residency program, the MAK Center has dedicated the Fitzpatrick-Leland House to the lodging of cultural thinkers, including the MAK Urban Future Initiative Fellows. It serves as an active hub for research, contemplation, and conversation about urban space.

For more information, please visit www.makcenter.org

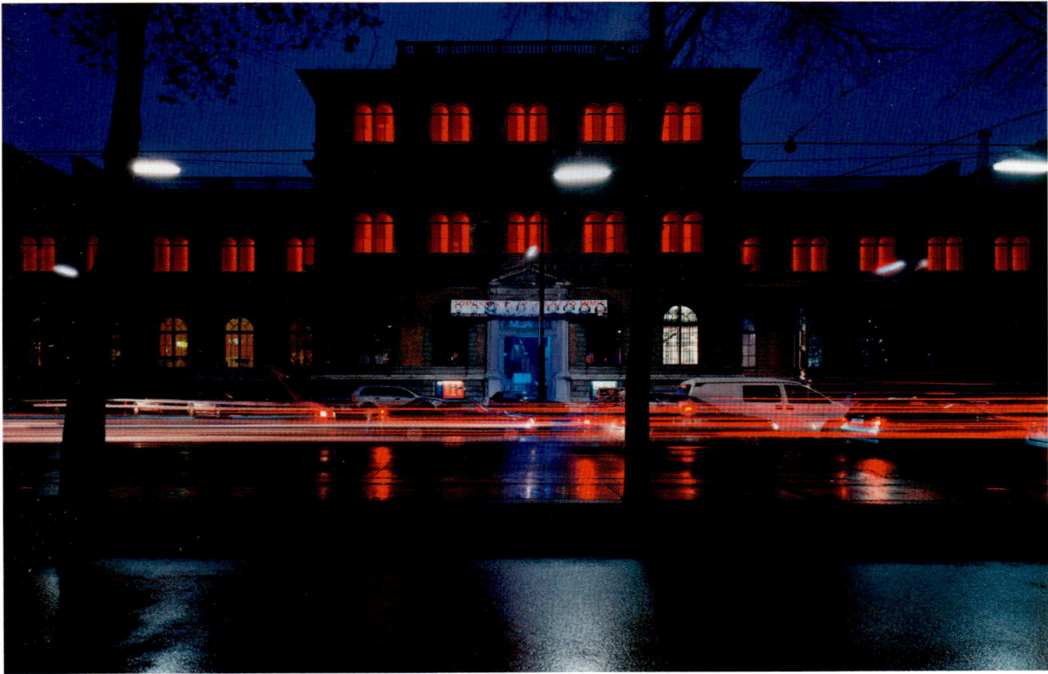

In James Turrell's permanent installation *MAKlite*, intensive light pulsates in the windows of the MAK. With the unreality of a dream, the brick façade loses its static solidity, appearing as a shimmering, translucent membrane that hints, wordlessly but emphatically, of transfers being made. By means of this inner radiance, the MAK communicates to its urban surroundings the complex proceedings being effected within. Permanent installation on the MAK Façade since 2004.

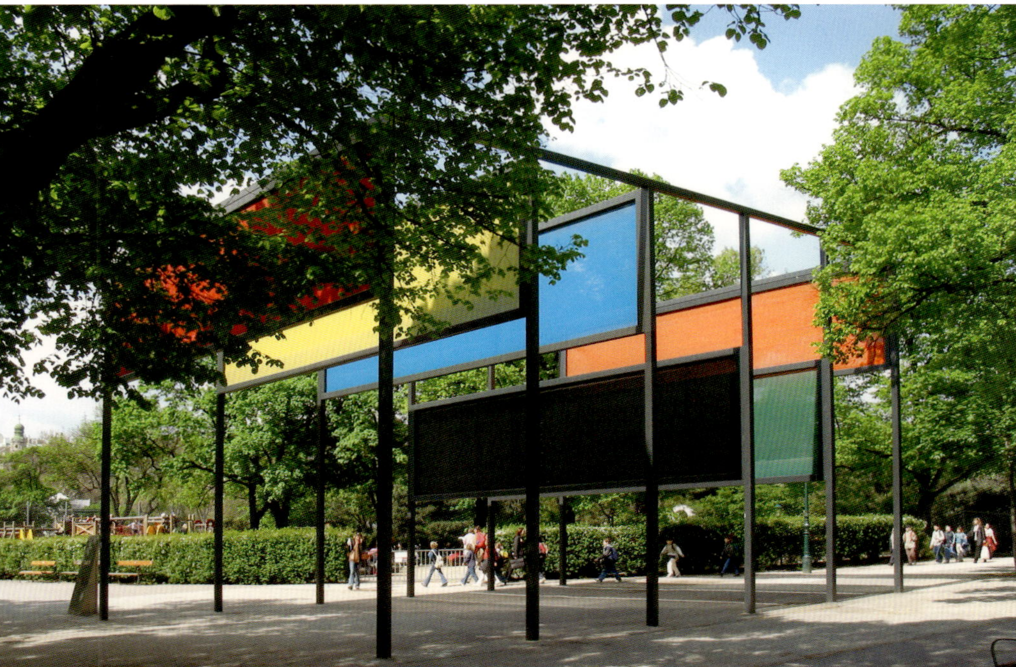

Donald Judd developed *Stage Set* for the MAK in 1991 on the occasion of his exhibition entitled Architecture. The sculpture was installed in Vienna's Stadtpark in 1996, and is an expression of Judd's uncompromising vision located between art and architecture.

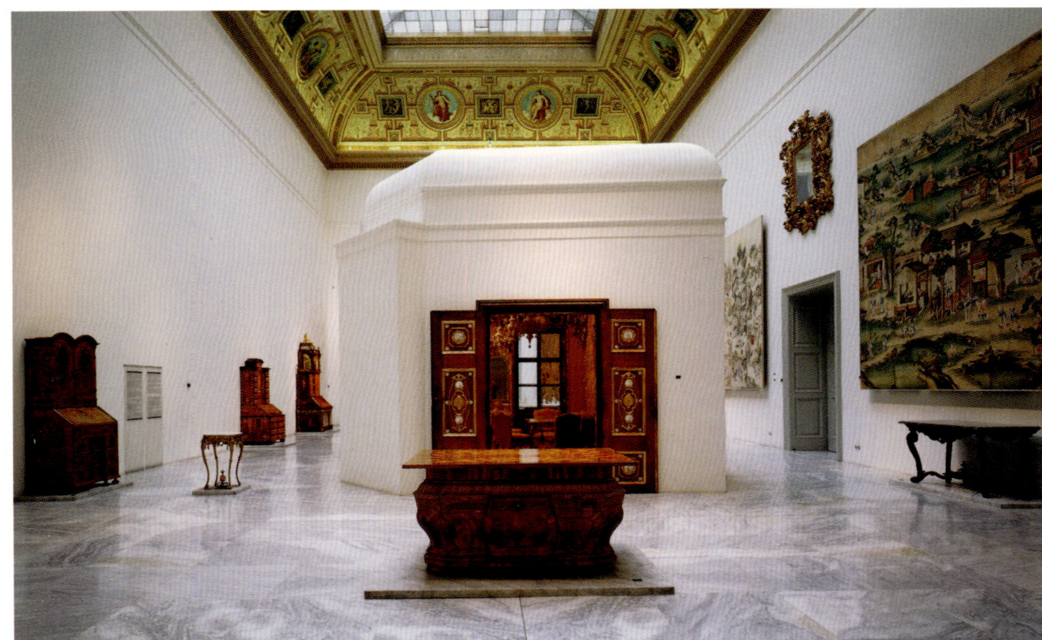

The reinstallation of the MAK's permanent collection and redesign of the gallery spaces by contemporary artists was the first experiment to be realized in the course of the museum's search for a new identity. Here, one can sense what the notion of fruitful confrontation between traditional collections and new artistic trends signifies.

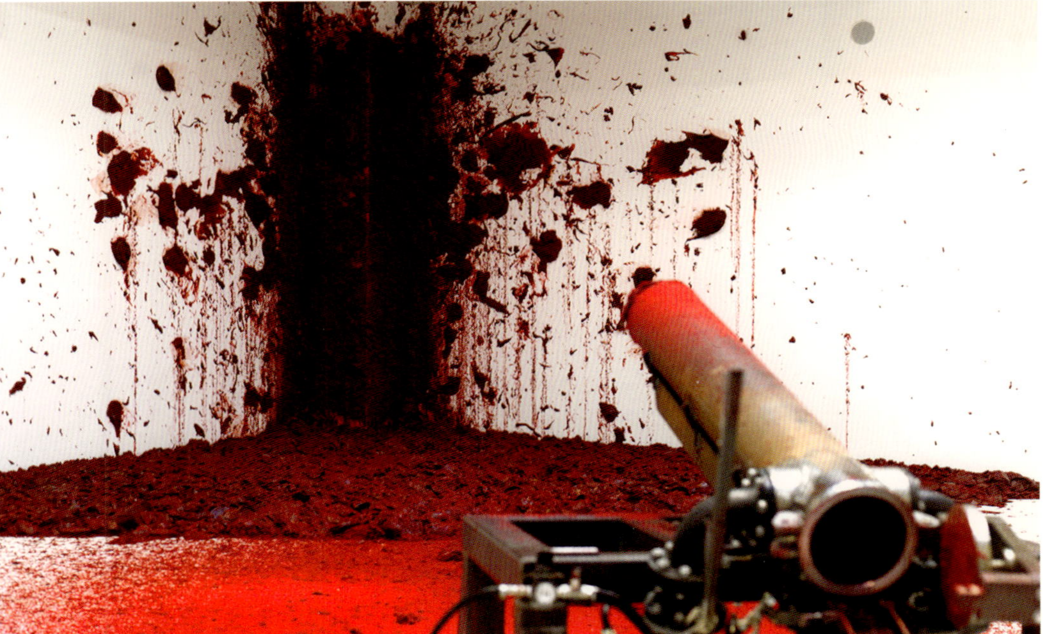

Anish Kapoor's *Shooting into the Corner* (2009) was especially created for his exhibition at MAK Vienna and donated to the museum by the artist. After the exhibition at the MAK, it was on view at the Royal Academy of Arts, London and the Guggenheim Museum Bilbao.

CREDITS

PHOTO CREDITS
Vivian Babuts - Page 155 (top row, left)
Anthony Carfello - Page 9
Sara Daleiden - Page 151 (bottom)
Kimberli Meyer - Page 155 (bottom right)
Nate Page - Pages 145, 147, 151 (top)
patricia parinejad - Pages 15, 25, 28, 29, 32, 33, 41, 45, 48, 49, 52, 53, 57, 61, 64, 65, 69, 73, 76, 77, 80, 85, 88, 89, 92, 96, 100, 101, 104, 105, 120, 126 (left), 131, 133, 140, 163 (middle column)
Gerard Smulevich - Pages 12, 13, 14, 16, 23, 24, 27, 31, 35, 36, 37, 39, 40, 43, 44, 47, 51, 55, 56, 59, 60, 63, 67, 68, 71, 72, 75, 79, 81, 83, 84, 87, 91, 93, 95, 97, 99, 103, 109, 110, 111, 112, 113, 114, 115, 122, 124, 125, 126 (right), 130, 132
Mimi Teller - Pages 155 (top row, middle and right; bottom row left and middle)
Joshua White - Page 163 (right column)
Gerarld Zugmann - Page 163 (left column)

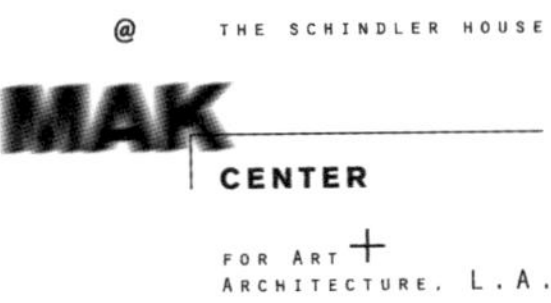